FRANCE AND MUNICH

FRANCE

AND

MUNICH:

BEFORE AND AFTER THE SURRENDER

by

ALEXANDER WERTH

It was the opinion of Marcian that war should be
avoided as long as it is possible to preserve a secure
and honourable peace; but it was likewise his
opinion that peace cannot be honourable or secure,
if the sovereign betrays a pusillanimous aversion to
war.   This temperate courage dictated his reply
to the demands of Attila, who insolently pressed
the payment of the annual tribute.
Decline and Fall of the Roman Empire, Chap. xxxv.

HOWARD FERTIG

New York   ·   1969

First published in 1939 by Hamish Hamilton

HOWARD FERTIG, INC. EDITION 1969
Published by arrangement with the author

Library of Congress Catalog Card Number: 68-9632

PRINTED IN THE UNITED STATES OF AMERICA
BY NOBLE OFFSET PRINTERS, INC.

PREFACE TO THE 1969 EDITION

I was pleasantly surprised when Mr. Howard Fertig recently proposed to reprint *France and Munich*. Very few people, except specialists, know this book.

I was Paris correspondent of the then *Manchester Guardian* from 1932 to the Fall of France in 1940, and *France and Munich* was the third part of my three-volume chronicle on that last prewar decade of French history. Its two predecessors were *France in Ferment*, published at the end of 1934, with the Stavisky Scandal and the Concorde Riots—that first violent flare up of the various French brands of Fascism and anti-parliamentarism—as their central episodes; and *Which Way France?* (entitled *The Destiny of France* in England), published toward the end of 1937. This carried on the story of the rise of Fascism—and what we might now call future Vichyism—in France, and also gave an account of the sharp reaction against it, which took the form of the Popular Front. One of the central episodes of this second volume concerned the fantastic pacifism and inertia that the French Government and, with it, the greater part of French public opinion displayed in March 1936, when Hitler marched his troops into the demilitarized Rhineland Zone, thus tearing up not only a vital part of the Treaty of Versailles, but also the Treaty of Locarno. By taking military possession of the Rhineland and preparing to fortify it, Hitler gravely endangered France's whole system of alliances; but, instead of sending her troops into the Rhineland and throwing the Nazis out, France proceeded to consult London which, being equally pacifist and even more shortsighted, advised her against any military action. The fortification of the Rhineland Zone by the Nazi regime thus became part of its drive toward war and made it increasingly difficult for France to intervene—either to protect Austria in March 1938, or, worse still, to defend Czechoslovakia in August-September 1938,

v

despite the firmest treaty obligations France had entered
into to defend that country. Instead, she was only too happy
when Mr. Chamberlain, Hitler's and Mussolini's arch-
appeaser, who had already given Hitler a free hand in Austria,
took it upon himself, by hook or by crook, to "free" the
French of their obligations toward Czechoslovakia. When I
say "France," I do not mean every Frenchman; there were
many—among them M. Paul Reynaud and the then Colonel
Charles de Gaulle—who saw only too clearly that, by abandoning Czechoslovakia, France was in danger of finding herself (together with an armyless England) wholly isolated in
the event of a German attack in the West. But twenty years
after World War I, in which France has lost 1,500,000 men,
the country, on the whole, was anxious to avoid war at almost any price, and the near-readiness to write off the Eastern
allies—Czechoslovakia, Russia, Rumania, Yugoslavia and
even Poland—went together with the foolish conviction—
which official propaganda had drummed into her for years
—that whatever happened in Eastern Europe, France was
"safe behind the Maginot Line." In 1938, just about the
time of Munich, there appeared an incredible book by a certain General Chauvineau, *Is an Invasion of France Still Possible?*, with a laudatory preface by one of the most revered
generals of World War I, Marshal Philippe Pétain, the future
head of the Vichy regime. Pétain debunked any idea of a
blitzkrieg against France, declared that tanks and aircraft
could not be of any decisive importance, and placed the
greatest confidence in the Maginot Line and a "continuous
front," after the model of World War I. The idea that
the Germans might break through neutral Belgium[1] and so
turn the Maginot Line was scarcely even considered.

France and Munich has a strange history. The manuscript
was completed at the end of April 1939, and the book was
published in England in July, that is, only a few weeks before the beginning of World War II. There were so many

---

[1] After Hitler's Rhineland coup of 1936, Belgium broke her military alliance with France and declared herself neutral, thus making France's northern
frontier even more vulnerable.

worries during that fateful summer that readers were not particularly interested in a post-mortem of the Munich period. Nor was the subject a fashionable one once the war— the "phoney war" of September 1939 to May 1940—had begun. By the fall of 1940, some 2,000 or 3,000 unsold copies of *France and Munich* were still in existence; most of these were stocked in a great warehouse in Paternoster Row, near St. Paul's Cathedral, and this warehouse was completely burned out in one of the December air raids on London. Thus, a large proportion of the printed copies of *France and Munich* were burned, along with millions of other books, in what was probably the biggest book bonfire in history, well worthy of the Nazis! I watched the fire from a roof in Fleet Street.

In a short preface to the original edition I explained why and how *France and Munich* had been written:

> I have not attempted here to give a brilliant and lovely account of my experiences and sensations at the sight and sound of crumbling bastions. This book is mainly concerned with some of the chief causes of these catastrophes, rather than with the catastrophes themselves.

By "catastrophes" in this context I meant, of course, the fall of Austria, the fall of Czechoslovakia and the fall of Republican Spain.

I then continued:

> The task I set myself was a more modest and less exciting one. Having watched France day after day, for over ten years, I felt that I must try to understand the rather long and at times almost imperceptible process by which France came to accept Munich—so contrary to all that she had stood for since the War; and also the process by which she consciously contributed to the downfall of the Spanish Republic.

And then:

> . . . The 'Munich crisis' . . . is such an outstanding land-

mark in the life of France that every little human detail, every little newspaper cutting throwing some light on the workings of French minds during those days is of some interest. . . . [Here then] is an examination of French foreign policy during the past eighteen months, and of the currents of French opinion in relation to the tragic events of 1938 and the early part of 1939.

Many books have been written since then about Munich, but I believe that this is still the only one which specializes, as it were, in the supremely important "French angle" of Munich—the currents of French opinion, as reflected in private conversations, in parliamentary debates, and in the French press, the great majority of which, it must be said, tended more and more, as the danger of a collision with Hitler approached, to support the appeasement-and-surrender policy[2] personified by the ideological leader of appeasement, M. Pierre-Etienne Flandin, and by the Prime Minister and the Foreign Minister, MM. Edouard Daladier and Georges Bonnet. While refraining from the more cynical remarks of M. Flandin (who had, throughout, been Chamberlain's—not to say Hitler's—stooge in France), what they did in actual practice was little different from what Flandin was preaching.

Flandin spoke, at various moments, of "imperial retrenchment"—in other words, the surrender of Eastern Europe to Hitler and France's "retrenchment" behind the Maginot Line complete with her Mediterranean, African and Asian possessions. When, some months after Munich, Daladier went on his trip to Corsica, Tunisia and other Mediterranean possessions and shouted defiance at Mussolini, it was, somehow, assumed that he was departing from the appeasement policy symbolized by Munich. But in reality his screaming over France's sacred rights in the Mediterranean suggested only too clearly that *that* area, and not Eastern Europe, was Daladier's chief concern.

As readers will see, the whole Chamberlain concept of

[2] Needless to say, German propaganda spent vast sums on subsidizing certain French newspapers.

"peace in our time" born at Munich collapsed like a house of cards barely six months later when Hitler marched into Prague and took over what was left of Czechoslovakia after the Munich settlement. Now Poland was, clearly, next on Hitler's menu. Chamberlain hastened to "guarantee" Poland, though how she could be helped by Britain and France unless Russia was also brought into the alliance was by no means clear.

It was at this point, in April 1939, that my narrative stopped.

*   *   *

In the weeks that followed, Hitler tore up his non-aggression pact with Poland, as well as the Anglo-German Naval Treaty of 1935. And then began those tortuous Anglo-French negotiations with the Russians for which, to tell the truth, no eagerness was shown by either side—Chamberlain disliking, almost as much as ever, the very idea of an alliance with Russia, and the Russians being highly distrustful of France and Britain after what had happened at Munich, with its "free hand for Germany in the East" undertones. Moreover, the Russians, with an eye on the German Siegfried Line in the West, already then foresaw the possibility of a "phoney war" in the West—a kind of "phoney war" which would help them no more than it was to help Poland when it came to the test in September 1939.[3]

Hitler's war could obviously have been checked in 1936 if France and Britain had not allowed him to occupy the Rhineland. It could still—almost certainly—have been stopped during the Czech crisis in 1938. Even had it not, France and Britain would (with Czech and Russian support) have been in a better position to fight than in 1939 when there was no longer Czechoslovakia or Russia to depend on, and when any direct military aid to Poland was far less feasible than direct military aid to Czechoslovakia a year earlier. I might add that the morale of the French soldiers in 1938 was still very

[3] These strange negotiations, which ended with the Soviet Nazi non-aggression pact of August 1939, are described in some detail in my book, *Russia At War 1941-45* (Dutton; also Avon Books paperback).

much better than it was to be in September 1939—to say
nothing of 1940, when the Germans overran Western Europe,
and the French (or most of them) lost their heads completely
as the Maginot Line myth burst like a soap bubble overnight.

The pacifism and defeatism of the Munich period, as described in this book, were to prove psychologically fore-
runners of the even stronger defeatism of 1940, after the
collapse of that Maginot Line which had been the supreme
—if secret—excuse for the surrender of Czechoslovakia.

The aftereffects of Munich did not end there. If the Czechs
and Poles entered the Russian orbit without much resistance
after World War II, the memory of how the one country
had been "let down" by the West in 1938, and the other in
1939, had something to do with it. A common argument in
both countries, which I visited soon after the war, was that
much as many of them disliked the Russians, they felt they
would at least protect them against a new German invasion
—which was more than France and Britain had done in 1938
and 1939.

So, in a sense, Munich is still with us.

The 1939 edition of the book is reprinted here without
any changes, even though there are, in it, a few weaknesses
which are obvious after more than twenty five years and
which I am ready to recognize: (1) I did not, at the time,
dwell sufficiently on the folly of the Maginot Line myth and
the inadequacy of the French army; (2) I dealt perhaps
rather too briefly with the Russian factor—that is, with the
role Russia might well have played in making Hitler abandon his demands on Czechoslovakia if the Western powers
had not hastened to surrender to Hitler and had entered,
instead, on serious military talks with Russia; (3), in retro-
spect, Franco Spain did not become to France as great a
menace as she potentially seemed to be in 1938-39. But then
what did Franco Spain matter in 1940 to France when the
latter was defeated by the Germans in a few weeks, anyway?
All one can say in Franco's favor is that, even after the French
débâcle of 1940, he had the sense to see (as, indeed, the
Russians also did) that so long as Hitler had not yet defeated

an American-supported Britain, he could not claim to have won the war. But the very real danger of a "third" (Spanish) front, in addition to the German and Italian fronts, could not be ignored in 1938 or 1939.

I have preserved here the detailed account of the British royal visit to Paris in July 1938. In itself it is no more than a period piece, except that the chapter ends on a very ominous note: the joy with which the French leaders learned, in the midst of the royal festivities, of the British offer to send Lord Runciman to Czechoslovakia—that number one gravedigger of France's faithful and trusting ally.

The only change I have made in this edition is to omit the last few pages, written in April 1939, in which I expressed the pious and over-optimistic hope that after Britain's "guarantee" to Poland, France and Britain would now make every effort to organize a big anti-Hitler coalition, complete with Russia, so as to paralyze the German attack on Poland which then seemed imminent. As we know, nobody was very wholehearted about the Grand Alliance, and the Poles themselves did their best to sabotage it. However, that is a different story. I have replaced those last pages by a short postscript.

A.W.

Paris, October 1968

CONTENTS

Book I

BEFORE SEPTEMBER

11

BOOK II

SEPTEMBER

Book I

BEFORE SEPTEMBER

CHAPTER I

FRANCO-CZECH IDYLL

A T 8.52 a.m. on December 19, 1937, a train steamed into the Gare de l'Est. It was bringing back to Paris M. Yvon Delbos, France's Foreign Minister, after his three weeks' 'tour of friendship' in Central and Eastern Europe. Two members of the Cabinet, and representatives of the Quai d'Orsay, of the Polish Embassy and the Czech and Rumanian legations had come to meet him. Behind a police barrier a small crowd of people were shouting: *'Vive Delbos! Vive la Paix!'*

M. Delbos, smiling his gentle smile, came out of the train and said: *'J'ai fait un excellent voyage.'* That was for the afternoon papers. A few days later, before the Foreign Affairs Committee of the Chamber, M. Delbos, as an honest man, admitted that the *voyage* had not been as *excellent* as all that. In fact, he was obliged to confess that France's credit among her friends and allies in Central and Eastern Europe had fallen lower than most people in Paris suspected. No doubt, the ordinary people in Poland and Jugoslavia and Rumania still felt deeply attached to France and all that France stood for; but the Governments—no, the Governments were not the same. The Czechoslovak Government alone was as whole-heartedly pro-French as were the Czech people.

Eighteen months had made a world of difference. France, absorbed in her domestic problems during these eighteen months, had almost forgotten the Rhineland coup of March 7, 1936; but in Warsaw, and Belgrade and Bucharest they remembered it well. The remilitarisation of the Rhineland had been a savage blow to collective security, and to the whole structure of France's Eastern alliances. It had weakened France strategically in relation to Central Europe; and if the Czechs continued to place absolute confidence in the French alliance, it was partly because they had no other choice, and partly because the French assurances were eloquent in the extreme. The Czechs knew, of course, that France's military aid to their country had been rendered more difficult by the re-militarisation of the Rhineland—but, after all (they reflected) the 'Bohemian bastion' was as essential to France as the French alliance was indispensable to the integrity of Czechoslovakia.

But in Warsaw (where the Polish Government had offered to 'march' on the day of the Rhineland occupation, but had met with no response from the Sarraut-Flandin Government), in Belgrade, and in Bucharest they regarded the Rhineland coup as a turning-point in the post-War history of Europe. And with it also went the relative weakening of France as a military power; for since 1935 Germany had been rearming on a stupendous scale. And there were also other reasons why the Jugoslavs and the Rumanians and the Poles were dissatisfied with France. About the middle of 1936, Blum had turned a deaf ear to the proposals for a mutual assistance pact made to Paris by Belgrade and Bucharest. Blum had said that before France could commit herself to defending Jugoslavia and Rumania, she desired the three Little Entente countries to sign a mutual assistance pact among themselves. Aware of Germany's designs on Czechoslovakia, Rumania and Jugo-slavia said they would rather not. Moreover, Nazi propaganda had been active in these countries; and their ruling classes were in any case prejudiced against the Front Populaire, which had governed France for sixteen months; they considered it to be revolutionary and socially disruptive. The stay-in strikes of 1936 and the labour unrest generally had given them the idea that if France was not exactly 'Communist', the 'Reds' were playing too important a part in her internal affairs. You never could tell. . . . In Jugoslavia there was also an influential set around Prince Paul who, largely owing to its past associations with Tsarist Russia, was strongly prejudiced against the Soviets, and so against the Franco-Soviet Pact—whatever it was worth in a military sense.

Such were the ideas prevalent in the ruling circles of the 'allied and friendly' powers which M. Delbos set out to visit during that month of December.

It was a curious journey. Shortly before leaving Paris, M. Delbos had, together with M. Chautemps, the Premier, gone to London; and there had been much talk of a 'general settlement' with Germany. Lord Halifax had returned from Germany, where he had seen Hitler at Berchtesgaden—only it is doubtful whether Lord Halifax fully reported to the French Ministers all that Hitler had said to him about Austria and Czechoslovakia. He had listened politely to what the Führer had to say; and the Führer—if one is to judge from his subsequent behaviour—seems to have interpreted Lord Halifax's politeness as complacency. In any case, it does not seem that, when M. Delbos set out on his tour, he had any grave misgiving about Germany's intentions; and Germany, indeed, had no desire, at that point, to be suspected by the French.

A surprise was awaiting M. Delbos. In passing through Berlin the Nord Express stops at three different stations. At Bahnhof Zoo M. Delbos was welcomed by M. François-Poncet, the French Ambassador, who took a seat in his compartment and said he would accompany him as far as Frankfort-on-the-Oder; at the Bahnhof Friedrichstrasse, the Polish Ambassador and Czech Minister in Berlin welcomed him; then came the last stop—the Schlesischer Bahnhof, far out in the East End of Berlin. And here, on the platform, as the train stopped for a quarter of an hour, was Herr von Neurath in person! He entered M. Delbos's compartment and there, in the presence of M. François-Poncet, they talked for over ten minutes. Then, according to the *Temps*:

> The three personalities stepped on to the station platform and obligingly posed to the photographers. In the process of this operation one of the photographers broke a bulb of magnesium. M. Yvon Delbos turned to Baron von Neurath, and said with a smile, 'In France broken glass is considered lucky.' M. Delbos and M. François-Poncet then re-entered the carriage, and a few minutes later the train began to move out of the station. Standing on the platform, Baron von Neurath saluted *à la hitlérienne*.[1]

The French were pleased and flattered by the courtesy of the German Government.

'When M. Barthou and M. Laval passed through Berlin,' The *Temps* wrote, 'they were welcomed at the station only

[1] *Le Temps*, December 4, 1937.

by an official of the German Foreign Office. When one con-
siders that Herr von Neurath took this initiative so soon after
the London talks, one is tempted to see in his presence at the
station more than just an act of courtesy. Herr von Neurath's
gesture marks in any case a real *détente* between France and
Germany. During their brief talk the two ministers were
glad to note that in recent months there had been more
frequent contacts between ex-servicemen and the young people
of the two countries, and that the Press comments had been less
violent on both sides. They agreed that such contacts increased the mutual comprehension between France and Germany and helped to prepare the way for a subsequent discussion
of political problems by the two Governments.'[1]

And so on. Compliments about the Paris Exhibition and
what not. This extraordinary display of German courtesy and
goodwill is curious when one thinks that the Austrian tragedy
was to start barely two months later—when the unfortunate
Schuschnigg was summoned to Berchtesgaden. However, it
is only fair to say that Von Neurath was to be replaced by
Ribbentrop in the interval.

In Warsaw M. Delbos was met by Colonel Beck and other
personalities, and outside the station there were large crowds
who waved flags and shouted '*Vive la France!*' The Democratic
Club of Warsaw passed a resolution that night, which said:

> M. Delbos personifies the moral strength of his country—a
> strength born from the masses of the people. In these days
> when European civilisation is threatened by barbarism,
> France continues to represent the purest democratic ideal.

Words, words?—no. France, that source of generous ideas,
France with her immense cultural heritage still meant a
terrible lot to these people—to liberals, intellectuals and to
all civilised human beings generally, in all those countries
east of Germany. The Polish Government, however, was less
enthusiastic. Beck, no doubt, referred to the Franco-Polish
alliance, and said that this was a particularly suitable time for
'demonstrating its vitality, its strength and its permanence',
but in his speech at the Foreign Office banquet he defined the
nature of friendship as follows:

> The peculiarity of friendship is that while each of the friends
> pursues his own aims and defends his own interests, he is able

[1] *Le Temps*, December 5, 1937.

to consider with the greatest benevolence all the problems concerning the other.

It might have been better put. The Poles showed much interest in the prospect of a return of colonies to Germany, and said that Poland ought to be given some too. Colonel Beck also attached great importance to Neurath's 'gesture'. The League of Nations was not mentioned in his speech; but at the same time he said that Poland had no intention of adhering to the Anti-Comintern Pact. All this was neither here nor there. But the chief object of Delbos's visit to Warsaw—his proposal to mediate a friendly settlement between Poland and Czechoslovakia—was completely unsuccessful. Beck said in effect that the Polish Government preferred 'bilateral' talks to any kind of mediation.

The Correspondent of the *Deutsche Allgemeine Zeitung* claimed that he had asked M. Delbos

> whether the Polish Government had shown any interest in the Czech problems.
>
> M. Delbos made an evasive gesture, which was greeted by an outburst of hilarity from those present.[1]

Delbos's talks with President Moscicki and Marshal Ridz-Smigly (who had gone to Paris a year earlier, been very enthusiastic about the French alliance, and had carried off a large armaments loan) were little more than *protocolaires*.

And so M. Delbos went off to Bucharest, feeling none too pleased. Rumania was, just then, on the eve of a general election, and in a state of great agitation. Shortly afterwards the Goga Government was to come into office. But at that time M. Tatarescu was still Premier and M. Antonescu Foreign Minister. They were friendly—friendlier than Beck—and the Rumanian people were enthusiastic about M. Delbos. At Cernauti, the first Rumanian town, he was presented with the traditional loaf and salt cellar—and he was cheered by peasants and other people at all the stations through which he passed.

The intellectuals were equally friendly. 'In the realm of culture,' the *Temps* wrote, 'it seems certain that the Rumanian *élite* has remained faithful to the French language and to

[1] *Deutsche Allgemeine Zeitung*, December 7.

French culture, in spite of all the efforts of hostile propaganda; and the French Institute at Bucharest remains a spiritual and intellectual *bourse* between the two countries.'[1]

Only 'hostile propaganda' had made much headway in the last year. The leaders of the opposition parties boycotted all the official receptions given in M. Delbos's honour—which was all the more deplorable when one remembered how three years earlier M. Barthou, during his visit to Bucharest, received a unanimous ovation from the Rumanian parliament. Only during the last day of his visit did M. Delbos have an opportunity to meet M. Lupu, the leader of the National Peasant Party, and the other opposition leaders—with the exception of M. Codreanu, the leader of the Iron Guard.

King Carol was friendly and so were M. Tatarescu, and M. Antonescu. Trade relations—oil against armaments—were discussed, and so was the mechanisation of the Rumanian army, on the development of which General Gamelin, during his visit a few months earlier, had insisted. But there was an undercurrent of uncertainty in all the talks. M. Antonescu, the Foreign Minister, in his speech of welcome at the Foreign Office banquet said that Rumania was loyal to the Little Entente and to the ideals of the League of Nations, and was also trying to maintain good relations with her Russian neighbour despite her horror of Communism. But he clearly indicated that she did not wish to enter into any new commitments for the present; the reoccupation of the Rhineland had been a terrible blow to collective security, and the foreign policy of London and Paris was full of uncertainties.

'Collective security,' M. Antonescu said, 'can exist only if the security of Central and Eastern Europe is not detached from the security of Western Europe.'

M. Antonescu was looking far ahead. And there was one thing that was disturbing him, as it was disturbing many other people in that part of the world. In the last eighteen months Blum and Delbos and other French leaders had repeated a thousand times that the British *entente* was the corner stone of France's foreign policy. France had tied herself to the apron strings of England; she had allowed England to force upon her the policy of non-intervention (even before anybody else

[1] *Le Temps*, December 11.

had agreed to it);[1] owing to the British Government's dislike of Russia, France had consistently cold-shouldered the Soviets, and had refused to enter into staff talks with them; and although M. Blum and M. Delbos had sworn a hundred times that nothing was more sacred than the Franco-Czech alliance, M. Antonescu (and many others) wondered how it would really work if it ever came to the test. Would not France again ask England's permission to mobilise, as she had already done on the fateful day of March 7, 1936, when the Reichswehr reoccupied the Rhineland? It was all very well for Delbos to ask Rumania to enter into mutual assistance pacts with Czechoslovakia and Jugoslavia and perhaps the Soviets—but M. Antonescu was not so sure that 'the West' would help when it came to the point. He did not say all this, but he certainly implied it.

In his farewell speech M. Delbos concluded by saying that 'Rumania was faithful to France just as France was faithful to Rumania;' he said he was delighted to see how 'Rumania was impregnated with French culture,' and added that 'when two countries are linked by such solid spiritual bonds, one need feel no anxiety for the future of their relations.' But the bonds were spiritual, more than military, and the French Foreign Minister's attempt to strengthen collective security among the Little Entente countries met with no success.

The most dramatic episode during the 'tour of friendship' occurred at Belgrade. As M. Delbos, accompanied by M. Stoyadinovitch was leaving the station, he was greeted by an incredible chorus of cheering (*un concert inoui d'acclamations,* said the *Temps* correspondent) from the enormous crowds who had gathered in the vast square outside. They were waving frantically innumerable French flags, large flags and small flags, and they had also brought with them a huge panel with a portrait of M. Delbos.

> This cordial—perhaps too cordial—demonstration (the *Temps* correspondent wrote) had a deplorable sequel as soon as the official carriages had driven past on their way to the French legation. Four or five thousand demonstrators formed themselves into a procession, and breaking through the police cordons, marched through the town shouting '*Vive la France!*'

[1] See *The Destiny of France,* Chapter XXII.

'*Vive la Démocratie française!*' '*Vive Delbos!*' They were
charged by mounted gendarmes who tried in vain to disperse
the crowds. There were some short but violent clashes at
several points between the Premier's Office and the Skupt-
china, and near the Czech legation. In one place the rioters
barricaded themselves against the gendarmes and threw stones
at them. The gendarmes fired. At the moment of writing
there is one dead and several wounded.

Not without a touch of officially inspired hypocrisy, the
Temps 'severely condemned this demonstration whose organ-
isers,' it said, 'had shown themselves guilty of an *abus de
circonstance*,' (a lovely phrase!). 'They should have known
that it was absolutely impossible for M. Delbos, as the official
spokesman of France and England, to make any distinction
between the Jugoslav people and its Government.'

Granted that it was tactless and all that; granted also that
the demonstration was essentially an anti-Stoyadinovitch
demonstration, the eloquent fact remained that in the minds
of the Jugoslav students the notion of liberty was associated
with their idea of France, and Stoyadinovitch was both
'against France' and 'against liberty'.

Delbos and Stoyadinovitch—the latter had just returned
from a visit to Rome—had hardly anything to say to each other.
except some courteous platitudes. In his speech that followed
the usual banquet Stoyadinovitch (no doubt out of respect for
Italy, which had just left the League) did not mention the
League at all; worse still, he did not even mention the Little
Entente. The omission rather suggested that the Little
Entente was none of France's business.

In the meantime, the pro-French rioting was spreading right
through Jugoslavia.

'Everywhere,' the *Sud-Est* Agency cabled on December 13,
'the population is organising pro-French demonstrations in
honour of M. Delbos. Obeying orders from Belgrade the
police are trying, but with great difficulty, to contain the
demonstrators. Numerous arrests, amounting this evening
to four hundred, have been made in all the principal towns.
The Government seems to be determined to prevent at any
price that to-morrow's demonstrations in honour of M. Delbos
should take the form of mass demonstrations against the
Government and its new foreign policy.'[1]

[1] *Le Temps*, December 14.

In the great naval harbour of Split large crowds assembled outside the French consulate singing the 'Marseillaise'.

Through the whole of Jugoslavia they were singing the 'Marseillaise'. The Serbian *intelligentsia* were passionately pro-French. During his last day at Belgrade M. Delbos attended a reception organised by the Society of the Friends of France.

> The hall was packed with over fifteen hundred persons. The president of the Association, Professor Stevan Pavlovitch, a former Minister, exalted, amidst loud cheering, the greatness of France and the strength of Franco-Jugoslav friendship. A choir of children and young girls sang the 'Marseillaise'; which led M. Delbos to exclaim: 'The 'Marseillaise' is the hymn of all nations devoted to liberty and justice; it is therefore the hymn of France and the hymn of Jugoslavia!'[1]

By that time M. Delbos must have been thoroughly fed-up with Stoyadinovitch. The *Völkischer Beobachter* claimed that when Delbos asked Stoyadinovitch whether in case of war Jugoslavia would be on France's side he received the evasive reply—'We want peace.'[2]

As the train on its way to Prague, was crossing the Hungarian plain, Delbos remarked wistfully to one of the journalists in his carriage: 'At last we are going to see some real friends.'

At Prague, richly decorated with French and Czech flags, the popular enthusiasm was as great as in Belgrade, but this time with the full approval of the Government. It was to be the last French State visit to that Czechoslovakia which France had in 1919, done so much to create. Beneš, Krofta, Hodza— here at last were real friends. Masaryk was mentioned affectionately in all the speeches, and M. Delbos travelled out into the country to lay a wreath on the old man's grave.

> 'France and Czechoslovakia,' M. Delbos said at one of the functions, 'see completely eye to eye on all questions. They are deeply conscious of the close community of their interests, and this community is reflected in the treaties we have signed. France is firmly and faithfully attached to her treaties with Czechoslovakia, and she sees in them the public expression of the solid bonds and the mutual obligations which unite our two nations, both of which are resolved to make every sacrifice for their common defence.'

[1] *Le Temps*, December 14.
[2] *Völkischer Beobachter*, December 16.

And in another speech, which was going to cause great
annoyance to the German Press, he declared:

> 'Fraternity is a word which is often used in after-dinner
> toasts; but it sometimes means little.   But in the case of France
> and Czechoslovakia it defines perfectly their relations.   While
> casting aside every idea of domination, I may say that Czecho-
> slovakia is like an extension (un prolongement) of France.   We are
> united by so many ties, we feel things in such a similar way, and
> our régimes are so similar that a Frenchman in Czechoslovakia
> feels as though he were in France, and a Czechoslovak in
> France feels as though he were in Czechoslovakia.

The German Press was much annoyed.   The *Berliner
Tageblatt* said: 'In proclaiming that Czechoslovakia is "an
extension of France" M. Delbos is taking a great responsibility
in Europe.'   It was also angry—and this was a more serious
matter—because M. Delbos, it said, had done nothing about
the German minority.   It claimed that, in London, the British
Government had strongly urged M. Delbos to examine the
matter in all seriousness with the Czech Government, and to
give them some friendly, but firm advice.

Actually in the course of one of the official receptions M.
Delbos did meet two of the Sudeten leaders, Herr Kundt and
Senator Pfrogner.   They told him that they did not wish to be
treated as a minority any longer, but emphasised their loyalty
to the Czechoslovak state.   It does seem certain that the Czech
Government easily persuaded M. Delbos not to worry about
the matter; and leave it for them to settle.   They would do
the best they could; but territorial autonomy would be a
menace to the integrity of Czechoslovakia, and could not
possibly be agreed to.   M. Delbos did not 'insist'.   According
to another report, M. Delbos hardly discussed the Sudeten
question at all.

> With all the respect due to a sovereign and friendly Power,
> which was receiving him in such a moving manner, and aware
> of the wisdom and clearsightedness of the Czech Government,
> M. Delbos refrained from offering any suggestion—even a
> friendly suggestion—on a question which he considered to be
> essentially an internal Czechoslovak problem.[1]

Czechoslovakia gave France's Foreign Minister an affectionate send-off.

[1] *Le Temps*, December 18.

Here is a Havas message from Cheb describing M. Delbos's homeward journey:

> In all the stations, decorated with flags, through which the train slowly passed, schoolchildren, Sokols, young girls in their national costumes, and many other people, who had assembled on the platforms, were cheering the representatives of France. In one of the stations a group of young men were displaying a large banner with the French inscription: '*Salut à notre grande patrie.*'
>
> The first stop was at Plzen [Pilsen]. The platform was decorated with French flags, and in the middle of it all stood a Christmas tree. The mayor of the great industrial city and a Czech legionary wearing the uniform of a French airman of the last war welcomed M. Delbos, who replied: 'There are no two peoples in the world so fraternally united as the peoples of France and Czechoslovakia.' At Cheb, on the German frontier, M. Delbos was greeted with the playing of the *Marseillaise* and of the Czech national anthem. Once more he expressed his gratitude for the reception given him in Czechoslovakia and emphasised the indissoluble bonds uniting the two countries.[1]

Without comment.

Except that it was through Eger (or Cheb as the Czechs called it) that Hitler made his triumphant entry into the Sudetenland in October, 1938.

[1] *Le Temps*, December 20.

CHAPTER II

THE TROUBLE STARTS

THE tragic year of 1938 which was to see the end of Austria and the dismemberment of Czechoslovakia, began with a setback for the Fascist cause. After a deadly battle that had lasted nearly a fortnight—part of it was fought in a blinding snowstorm—the Government troops entered Teruel. It was a very costly victory, and perhaps it facilitated the great Franco advance on the Aragon Front three months later. But superficial observers and optimists saw in the Teruel victory not only the long-awaited demonstration of the Republicans' capacity to conduct offensive warfare, but a turning-point in the Spanish civil war. Never had the outlook for the Spanish Government looked better than during those first weeks of 1938.

But during that month of January France took little interest in foreign affairs. She was stewing in her own juice.

There had been a wave of strikes at the end of December; and the first half of January saw an abortive 'industrial peace conference'; the resignation of the Chautemps Cabinet; a Cabinet crisis that lasted nearly a week—in the course of which M. Blum, aware of the grave international situation, first proposed a national Government 'around the Front Populaire', and M. Bonnet tried for the first time his hand at Cabinet making—and, in the end, the formation of a new Chautemps Government, only without the Socialists in it any longer. It was a very weak and unrepresentative Government—and this was the Government which was going to face the beginning of the great international crisis of 1938. It was one of those stop-gap Cabinets which have often proved unlucky internationally. It was while the stop-gap Cabinet of M. Sarraut was in office in 1936 that Hitler invaded the Rhineland.

Already two days before the Government was formed M.

Archimbaud, one of the leading Radicals, remarked in the Chamber lobbies:

> France is waiting impatiently for a Government. Party quarrels should be relegated to the background. The first thing to think about is the future of France and of the Republic, *especially in view of the intrigues going on against France in Central Europe and the dangerous activities of Germany.*[1]

But it was no use. Cabinet-making continued to be dominated by party politics. As for Europe, everything still *seemed* quiet.

The Chautemps Government was anything but impressive. It nevertheless received from the Chamber, not exactly a vote of confidence, but the benefit of the doubt. The vote was an unusual one—501 for the Government—and one (the irrepressible M. Bergery) against. There were about 100 abstentions on the Right. But this overwhelming vote did not mean anything, except that the Centre welcomed the departure of the Socialists from the Government bench, and the Socialists and Communists were still unwilling to break up the Front Populaire majority. M. Chautemps had, in fact, undergone a complete metamorphosis: a week earlier he had attacked the working class; now he was all honey to the Left. In reality it meant little, except as a demonstration of remarkably slick parliamentary acrobatics. The Government meant, above all, a further step in the disintegration of the Front Populaire. Looked at from the international point of view the whole Cabinet crisis—*de Chautemps à Chautemps*—was something wretchedly frivolous. So also was the overwhelming 'vote of confidence' given to the new Chautemps Cabinet. André Albert, the youngest deputy at the Chamber, and something of an *enfant terrible*, remarked before the vote: 'The bigger the Government's majority, the less time will it last.'

The Ministerial Declaration was full of good intentions and included some promises which were calculated to sweeten the temper of the Left, as well as some passages in praise of the Front Populaire:

> The Front Populaire, that spontaneous outburst of the democratic instincts of the people—an outburst which followed

[1] *Manchester Guardian*, January 18.

the bloody incidents [the riots of February 6, 1934] which re-
vealed a threat to the régime—a régime to which the nation
is profoundly attached, has the double significance of a powerful will to defend the Republic and of an ardent desire for
social justice.

M. Chautemps went on to say that the working class would
be given the 'complete certainty' that nothing would be done
to diminish the social advantages they had legitimately acquired.   And M. Chautemps actually promised to introduce
'within the shortest time' a Bill providing Old Age Pensions
for needy workers—a substantial sop to the Left, but a promise
that was actually never going to be carried out.

The Declaration said that France would remain loyal to the
Tripartite Agreement, and the passage on foreign policy was
still in the best League tradition:

> Our foreign policy will be based on France's loyalty to the
> League of Nations, which despite many obstacles, remains the
> best safeguard of peace in the world.   We shall spare no effort
> to revive the confidence and the will of the nations who intend
> to remain faithful to the League. . . .   Faithful to the ideal
> we share with the great democracies, and to the friendship that
> unites us so cordially and so completely to Great Britain,
> *and resolved to uphold and respect all the treaties with which we are
> linked to friendly nations*, France is at the same time sincerely
> anxious to develop normal and peaceful relations with all
> nations, and to seek a loyal basis of agreement with them,
> through an effort of mutual comprehension.

Words, words, 'words.

The League Council met on January 27.   It was the 100th
Session of the League Council.   It was perhaps the last meeting
where some faint illusions were still entertained on the future
of the League.

As the Geneva Correspondent of the *Manchester Guardian*
wrote on January 27:

> At the public meeting of the League Council, this evening
> the fourteen members celebrated the hundredth session of the
> Council by making fourteen speeches in which most of them
> declared their attachment to the principles of the League,
> with reservations in many cases concerning their application
> in practice.   It was not an exhilarating ceremony.

The main task M. Delbos and Mr. Eden had undertaken

was to prevent the League Covenant from being wrecked. The discussion on the Committee of Twenty-eight on an eventual revision of the Covenant resulted in the dossier on the revision being sent to the Assembly, which would in due course give the Committee further instructions. Until then, the Committee would suspend its labours. This decision was taken on the proposal of Lord Cranbourne.

On February 3, the *Temps* wrote that thanks to Britain and France 'no rash decision was taken which would have increased still further the difficulties of the League of Nations'.

It was a tame Council session. In the opinion of the British and French Governments, the best that could be done was to postpone and avoid all important decisions, in the hope that conditions *might* improve in the next few months. Naturally, nothing was settled about either China or Spain—except that in the case of Spain M. Chautemps, on January 31, launched from Paris an appeal to both sides to refrain from bombing open towns; while two days later, in view of a revival of piracy in the Mediterranean, the British and French Governments decided to reinforce the Nyon patrol, and to attack all submerged submarines. Weak as was the foreign policy of the British and French Governments in those days, there were still certain things which they would not tolerate—one of them was Italian piracy in the Mediterranean. With the Chamberlain régime establishing itself in England, the most Mussolini and Franco had to fear was a British inquiry, or—in very bad cases—British 'representations' at Burgos! When one looks back on February 1938, that Anglo-French decision of February 2, to 'attack all submerged submarines' seems like the last action taken by France and Britain without any regard to the feelings of the Dictator countries.

It was during the first week in February that reports came from Germany which gave England and France something of a shock. Hitler had been expected to speak at the Reichstag on January 30, the fifth anniversary of the Nazi régime. But the meeting did not take place. Something was in the air. There were rumours first, of General Blomberg's resignation because of his *mésalliance* with his typist; then there was a rumour that General von Fritsch had fallen into disgrace. Stories went round of a monarchist plot. But a day or two later, there was no longer much doubt of what had happened, especially when it was learned that Ribbentrop had been appointed Foreign Minister in place of Von Neurath. The Nazi extremists had gained the upper hand, both in the army and at the German Foreign Office. It is true that Paris was to remain puzzled for a day or two longer than any other capital; for on February 7, an 'occasional correspondent' claiming to write from Bâle, gave an entirely different version in the *Temps* of what had happened.

> Himmler, according to the story, had discovered a monarchist plot in the Reichswehr, a plot which aimed at putting the second son of the Crown Prince on the throne. This plot was headed by Von Fritsch. Von Fritsch was placed under domestic arrest, while on behalf of the Reichswehr Von Keitel negotiated with Hitler. He accepted the dismissal from the Reichswehr of the 'Royalist group', but demanded the complete autonomy of the Reichswehr. Goering's and Himmler's attempts to place the Reichswehr under Party control were thus foiled. Further, the Reichswehr demanded that they be given an important role in the conduct of German foreign policy; they demanded, above all, a friendlier policy in relation to England.
>
> The theory that the appointment of Von Ribbentrop to the post of Foreign Minister meant the beginning of a 'wild' foreign policy was dismissed by the 'occasional correspondent' at Bâle with the remark that 'perhaps it was, above all, necessary to clear the German Embassy in London of Ribbentrop's presence'.

This article in the *Temps* of February 7 aroused no end of comment in Paris. Partly because its authorship was widely attributed to a high official at the Quai d'Orsay. Why did he write this article? The only plausible explanation was that the Government—or certain members of the Government— were anxious that French opinion should not become too worried about the developments in Germany.

No doubt a kind thought, but a useless one; for this optimism was soon belied by the Berchtesgaden ultimatum to Schuschnigg.

In this case, however, the Press tried again to be optimistic. The *Intransigeant* claimed that Schuschnigg had stuck to his guns, and had pretty well told Hitler where he got off. It was not until several days later that the ugly truth of the Berchtesgaden meeting began to leak out.

And then came the twentieth of February. There had been Press rumours of a conflict within the British Cabinet; but the man in the street knew nothing definite. But certain people in France had nevertheless smelt a rat; among them was M. Flandin, who was in close contact with certain London Press lords; and these kept him informed.

It was about the tenth of February that M. Flandin came out, with renewed vigour, in favour of a 'retrenchment' policy. He blamed everything on the Communists and on the Franco-Soviet Pact. But for the Communists, he said, France could live in happy harmony with Germany and Italy. His meaning was perfectly clear. Free hand for Germany in the East. In Germany, too, the Government must have been informed of the way the wind was blowing in London; for it is otherwise inconceivable how Hitler could have attacked the British Foreign Secretary with such personal violence on the afternoon of February 20. Flandin in France and Hitler in Germany seemed to know more about the doings of the British Cabinet than almost anybody in England.

Hitler's speech that day was the most violent he had ever made. In Paris the following were the principal points noted:

(1) Hitler no longer made any serious pretence of being a defender of European peace;

(2) he virtually declared that the policy of Berchtesgaden would be persevered in, and that woe to the Czechs if they did not submit to his demands in favour of the Sudetens;

(3) he declared more explicitly than ever before Germany's refusal to tolerate a victory of the Spanish Government;

(4) the speech, with its attacks on Mr. Eden showed that he knew that something was brewing in London; and he no longer thought it necessary to keep up even the illusion that Germany might, in certain circumstances, return to the League;

(5) he gave unqualified support to Japan;

(6) the speech did not contain the slightest guarantee of Austrian independence; and there were particularly menacing references to the ten million Germans living close to Germany's borders [seven million Austrians and three million Sudetens], and

(7) France was treated merely with contempt as a country clinging to a dead democratic ideology and incapable of putting her house in order.[1]

[1] *Manchester Guardian*, February 21.

And, on the night of the same day, after an interminable
Cabinet meeting at 10 Downing Street, the B.B.C. announced
with laconic brevity that Mr. Eden had resigned.

Every editor in Paris that night was puzzled as to which of
the two items of news was the more important—Hitler's speech
or Eden's resignation. In the end most of them decided in
favour of Eden's resignation.

The reactions in Paris next day were described as follows
in a Paris message in the *Manchester Guardian*:

> Mr. Eden's resignation has caused the deepest commotion
> in Paris, deeper even than is outwardly shown in French
> Government quarters. In the view of many observers it is
> perhaps the final blow to all the beliefs and political principles
> the majority of the British and French people upheld together
> for so many years.
>
> One may ask: 'Tell me who are your friends—and your
> enemies—and I will tell you who you are.' It is clear who Mr.
> Eden's enemies are, and it is clear what he represented. Italy
> is rejoicing, Germany is rejoicing, and in France all the pro-
> Fascists, Royalists, and Cagoulards—that is, the small anti-
> democratic minority who now hope to gain in importance
> —are overjoyed.
>
> 'Having seen the light at last, England has sent Eden back
> to the crazy old spinsters (*les vieilles folles*) and to Lord Cecil's
> clergymen,' the *Action Française* prints at the top of its front page.
> This is the very paper which during the Abyssinian war
> constantly spoke of 'Bloody Eden'.
>
> Perhaps the general sentiment is best expressed by the head-
> line of the *Intransigeant* which says: 'Hitler has driven Eden
> out of office.' The statement is crude, for by 'Hitler' is meant
> not only the Führer but Nazi-Fascist blackmail in general
> and those forces in England which two years ago supported
> the Hoare-Laval plan, which struck such a blow at the League
> of Nations.
>
> They have now had their revenge. The Italians, as seen
> here, played skilfully on the differences in the Cabinet in order
> to squeeze Mr. Eden out. Mr. Eden believed that peace
> could still be saved if Great Britain and France (increasingly
> supported by the United States) showed that they were firm
> and would not be intimidated by Germany and Italy. His
> style was constantly cramped by his Cabinet colleagues, but
> still he was not without influence, and the greatest desire of
> Germany and Italy was to see him go.
>
> It is deeply felt here that Mr. Eden, who knew the dictators
> from personal experience, understood their mentality better

than Mr. Chamberlain can understand them yet. He knew that Mussolini and Hitler were not open to moral suasion and that they could not be trusted to keep promises without solid guarantees being given first. He understood that there must be withdrawal from Spain first and not afterwards, for if it was to be 'afterwards' it would never be at all.

'Back to the Four-Power Pact of unholy memory?' one observer at the Chamber remarked this evening. 'And it is clear what the Four-Power Pact means: the perpetuation of Berchtesgaden diplomacy at the expense of the smaller Powers. And once these are swallowed up it will be our turn—with the odds then overwhelmingly against us.'

For all this places France in a singularly delicate position. No doubt she will have to co-operate with Britain whatever its Government, just as Britain will have to co-operate with France whatever hopes Lord Halifax may have of gaining Germany's friendship. But what, it is asked, about France's allies, Poland and Czechoslovakia? And what about the League? If the new British Government pays only lip-service to the League and adopts Four-Power Pact methods must France follow—which would amount to following the precepts of M. Flandin and other Right-Wing politicians?

The repercussions of such a state of affairs, were it ever to come about, are incalculable. But the instinct of the great majority of French public opinion is that a Four-Power Pact policy, or anything like it, would be suicidal. And is Spain, it is also asked, to be handed over to German and Italian domination? For Hitler's speech left few illusions that he and Mussolini would abandon Spain out of pure kindness of heart. The matter is of the most immediate and vital importance to France's security.

The less nervous among the French hold that since Mr. Chamberlain could not be dissuaded by Mr. Eden from adopting his new policy nothing else can, and that he had better find out for himself that neither Mussolini nor Hitler is possible to deal with unless he is prepared to surrender to them all along the line.

In the meantime, it is felt, France should at least try to strengthen her own authority in European affairs. A more representative Government than the present one is now considered to be a matter of only a few weeks, and there is indeed a strong suspicion that the unimpressiveness of the present French Government and also the needlessly exaggerated reports of France's military weakness, especially in the air, have helped to precipitate the Cabinet crisis in London.[1]

It was a fearful blow to M. Delbos. It looked as though

[1] *Manchester Guardian*, February 22.

his policy to which he had clung in spite of everything, was
finally crumbling.   Since his tour in Central Europe he had
become increasingly pessimistic.   On February 16, a few days
after the Berchtesgaden ultimatum, he had remarked to a
number of French journalists—'How can we interfere in a
quarrel between a country of 70,000,000 and a country of
7,000,000, and with all the guns on the side of the former?'
It was a phrase with terrible implications; but M. Delbos was
a tired and disheartened man.   On February 18, however, he
was given to understand that Mr. Eden was prepared to make
at least an attempt to stop the rot in Austria, especially if France
took the lead; and it was while M. Delbos was considering ways
and means of saving Austria's independence, that the news
reached him of Mr. Eden's resignation.   Later it was learned
that not only the Italian issue, but also the Austrian issue
had precipitated Eden's resignation.   Perhaps M. Delbos and
Mr. Eden would have done nothing in the end; but it is certainly possible to argue that, without the complete indifference
shown for Austria by Mr. Chamberlain and Lord Halifax,
the Anschluss would not have come so soon, or with such suddenness, and that Hitler would have hesitated to march his
army straight into Austria.   With Mr. Eden in office, Hitler
was still kept guessing.   But Mr. Chamberlain's speech of
February 22 gave him a completely free hand.

The speech was as bad as anyone in France could have anticipated.   It implied that England cared nothing for what happened to any country east of the Rhine.   Hitler could help
himself to Austria and Czechoslovakia for all he cared.   For
that night Mr. Chamberlain said:

> If I am right, as I am confident I am, in saying that the
> League as constituted to-day is unable to provide collective
> security for anybody, then I say we must try not to delude
> small weak nations into thinking that they will be protected
> by the League against aggression—and acting accordingly
> when we know that nothing of the kind can be expected.

It was like giving Hitler a free pass to Vienna.

And on the previous day Mr. Chamberlain had expounded
a theory which, for all his friendly references to France, disturbed many Frenchmen—for it looked exactly like a return
to the Four-Power Pact of unholy memory:

The peace of Europe must depend upon the attitude of the four major Powers—Germany, Italy, France and ourselves. For ourselves, we are linked to France by common ideals of democracy, of liberty, and Parliamentary government. France need not fear that the resignation of my right honourable friend upon this issue signifies any departure from the policy of the closest friendship with France of which he has been such a distinguished exponent. I count myself as firm a friend of France as my right honourable friend. The difference between him and me will never mean that there is any difference between us about our relations with France.

On the other side we find Italy and Germany also linked by affinities of outlook and in the form of their government. The question that we have to think of is this: Are we to allow these two pairs of nations to go on glowering at one another across the frontier, allowing the feeling between the two sides to become more and more embittered, until at last the barriers are broken down and the conflict begins which many think would mark the end of civilisation? Or can we bring them to an understanding of one another's aims and objects and to such discussion as may lead to their final settlement?

If we can do that, if we can bring these four nations into friendly discussion, into a settling of their differences, we shall have saved the peace of Europe for a generation.

Poor Delbos! It must be said that he faced the new situation bravely. There was to be no change in France's foreign policy, he said to the Foreign Affairs Committee after Mr. Chamberlain's speech, and he stressed France's determination to preserve her Eastern alliances.

．　　．　　．　　．　　．　　．　　．　　．　　．

The great foreign affairs debate at the Chamber that began five days after Mr. Eden's resignation is of particular interest; for it shows that French opinion was still, on the face of it, almost unanimous in reaffirming France's 'traditional' policy. Only, reading to-day the verbatim reports of the speeches, we have the impression that the Chamber displayed great vigour and determination in reaffirming this policy. In reality the debate took place in a morose and gloomy atmosphere. The Chamberlain speech of the previous Tuesday was rankling in many minds, and if, as a matter of courtesy, Mr. Chamberlain was not directly criticised, M. Flandin was used as Mr. Chamberlain's whipping boy.

．　　．　　．　　．　　．　　．　　．　　．

I have dealt with M. Flandin's earlier career in *The Destiny of France*. It is sufficient to recall here that after being closely associated with M. Tardieu and political reaction in 1930-1, and being violently attacked by the Left for the part which, they alleged, he had played in the Aeropostale scandal, Flandin managed to become, in the next few years, something of a *persona grata* with the Left.

He quarrelled with Tardieu and came to be regarded as the leader of the democratically-minded part of the Centre. He acted as an exponent of political and economic liberalism. In 1933 he hurried to the support of the Radical Cabinets of MM. Daladier and Sarraut when these were attacked by the Socialists. In 1934 he was a member of M. Doumergue's National Government and was accused by Colonel de la Rocque of having plotted, together with M. Herriot, for its downfall. He became Premier in November and his Government was welcomed by M. Blum as 'the first victory over Fascism'. He dropped M. Doumergue's highly suspect Constitutional Reform proposals, and by contrast with M. Doumergue, he came to be regarded as being almost one of the saviours of Democracy. He was disliked by the Right, and when, in a spirit of impartiality, he attended a memorial mass at Notre Dame on the first anniversary of the Riots of February 6, 1934, he was spat on by an *Action Française* thug.

On the whole, however, he failed to impress himself upon the public imagination. Looking like a fat opulent stockbroker, his personality was singularly colourless, and he was completely eclipsed by Laval, his Foreign Minister. It was during this Flandin Government that the Franco-Soviet Pact was signed in May 1935, a pact which was to be ratified in the following February, when Flandin was Foreign Minister in the short-lived Sarraut Government.

In the interval, Flandin was Minister of State without portfolio in the Laval Cabinet of Abyssinian fame, but, having been badly injured in a motor accident in April 1935, he played little part in public affairs for some months.

However, by the time the crisis had reached its height in October 1935, Flandin had become very active again, and—this was a surprise to many who had considered him as a good liberal and as a staunch supporter of the League—he showed himself, at the famous Cabinet meeting of October 3, on the day after war had broken out in Abyssinia, more grimly opposed to sanctions than even M. Laval himself. The Laval Government fell on the issue of foreign policy in January 1936; and the Sarraut Government took its place—with M. Flandin as Foreign Minister. 'Such as you are, I welcome you,' M. Blum said to the new Government; 'for you represent a reaction against the disastrous Government of M. Laval.'

By what aberration Flandin was appointed Foreign Minister 'as a reaction against Laval' remains a mystery. It must have been known that he was a complete anti-sanctionist; and soon after becoming Foreign Minister, he frankly announced to his party, the Alliance Démocratique that 'except for some points of detail, he agreed with the foreign policy of M. Laval'. Nevertheless his protestations of loyalty to the League and of his belief in collective security and in the Franco-Soviet Pact (the ratification of which he urged) continued to be taken at their face value. On March 3, the question of the oil embargo against Italy arose once again at Geneva, and Mr. Eden seemed to be strongly in favour of this step. It was M. Flandin who refused to subscribe to it. A story told by competent observers was that Hitler was anxiously waiting for the outcome of these discussions on the oil embargo, in order to see whether France and England were united or not. The breach between France and England on this issue convinced him that he would have nothing to fear from England if he occupied the demilitarised Rhineland zone.

France could, nevertheless, have taken the initiative in reacting sharply to this capture of her 'first line of defence'—a capture which—it was only too clear—was a savage blow to collective security and to France's whole system of Eastern alliances.

In *The Destiny of France* I described in detail the hesitations and divisions in the French Cabinet on that fatal day of March 7. Some Ministers stood for mobilisation, others for inaction—and M. Flandin was among the latter. Instead, he decided to submit the matter to the League Council. That Council Meeting in London was a complete getaway for Germany. For the moment for doing anything had clearly been missed. On Monday, March 9, Mr. Eden gave a pledge of

unqualified support to France in the case of German aggression; it was the least England could do, and it was done spontaneously. This declaration was followed by a more detailed
agreement. Though all this was inevitable M. Flandin never
ceased to boast that it was he who had brought about the Anglo-
French alliance.

Under the Front Populaire Governments of 1936-7 Flandin
became one of the principal leaders of the Opposition; and it
was towards the end of 1937, after a visit to Berlin, that he
began to preach openly his New Policy of 'retrenchment'.
Flandin, who had never succeeded in impressing himself upon
the public's attention, had now discovered a way of being
'talked about'. The reactionary Press eagerly published his
articles, and, thanks to important connections with London
Press lords, he was also given a great deal of publicity in England. Before very long he was recognised to be the principal
French exponent of the New Policy, and the fall of Eden was,
of course, a godsend to him. In the course of the year he was
to become the central figure in the French movement against
Czechoslovakia and also against the Spanish Government; and,
since foreign politics and home politics run in more or less
parallel lines, he also became one of the principal figures in
the movement of Political Reaction in France itself. Though
at first seemingly hostile to the Daladier Government—for the
Premier had a certain distrust of him—he was going to be on
increasingly good terms with M. Bonnet, the Foreign Minister.
He came to be more and more associated with Four-Power
Pact ideas and in reply to a telegram he was to send to Hitler
on the day of the Munich agreement Hitler complimented him
on the good work he had been doing in France. If in the
February debate M. Flandin acted as Mr. Chamberlain's whipping boy, in the year that followed he was to go a good deal
beyond Mr. Chamberlain's 'appeasement' policy.

THE BATTLE OF IDEAS IN FEBRUARY 1938

A fairly detailed account of this February debate is justified;
because it was the only full-dress foreign debate of the year,
and it reflects in an interesting way the state of French parliamentary opinion at an extremely difficult moment—ten

days after the Berchtesgaden ultimatum, five days after Mr.
Eden's resignation; and barely a fortnight before the German
troops were to march into Vienna. It is true that at that
moment, there was probably nobody in France who was expecting the Anschluss to happen so soon and so brutally; there
were actually still some illusions that Italy was 'against it', and
it was still believed that this Italian hostility would act as a
safeguard of at least Austria's nominal independence. One
speaker warned the French Government against the danger of
—not the Anschluss—but of an Austro-German customs
union! On the whole, however, nobody saw clearly how the
Anschluss could be prevented, if it really came to the point.

The debate opened in the morning of February 25 with a
speech by M. Pezet, a member of the Catholic *Démocrates
Populaires,* a vice-president of the Foreign Affairs Committee,
and a personal friend of Schuschnigg's. Large sections of
the French Catholics were deeply concerned about the fate
of Catholic Austria.

Pezet, who had, clearly, given much thought to the international situation, plunged straight into the subject; and
sounded in the very first sentence the Chamberlain-versus-anti-
Chamberlain *motif;* though Mr. Chamberlain was disguised
as M. Flandin.

> 'Mr. Winston Churchill,' Mr. Pezet said, 'has highly praised
> the valour and the power of the French Army; while M. Flandin
> [Mr. Chamberlain] is basing his policy on the temporary
> abdication of France and on our present helplessness. . . .
> The French Government is speaking well and firmly; but it is
> acting without authority; and it has had bad luck.'

This was obviously an allusion to Mr. Eden's resignation.

> M. Pezet recalled how, before the Foreign Affairs Committee
> of the Chamber, soon after his return from Central Europe, M.
> Delbos had said: 'It would be tragic if France were in the
> dilemma of abandoning to their fate the States of Central
> Europe, in spite of our agreements, and of coming into conflict
> with England in our determination to be faithful to our allies.'

Here was France's tragic dilemma in a nutshell.

M. Pezet then came to the Austrian problem and to the
Berchtesgaden ultimatum of a fortnight before.

'And what now? We are groping in the dark. We don't know where we are going. For we know nothing of England's intentions. We must give an answer worthy of France. Are we entering to-day into a new era of French foreign policy? And what is this new era to be?

'But suppose the Government is unable to give a clear answer, suppose it feels obliged to cover up the truth behind a screen of pious words, and suppose that in reality we are going to be compelled to change completely our foreign policy—then, I think, it is only right that I should say to you: this change will in reality have come about as a result of Lord Halifax's visit to Berlin, of M. Stoyadinovitch's visit to Berlin, and of M. Flandin's visit to Berlin;—what a succession of journeys to the bank of the Spree! Before these journeys and before M. Delbos's tour in Central Europe the successive Governments of France always spoke a different language.'

And M. Pezet recalled how the Belgrade paper, *Vreme*, wrote at the time of the Stoyadinovitch visit to Berlin:

'This journey is taking place at a time when in France a movement in favour of a new foreign policy is coming into being.'

'Who informed the Jugoslav Government? Was it Paris, or was it Berlin?' M. Pezet asked. It sounded like a pointed reference to M. Flandin.

M. Pezet, who would to-day be called an anti-Munichite quoted from the *Frankfurter Zeitung* of May 23, 1937:

'France's Danubian policy is really the question which will determine not only the future of Franco-German relations, but the future of Europe.'

And he added that there were plans which had gone far beyond the Anschluss; M. Beck, he said, had already talked to M. de Kanya about a common Polish Hungarian frontier in Subcarpathic Russia! In short, *the dismemberment of Czechoslovakia was already being planned.*

And Austria?

Mussolini, M. Pezet said, had informed M. Stoyadinovitch in December: 'I am still against the Anschluss, but I have my hands tied.'

'And now,' he continued, 'the Anschluss has become a grave and real danger, in spite of the courage of the patriotic Austrians; and it can scarcely be prevented if France and

England are again too late in helping Austria *by all the peaceful means at our disposal* to preserve her independence.'

Clearly, M. Pezet, like most Frenchmen, still failed to visualise, at that moment, a German march into Austria.

But what did 'peaceful means at their disposal' mean?

There followed the familar argument about the road to India; a road on which Austria was the first and most essential obstacle. 'How blind England is!' M. Pezet cried, and, after recalling all the guarantees given by England to support Austrian independence, he said:

> 'I cannot recall without some melancholy and a touch of irony the words used by Sir John Simon when in announcing the results of the Anglo-French talks of February 3, 1935, on the necessity of guaranteeing as well as possible the independence of Austria: "We have the reputation" (he then said) "—and I trust it is a well-deserved reputation—for keeping our word." . . . Are all these agreements, treaties and protocols to be turned into so many scraps of paper in the name of realism, and with our helplessness as an excuse? Are France and England to turn a deaf ear to the appeal Chancellor Schuschnigg addressed to them yesterday? Oh, I know only too well that certain members of this House will say to me: "Read Mr. Chamberlain's speech. Does it sound as if we could expect any help from England if we tried to save Austria and Czechoslovakia? Did not Mr. Chamberlain say: 'We must not delude either ourselves, or the small nations into thinking that the League of Nations can do anything for them.' "
>
> 'I only say that these small nations have been deluded for nineteen years; they have been told to hold out, and resist and organise themselves; they have been told that they would be helped if the occasion arose. And now when the moment has come, are we to drop them? That is what I call "deluding" them.'

And M. Pezet concluded by asking:

> '*If the same technique of pressure and interference that Germany is now applying to Austria is also applied to Czechoslovakia—will France carry out her obligations under the Franco-Czech treaties of January 25, 1924 and October 16, 1925?* What advice did M. Delbos give the Czechs? Did he advise them to resist or to yield and resign themselves?'

His remark produced what the *Journal Officiel* called *mouvements divers.* If I remember rightly, the main reaction was to say that 'the Czechs would naturally be expected to resist'.

M. Pezet's speech created a deep impression at the Chamber. Only, it left an undercurrent of anxiety. He had spoken of 'peaceful means' of protecting Austrian independence; he feared that England would not agree even to 'peaceful means'; and throughout his speech he avoided even contemplating the circumstances in which 'peaceful means' would be of no good.

The suggestion of France's helplessness in the face of the Berchtesgaden ultimatum was very apparent. Peaceful pressure *might* have worked—but no longer with Mr. Chamberlain in charge of British foreign policy.

M. Marcel Boucher and other speakers of the Right took a more partisan line. If France was unable to help Austria it was because she had lost Mussolini's friendship. If only France had stuck to Stresa, and had not associated herself with the folly of sanctions!

These French illusions about Stresa were pathetic; and almost to this day it is impossible to convince many Frenchmen that Stresa was nothing but a piece of Italian trickery; for, whether he was later to get a free hand in Abyssinia or not, there is nothing to show that the Duce had the slightest intention of sticking to the 'Stresa Front'.[1]

The Socialists were poorly represented in that debate. M. Blum's wife had died at the end of January (a reason, by the way, why M. Blum had not persisted in his Cabinet-making shortly before), and the Socialist speaker was M. Salomon Grumbach, a man of great ability, but one whose slightly unfortunate music-hall manner irritated the Right, who on several occasions broke out into loud anti-Jewish abuse.

M. Grumbach quoted large chunks of *Mein Kampf* and attacked M. Flandin.

> 'For some days past,' M. Grumbach said, 'a big campaign is being conducted by a former Premier. Being a former Premier his responsibility is three times heavier than that if he were an ordinary mortal like myself. The phrases he utters constitute, throughout the world, the material for a peculiar kind of propaganda. I can hear his words in every language on the wireless, and see them in every foreign paper I can read.

[1] See *The Destiny of France*. Extracts from a Stresa Diary, pp. 134–40.

And I am profoundly convinced that if the world is left with the impression that the statements of M. Pierre-Etienne Flandin are of considerable importance, the danger to peace would be enormous, for it would be an encouragement to all the enemies of peace, and to those who wish to demoralise the French nation.' (Cheers on extreme Left. Protests on Right and Centre.)

And if we were to follow M. Flandin's policy of retrenchment, France would disappear not temporarily, but for ever from the world chessboard.

This phrase was again cheered on the Left and booed by the Right and Centre.

Not that the Right and Centre were unanimous. The next speaker was M. Ybarnégaray, of the P.S.F. (the former Croix de Feu), and the chief representative in the Chamber of Colonel de la Rocque; and he joined in the attack on M. Flandin—and on Mr. Chamberlain for that matter. For M. Flandin—in himself a person of no great importance—acted at the Chamber as though he were the representative of Mr. Chamberlain.

'There is no lack of people,' M. Ybarnégaray said, 'who will crowd the waiting rooms of Ribbentrop, Goebbels and Goering, and who, without any mandate, and without any authority from the Government, go there, like so many pilgrims, to collect promises and assurances. It is their lookout. But I shall venture to suggest to them in a friendly way that in doing so they are not serving the interests of France. Peace? Yes. There is not a Frenchman who does not want peace passionately. But peace at any price—No!'

The Croix de Feu man, who is also one of the most respected men at the Chamber, was cheered by the entire Left and (in the words of the *Journal Officiel*) 'on various benches of the Right and Centre.'

M. Ybarnégaray then spoke of Austria and of Hitler's ultimatum to Schuschnigg:

'He was given three days. And during these three days not a word of moral support came to him from London or Paris, or anywhere. It is a regrettable silence, but one that Hitler anticipated when, at Berchtesgaden, he said sneeringly to Schuschnigg: "Are you counting on France and England? You are wrong. When I occupied the Rhineland in March 1936, they didn't budge. Do you imagine they are going to budge for you?"'

M. Fernand-Laurent, a leading member of the Right, taking

a party line, interrupted M. Ybarnégaray and proceeded to
recall the unworthy treatment Austria had on so many
occasions received from the French Left (who, it is only right
to explain, could not quite forget the massacre of the Socialists
in February 1934).

He recalled how on February 22, 1935 Schuschnigg arrived
at the small Gare de Reuilly in Paris, for the Government was
afraid of a hostile demonstration at a bigger station; and the
Humanité wrote the next day: 'It's a wonder they didn't
smuggle him in through a goods station.'

> 'There is not a man with a heart,' M. Fernand-Laurent
> said, 'who did not read, with tears in his eyes, the simple and
> poignant speech that was made yesterday in front of the bust of
> Dollfuss, the martyr of his country, by the leader of a small
> people, who proclaimed with calm dignity his faith in his
> country, in its destiny, and in its will for independence. And as
> I read this speech this morning, with tears in my eyes, I blushed
> with shame at the contrast between that nobility, and the coarse
> insults with which Schuschnigg was received in Paris.'

M. Ybarnégaray resumed his speech, and said:

> 'There are some blind or cowardly men who say: "We shall
> never mobilise for Austria and Czechoslovakia." At the risk of
> making myself unpopular I reply to these people: "we shall not
> mobilise *for* Austria or *for* Czechoslovakia; for it is on the Danube
> to-day that the fate of our frontiers is being settled." '

And then M. Ybarnégaray turned to M. Delbos and asked:

> 'What are you going to do about Austria? I do not want any
> humming or hawing from you. You must speak up. What
> will you do? What can you do? The independence of Austria
> has been guaranteed by the League of Nations. Yet after so
> bold a violation of international agreements as the Berchtes-
> gaden ultimatum, nothing has yet been done to call a meeting
> of the League Council.[1]
>
> 'Is it true then, as Mr. Chamberlain said the day before
> yesterday, that collective security is dead?
>
> 'If so, say it. It is better to be frank than to cling on to
> illusions. My question is a simple one: are you going to save
> Austrian independence? Can you do it? Do you want to do
> it?

[1] During the Czech crisis M. Ybarnégaray, and the P.S.F. generally were not
going to take any firm stand.

'If I ask this question about Austria, it is because *you are now in a far better position than you may be very shortly, when Czechoslovakia is, in turn, involved.* Remember that Hitler's offensive has scarcely begun. Nothing essential has yet been achieved by Germany. Moreover, Austria is organising her own resistance. It was with profound relief that I listened yesterday to the magnificent words that the Austrian Chancellor was addressing to the world: "We shall do everything, everything that depends on us; we shall sacrifice everything for this freedom and independence of Austria."

'The Anschluss has not yet been achieved. And I persist in believing that an energetic reaction by France and Britain could yet prevent it. *To threaten Chancellor Schuschnigg is one thing, to decide on a military invasion of Austria is quite another*, and I am not sure that Hitler would risk it. Are France and England ready to unite on the Danube, as they have united on the Rhine and to defend nations whose independence they have guaranteed?

'If so, let them say so openly; *everything may yet be saved. If not, let them say so just as openly. But in that case, it will be a different policy, a policy of weakness and abdication—a policy of retrenchment behind the Maginot Line.* If that is your policy, say so, M. Delbos!'

All that, as it would be called to-day, was good anti-Munich stuff; and M. Ybarnégaray stated the dilemma very clearly. Only, like many other men of the Right, he continued to entertain illusions about Italy: 'If we had not helped the Negus,' he said in effect, 'there would have been no Berchtesgaden ultimatum.' And he asked that France should send immediately an Ambassador to Rome.[1]

It was a widespread illusion which was not to be killed until November 1938, when an Ambassador *was* actually sent to Rome. No sooner had he arrived there than the Italian deputies organised their famous demonstration with their clamour for 'Corsica and Tunis'.

The debate continued. M. Mistler, the young president of the Foreign Affairs Committee, who was later to be among the most ardent defenders of a Munich policy, spoke. On the

---

[1] M. de Chambrun, who was strongly biased in favour of Mussolini during the Abyssinian crisis was withdrawn by the Blum Government ; and the new Ambassador, M. de St. Quentin, could not go to Rome as the Italian Government insisted that in his credentials he should address the King as 'King of Italy and Emperor of Abyssinia.' It was not until after Munich that the Abyssinian 'Empire' was officially recognised by France.

whole, he agreed with M. Ybarnégaray; but there was a difference in tone, a difference in emphasis. The speech was, somehow, more philosophical; M. Mistler dwelt on the unfortunate
fact that the democracies lacked both the organisation and the
dynamic vigour of Germany; and said that France ought to
pull herself together. And he added cautiously:

> 'At the present time, we cannot pursue a policy that would
> commit us to automatic action everywhere. But, there are
> certain vital areas—the Rhine, the Mediterranean and Central
> Europe—where, after consulting our allies, we must say that
> there is a point at which great risks begin, and beyond which
> this country must throw in her whole weight.'

'Only,'—and here M. Mistler became even more cautious—
'we cannot pursue such a policy alone, and we must be sure
to act in close agreement with Great Britain.'
And still more cautiously he added:

> 'But I think it would be a mistake to be in too great a hurry in
> adopting an attitude which would not be without danger.'

One can leave out the speech by M. Péri, the Communist
speaker, which was a good exposé of the policy of No Surrender
to the Fascist dictatorships. He quoted Mr. Churchill on
several occasions, complained that the Government had neg-
lected the Soviet Pact, and spoke scathingly of the City of
London and 'those who advise you to adopt the theories of
the grouse-shooting pro-German Press lords of Great Britain'.
He was loudly cheered by the Left, while several members of
the Right shouted: *Sac au dos!*

M. de Monzie, who was to be another ardent protagonist
of a Munich policy later in the year, spoke quite differently
in February.

He admitted that Austria had always striven to unite with
Germany; and the Austrian Socialists were in 1931 among the
strongest supporters of the Anschluss. But now the position
was different.

> 'For the first time since 1918 the people of Austria have
> affirmed with great unanimity their desire of independence.
> For the first time the Socialists of Vienna and other towns and
> the Conservatives and legitimists of the rural areas have re-
> vealed a profound national consciousness. There is no longer
> any identity of temperament between Austria and Germany.'

And it was particularly sinister, that at such a moment, M. de Monzie said, Hitler should have proclaimed his intention to 'protect' his racial brethren. An astonishing pretension. It was as if France suddenly claimed a right to exercise control over the French Canadians!

'I shall not be childish enough to imagine that this revival of the national sentiment in Austria is sufficient to resist violence coming from outside. But what shall we do? Shall we do nothing? I do not think that is M. Flandin's intention. Yet M. Flandin has been talking of "retrenchment". And he has expressed these views in a dangerous way; especially *because his views reflect the feelings of many people in this country who see in every diplomatic démarche a risk of war.*

'M. Flandin tells us: France will become more Imperial that European. I reply to this that there can be no Empire without a head. What would be the British Commonwealth without the greatness of England, without those forces of cohesion that exist in the City and in English life, without that head which rules the body.

'A French Empire run by a Little France—a France without European prestige? No, it's out of the question.'

A remarkable statement in the light of Munich, and in the light of that smug post-Munich atmosphere into which France sank for a time—with the blessings of M. de Monzie. Like many other of his countrymen, he was going to undergo a radical change.

In February, however, he was still determined to defend Austria—how? He was glad to think that there was going to be a brief spell between the Berchtesgaden ultimatum and the final destruction of Austrian independence. And this respite, M. de Monzie said, must be used by France to save Austrian independence, and her freedom of action in Europe.

And M. de Monzie's remedy was simple. Apart from the Franco-Soviet Pact, which, he said, ought to be developed into real military alliance;[1] he said that Mr. Chamberlain's England had entered into negotiations with Italy; it was for France to join in. And he quoted with approval Mr. Churchill's phrase: 'Oh, if Italy will consent to return to the Brenner, I'll forgive her everything.'

[1] Turning to M. Péri, M. de Monzie remarked that although the Communists were now lamenting the departure of Mr. Eden, it was Mr. Eden who had always opposed a regular Franco-Russian alliance.

'It is a British opinion; and I quite agree with it. And if you will forgive me, I'll say in the good Gallic style of Henri IV—*Vienne vaut bien une messe à Genève.*'

M. Marin, the Right-Wing leader, and once an ardent supporter of the Ruhr policy, and a man who had ceaselessly warned France against Germany when Germany was still disarmed, also saw the last hope in an attempt to 'return to Stresa'. *Sancta simplicitas!*

On the following day the debate began on the same note. M. Gaston-Gérard, and other members of the Right, said that if Austria was going to be lost, it was because France had stupidly thrown away Italy's friendship. He, and the next speaker, M. Frédéric Dupont, also argued that friendly relations should be established not only with Mussolini, but also with General Franco.

M. André Albert, who spoke after them, the *enfant terrible* of the Chamber, made one sensible remark. He said he had listened to all the speeches and had come to the conclusion that nobody had any guts at all. The very people who in the past had thundered against Germany at a time when Germany was weak, and who had prevented an understanding with Germany, were now bleating helplessly.

> 'In the past M. Franklin Bouillon[1] used to frighten everybody with the Anschluss, and that at a time when it hadn't a ghost of a chance of becoming a reality. I must say that I am rather surprised that the man who had so many disciples when he fought against Briand's peace policy, should to-day be left without any spiritual heirs. Is it not because the French patriots have fallen into Hitler's snare, and are ready to support his Anti-Comintern crusade?'

The two speakers who in that February debate came nearest to the 'Munich' outlook were M. Montigny—who is, as it were, M. Caillaux's representative in the Chamber—and, naturally, M. Flandin.

M. Montigny said:

> '*Since, rightly or wrongly, we have not created an army fitted for our foreign policy, and since it would take years to create one, we must— unless we are mad—adopt a foreign policy compatible with our military possibilities.*'

[1] The impetuous ultra-nationalist Deputy who died in 1937.

He refrained, however, from revealing the enormous implications of his phrase.

As regards Austria M. Montigny merely said:

> 'It would be desirable—and I mention this incidentally—to
> clarify the situation in Austria, and to propose—and there is no
> reason why France should not take this initiative—the organisa-
> tion of a clear and loyal plebiscite.'

The suggestion created *mouvements divers,* that is, something of an uproar.

> *M. Pezet:* 'How are you going to guarantee the loyalty of such
> a plebiscite?'
> *M. Montigny:* 'It might be controlled by Americans, or
> Swedes or Norwegians.'
> *M. Pezet:* 'The plebiscite will be run by Hitler, who knows
> that if he is allowed to go on like this a little longer he will
> be in a position to conduct the plebiscite under his own
> exclusive control.'
> *M. Montigny:* 'That is precisely why I want a plebiscite now,
> under neutral control.'
> *M. Oberkirch:* 'It would set up a dangerous precedent.'
> *M. Montigny:* 'Well, if you won't have a plebiscite, let me give
> you my main conclusion: if the Government is to be urged to
> use physical pressure in its attempt to stop the Anschluss, I
> think we must all agree that, in any case, France cannot act
> separately, and that she can only join in a concerted action—
> an action which remains impossible without the support of
> Italy.'

Here we were again—Italy, Italy—nothing could be done
without Italy. Oh, that unforgettable vision of Italy on the
Brenner, where she had frightened off Germany in 1934 when
Dollfuss was murdered.

The biggest uproar during the debate occurred when towards the end of the second day M. Herriot, the Speaker,
announced:

'*La parole est à M. Flandin.*'

The Left, and particularly the Communists rose to their feet
and greeted M. Flandin with the Nazi salute, shouting: 'Heil
Hitler!' 'Heil Flandin!' and '*A Berlin!*' and 'Seiss-Inquart!'
The Right and part of the Centre cheered.

At last silence was restored and M. Flandin spoke.

This debate, he said, was the gravest that had been conducted at the Chamber since the War. One had to get down to

fundamentals. Events in Europe were developing in such a way that France was faced with the choice between war and peace.

> 'For some weeks past,' he continued, 'I have been treated as the mouthpiece of pro-German Press lords; I am called pro-Nazi, and pro-Fascist; and that reminds me of the time when I was treated as an agent of the Soviets.'[1]

After saying, with his hand on his heart, that he had never cared for anything but the interest of his country (loud cries from the Left of '*Aéropostale! Aéropostale!*'), M. Flandin gave a long quotation from 'the noble speech of Sir (sic) Neville Chamberlain'.

> 'Sir Neville Chamberlain knows that the time has come to act. Because peace—the Peace of Versailles—is on its deathbed.'

France, M. Flandin said, had concluded a number of pacts. All these pacts and alliances were concluded within the framework of the League Covenant. What was the value of these pacts when the League Covenant was dead? France, as he had said some time ago, could not accept the risk of acting single-handedly the policeman of Europe.

> 'When Mr. Baldwin proclaimed that Great Britain's frontier was on the Rhine, he entered into a serious obligation.
>
> 'Some of you gentlemen complain because British opinion is rather reserved about intervening in Europe. But remember that Britain is rearming, while our armaments works, our economy, our finances and our morale, all need adjusting. It is not until these are adjusted that you can try, together with England, to practise a policy of intervention.'

France's inadequate armaments—here was already in substance one of the chief pro-Munich arguments used by the advocates of surrender in September 1938.

> 'In the circumstances, let us, for heaven's sake, stop striking heroic attitudes because Austria is being *gleichgeschaltet*. When the question of peace and war arises, nothing can be worse than not to look the facts in the face.
>
> 'M. Delbos has once again proclaimed his faith in the League

---

[1] M. Flandin was Foreign Minister in February 1936 when the Soviet Pact was ratified.

of Nations.   That is all very well.   But what did Mr. Chamberlain say?

'No doubt, he hoped that the League of Nations would have a future.   Only not without being overhauled and strengthened. And he added that the League could not perform its peaceful task so long as it and its members were nominally committed to applying sanctions.'

There followed long streams of quotations from Chamberlain's speech of February 22.

After that M. Flandin spoke about Italy.   In January 1935 M. Laval had signed an agreement, which included a Franco-Italian convention for the defence of Austrian independence. The Abyssinian affair had ruined everything, and since then France had done nothing to restore friendly relations with Italy.

And, turning to M. Delbos, M. Flandin said:

'Your policy is out of date.   It is based entirely on old-fashioned formulae about the League of Nations, collective security and mutual assistance.'

What, then, was M. Flandin's attitude to, say, a German attack on Czechoslovakia?   Did he wish France to repudiate her treaty?   He was cautious, very cautious on this point— even though he had already questioned the value of pacts 'within the framework of the League Covenant' at a time when this Covenant no longer meant anything.

'*Messieurs*,' he said, 'far be it from me to suggest that we should repudiate our obligations; but we ought to make sure whether we are able to observe them.   And I believe that we must not base our entire policy on these commitments, especially when we look at them in the light of Mr. Chamberlain's statement on British foreign policy and on the League of Nations.'

M. Flandin admitted that Germany was 'a nation of conquerors; but France also was a nation of soldiers'.   And he tried to console himself with the following thought:

'European hegemony may be the dream of an ambitious dictator; but it was also the dream of Napoleon, and his imperialist attempt failed when it was faced with a coalition. No attempt at European hegemony can succeed any more than it did under Napoleon.'

And then he came to the Maginot Line.

'To-day we are sheltered behind the Maginot Line. If ever we are attacked, we shall be strong enough to hold out until the freedom-loving countries of Europe come to our aid as they did in 1914.'

And M. Flandin argued for à *rapprochement* with Germany, which would tend to put an end to the armament race.

M. Flandin, aware of the hostility of the Chamber, was more cautious in his choice of words than he had been in speaking before the Foreign Affairs Committee in December. But, reading between the lines, his speech contained the 'Munich' argument in full. His weakest argument, of course, was the argument about the Maginot Line and about the coalition that would inevitably come to France's aid were she attacked. For in 1914 France was supported from the very outset by a coalition, and Germany had to fight on two fronts —which might not be the same next time. For Hitler's great ambition is always to 'localise' war as far as possible.

M. Reynaud undertook the task of smashing M. Flandin's arguments:

'We all want peace,' M. Reynaud said, 'and it is only a question of method; and let no one come and tell me that I represent the "War Party".'

The abdication of France in Central Europe would be fatal. For,

'having, without firing a single shot, gained control of Rumanian oil, Hungarian wheat, and the Czechoslovak war industry, and having established a common frontier with Italy, what would Germany do next?

'Hitler wrote in *Mein Kampf:* "Before launching ourselves upon the great adventure, toward the steppes of Asia, we must make certain not to be attacked by France in the rear." Let us therefore imagine this vast Germanic Empire, which, in addition to its own resources, has full control over vast supplies of oil, wheat and arms. In addition to that, Germany will have obtained from us the denunciation of the Franco-Soviet Pact. Would it, in that case, be possible to defend France? If it is not possible, you see the consequences of your [meaning M. Flandin's and Mr. Chamberlain's] policy. You say: there is the Maginot Line. Quite right, and no one knows better than I do how precious it is in our national defence. *But there is not a single expert who will claim that any line of fortifications can resist indefinitely against an indefinite accumulation of tanks and artillery*. It is also said that defensive warfare is easier than aggressive warfare, and the case of Spain is quoted. But in Spain the forces are more or less equal; but what chance would France have if she had half of Europe against her?

'Are we then to yield without war in the name of "fairness"? The Germans will say that it is only fair that they should have colonies, and the iron ore of Lorraine, and that they should be handed over Alsace.

'And then the day will come when our colossal neighbour will make things so unbearable to the pride of a noble people that we will be thrown into war, without friends, without honour.'

And England?

M. Reynaud deplored the departure of Mr. Eden, but believed that England would not stand aside if France defended her vital interest in Europe. 'England cannot afford to see France crushed, whatever may be the personal feelings of the men in charge of her public affairs. *Only we must remember that in the matter of Central Europe it is France who must take the initiative and take her responsibilities.*'

'If Germany believes that this debate will result in a reversal of France's foreign policy she is making a great mistake. The outstanding feature of this debate is that nobody has proposed a repudiation of the treaties that France has signed. Nobody is opposed to a Franco-German agreement, but on what basis, I ask you, and by what means is it to be achieved?

'There are some who believe (a reference to M. Flandin) that France could save peace by surrendering her role in Europe. I maintain, on the contrary, that such surrender would lead to war. France has the choice between two policies. Either she maintains the balance of power in Europe or she retreats to the Maginot Line, to begin with. Is France really incapable after spending 372 milliards on armaments, of standing her ground? I say "No".'

After referring to France's friends and allies, who, taken together, represented a formidable military force, and to the rearmament of the United States, which was 'a terrible warning to the dictators', M. Reynaud said:

'There is only one way of killing France, and that is by isolating her. That is what some are proposing.'

M. Flandin fidgeted uneasily on his bench.

M. Reynaud then added:

'Between the movements of opinion in the United States and

the admirable spirit of the working class of Vienna there is a powerful moral link. What the false realists do not see is the greatest of all realities—the moral reality.'

One of these 'moral realities' was the moral unity of the French people. Alluding to the probable ·formation in the near future of a large National Government, M. Reynaud said:

> 'The world will soon be startled to see that it is impossible either internally or internationally to speculate on France's lack of unity.'

A large part of the Chamber rose and cheered.

Though M. Reynaud was not in the Government, this was the best 'government' speech.

M. Delbos, a tired and disappointed man, was less dazzling —though his arguments were of the same order.

'Those advocating a policy of abdication,' he said, 'forget that France has something more to defend than her own frontiers. Must we throw to the winds France's greatness, her history, and the ideals that inspire her, ideals which will not allow her to forget her mission in the world? Are we to throw to the winds the respect of our signature, our loyalty to our friends, our feeling of European solidarity?'

M. Delbos spoke respectfully of Mr. Chamberlain, paid a tribute to Mr. Eden, but preferred not to dwell on the implications of Mr. Eden's departure.

And while—significantly enough—he refrained from saying much about Austria except that 'Austrian independence' was 'essential to the balance of power in Europe', he was completely categorical about Czechoslovakia:

> 'I wish to reaffirm once again—and I think I voice your opinion in doing so—France's affection for the brave people of Czechoslovakia and their Government, who combine, with so much wisdom, their will for independence and their concern for peace. And I desire to say once again that our obligations to Czechoslovakia will, if it comes to the point, be faithfully observed.'

And, later in the debate, M. Chautemps the Premier, reaffirmed M. Delbos's pledge to Czechoslovakia and attacked the defeatists.

> 'It is my duty to associate myself with the statement of the Foreign Minister, and to affirm clearly that France cannot

abandon Central Europe to its fate, or to fail in her alliance which makes it an obligation of honour for her to protect the independence of Czechoslovakia. Nor can she allow, *without reserving her right to regain complete freedom of action, the intervention of other powers in Spain (!!!)*'

After attacking M. Flandin and saying, amid loud applause, that France would not yield to any threats, he continued:

'France must remain faithful to her historical policy based on the union of peaceful nations, on human liberty and on the respect of treaties. It is always a weakness to betray the moral principles which dominate both the collective life and the individual conscience. The French Republic will overcome not through war, but in peace, the obstacles on the road of her destiny.'

M. Chautemps, who, in the Spanish affair, had been all along a 'non-interventionist at any price', was also going to be one of the principal supporters of a Munich policy in September.

The motion on which the Chamber voted said:

The Chamber approves the statements of the Government and trusts that it will safeguard national dignity, assure the maintenance of peace, and the respect of treaties within the framework of collective security and the League of Nations.

This motion was adopted by 439 votes to two. But—there were about 150 abstentions. And these abstentions—though they also included simply opponents of the Government, such as M. Ybarnégaray of the P.S.F.—also included a great many people who were already *Munichois* at heart. Openly, at any rate, the 'defeatism' on the Left was not going to develop until later. It is true that nobody was openly against the repudiation of treaties—a point M. Paul Reynaud emphasised; and yet—M. Flandin was cheered by a large part of the Right and Centre. And what they were cheering was not so much his cautious platitudes as their grim implications.

Such was the battle of ideas at the end of February 1938.

On the face of it, France's 'traditional League policy' triumphed all along the line—in spite of Mr. Eden's resignation and the New Policy proclaimed by Mr. Chamberlain. But below the surface there was a feeling of deep uncertainty in France; and, when, a fortnight later, the Anschluss came,

France did not budge. During the Chamber debate no answer was given by the Government to the question: 'How are you going to help Austria?'

March 11 provided the answer: 'We cannot help Austria.'

In fact, there was no Government in France that day; and the state of confusion in France at that time acted as an additional incentive to Hitler to march into Vienna without delay. For four days before the Anschluss, M. Chautemps quarrelled with the Socialists over the question of plenary powers; and without waiting for a Chamber vote he resigned—in even stranger circumstances than he had resigned less than two months before.

Cynics remarked that M. Chautemps was expecting grave developments in Austria in a few days, and that he was not prepared to face the music. M. Chautemps himself hotly denied this charge. But the fact remains that but for his surprising and sudden decision to resign, France would not have been without a Government on the day Hitler's troops marched into Austria, and so began the revision of the *territorial* clauses of the Treaty of Versailles. Until then the violations had not gone outside Germany's borders.

CHAPTER III

SPANISH INTERLUDE

I VENTURE to change the subject for a while. The rest of the long story of France's journey along the road to Munich will be told later. Czechoslovakia was not the only great foreign issue in 1938; an issue at least as great was Spain. And here are some notes written during a visit to Government Spain in November and December 1937, shortly before the battle of Teruel—at a time when the outlook for the Spanish Government looked fairer than at any time since the beginning of the war. True, the Basque Country and Asturias had been lost during the previous summer; but these had long before been isolated from the main part of Government Spain; and once Franco had reached Gijon, and liquidated the northern front, he got stuck. Madrid, though already suffering severe hardships for over a year, and having lost 10,000 dead in bombings and shellings, was facing the future with cheerful heroism, while Barcelona, despite occasional air-raids, did not yet, properly speaking, belong to the war zone. The enemy was still far away, beyond the mountains, at Saragossa. He was being helped by Germany and Italy, but not on the scale on which he was going to be helped in 1938 and in the early part of 1939 under the cold placid glance of Mr. Neville Chamberlain—and M. Bonnet.

All the way from Almeria to the Pyrénées, the front was 'stabilised', and when the next offensive came at last, it came—from the Government side. Teruel was captured in the last week of 1937.

It was shortly before Teruel that Richard Mowrer and I went to Spain—and here are some of the notes written at the time.

A VISIT TO 'RED' SPAIN[1]

Has the Spanish Republic lost the war? Has Franco, as one so often hears, 'practically' won it? That is the question I was asking myself when, on a sunny day at the end of November, Richard and I crossed the frontier at Le Perthus, south of Perpignan, into Republican Spain. That morning, at Marseilles, we had bought a paper displaying an article on 'The End of Red Spain'. It was a gruesome production; the Republican forces, it said, were totally demoralised; Barcelona was starving, and its people, like those of Madrid, were almost in open rebellion against the Government. In fact, there were so many Governments in Barcelona that nobody knew which the real one was.

Had not many other papers, in France and in England, published articles of the same sort? Since the collapse of the northern front, after the fall of Gijon, the Spanish Republic had had an almost universally bad Press, and Mr. Eden's speech early in November had only too widely been interpreted as meaning that the Spanish Government had as good as lost the war. For weeks there had been talk of Franco's 'final' offensive.

But I may say at once that, whatever the difficulties, they are offset by two immensely important factors: (1) the Government's power of physical—that is, military—resistance has vastly improved, for instead of the militia of a year ago it has a highly trained and well-organised modern army; and (2) the spirit is good—good among the great majority of the civilian population, and supremely good among the army and among the people of Madrid.

Fascist propaganda, supported by such 'obvious' facts as the collapse of the northern front (for which the Central Government could do nothing), ignores all the factors which constitute the Government's strength and dwells only on its obvious and undeniable difficulties. And Fascist propaganda is more effective than Republican propaganda, all the more so as it

[1] What follows are articles published in the *Manchester Guardian* in December 1937 and January 1938. I believe they are still of topical interest; the inferiority in war material, the moral weakness of Catalonia, the food shortage were problems which already existed in December 1937, and which—by increasing instead of diminishing—were to play a decisive part in the final collapse.

has conscious and unconscious friends and accomplices on only too many sides. The effect of it all has been to create a widespread impression in England, as well as in France, that Franco has 'practically' won. The information on which the British and French Governments largely base their information is not always reliable, impartial information. Are most French and British diplomatists 'class-conscious'? I do not know, but what I do know is that in Republican Spain the two great Western democracies are sometimes represented by men who not only lack sympathy or understanding for the Spanish Republic but who hate it with a personal hatred. And these are some of the people who in their 'objective' reports 'inform' the democratic Governments of Europe on conditions in Spain. And it is largely on the strength of these reports that the Governments shape their policies. It is an important and grave matter. In Madrid, for instance, the sole representative of H. M. Government is a vice-consul notorious throughout Spain for his openly avowed Franco sympathies.

THE ROAD TO BARCELONA

In crossing the frontier into Catalonia we did not notice anything very unusual. No doubt the red star—the Soviet star!—on the caps of the carabiniers and *asalto* guards—the latter mostly Communists, some of whom were actually wearing the famous leather jacket popularly associated with the Ogpu—might have suggested to some travellers that they were entering another Soviet State, but actually these guards are under the orders of the Negrin Government, whereas not much more than six months ago the whole North of Catalonia was ruled by the Anarchist syndicates, and the black-and-red flag of the F.A.I. and the C.N.T. flew on every public building. But the country beyond the frontier looked just like a continuation of the rich Roussillon Plain, with its vineyards, its flocks of sheep, its peasants ploughing the fields lined by long rows of cypresses. It was a warm day, and in the small towns[1] women were sitting on their doorsteps, playing with their children or knitting. The children looked healthy and well

[1] Such as Figueras, the scene of the fearful last act of the Catalan tragedy in February 1939.

dressed. A large number of lorries were coming in from
France, mostly laden with chassis or with complete motor-
cars; others carried small but substantial-looking cases marked
'Le Havre'.

We discovered the first signs of abnormal conditions when
we stopped at Gerona, with its beautiful cathedral marked
'National Monument' and with one of its churches turned
into a military hospital. At Gerona we could get no lunch.
One hotel had been requisitioned for the Air Force, and
through the window we could see the dining-room, with its
ceremoniously folded napkins; but the other hotel had not
provided lunch for any visitors. In the dark hall the old
woman in charge merely shook her head. So we sat in the
sunny square outside the 'Bar Express', on the river embank-
ment, sipping a doubtful vermouth. The local inhabitants
also sat round tables drinking their vermouth or a black liquid
that looked like coffee. Among them were many young
civilians of military age.[1] Nobody ate anything and nobody
smoked. Cigarettes are almost non-existent in Spain, except
among the troops. Two oranges were displayed in a shop
window in solitary glory. Nearly all windows were pasted
over with strips of brown paper—an anti-air-raid precaution.
'Immortal Gerona' had been bombed once or twice. On the
other side of the square there was a public building decorated
with the Spanish red-yellow-and-purple and the Catalan
yellow-and-red flags, and on the wall were painted the hammer
and sickle and the words 'A Fascist at large is a spy in action'.
Along the river front were two competing bookstalls—one
Anarchist, with books by Bakunin, William Morris, and
Kropotkin, and the other Communist, with pamphlets on
Stalin, the Soviet Union, and Léon Blum, and postcards with
portraits of Galan and Hernandez, the two leading Spanish
Communists, in an orgy of Republican flags. The newspapers
the people outside the café were reading were printed on
dirty grey paper. At the other end of the town were several
streets recently renamed after Garcia Hernandez and the 19th
of July (the suppression of the military rebellion in Barcelona).

Driving on to Barcelona we went through a vast beech and

----

[1] At that time Catalonia—as the subsequent description of Barcelona will
show—was by no means fully 'war-conscious'.

pine forest, and then took the road along the sea. The Mediterranean, without any ship in sight, was a dazzling pattern of blue and gold. We passed several bathing resorts; it was like any road on the Riviera. Everywhere the food shortage was apparent. In one small town we tried to buy some green apples we had noticed in a window, but in vain. Not only was food scarce, but its delivery was most irregular; on some days a great deal could be bought, on others nothing at all. This faulty distribution largely paralysed the official rationing system. Manufactured goods, on the other hand, were plentiful: there was no lack anywhere of shirts and ties and socks, and hair oil and perfume; and even soap, unobtainable a few months ago, was plentiful though expensive. Outside Barcelona, whose hundreds of smoking chimneys we could see miles away, there are miles of allotments, and we passed scores of donkey-carts and mule-carts filled with cabbages and salad going to town. We also passed a funeral procession with a regular black hearse with a yellow crown, but without any cross or other religious marks, and followed by some fifty working people, but without any sign of a priest.

Just outside Barcelona we saw the first double-decker bus, almost exactly like a London bus, but painted in the Anarchist colours of black and red and with 'C.N.T.' (the Anarchist trade union federation) painted in white on the radiator. The buses and trams, and many other things besides, are still run by the Anarchists in Barcelona. We entered Barcelona from the east, through a grimy working-class district. The tobacco-shops had notices pasted on their windows saying that there was no tobacco. Outside the food-shops there were long queues of women, some of them looking distinctly bad-tempered. The tram-cars were over-crowded, with human 'bunches of grapes' clinging on to the footboards and buffers—a sight strangely reminiscent of St. Petersburg in 1917. The vast bull-ring, where they still have bull-fights ('only the bulls are badly fed, and aren't much use', I was told), marks the border between the east end and the centre of Barcelona. There is perhaps more absurd architecture along the Ramblas of Barcelona than in any other town in the world—houses looking like wedding-cakes, houses with domes and cupolas and mounted by eagles, houses in the 'style moderne' of 1900, with

metal ivy railings, and shell-shaped balconies, and 'stalactite'
porticos, and tiled fronts, dotted with little blue flowers. We
stopped at the Hotel Majestic, near the Plaza de Cataluña, one
of the few big hotels commandeered by the Government, the
rest having been turned into hospitals or trade union headquarters. The windows were pasted over with zigzags of brown
paper, and there were many bullet-holes in the walls and shop-
windows along the street—a memory of the Anarchist rising
of last May, 'the tragic days of May 1937' as the Anarchists
themselves call them. It was night now, and the streets were
pitch black except for the lighted tram-cars and the dazzling
lights of passing motor-cars.

ANARCHISTS AND OTHERS

For over a month Barcelona has been the provisional
capital of Spain. All Government offices have been moved
from Valencia to Barcelona. The situation is paradoxical,
on the face of it. It is a little as if, in an emergency, the
British Government had moved to Dublin. And yet most of
the people of Spain agree that it was a stroke of genius on the
part of the Negrin Government to settle in the Catalan capital.
Under the severe glance of the Central Government turbulent
Barcelona has become less turbulent and less restless. It has
become more conscious of its share and responsibility in the
common war. The Government can keep a vigilant eye on
the war industries, which are concentrated in Barcelona, and
see to it that the arms made there really go to the front and
not elsewhere, as they frequently did some months ago. It
is in a better position in Barcelona to prepare for such
emergencies as a naval blockade; for if such a blockade were
attempted it would be sufficient for the Government to keep
the coast clear between the French frontier and Barcelona—a
matter of 100 miles—instead of the coast all the way down to
Valencia.

No doubt in their more disagreeable moments the Catalan
autonomists assume an air of resignation and say: 'Well, since
the Government thought it necessary to move to Barcelona,
we couldn't say no. After all, we also put victory above all
other things.' And the more extreme Anarchists shrug their

shoulders and say: 'It's all very well; but it has made a most deplorable impression among the people of Catalonia. The next capital will, no doubt, be Figueras, closer still to the French frontier; so that they can get away still more easily if things go wrong.'[1] But such bad temper, bordering on defeatism, is by no means widespread; it is, indeed, exceptional; though it would be idle to deny that many of the Anarchists are not at all happy.

The position of the Anarchists is very curious.[2] They and their trade union federation, the C.N.T., virtually dominated Catalonia for several months after July 19, 1936. They took full credit for the suppression of the military rebellion in Barcelona that day, and in the months that followed they engaged upon a vast scheme of both urban and rural collectivisation. This collectivisation received a legal basis through the Catalan law of October 24, 1936, but actually the collectivisations carried out by the Anarchist committees both before and after went far beyond the letter and the spirit of that law, and in the rural districts in particular the 'voluntary' collectivisations carried out by the F.A.I. and the C.N.T. were voluntary only in name. Much of this work has had since then to be undone.

The 'conquests of the 19th of July must be preserved above all things,' the Anarchists said. They were also opposed to conscription and militarisation, and intended to fight the war against Franco on a militia basis. To many Anarchists the war against Franco was not the primary consideration; if the war was to end in the establishment of a democratic 'bourgeois' régime in Spain, it was hardly worth fighting. As Augustin Souchy, the well-known Anarchist leader, wrote in a pamphlet on *The Tragic Week in May*, 'Anti- Fascism is neither a theory nor a doctrine.' No doubt other Anarchist leaders took a more realistic line, above all the famous Durutti, who was killed at the front in mysterious circumstances on November 20, 1936. 'We abandon everything,' Durutti had said shortly before his death, 'except victory.' A grave conflict was inevitable between the 'purer' Anarchists with their conception of

[1] To-day there is a grim irony in this phrase.
[2] The peculiar mentality of the Catalan Anarchists perhaps helps to explain in some measure the suddenness with which the defence of Barcelona collapsed in January 1939.

'simultaneous revolution and war,' and the conception of 'victory first'—a conception advocated by the political parties now represented in the Negrin Government, including the Communists. The conflict broke out in Barcelona on May 3, and there were five days of bloody battles between the more extreme Anarchists and the Poum on the one side and the police and *asalto* guards on the other. Ultimately the Anarchists yielded when the Valencia Government rushed 1,500 troops from the Jarama front to Barcelona—at the treacherous request (so the Anarchists said) of the Catalan Left.

What annoyed the Anarchists above all was that the Communists should, on that as on many other occasions, have taken sides with 'the privileges of property and capitalism'. The Communists, with their conceptions of centralisation and nationalisation, had never agreed with the Anarchists, and with their programme of trade union federalism and collectivisation; but the conflict now went much deeper. The Anarchists actually accused the Communists of conspiring against them, and of having 'provoked' the Barcelona riots of May 3. Be that as it may, the Communists, acting as a party of law and order, and as the advocates of 'victory first' were enormously strengthened by the events in Barcelona during that first week in May. The Government of Largo Caballero who had had a soft spot for the Anarchists and the Poum, resigned, and in the new Negrin Government the extreme Left was represented by the Communists only.

The Communists, though numerically unimportant at first, appeared to wide sections of Spanish public opinion as the most dynamic element among the 'anti-Fascist' forces. Their influence grew, especially in the Army and among the carabineros—an influence which prompted the Anarchists to treat the guards as 'Spain's G.P.U.'. The Poum, an important rival of the Communists, was dissolved after the May riots. The Poum, a party with strong Trotskyist tendencies, was declared by the Communists to be the chief instigator of the May riots, and was accused of being plainly defeatist. Not being numerically comparable to the Anarchists, it was easy to dissolve. It was alleged that the Poum had for a long time been the rallying-point of all defeatist elements, and that it was teeming with *agents provocateurs*. Andreas Nin, the Poum leader,

who at one time had been a member of the Catalan Government, disappeared mysteriously in July; hundreds of Poum
members were arrested, and the pro-Poum Anarchists allege
that a number of Poum members, such as Kurt Landau, an
Austrian Socialist who joined the Poum in November 1936,
had been put to death by the Barcelona 'G.P.U.'. It is true
that there had been an abnormally large number of foreigners
in the Poum—Germans, Austrians, Russians, and so on. I
saw Landau's wife, a delicate little woman with feverish eyes,
in Barcelona; she had been released after three months' imprisonment and a week's hunger strike. Mr. John McGovern,
M.P. of the I.L.P., and M. Félicien Challaye, of the *Ligue des
Droits de l'Homme*—whom I also saw at Barcelona—had
apparently worked hard to secure her release.

The persecutions of the Poum are, no doubt, deplorable;
and it is probable that the Communist carabineros do more
than what the Negrin Government would like them to do; but
it would be idle to deny that, in the midst of the gigantic
struggle against Franco, the Poum has acted as a disruptive
influence in Catalonia. Even many Anarchists are now aware
of it.

The Communists have also greatly gained in influence since
last May in the U.G.T., the principal trade union federation
apart from the Anarchist C.N.T., as well as in the unified
Socialist-Communist party of Catalonia, which joined the
Third International at the end of 1936. Their 'victory'
propaganda, and, above all, the substantial deliveries of
Russian war material throughout 1937, which made people
feel, at a time when 'non-intervention' was at its height, that
the Soviet Union was the only friend of Republican Spain,
heightened enormously their prestige as the most active and
most determined anti-Fascist party.

And yet, in spite of much grumbling among the Anarchists,
it would be wrong to imagine that they are in a state of latent
rebellion. They have lost many of their members to the
U.G.T. (which now claims to be stronger than the Anarchist
C.N.T., even in Catalonia, where it now has 600,000 members),
and they feel that the great majority of Spanish Republican
opinion would be against a repetition of May 3. They are
lying low, very low. They are becoming rather more 'war

conscious' than they were; their members, despite difficult
food conditions and the rise in the cost of living, are refraining
from strikes and even wage demands, and are content with
their 100 or 150 pesetas a week.   The Anarchist militias of
the early days of the war have been incorporated in the
Regular Army; true, not as single units, but mostly scattered
through the army as a whole, for their military enthusiasm is
not always considered to be whole-hearted.   Yet many of the
Anarchists are to-day serving the anti-Fascist cause as well
as anybody.   There are Anarchist war commissars and Anarchist army commanders (such as Mera, on the Guadalajara
front), men of great personal courage and austere idealism,
who hold the views of their dead leader, Durutti—'renunci-
amos a todo excepto a la victoria.'[1]   Men different from some
of the young unshaved ruffians with uneasy eyes who haunt
the headquarters of the C.N.T.-F.A.I. in the immense eight-
storey building—a former hotel—in the Via Durutti, in the
heart of Barcelona.

LIFE IN BARCELONA

Except for the Cathedral and one or two other churches
'of artistic value' all the churches in Barcelona have been
destroyed; and although by a recent decree several thousand
priests have been 'reinstated', it does not mean much in practice.   They are allowed to say Mass in private houses, but anti-
clerical feeling is still so strong in Barcelona that the
authorities hesitate to allow Mass to be said in any public place
of worship.   The same applies to the other towns; it is true
that Presbyterian and other Protestant services are tolerated
both in Madrid and in Barcelona; but the only Catholic service
I heard of was that held at the Basque Legation at Valencia.
But none has been held in the Basque Legations either in
Barcelona or in Madrid.

Barcelona is not a pleasant city.   Unlike Madrid, with its
wonderful unity of spirit, it seems tormented by doubts and
contradictions.   The memories of the May rising, when 5,000
people were killed in street fighting, are still fresh; in the
wide luxurious ramblas of Barcelona walls and windows are

[1] Yet even Mera was among the first to rebel against the Negrin Government in March 1939.

riddled with bullet holes, and although by moving to Barcelona the Negrin Government has made Barcelona more 'war conscious' than it was before, there is still much political tension below the surface. It is a city of contrasts. 'In Madrid,' an Anarchist remarked to me, 'one says "comrade"; here one still says "señor". Barcelona is still dreadfully bourgeois.'

The wide avenue in front of the Basque Legation is crowded from morning till night by pitiful Basque refugees. Food is, generally, scarce; and yet by paying exorbitant prices—fifty pesetas—one can still dine luxuriously in one or two Barcelona restaurants. And round the corner from the Basque Legation with its refugees you hear at night while the streets are pitch dark the shrieking and bellowing of a jazz band. For the night life of Barcelona goes on. The hall is crowded with young officers in suspiciously spotless uniforms and well-groomed young men with perfectly creased trouser legs, and good-looking women with bare backs and shoulders. 'Valencia!' (oh, irony!) the trumpet blurted. 'Valencia!' the saxophone wailed in reply. An old, old jazz tune. And the couples on the floor and the men at the bar roared the refrain of 'Valencia' as though it meant nothing more than an old, old jazz tune. But a tough-looking man in uniform, looking at the well-groomed young men with the creased trousers, could be heard growling: 'Fascists . . . machine-gun. . . .'

It is true that the distribution of milk among children is well organised and the children of Barcelona look well and cheerful. But grown-up people are often short of food. An elderly woman, working in an office, told me of her 'miraculous experience'; for the first time in a month she had been able to eat an ounce of butter with her bread that morning. 'The hotels and restaurants get first choice,' she complained bitterly. 'It isn't right.' Actually, in the hotel where I stayed the food was worse than mediocre; the hard grey bread was strictly rationed; nevertheless each meal invariably included a meat course. It was abnormal. But oranges, of which there are plenty in Valencia, are often unobtainable in Barcelona, and even at our 'privileged' hotel we were served only tiny green apples, mostly worm-eaten.

The problem of food is largely a problem of transport— petrol for the lorries and coal for the railways. People who were here three months ago tell me, however, that great improvements have been made in that direction; and that petrol, in particular, is much more plentiful than before. In fact, during our travels in Spain we never had the slightest difficulty in having our tank filled. Apart from that, Government Spain does not produce enough to feed its increased population, and the Government is reluctant to buy more food abroad than is absolutely necessary. No doubt the food shortage has created some discontent; but it is important to emphasise that the food shortage in Government Spain is still mild compared with the hardships suffered by Germany at the end of the War, or by Russia during the first three years of the Revolution. Shortage, yes; famine, no. The word 'famine' can apply only to tobacco, and to any inveterate smoker Government Spain is a fearful place. One is entitled under the rationing system to one packet of cigarettes a week; but even this cannot always be obtained. People smoke weeds, and hay, and old tea leaves; most of the thirty packets of French cigarettes I had brought with me vanished in a short time into the pockets of overwhelmingly grateful Spaniards. A person smoking in the street is often followed by somebody waiting for the 'fag end' to be dropped on the pavement. At my hotel Lucky Strikes were privately sold at thirty pesetas a packet. The Lucky Strike people, have, by the way, made a present of a million cigarettes to the Spanish Government.

The streets of Barcelona are crowded and there is a great deal of traffic—cars, buses and tram-cars—though no taxis. In the evening, before it becomes completely dark, animated crowds walk as usual along the ramblas. Many of the larger buildings in the main streets of Barcelona have been turned into Government offices or are used as the headquarters of trade union and party organisations. Flower stalls are still plentiful, and most of the shops—except food-shops—are full of textile goods, clothes, shirts, ties, socks. Barcelona continues to be a well-dressed town. The Sepu, a Spanish variety of Woolworth, where khaki shirts are sold at twenty-five pesetas and ties at three pesetas, is as popular as ever. The cafés are crowded, though often people have to bring along their own sugar; and there are also plenty of open-air bars, where numerous soldiers are seen drinking vermouth and other concoctions, and eating olives out of a glass bowl on the counter. Sunflower seeds—oh, holy Russia!—are also sold in large quantities. With no cigarettes, almost anything to nibble and chew is welcome. Most of the confectioners have nothing in their shop-windows but gorgeous displays of empty chocolate boxes; and it was a pathetic sight to see the owner of one of them carefully clean and scrub the window. And yet in a few shops excellent chocolate can still be bought, only the day's supply is invariably sold out by 9 a.m.

Nearly all the bigger shops have been 'collectivised' and are run by the trade unions; their owners are said to be 'on the other side'; but an Anarchist complained to me bitterly of how, since the Negrin Government had come into office, several shops had been handed back to their owners—even to those who had 'come back from the Fascists'.

I went down to the harbour one day; eight British ships had come in that morning. In spite of non-intervention the Spaniards are grateful to Britain for not having yielded to Franco's threat of a blockade. 'After all,' a Spaniard told me, 'England is still keeping Valencia and Barcelona going.' The Spaniards themselves scarcely ever venture to go to sea; so much so that all along the coast fish is scarce.

Madrid is shelled almost every day; in Barcelona sometimes nothing happens for weeks on end, but when the air raids come they are often deadly. During one of the days I was there— clouds were lying low over the town and the anti-aircraft guns and fighting planes could do little—fifty people were killed in a café by one bomb. I do not know, if it came to the test, whether the Catalans would have the superb courage of the people of Madrid, but for the present they have taken even the worst air raids philosophically. Half an hour after the air raid I have just mentioned the ramblas were again full of people and a large crowd was standing around a quack doctor looking singularly like Mussolini. Giving his stomach terrific thumps he was explaining with Ciceronian eloquence the miraculous effect of his medicine 'on your guts'.

NEGRIN AND COMPANYS

The Premier's office in Barcelona occupies a large private

house in the Pasea de Gracia which once belonged to a banker who is now on 'the other side'. The entrance, which is guarded by two soldiers with fixed bayonets, is decorated with a religious panel in blue and golden majolica. In the courtyard there usually stands a large limousine, flying the Republican flag. It looks an efficient, up-to-date office. The day I called there they were unpacking several large cases of American dictaphones. Negrin's office, with wood-panelled walls, a horseshoe desk with a row of telephones on one side, modern lighting, and soft leather armchairs, is like that of an important American business man.

Nothing is more refreshing than a talk with Negrin. He joined politics late in life, and still looks more like a lecturer in biology than like a professional politician. He smiles kindly through his horn-rimmed glasses, and when he speaks (in excellent English) he speaks with quiet assurance and self-confidence.

I began by referring to what somebody had described to me as 'Negrin's three-year plan'. 'No,' he said, 'there is really no such thing as a "plan". The "plans" will come when the war is over, and when it will be possible to have them sanctioned by Parliament. What we have for the moment is merely a plan of expenditure. Our gold reserves are much more important than is generally thought, and with care they should last us a couple of years; and then there are other forms of wealth besides. Yes, we have to buy food abroad, but I am not going to spend more money on that than is absolutely necessary. If last year I had yielded to all the pressure to spend money on this, that, and the next thing we should have had none left for the war by now! But the food problem must be solved through organisation and restriction, not through thoughtless spending. We are busy organising our exports in such a way as to provide us with substantial funds for purchases abroad; we already sell ores and oil and fruit and Almaden mercury and potash, and in the next six months we hope to increase substantially our exports of industrial products.

'What we need in exchange is petrol, coal, food, and army equipment. As regards food, you have to remember that most of the wheat and meat in Eastern Spain came from parts now occupied by the rebels, and moreover, we have 800,000 refugees

to feed in Catalonia alone and over 3,000,000 in the whole of
our territory. And the problem of feeding Madrid, with its
population of 800,000 is no easy one. As for armaments, I
can assure you that if only we could buy abroad all we really
need the war would be finished before next summer. Our own
production of armaments is increasing steadily, but it is not
easy to keep up with the requirements, and if we could we
would rather buy more abroad and finish the war more quickly.
I do not think we shall be able to produce ourselves all we
need before six or twelve months. The aeroplanes and the
Hispano-Suiza aeroplane engines we make are excellent; we
also make tanks, but we are short of heavy artillery. It is
often said abroad that after the fall of Gijon the Government
should have scored some tangible success—for instance, by
taking Saragossa—but we shall not take the offensive until we
are sure that we are fully prepared.'

'So you are optimistic?'

'No, I am not "optimistic"; optimism is merely a contem-
plative attitude. We are not waiting. We are working hard.
We know that the war can be won. We know what the possibilities are, and we know that the people are behind us. Our
real enemies are the Italian and German invaders; and we are
prepared for all eventualities, a blockade and even a gas attack.
Emergency food stores for several months are being accumulated both in Madrid and in Barcelona; and if they use gas we
have our counter-measures ready, not only passive but also
active. Of course,' Negrin smiled a little ironically, 'if they
do that we shall also appeal to the League of Nations. As for
belligerent rights, we hope they will not be granted to Franco;
it will be tantamount to a recognition of his "Government",
and it will enable Germany and Italy to blockade us. The
credits that Franco may receive now or later from abroad we
shall not recognise once we have won the war, so the money
will just be wasted.'

Negrin also spoke of the inhumanity of the rebels—of the
shelling, bombing, and machine-gunning they practised daily
against civilians, against women and children. By way of reprisals for the fearful bombing of Lerida, where twenty school
children were killed by one bomb, the Government had been
obliged (for public feeling against the rebels was running high)

to bomb Saragossa. 'But we avoid it as much as we can, for
out of 100 people killed eighty are our own people.' The
refugees who had returned from France to Asturias had, despite the assurances given them, suffered terrible persecution,
with hundreds being shot down or thrown into prison.

I referred discreetly to the complaints made by the Poum
people.

'For my own part,' Negrin said, 'I do not believe that Nin
was killed. But, in any case, why all this agitation about
Nin?' And, alluding to the terroristic activities in Madrid
and Barcelona last year, Negrin said, 'What is one man compared with the thousands of innocent people who were ruth-
lessly killed before the Government was in control? To-day
in Madrid and Barcelona you are as safe as in London or Paris
and' (turning with a smile to Richard of the *Chicago Daily
News*) 'safer than in Chicago!'

We also saw Señor Companys, the President of Catalonia,
that day. He received us at his official residence in the
Rambla de Cataluña, a sumptuous building, protected by
Catalan guards in red and yellow—slightly 'Ruritanian'—
uniforms. Companys is quite different from Negrin,—a wily
Mediterranean politician, whose vivacious manner and exuberant French reminded me of Veniselos. He hotly denied
the report that he had gone to Brussels to enter into contact
with the rebels. 'That I, the man who proclaimed the Republic and spent fifteen years of my life in Alfonso's gaols,
should do such a thing,' he cried, 'no, never!' Apart from that
he made no statement for publication, and I can only record
general impressions of my visit. Companys seemed to think
that even if, in theory, *Franco might be reasonable the people
around him were certainly utterly impossible* and that there
could be no question of any negotiations. Companys constantly referred to the loyal co-operation between the Catalan
Government and the Central Government, and suggested that
the Catalan Government, with its great experience in such
matters, was helping Negrin as much as possible to overcome
the food difficulties now that the Central Government had
taken the matter over, though he also seemed to think that it
was not perhaps a bad thing that people should not be 'too
comfortable' in war time. His view appeared to be that

Catalonia had, after all, 'liquidated' the rebellion of July 1936, in a day; that there was, therefore, no 'Fascist problem' as far as Catalonia was concerned; and that if the Catalans were fighting the common enemy they were doing so 'for the sake of democratic Spain as a whole'. All of which seemed to mean that, far from criticising the Catalans, the Spaniards should be grateful to them.

Companys is a politician who does not like to burn any bridges. In the past he had a soft spot for the Anarchists, and, being conscious of their numerical strength in Catalonia, he seems even now reluctant to quarrel with them finally. While agreeing that they have misapplied the collectivisation law of October 24 and that much of their collectivisation has had to be undone, Companys is unwilling to attach to the Anarchists much blame for the 3rd of May. In his view the revolt was deliberately fostered by the Poum and joined by the more irresponsible elements among the Anarchist rank and file, and without the approval of their leaders.

THE ROAD TO MADRID

He had the fine, long hands of a pianist, but he was only our chauffeur. His face and his nose were also long and narrow, and his small mouth was surrounded by the everlasting stubble of Spanish plebeian chins. The stubble was turning grey, and so was his long, dark hair, and his eyes were kind and terribly sad. Perhaps they were sad by nature; or perhaps they were sad because his brother had been shot by the rebels at Malaga and because his old father and mother and his three sisters were 'on the other side', in Seville, and he had not heard from them for more than a year. Were they still alive? We used to call him Oleander; it was something like that, but we could never remember exactly. He wore the large blue cap of a carabineer, but this did not make him any more soldierly. He was an elderly man, and they used him for driving Government cars. He drove them slowly, very slowly; though sometimes he would be seized by fits of recklessness. Spanish drivers seem to be made that way; or why else should so many corpses of cars lie along the edge of every road in Spain?

Oleander had a great contempt for mechanics—or, rather,

he had his own ideas on the subject.   Once the exhaust pipe
of our little Vauxhall car became all rattly and noisy, whereupon Oleander detached it and battered it as flat as a wafer
with a piece of rock. 'It's the fumes that make all the noise,'
he explained.   And when we told him he would blow up the
car he cried, 'Heaven forbid!   Do you think I want to die any
more than you do?'   In the end we threw the flattened exhaust
pipe into a ditch—a gesture Oleander received with bad grace,
but with a certain feeling of resignation.   For a time he continued to mutter things to himself. We never saw Oleander
read a paper; he was probably illiterate. Nor did he think anything of coming at eleven when we had told him to fetch us
at nine.   When, after a fortnight's travelling, in the course of
which we had shared with him loyally our meagre supply of
biscuits, cheese, and cigarettes, we said good-bye to him he
patted us lovingly on the shoulder and cried like a little boy.

   That morning we had left Valencia in a happy mood.
Compared with Barcelona, Valencia was gloriously cheerful.
The streets were half-lighted at night, the cafés were crowded,
in the fruit-shops glorious Valencia oranges, at a peseta a kilo,
were piled to the ceiling, and in the market there was any
amount of fruit and vegetables and dried figs—though very
little meat and fish.   There was laughter in the streets of
Valencia.   The rosy-coloured baroque portal of the Church of
San Andrea was intact, and all the saints and angels and
apostles had their heads on the right way, while inside the
church cases of munitions, machine-guns, and trench mortars
(these looked a bit trashy; were they Spanish-made?) were
piled fifteen feet high. At the Victoria Hotel, hopelessly
packed while the Government was in Valencia, we were offered
a whole selection of rooms, and we were served an excellent
dinner, though the next morning at breakfast there was no
sugar for our tea.   And—this seemed the height of 'normality'
—I saw a man in a workshop binding books!   There were
many bookstalls in Valencia, and these sold not only Marx
and Lenin and Gorki and Zola and Dickens but also the Bible,
at seven pesetas a copy.

   I disagree with those who say that the journey from Valencia
to Madrid is dull.   At first you travel for miles through the
olive and orange groves west of Valencia; then the road begins

to climb, and after crossing, over a stretch of fifteen miles, the superb canyon of the Rio Gabriel, you reach the high Castilian plateau. The earth here is of a bright brick-red colour, dotted with dark-green shrubs. An immense pale-blue sky hangs over this wild, brick-red country, where you travel for miles without seeing a human dwelling. Here and there you pass a flock of brown sheep, guarded by the still, gaunt figure of a shepherd wrapped in a long, brown checked plaid. Brick-red and brown and dark-green and an indifferent, pale-blue sky above—a raw landscape that Cézanne and D. H. Lawrence would have loved. Parts of Mexico must be something like this.

We passed whole caravans of mule-carts and donkey-carts taking vegetables and flour all the way to Madrid—250 miles. It is not always a safe journey. It has happened that rebel aeroplanes have swooped down on these caravans and machine-gunned the peasants. There is nothing worse than being machine-gunned from the air; it is so personal; you feel that you, and you only, are the target. A shell or a bomb, at least does not aim at you individually. The reflection was made to me by a man who had experienced all three. His recipe against being machine-gunned from the air was to stop the car, run at least 500 yards off the Madrid road, and lie down in a ditch. 'If you get there safely you'll be all right. The bullets come at a certain angle which makes a ditch perfectly safe.'

But the morning we travelled from Valencia all these reflections seemed irrelevant. There were no aeroplanes in the sky; in the army lorries we passed the soldiers were laughing; and over the edge of a petrol van two soldiers were dangling their legs. All along the Castilian plateau the land seemed barren except for a few patches of cultivated soil here and there. The villages seemed to have grown out of the earth, with their houses the same brick-red colour as the earth itself. These villages on the Madrid road, where dark-skinned urchins play in the street, where old women in black bonnets sit on their doorsteps surrounded by grand-children and cats and dogs, where donkey-carts move slowly along the road, cannot have changed since the days of Don Quixote. Except for the petrol pumps. At Minglanilla, a village that seemed as old as the earth itself, a girl looking like a Goya model pumped petrol into our tank. She wore a scarlet dress and

coral earrings, and as we drove off she smiled at us with her
strong white teeth and cried '*Salud!*' as she raised her little
clenched fist.

On and on we drove along the still Castilian plateau. The
milestone showed 100 kilometres to Madrid. 'We are in the
war zone now,' one of us facetiously remarked. The next town
on the road map was Tarancon. The name meant nothing
to us. But a surprise awaited us. As we turned into Tarancon we were suddenly stopped by a crowd of guards. We
must branch off the main road, they said, for this road had been
damaged. We soon realised what had happened. There had
been an air raid on the town barely two hours earlier. We
wandered through the streets of Tarancon. They were strewn
with wreckage. A hundred houses had been wrecked. In one
of the streets, cordoned off, the solitary remaining wall of a
house was being brought down with a crash. The whole front
of several other houses had been blown in—we counted over
fifty wrecked houses in less than five minutes; in one of them
the washing was still hanging from the second floor. In another house the whole front had been blown away, and the
pink bedcover from the second floor was protruding through
the ceiling of the floor below. Outside the post office there
was a bomb-hole four feet deep; all the windows around had
been shattered; a woman in the house opposite was sweeping
the glass debris on to the balcony. In one street we waded
through large pools of red wine; a bomb must have hit a load
of wine barrels. Outside a small miserable house we saw a
woman clutching the remains of a broken chair. There was
also a visibly well-to-do house, one side of which had been
blown away. A large bronze chandelier was still hanging from
the ceiling on the first floor, and—a strange sight—a large oil-
painting of a man in uniform was dangling from the same
ceiling over a void. The wall on which it had rested was gone.
We also went into another prosperous-looking house, with an
inner yard surrounded by a white colonnade. The top of the
house had been blown away. The yard was filled with heaps
of debris. A sad, elderly woman, to whom the house belonged,
looked on in bitter silence. There were three palm-trees in
the yard; two of them were intact. The woman's two children
and a dog were playing among the debris. In another street

a house had completely collapsed and soldiers were still looking for bodies among the wreckage. Opposite, at a window,
a woman was looking down on them, pressing a small, dark-
eyed child to her bosom.

When the air raid began most of the inhabitants had rushed
into the underground refuges, and only four people—one soldier and three civilians—had been killed that day. Eighteen
aeroplanes, in groups of three at three or four minutes' interval, had swooped down on the town and bombed it. This was
the second raid on Tarancon. There had been another raid,
a week earlier. We asked a man about it. There was a grim
and bewildered look in his eyes. Yes, twenty bombers had
come that time, he said, and ten or twelve people had been
killed—five people in one house only: father, mother, and the
three daughters. Some of the others had been machine-gunned
as they were running away across the fields.

We drove on to Madrid, no longer feeling as cheerful as
before. It had grown dark. Some twenty miles outside
Madrid we turned off the main road, which, nearer Madrid,
is being constantly shelled from the rebel lines. Only dispatch riders take that road. We drove through the dark, following a long procession of army and food lorries. One of
them carried olives sent by some labour organisation in Catalonia 'to our Madrid brothers'. At length we saw the first
Madrid tram-cars. At one of the tram-stops, below a tree, we
saw a couple—kissing.

MADRID

Over thirteen months have passed since General Franco's
troops were thrown back after entering the outskirts of
Madrid. Since then Madrid has successfully resisted the rebel
onslaught: thirteen months of heroic resistance by the troops,
thirteen months of unparalleled courage and endurance by
the people of Madrid. Never has a city of nearly a million
people lived through what Madrid has endured. To-day
Madrid may feel the physical strain of it, but its spirit is un-
broken.

Until last spring air raids were a frequent occurrence; since
then these air raids have ceased completely. But once, twice,

three times a week, sometimes day after day, the capital is shelled from the rebel batteries to the north, west and south. On three sides Madrid is surrounded by rebel trenches, and only the east is open. Will this bottle-neck ever be closed through another, this time more successful, offensive at Guadalajara? That is one of the most vital questions on which perhaps the whole future course of events in Spain will depend. The fact that only the eastern exit is open and that Madrid is connected with the rest of Spain only by road does not make it easy to supply it with food. But, considering the enormous difficulties, the Government has dealt with this problem in a highly creditable manner, and the food situation in Madrid today is, if anything, rather better than two or three months ago.

But Madrid's resistance has been not only passive. Immense improvements have been made in fortifying the outskirts of the city; the trenches around Madrid are incomparably more solid than they were six months ago; and the fact that air raids have ceased and that the rebels now resort only to the more cowardly but less deadly method of shelling, shows that there are a sufficient number of chaser planes and anti-aircraft guns to discourage the bombing of Madrid from the air. Further, a new railway line is being built to connect the Madrid-Guadalajara line with Albacete and the south-east. 'If a year ago, when we were, materially, almost undefended, Franco was unable to take Madrid, how can he possibly take it now?' I have heard many people in Madrid make this reflection.

We stayed in the Hotel Victoria, some five minutes' walk from the Puerta del Sol. Most foreign visitors stay there now. The windows of the Victoria face east (the best direction) and south (the second best). For, in Madrid, with the shelling coming mainly from the north and west, there are degrees in the security (or insecurity) of houses, just as there are also parts of the town—said to be largely inhabited by Franco sympathisers—which have suffered far less than others. No place, however, is as perfectly safe as the underground vaults of the Bank of Spain; and it was in this exclusive place that we attended the luncheon that General Miaja gave in honour of Mr. Attlee, Mr. Noel-Baker, and Miss Wilkinson. The famous soldier, enormously popular in Madrid, looks like a kindly old bishop.

The first night in Madrid, groping our way along a dark, narrow lane littered with debris—for there had been some shelling that morning—we went to see Ernest Hemingway, one of the three remaining tenants of the Hotel Florida, whose 'modern comfort' we had seen advertised on the way up to Madrid that day. The Florida forms the angle of two of the principal Madrid avenues, and the side facing north-west is almost completely wrecked. The room Hemingway occupies is on the first floor in the south-east corner of the hotel, the only 'relatively' safe room in the place. Hemingway, with his exuberant Douglas Fairbanks laughter, loves movement, action and human courage. He is immensely popular both in Madrid and in the trenches. He takes a boylike joy in collecting all the bits of shell that have landed in the Florida, and labels them lovingly according to the number of the room which they had wrecked. One of the 'duds' that had landed in the Florida has now been turned into an electric lamp on Hemingway's desk, with a lampshade painted by an anti-Fascist artist.

That night there were two other people in Hemingway's room. One was 'John the Greek', who spoke a boisterous New York-Greek jargon and who had not yet fully recovered from the shock of being buried by a shell which had at the same time killed five of his comrades in the International Brigade. The other was a young American poet, Evan S., shot through the thigh at Brunete, a delicate consumptive boy, quiet and modest. He was going back to the front, against 'doctor's orders'. To these two, as to many others, Hemingway was like a father. Some days later I saw Hemingway again at Chicotes Bar, in the Gran Via. There were crowds of soldiers around him; everybody in Spain seemed to know him. Chicotes Bar figures in *The Fifth Column*, the play about Madrid which Hemingway has just completed. (The 'Fifth Column' is that which, in Franco's own words, was waiting inside Madrid to join the other four as they entered the capital.) The proprietor of Chicotes is 'on the other side', and the place is run by the waiters.

It was cold and sunny the next morning, and we went down to the Puerta del Sol. It is a sort of Piccadilly Circus of Madrid, and, like Piccadilly Circus, undistinguished by any outstanding

monument or building.   A big yellow block of offices on the
north side had been completely gutted by a bomb; nothing
was left but the bare walls, with the sky showing through the
glassless windows.   But the other houses seemed moderately
intact or had, rather, been patched up.   Franco has a predilec-
tion for the Puerta del Sol.   Last New Year's Eve, on the stroke
of twelve, twelve shells landed there—an example of rebel
humour.

   That morning, however, the tram-cars jingled and the
motors hooted as they would anywhere else, though the place
was barely a mile away from the enemy trenches.   On the
bookstalls along the pavements there were large piles of the
seven or eight daily papers published (on rather grey paper)
in Madrid.   There were some blank spaces—the work of the
censorship—in the Anarchist paper.   The shoe-cleaners were
doing a brisk trade on the north side of the Puerto at the foot
of the wrecked yellow house, and we got the best shoeshine in
the world for our sixty centavos.   We went into a café where
crowds of people sat drinking wine and vermouth and some
eating nasty looking bits of raw mule flesh.   All the shops except those selling foodstuffs were well stocked.   In the wine
stores there were respectable arrays of bottles, including
genuine French champagne at twenty-five pesetas; and there
must be enough shirts and shoes and ties and handkerchiefs—
some in Republican and even Anarchist colours—to last a
generation.   But food-shops look rather miserable; for instance, a famous grocery store to which we went, in the Calle
Alcala, had little to show except bottles of wine and one big
bag of rice, part of its contents wrapped up in little half-pound
parcels, and innumerable bottles and jars of Worcester sauce,
mustard, and pickles!

   Madrid is supremely war-conscious.   In the food queues
there is far less grumbling than in Barcelona, where grumbling
is often deliberately stimulated by *agents provocateurs*.   In
Madrid such tactics do not work.   Madrid is also strangely
cheerful.   Ten thousand people have been killed by bombs
and shells, but people do not speak of the dead; everybody
will prefer to tell you of his own 'miraculous' escape.   It makes
for optimism.   So also does the important fact that children,
at any rate, are getting enough to eat.   These healthy children

playing in the streets of Madrid are a truly happy sight. And what is more cheerful on a fine day than the wide, sun-lit avenues of the Prado and the Castellan, where one still sees some old horse-cabs standing in a rank; Madrid is a clean city, and the rubbish carts are active every morning. In the wide eastern avenues—finer almost than the Champs Élysées—the Prado Museum is closed to visitors, the best pictures having been taken to Valencia and other places and the rest being carefully stored in the basement; the statues in the streets are carefully covered up with brick masonry, with a little Republican flag flying on top of these strange pyramids. The large building of the General Post Office is badly damaged by bombs and shells, but people continue as usual to drop their letters into the boxes. And, strangest of all, the Zoo goes on as before and is open to the public on Sundays. The lions still get meat, but the lady zebra was seized with panic during a shelling and battered her head fatally against a stone wall, and there are a few other little anomalies. The hippopotamus —or so at least the story goes, for Madrid is full of jokes— developed a skin disease after being fed for weeks on bird seed, and the cockatoo, I am told, is the most unpopular creature at the Madrid Zoo, for he has learned to imitate the noise of exploding shells.

One may wonder how the 'ordinary' person lives in Madrid after a year's bombing and shelling and privation. Having had the good fortune of being able to visit some private houses, I shall describe a couple of typical cases.

In the Via we called on a 'middle-class' Spanish family to whom I had an introduction. The house was a large seven-storey block of flats, and since lifts are not allowed to work in Madrid we had to climb all the way, for they lived on the top floor. Like all stairways in Madrid, it smelt of rancid oil. The man to whom I had a note was an artist. But the door was opened by a delicate little dark-skinned woman, with a strained, careworn look on her face. No, she said, her brother was not in Madrid; he had left some months ago for Murcia, where he had a job with a trade union organisation. She herself was working with a cinema firm in the Gran Via. She also had another brother in Madrid. 'But he is a bit more nervous than I am,' she said, 'and, on account of the shells, he doesn't like coming home at night. So he lives near his office. Nor does he like this flat, which he thinks is a little too exposed.' She took us on to the balcony. Right below us, half a mile away, with nothing in between, were the rebel trenches, from which, with a dry noise, a little flare of smoke would go up every few minutes.

'You must be brave to live here,' I remarked. 'You might as well live on top of the Telefonica building.' 'Why?' she said. 'What's the good of moving? I like this little house of ours. We've got all our furniture, and my brother's belongings are here. And look at this,' she said, pointing to a whatnot filled with porcelain, 'everything completely intact!' 'What do you do when the shelling starts?' 'Oh, nothing; I just stay here. What's the good of running downstairs? A shell might hit me while I was running down the stairs, and the people would then just say, "Serves her right for being a coward!" So it's better to stay where you are. Don't you think so?' The girl had a typically Madrid mentality. She firmly believed that Madrid would never be captured by the Fascists. 'If they couldn't capture it a year ago, how can they possibly capture it now?' How often had I already heard that refrain!

'Oh, it is no use denying it,' she said, 'it is tiring, terribly tiring;[1] and we know the war must go on for another three years. And we do not get much to eat. Beans and split peas, and a little rice, day after day. And no cigarettes. But we must stick it, and we shall stick it; and, except for the Fascists, everybody in Madrid feels exactly the same.'

'How many people in Madrid, would you say, are Fascist?'

'Oh, quite a lot; twenty-five per cent, I should say, though many of them have gone away in the last few months—to Valencia, to Barcelona, to other places which are more "comfortable". Murcia is full of Fascists.'

The Government has to keep an eye on the 'Fascists', and although there are frequent arrests and house-searches among potential members of Franco's 'Fifth Column'—can one blame the Government for it?—there is no Terror in Madrid to-day

---

[1] How much more 'tiring' it must have become after fifteen more months of such a life!

and no 'atrocities'. Until this spring, before the Government was in proper control, there was a great deal of private and semi-private terrorism in Madrid and many fearful things happened. People would be dragged out of their houses by unknown men, and their bodies would later be found somewhere outside the town. But the Negrin Government has put an end to all this.

No doubt people of the middle and upper classes in Madrid, incapable of adapting themselves to new conditions, or unwilling to do so in the expectation of an early rebel victory, are having a thin time; and old people of that class suffer great hardships, though a considerable amount of relief has been organised for them, chiefly with the help of the various Consulates and Legations, mostly South American, but also some others. So long as this relief, which also includes evacuation to rebel territory, is dictated by purely humanitarian motives and is not calculated to keep the 'Fifth Column' going it deserves nothing but praise.

Here is a concrete example of how a man who a year ago was in danger of being murdered by terrorist gangs is now living normally again. Señor N. is an elderly man, something of a literary dilettante, who never took any part in politics, but who, through his family connections, could be ranked as a member of the aristocracy. Worse still, having been the member of a Conservative club (which was enough to make him a 'Fascist' in the eyes of the terrorists), he believed himself to be in serious danger of being murdered. His friends abroad tried a year ago to help him to leave Madrid, but for some reason he remained there. When I called at his house I found that he was not in. The door was opened by an old woman—a housekeeper or a 'nanny'—who, judging from the way she talked about her master, must have been in the family for a couple of generations. The house was tidy and well furnished, though the floor just above it had been wrecked by a shell. Oh, Señor Alfonso was very well, she said, thank you. Unfortunately he had gone to Barcelona and wouldn't be back for a few days. He had gone there to buy the raw material for the shoe polish he was now manufacturing. It wasn't easy, she said, but he was making ends meet.

'Have you enough food?' I asked, as a matter of course. The

old woman's answer was sublime. 'Yes, would you like some?'
she asked sympathetically. And, in spite of my grateful
refusal, she urged me to sit down, as she would make me 'a
nice cup of tea'. And outside, at some distance, a machine-
gun was going pat-pat-pat.

.   .   .   .

Few parts of Madrid have escaped bombing or shelling, but
the actual 'devastated areas' of Madrid are in the west, on the
hill around the Royal Palace, and in the north-west around
the University City, through which the 'front' still runs. Both
devastated areas are within fifteen or twenty minutes' walk
from the Puerta del Sol. Armed with passes signed by Señor
Prieto, the War Minister, in person, we set out for the University City 'front' one morning.

Along the Calle Blasco Ibañez the tram-cars still run almost
as far as the front, even beyond the point where they have
to run through a gap in the solid stone barricades built right
across the street. All the side-streets, both east and west, are
also barricaded, and these barricades are now being strengthened and reinforced as an additional precaution. The houses
throughout the district—mostly modern working-class tene-
ments—have been horribly damaged by bombs and shells,
though in few cases completely destroyed. People still live in
some of them, with planks or sheets of cardboard taking the
place of window-panes. Shattered green wooden blinds hang
out of many windows, fan-shaped, like the branches of some
fantastic palm-tree. And yet, even among these scenes of
desolation, we could see a crowd of people standing outside a
bakery while firing was going on barely a hundred yards away,
and the street cleaners were taking away the stone wreckage
in the street caused by a shell an hour or two before. From
all these barricaded side-streets one looks down on the green
fields below, where the rebel trenches are. Nobody worries
about stray bullets.

The real front begins at the prison. A little soldier, with
fair hair and a pock-marked face, cheerfully volunteered to
take us down to the trenches on the slopes of the Parque del
Oeste. Some sporadic firing was going on in the trenches north
and west of us, but it was, on the whole, an 'all quiet' day.
The little soldier took us through the yard of the prison, its

walls battered by shells, and then on to the square outside the prison, with dug-outs on both sides. There were parapets on the north side of the square, opposite the rebel lines, composed of trunks, suitcases, and wooden drawers filled with sand. We were then taken down a long, low, underground passage, at the end of which were the trenches. The trenches and the dug-outs inside the gallery, where we found several soldiers sleeping, were as solidly built as any on the Western Front, and the trenches were fully seven feet deep. A little sniping was going on, and we heard a couple of bullets whizz past a good safe distance above our heads. There were few soldiers in the trenches that morning. One of them was testing, rather than actually 'working', a new trench-mortar.

Passing down a slope from the second to the first line of trenches we got a good view of the rebel lines and of the various buildings of the University City, whose ruins were battered into the shapes of some fantastic giant animals—some white others red. It was at this unfortunate point that our little soldier, unperturbed by any snipers on the other side, began to explain to us, with the thoroughness of a Cook's guide, all about the rebel lines fifty yards away. His explanations went on for a time that seemed interminably long.

After spending a singularly uneventful hour or so in the trenches we went back through the same galleries to the square outside the prison, with the fearfully wrecked tene-ment houses on the other side. First we went into a dug-out on one side of the square, where we were shown a German 1918 anti-tank gun pointing through a loophole at the rebel trenches. How, one wondered, had this old German gun got here? On the other side of the square was another dug-out, with a much more up-to-date American anti-tank gun, with two-inch shells stamped 'U.S.A.'. Five soldiers were sitting around a *brasero* (or, rather, a basin filled with burning logs) eating a good lunch—the best I had seen in Madrid. We talked to them for a long time, and they seemed as cheerful and contented as anyone at the front could be. They demon-strated to us their anti-tank gun with loving care and offered us a 'dud' shell as a present.

There was an upright piano in the dug-out, with broken and grimy keys, and we played them some popular songs and

the 'Internationale' and the 'Marseillaise', even 'God Save the
King' and—this seemed a bit absurd—some bits of Chopin
and Beethoven. But they seemed to like it and asked us to go on
and on. A red-haired mongrel limped into the dug-out. The
soldiers had a fellow-feeling for the dog and stroked his injured paw, wounded by a stray bullet, and patted him and
fed him on bits of meat. 'It's a dangerous bit of ground,' they
said, pointing to the square outside. 'Hardly a day passes
without some shelling.' 'Are there many wounded?' we asked.
One of the soldiers shook his head. 'Quite a few,' he said.

Before we had left the dug-out we were laden with presents
—two dud shells and another shell sawn in two and turned
by one of the men into a cigarette lighter, its lower half
stuffed with cotton wool. We were then taken to another
dug-out on the other side of the square, below the wrecked
tenement, where we paid our respects to the captain, an
elderly man in a smart khaki uniform looking very like a
British officer. There was a picture of Lenin on the wall,
and the captain produced a bottle of Spanish brandy, which
we all drank from the same glass to the Spanish Republic.
What cheerful, lovable and earnest people they all were, these
little peasants from Valencia and Castile!

Our second attempt to go to the front, this time in the Casa
de Campo, at the foot of the hill below the Royal Palace, was
less successful. The whole area around the Royal Palace,
which has been turned into a sort of fortress overlooking the
rebel plain below, forms another piece of 'devastated Madrid'.
The Opera House, now used for storing army material, behind
the Royal Palace, and all the houses around it are badly
damaged by shells. The wide avenue along the front of the
hill on either side of the Royal Palace and the adjoining streets
are barricaded. The statues of the Spanish kings are used as
supports for these barricades, with the royal bodies half-
cemented into them. There was a great deal of rifle and
machine-gun firing that evening when, conducted by a guard
who had been impressed by our Prieto passes, we went down
the wide barricaded avenue which runs, south of the royal
park, down to the Casa de Campo, a wood on the other side of
the Manzanares River. We were taken through the wood to
the battalion commander's headquarters in a building that

looked like a farm-house. But nobody would deal with us there, and we were sent to another house at the other end of the wood. It was strange to walk through this peaceful wood, over a thick carpet of brown and yellow leaves, with a shell whizzing over us from time to time and the rifle fire, a few hundred yards away, becoming more and more active.

The little white house to which we were taken was like a gamekeeper's lodge. We presented our Prieto passes and were taken into a small room, where we were told to wait. And as the door opened and we were shown in we heard an extra-ordinary thing: 'King's Park, 1; Dunfermline, 3; Montrose, 1; Dundee United, 2;'—London broadcasting the football results, while outside the rebels were firing shells at Madrid. It was an expensive wireless set, and the little room itself was expensively furnished with heavy drawing-room chairs covered with crimson silk—no doubt from the Royal Palace. At the desk, dressed in khaki, sat a slim young officer, with dark hair and a fresh scar on his forehead, taking notes. There was a large desk in the room, and above it, a pair of antlers, and a clock, and a bottle of wine on it, with two glasses, and various objects were hanging on the wall—an old sword and a mandolin and a framed picture of Napoleon's retreat from Moscow and a crudely coloured print of that meek-looking man President Azaña, with his goggles and puffed cheeks. In a corner there was a pile of brown army pull-overs. And the wireless wailed:

> You are my lucky star,
> I'm lucky in your arms,

drowning the noise outside.

There seem to be no definite rules in Spain about passes, and this time we were told that our Prieto passes were no good at all and that we had no business to be in the Casa del Campo and that, in fact, we were liable to be arrested. But we were not arrested, and with great courtesy we were put in the captain's own car and driven back to Madrid.

.   .   .   .

The Republican offensive on the Teruel front came almost to everybody as a complete surprise. The plans had been kept very dark; and the watchword I used to hear both in Madrid

and Barcelona was: 'Franco's next offensive must be another
Guadalajara.' In other words, Franco must not pass; it did
not seem that the Government's plans went beyond defending
its own positions—at least not for a good long time. As Dr.
Negrin told me: 'We shall not take the offensive until we are
sure that we are ready for it. Time is working in our favour.'
Brilliant as Teruel was, it does not change this fundamental
view that the Government was not yet ready for a big offensive;
though it does suggest that the Government troops are already
admirably trained and equipped for manœuvring and for comparatively small-scale operations calculated to upset the
enemy's plans. And one may well wonder what rebel plans
were undone by the attack on Teruel.

The Government has an army of about 500,000 men, with
an admirable moral, and—an important recent development—
a highly-trained and highly mobile reserve force of completely
fresh troops, numbering between 100,000 and 120,000 men.
These can be thrown into battle at the shortest notice, to any
critical point of the front. The international troops whose high
fighting quality was demonstrated at Brunete and on a hundred other occasions, do not exceed 15,000 men, and they
are now scattered through a large part of the army; for the
opposite reason (for they form, from the point of view of moral,
the least reliable element) the Anarchists are also scattered
through the army and do not, as a rule, form any separate
fighting units. The Spanish army is no longer a militia
and is ruled by a strict though human and comradely
discipline.

The armaments position of the Government is improving.
A large part of these armaments is now manufactured in
Catalonia, not only the smaller weapons but also tanks, and
some thirty aeroplanes a month—a figure which, it is hoped,
will be doubled in a few months. There is still a certain shortage of good pilots, but Spanish pilots are being intensively
trained both in Spain and—why deny it?—abroad. In the
heyday of one-sided 'non-intervention' Russia and, to a lesser
extent, Mexico were practically the only sources of foreign
arms, and Russia literally saved the Spanish Republic, a fact
which has not been without political repercussions there. To-
day the Republic is finding it less difficult to procure arms

elsewhere, in addition to those she manufactures herself though the French, I was often told, 'are still a bit sticky'.

Republican Spain to-day is an immense fortress with its battlements stretching, often in strange zig-zags drawn by geography herself, from tropical Almeria to the crest of the central Pyrénées. Along hundreds of miles of this 'front' there is no fighting, for the natural barriers make this useless. But there are vital points at which the rebels may strike—if their loudly heralded offensive comes; an offensive that Teruel must have delayed. These vital points are Teruel itself, Madrid, and the Aragon front.

The hideous bombing of defenceless towns like Tarancon, in the Madrid sector, which, like Guernica, was calculated to 'demoralise' the civilian population, suggested for a time that an attack on Madrid was coming. Madrid itself is as good as impregnable; a direct attack on Madrid would cost the rebels 100,000 casualties and would probably fail even then. More probable would be an attempt to cut off Madrid through another Guadalajara offensive, accompanied by a simultaneous offensive from the south of the 'bottle-neck'. But this southern side of the 'bottle-neck' is as strongly fortified as Madrid itself; as for Guadalajara, the number and the mobility of the Government troops there are incomparably greater than during the famous rebel offensive in March (nothing, by the way, amuses Spaniards more than Mussolini's decision to name a street in Rome after Guadalajara).

From the Government point of view there are two real dangers in sight: a blockade, with the assistance of Germany and Italy, and immense new deliveries of war material to the rebels. In time the Government expects to equal the rebel armaments; but so long as they are able at least to maintain the present proportion (and everything shows that they can do that, *unless the rebels receive some unusually large shipments of both arms and men and unless there is a blockade*) they can hold out indefinitely. For the Government the most vital immediate problem is food; if the Negrin Government succeeds in improving the situation still further, in organising the distribution more rationally, and in obtaining food credits abroad (as it is now trying to do) the Spanish Republic will not break down. And in time, but not before they are ready, the defenders of Republican Spain will take the offensive. There may then be a deadlock—and an armistice. But what if Italy and Germany intensify their aid to an enormous extent and attempt a new blockade? Then, of course, anything may happen. But it is for the democratic powers to prevent it.

.   .   .   .

Our car was nearing the French frontier. Those two poplars and the hill beyond were France. I have known many people who at that moment felt like crying *'Vive la France!'* Instead I turned round and had a last look at Spain. And I thought of the small female figure looking down on the rebel lines from her lonely little flat in Madrid; and I remembered the soldiers in the dug-out and how they stroked the wounded paw of their friend, the little red-haired mongrel. The human side of these people is unforgettable.

.   .   .   .

Three months later, there was a great change for the worse in Spain. Heavily armed, and supported by Italian legionaries, Franco's men swooped down the Ebro valley to the Mediterranean. Government Spain was cut in two. And about the same time Barcelona became the object of the most horrible Italo-German experiments in human vivisection. High-explosive bombing was tried out—and its results were so frightful that London and Paris remembered them only too clearly when the German blackmail reached its height at the time of the September crisis.

And it was during the Aragon offensive that Mr. Chamberlain was to conclude his pact with Mussolini—and this pact was based on the assumption of an early, almost an immediate Franco victory.

But at Tortosa—now in ruins, Tortosa where Richard and Oleander and I cheerfully ate an oily, greasy and rather nasty Spanish lunch on our drive from Barcelona to Madrid early in December—at Tortosa Franco got stuck again.

Mr. Chamberlain was bitterly annoyed by the caddish conduct of the Reds who refused to oblige by allowing themselves to be exterminated in the name of Anglo-Italian friendship. The diplomatic correspondent of the *Times* recorded on May 20 the great anxiety felt in London because Chamberlain's calculations about Spain had gone wrong!

'To a large extent,' he wrote, 'the general depression of the past few days seems to have been caused by the uneasy realisation that the Spanish war is likely to drag on far beyond the easy estimates made a month or so ago. Then it was widely said in the Embassies that Franco would break the Government resistance within six or eight weeks, and that Signor Mussolini would soon afterwards recall the Italian combatants. Now it is expected that an end cannot be put to the main fighting before the late autumn. *Depression is turned into anxiety at the reports that General Franco can hardly hope for victory unless his backing of foreign combatants and foreign munitions is greatly increased.*'[1]

But in the months that followed (as shall be seen) the two things that Republican Spain feared became a reality. One was the immense intensification of Italo-German intervention in Franco's favour, the other was the blockade—which, with the tacit acceptance of the British Government, took the form of an air blockade. And this blockade was reinforced by the closing to arms of the Catalan frontier. Without this grim travesty of 'non-intervention' the Spanish Republic would not have been defeated. And I often wonder what has happened to Oleander. . . . He may have been killed by a bomb—or in a motor smash—or he may still be—alive or dead—in the Camp of Argelès. I wish I could remember his real name.

[1] The *Times*, May 20, 1938.

CHAPTER IV

1937 RETROSPECT

(Dealing mainly with the decline of the Front Populaire and other French internal matters)

IN my last book, *The Destiny of France*, which dealt with the events in France until the beginnings of 1937, I gave a detailed account of the birth and growth of the Front Populaire, of the General Election of 1936, of the great wave of strikes that summer, of the economic and labour reforms passed that year—the forty-hour week, holidays with pay, collective contracts, the *office du blé*, the nationalisation of the war industries and the semi-nationalisation of the Bank of France. I also dealt with the Tripartite agreement and the first devaluation of the franc. I told the story of the spectacular revival of French trade unionism; and, naturally, described in detail the great episodes of France's foreign policy—everything from Barthou's policy of 'encirclement' and Laval's Abyssinian adventure to the Reoccupation of the Rhineland and the birth of the non-intervention policy. As a witty Labour M.P. remarked, the mother of this monster was French, but its father British. And I concluded, at the end of 1936, by pointing to the grave new economic and financial difficulties that were awaiting France at home; and the new surprises that might be sprung on her from Berchtesgaden. Berchtesgaden!—Old Moore wasn't in it. Except that Berchtesgaden did not become Big News until 1938; in 1937 nothing much happened at Berchtesgaden.

Internationally, 1937 was another year of hesitations and surrenders by the Western Democracies in the face of the ever-growing arrogance of Berlin and Rome. The foreign policy of London and Paris during that year—and above all, in relation to Spain—was best summarised by Low, in his superb cartoon called 'Revival of Old-Time Melodrama'. The snarling villain, cloaked and top-hatted, stands there, with one foot resting heavily on the toes of sweet young Anthony. The figures around them are—the dead body of the League; Democracy, a damsel in distress; and the British Lion with all four paws in the air. 'Benito Mussolini!' says the young hero with a gesture of admonition. 'Benito Mussolini, have a care! You have ruined the woman I love, killed my aged mother, sunk the British Fleet, and set fire to the Empire—but BEWARE! Do not go TOO FAR!'

Looking through a pile of 1937 cuttings the other day, I could not help chuckling at the thought of Low's young man.

LAST CHANCE FOR NON-INTERVENTION.

FRANCE GROWS TIRED OF NON-INTERVENTION HUMBUG.

WILL FRANCE OPEN FRONTIER INTO SPAIN?

ENGLAND INDIGNANT AT MEDITERRANEAN PIRACY.

CALLING ITALY'S BLUFF?

And so on. Day after day, month after month.

However, all things considered, 1937 was not a very eventful year—at least not in Europe. It was, as it were, a year of transition, in which nothing really decisive happened. Germany was proceeding with her rearmament, but, except for the menacing *Deutschland* and *Leipzig* incidents in the Mediterranean, the Nazi extremists were still being kept in check by General von Fritsch and other cautious people. In Spain, by the end of the summer, the Government had lost the northern provinces of Bilbao and Santander; but the rest of Government Spain was holding out, and if the reinforcements in men and material which the rebels had been receiving all the year from Italy and Germany were enormous, they were not sufficient; for in the meantime the Government had been getting some help from Russia, and had not only organised a well-trained army of over half a million men, but had also built up its war industries; and by the end of 1937 the chances looked even. Not only was the Government able to defend every mile of its enormous front between Almeria and the Pyrénées, but in the last fortnight in December it showed itself capable of carrying out a successful offensive when it captured Teruel.

During the year Britain and France rendered at least one service to the Spanish Government—it was when they signed the Nyon agreement. For although it did not completely end

piracy in the Mediterranean, it at least prevented a regular
Italo-German blockade of Spain's Mediterranean coast. It also
had the psychological value of showing that, when it came to
the point, France and Britain were capable of acting independently of the Dictators. In the absence of Italy, which had
decided to boycott the conference, the Italian Press gleefully
prophesied a fiasco; when the agreement was signed in spite
of her absence, Italy promptly climbed down, and asked to
join in the agreement. It was said at the time that the agreement was in reality the work of Litvinov; by 'insulting' Italy
a few days before Nyon, the Soviet Government had induced
Italy to boycott the conference; the French and British Governments were very angry with Litvinov, whom they called tactless. Actually, if Italy had been there from the outset, the
conference would have been a much more troublesome business. So the Soviet manœuvre had its value. But much credit
is also due to Mr. Eden who acted at Nyon as he had not acted
for a long time. For at Nyon his style was not cramped by
the proximity of Downing Street. And this gave M. Delbos
some courage, too.

Though in a small way, Nyon was a real achievement, in
fact the only tangible achievement the Western Democracies
could boast of during the whole of 1937. The rest was little
or nothing. It may, however, be added that the rearmament
that continued in Britain during the year promised to increase
her international weight in the future; and one had a feeling
that it might be of decisive service to European peace if it
were properly used. Only how, one wondered, would this increased authority be used? The decisive moments came in
the early part of 1938.

.   .   .   .

And France? France muddled along. The apprehensions
of the financial difficulties confronting her (and referred to
at the end of *The Destiny of France*) were fully justified.
Already in February M. Blum realised that 'this could not go
on'. In a memorable speech at St. Nazaire on February 24
he proclaimed that the time had come for a halt, for a *pause*,
as he called it—a pause in the application of the Front Populaire programme, in the increase of public expenditure, in
the rise of prices—'so that we may consolidate the ground we

have conquered.' In the financial debate at the Chamber that followed the St. Nazaire speech, the Opposition behaved, for the first time since June 1936, with an air of extraordinary self-assurance. 'Ha, Ha! we've got you this time!' seemed to be written on every face on the Right and Centre. For a week or more there had been heavy pressure on the franc, and when, waving a cutting from the *Times*, M. Fernand-Laurent, a member of the Right, claimed that a milliard francs of gold a day had been leaving Paris for London for some days past, M. Vincent Auriol, Blum's unimpressive Finance Minister, became very angry, shouted that the affairs of the exchange equalisation fund were nobody's business, and then mumbled in conclusion an awkward and ambiguous denial.

Again, as in October 1936, Blum was in a dilemma. Would he order exchange control, adopt a more or less autarchist system, and so abandon the Tripartite agreement of September 25; or would he save 'financial liberalism' at the price of making some important concessions to the orthodox financiers, who were obviously not fully satisfied with the announcement of the 'pause'? The 'coercive' way was advocated not only by Vincent Auriol who, poor man, had his style constantly cramped by Blum's international considerations, but also by M. Labeyrie, the Governor of the Bank of France. But Blum still preferred to choose the 'liberal' way. With the 'coercive' way he might have gone boldly ahead with the Front Populaire programme: only—it would have meant much less harmonious relations with England, and a suspension in the work of *rapprochement* with the United States which, for the first time since the War, was showing signs of becoming an important, perhaps decisive, factor in international affairs. A speech like that of Mr. William Bullitt, the American Ambassador in Paris, at the end of February, in which he said that although America desired peace, 'there might be some madmen in the world who would drag her into war', and in which he spoke of the bonds between the democratic countries—such a speech was enough to give Blum serious qualms at the thought of tearing up the Tripartite agreement. Moreover, about that time, the British Treasury gave him a polite but firm warning; and on March 5 the Blum Government made its climb-down. This consisted in the following measures:

(1) The Government decided to restore the free importation of, and trade in, gold, and the renewal of the purchase of gold at the current price, and without personal inquiries, by the Bank of France; (2) It undertook not to increase ordinary budget expenditure during the year (which meant a 'pause' in the application of the Front Populaire programme)—an exception was made only for the lower grades of Government officials who were suffering severely from the high cost of living; (3) Extra-budgetary expenditure was reduced by six milliards,[1] (largely at the expense of public works); (4) To crown this return of confidence a *garantie-de-change* loan for national defence was to be floated; and (5) last but not least, a committee of highly orthodox experts, including M. Rist and M. Baudoin, were placed in charge of the Exchange Equalisation Fund.

This was perhaps most unwise; for the Committee in question had the Government well on the leash; but 'confidence' had to be restored; and that was the price High Finance demanded from M. Blum. He gave way. The Bourse went up; and the first $8\frac{1}{2}$ milliards of the Defence loan (which was as safe a bet as one could desire and was almost an admission that a new devaluation was coming) was bought up by the banks in no time. Blum, though feeling a little uneasy at heart, looked like a happy man, and said that France had never in the last ten years, been stronger; and never had the outlook been so hopeful.

.   .   .   .

His joyful mood did not last long. On the night of March 16 the Premier, wearing full evening-dress, was at the opera listening to a concert of British music, conducted by Sir Thomas Beecham, when the news reached him of bloody rioting at Clichy, the Paris suburb. The workers had arranged there a mass demonstration against the 'provocation of the Croix de Feu', 200 of whom, complete with wives and children, were attending a private show at the local cinema. M. Dormoy, the Minister of the Interior, had not considered the Croix de Feu meeting illegal, and had refused to prohibit it; in the circumstances the meeting had to be protected by police cordons; and there was a clash between the police and the workers' demonstration in the Place de la Mairie; six workers were killed, and a couple of hundred injured; among the injured

---

[1] This reduction was to prove largely theoretical

was M. Blumel, M. Blum's secretary, who had rushed to Clichy as soon as he heard that trouble had broken out. At midnight Blum drove to the hospital at Clichy, where his white tie and top hat contrasted strangely with the blood-stained caps of the Clichy rioters. His first reaction was to resign. He felt as though he had been stabbed in the back.

Clichy had a disastrous effect. Confidence was immediately shaken. The Trade Unions—who had been hostile to the 'pause', which they considered incompatible with the Front Populaire programme—arranged a six hours' general strike two days after Clichy; it was hardly a demonstration of friendship for the Government. Whoever was mainly responsible for Clichy (and it is hard to believe that it was all the work of *agents provocateurs*) it was clear that certain extremist working-class elements were in a vicious mood, and were taking Blum's 'surrender to the 200 families' very badly. · It seems that the Clichy 'demonstration' was organised by two local leaders—one Socialist, the other Communist—who were competing among themselves in 'extremism'. Extremism was the fashion of the time. Playing up to the extremists, Thorez, the Communist leader, thundered at a protest meeting at the Vel d'Hiv against 'Governments of the Left who pursue a policy of the Right' and against the police. And the *Libertaire*, the Anarchist paper, appeared with a headline:

LE SANG OUVRIER A COULÉ

and it compared Blum to 'bloody Noske'.

Clichy was not soon forgotten. For weeks afterwards there was serious labour trouble—especially at the Exhibition. It was officially to open on May 1; at the end of April only the German, Russian, Italian and Belgian pavilions (employing their own labour) were finished. The rest promised to be two or even three months late. The workers would not hear of overtime, and strikes were frequent. The *Œuvre*, though not a panicky paper, wondered whether this 'sabotage' was the spontaneous work of anarcho-syndicalists, Trotskyists and other revolutionary extremists who hated Blum and his 'pause', or whether it was not being deliberately encouraged by foreign agents—German and Italian—who would have welcomed a fiasco of the much-vaunted *Expo 1937*. A simpler—but, no doubt, incomplete, explanation of the delays was the hopeless depression in the French building trade, and the natural reluctance of the workers to finish the work sooner than they could help it. In any case, the trouble at the Exhibition was such that M. Campinchi, the Radical leader, and a member of the Blum Government, did not hesitate to brand it a 'national humiliation'.

During the weeks that followed Clichy the C.G.T. were, from Blum's point of view, as unhelpful as possible. Strikes continued to break out in various trades. M. Jouhaux, afraid of losing his grip on the rank-and-file, sent a sort of ultimatum to the Government demanding, among other things, a loan of ten milliard francs for a vast public works programme—an amount which could, obviously, not be found without exchange control or some other forms of coercion. Referring to the Defence Loan of March, Jouhaux said: 'If they can find ten milliards to finance death, surely they can find ten milliards to finance life.' A pretty phrase; but one which overlooked the fact that, barring the adoption of totalitarian monetary methods, *vast social expenditure was impossible in a time of heavy rearmament. That was the real tragedy of the Front Populaire.* In normal times the Front Populaire programme might have been carried out without undue strain on the financial system; in a time of rearmament, the possibility of simultaneous heavy social expenditure was excluded, *unless* the methods of totalitarian finance were adopted. And these, for international reasons, Blum could not persuade himself to adopt.[1]

The Government firmly rejected M. Jouhaux's demands, and in May there was a notable improvement in the general outlook. M. Blum succeeded in bringing about an 'exhibition truce'; the collective agreements, which were about to expire, were automatically extended for six months; and it looked as though the Blum Government would last at least until the autumn. The Exhibition, though far from ready, and with large flags hiding from M. Lebrun's sight so many

---

[1] There is, of course, the example of the United States, where a vast expansion of credit was possible without exchange control. But this was impossible in France; Caillaux foresaw it when in 1936 he scathingly described the Front Populaire programme as 'Rooseveltism for Liliput.'

skeletons of unbuilt pavilions, was nevertheless officially opened on May 24.

. . . .

But suddenly, in the first week in June, fresh trouble started. The Bourse went crashing downhill, the three per cent Rentes falling far below sixty francs—a level to which they had never sunk since the panic days of 1926. The flight from the franc started again with renewed vigour. 'A bankers' ramp,' the Left-Wing Press complained. The *Œuvre* told a strange story of a mysterious meeting on June 3 between a number of high financial personalities 'in a certain restaurant in the Place Gaillon'; and the resignation of Horace Finaly from the post of managing-director of the Banque de Paris et des Pays Bas looked particularly sinister. Finaly was a modern and 'liberal' banker, with many personal contacts with the politicians of the Left, and, on the whole, friendly to the Blum Government. He was replaced at the head of the Banque de Paris by M. Moreau, the ultra-reactionary financier, who shortly before, had boasted in an article in the *Revue des Deux Mondes* of how he had done his best to turn out one Left Government after another when he was Governor of the Bank of France in 1925. This change in the management of one of the most influential of the Paris Banks was generally regarded as a sign that the 'City' had sentenced the Blum Government to death. The Blum Government felt that the time had come to act. But without the goodwill of the banks what could it do? Where could it borrow money—even short-term money—to bridge the gulf? On June 10 the Government began to discuss ways and means of solving the crisis; but no agreement could be reached at first. In the meantime the Senate had already declared war on the Government. On June 10 a resolution concerning the forty-hour week in the hotel trade, and openly hostile to the Government, was passed by a large majority of the Senate. Several Senators claimed that Blum had cheated the Senate; that he had promised to be cautious in applying the forty-hour-week law. And then came what looked like the *coup de grâce*: On June 12, M. Rist and M. Baudoin resigned, saying they could not defend the franc any longer unless Blum accepted all their suggestions. It looked like part of the bankers' conspiracy.

Unable to agree with his colleagues on a detailed programme
of financial reform, M. Blum made on June 15 a bold move:
he decided to ask Parliament for plenary powers. It was an
unusual course to take; for in the election campaign no one
had attacked legislation by decree more severely than the
Socialists and Radicals. Was Blum to adopt Laval's methods?
It was unfortunate; and yet it was excusable. In his preamble
to the Bill, Blum said:

> We cannot tolerate and the country cannot tolerate that
> once again the will of the overwhelming majority of the French
> people should be opposed by a handful of speculators who
> through their newspapers and their pressure on the Bourse and
> on the foreign exchange markets spread panic among investors
> in order to cheat them.

No doubt, the speculator was not alone to blame; if he was
speculating, it was because the franc was overvalued, and its
eventual fall was a safe bet; but, even so, the crisis (which
would have come in any case) was certainly precipitated by a
political campaign against the Government.

The Chamber did not like the Plenary Powers Bill; but
voted it none the less after a stormy debate. It was believed
at first that the Communists would vote against the Government, or at least abstain, in which case the Government would
be defeated. In the end they voted for it, 'for the sake of
preserving the Front Populaire'. Paul Faure, the Socialist
Minister of State, jokingly explained as follows the sudden
change in the Communists' intentions:

> At five o'clock they rang up Moscow, and the fellow who
> spoke to them said they were not to vote for the Government.
> At midnight they rang up Moscow again to make quite sure.
> Another person answered the phone. 'You are to vote for
> the Government.' 'But you told us at five o'clock we were to
> vote against.' 'Yes, but the comrade who told you that has
> since been shot. You are to vote *for* the Government; do you
> understand?'

But the Senate was a different proposition. Ever since
June 1936 the Senators had borne Blum and the Front Populaire a savage grudge. The day of reckoning had come.
Already, during the previous week, M. Gardey had declared
that 'the French New Deal, with its purchasing power theory,

had proved a dismal failure'. But now the real fun started. M. Caillaux, the most influential man at the Senate, had the time of his life. Among the innumerable attacks he made on Blum there was one to the effect that

> If, in the past, the Government was hostile to plenary powers, and is now asking for them, what guarantee have we that M. Blum, who is favourable to parliamentary government to-day, will still be favourable to it to-morrow?

He also referred to the 'non-parliamentary outlook' of the C.G.T., and embroidered on M. Blum's admission that, 'although he was opposed to exchange control, he believed in the necessity of fighting against excessive financial freedom, and that there was a happy medium between the two'. In the final sitting on Sunday, June 20, he attacked the Government with even greater savagery. Wagging his bald head, and moving his arms stiffly from side to side, the old man looked like a tragic puppet. He spoke in an ironical Punch-and-Judy voice, which at times rose to the high pitch of an angry scream. His conclusion was that the Government was unworthy of the confidence it was asking for; in the words of Richepin, he said, the Government was:

> Comme une femme saoûle
> Qui dans l'infini roule
> Sans savoir pourquoi, ni comment!

True, he apologised for the adjective, but that was only *pro forma*. Vincent Auriol, speaking like a crucified martyr, became almost hysterical, and although Blum treated the Senate to some home truths, and told them, in effect, that they were not the true representatives of the French people, he gave it up in the end, and the Cabinet resigned.

And that was the end of the *real* Front Populaire Government. What came afterwards was Front Populaire only in bits—in diminishing bits. Except for the short-lived Blum Government of March 1938. *Et encore. . . .*

The truth perhaps is that Blum was riding for a fall. He would probably have been most embarrassed if the Senate had granted him plenary powers—especially the 'limited plenary powers' that some of the Senators were, at one moment, ready to grant him. These would have been no good at all. As for real plenary powers, there was a danger—and the Senate was fully aware of it—that the C.G.T. might drive him much further than he, with his *not* very revolutionary temperament, would like to go. In any case, the *Leipzig* incident in the Mediterranean, which coincided with the fall of his Government, was there to remind Blum that France was not living in a vacuum, and that this was not perhaps the best time for revolutionary experiments.

.   .   .   .

The next day it was generally felt that there was no time to lose. The *Leipzig* incident threatened to develop into a general war. Chautemps, suave and polite, was asked to form the new Government. He had been on good terms with Blum, and had often helped him in settling labour disputes. Blum went before the National Council of the Socialist Party, and implored them to let him enter the Chautemps Government. The Socialists, he said, must be loyal to the Radicals, as the Radicals had been loyal to them. If they refused to enter the Chautemps Government it would mean the end of the Front Populaire. And he spoke gravely of the *Leipzig* incident; and said that the most important thing of all was to provide France with a normal Government at once. The belief that France was going to pieces could only encourage Hitler. The Socialists grumbled, and were very angry with the Senate, but, in the end, agreed. Needless to say, they also deplored the proposed appointment of Georges Bonnet to the post of Finance Minister.

If ever there was a Radical who had no love for the Front Populaire, it was Bonnet. Bonnet, whom, some months earlier, Blum had appointed Ambassador in Washington largely in order to get him out of the way—for he was constantly conspiring against the Front Populaire, and was doing his best to demoralise the Radicals—now returned from Washington with a triumphant little smirk on his face. Chautemps's ministerial declaration was full of Front Populaire sentiment; but the presence of M. Bonnet on the front bench made it all sound a little hollow. But the Banks liked Bonnet, and so did the Senate; and it granted Chautemps plenary powers with the greatest of ease, and even with a touch of cordiality. The first thing Bonnet did was to devaluate the franc once again.

He made it a 'floating franc', but hoped to maintain it in the neighbourhood of 130 to the £. A fortnight after that M. Bonnet submitted to the Cabinet a number of decrees increasing taxation or reducing expenditure by nearly ten milliard francs. Income tax was increased by about twenty per cent, and so were tobacco and railway fares. It all savoured of Poincaré and orthodox finance—a complete reversal of the purchasing power theory. If Blum accepted it, it was mainly for international reasons. As a sop to the Left M. Bonnet agreed to the semi-nationalisation of the railways. The working class were disillusioned, and rather embittered. The Front Populaire procession of the 14th of July was a sad spectacle. The enthusiasm and vigour of 1935 and 1936 were gone. It was a big procession; but all the little shopkeepers of the Faubourg Saint-Antoine who had crowded the pavements a year before to cheer the procession had now stayed at home, or had gone to the Bois de Vincennes to lie on the grass. The workers were not even very sorry for M. Blum, and not even very angry with the Senate. For one thing, the cost of living had gone up a lot, and their wives grumbled— and some even blamed Blum for it. At the Socialist Congress at Marseilles that week Blum was howled down by the revolutionary extremists of the Marceau Pivert group. Marceau Pivert, the elementary schoolmaster with an ascetic's face, who combined revolutionary fanaticism with a gentle and slightly crazy smile, was going to gain in importance in the months that followed. He had already rebelled against Blum's 'pause'.[1]

·   ·   ·   ·   ·   ·   ·   ·   ·

But on the whole, it was not a bad summer for Paris. The Exhibition created a general holiday mood. No doubt, Picasso's panel of Gernika in the Spanish pavilion was a terrifying thing, and the German pavilion was ominously heavy and overpowering; but the aggressively nude Teutons in front of it were an object of loud mirth, especially to the young people who would photograph each other in the shadow of those formidable—loins; and the proletariat took a certain joy in

[1] Officially, the Pivertists did not break away from the Socialist Party until the Royan congress in June 1938. Being left to themselves, without the authority of the Socialist Party behind them, they later lost in influence.

scribbling in the visitors' book in the Soviet pavilion: *'Les Soviets partout. A bas Bonnet!'* True, it was a loose-leaf book; so that the Russian profanities by the White *émigrés* could be carefully weeded out every evening. And there was delightful coffee at the pretty Austrian pavilion, and good Pilsner at the Czech pavilion on the other side of the river. And altogether thirty-three million people visited the Exhibition; but it was built under the Front Populaire, and the Senate did not like it largely for that reason, and found some more or less good excuses of a financial nature for not allowing it to continue in 1938, and for having it pulled down after a brief four months' existence. It was a great pity.

For several months the Chautemps Government muddled along without any serious internal trouble. At the Radical Congress at Lille at the end of October M. Bonnet attempted a little manœuvre which, if successful, would have broken up the partnership between the Radicals and Socialists; but he was severely sat on by Herriot and Chautemps and Daladier. And Front Populaire Government No. 2 continued its unexciting existence until the middle of January.

Unexciting—that is perhaps an exaggeration. There was the whole international situation over which M. Delbos tried not to become too excited; but which was exciting for all that. And then there was the Cagoulard affair which was perhaps less funny than it sounded. A number of queer and, in some cases, tragic, things had happened in France during the year. One was the horrible murder, on a quiet country road in Normandy, of Carlo Rosselli, the brilliant Italian anti-Fascist journalist, and of his brother Nello; they were dragged out of their car and stabbed to death. That was in June. And then, one Saturday evening in September, while the Exhibition was blazing with coloured lights and crackling with fireworks, something that sounded like a couple of rockets went off in the neighbourhood of the Etoile. As a result, the headquarters of the Employers' Federation in the rue de Presbourg collapsed, and killed two policemen in the process; and another house belonging to another employers' organisation was wrecked in the rue Boissière, a few hundred yards away.

It was a complete mystery at first. The Press of the Right claimed that the Anarchists were at it again—after thirty or

forty years of inactivity. Others accused Moscow: Employers'
Federation—obviously the outrage had come from the Left.
The Press of the Left spoke of an act of provocation organised
by the employers themselves. But about the same time the
word *cagoulard* was first mentioned in connection with the
arrest of three or four nondescript characters alleged to belong
to a secret terrorist organisation. Cagoulards, the hooded men;
a French Ku-Klux-Klan! It sounded both funny and intrigu-
ing. But it took several weeks before the word came to mean
something more than a joke. It was when several large private
arsenals in Paris and other towns were discovered by the police,
as well as the existence of an organisation known as the
C.S.A.R. (*Comités secrets d'action révolutionnaire*). A number of prominent business men—among them M. Deloncle—
and men like M. Pozzo di Borgo, who in the past had played
a leading part in the Croix de Feu and other Fascist and semi-
Fascist organisations, before their dissolution, were arrested.
The police claimed that the C.S.A.R. numbered about 6,000
members.

The dissolution of the Fascist leagues and also their failure
to achieve anything by more or less legal means had inevitably
sent some of their wilder members underground. They were
prepared to fight the Republic by every means, and the financial support given to the C.S.A.R. by Germany and Italy did
not put them off. 'Hitler rather than the Front Populaire' was
a genuine reflection of a state of mind existing among these
people. Most of the arms came from Italy, Germany and
Rebel Spain and there were strange contacts existing between
the C.S.A.R. and certain agents of General Franco. The
attempt to capture the *C2*, a Spanish Government submarine
anchored at Brest was made by the notorious Major Troncoso,
the military governor of Irun, with the assistance of several
Frenchmen, including former Croix de Feu men. M. Chautemps in a speech at the Chamber in November referred
to the extreme gravity of the C.S.A.R. affair, 'especially in
view of the origin of the arms'. In Government quarters it
was openly said that the show was run from Italy, and the
name of a prominent Italian Fascist was freely mentioned.
No doubt, some French money had also been spent on the arms
dumps; at the time of the first Blum Government there were

any number of panicky and *bien pensant* people who were ready to contribute to any organisation calling itself anti-Red. As the police inquiry proceeded, and more arrests were made, the suspicions were confirmed that there was a link between the murder of the Rossellis, the rue de Presbourg explosion, and a number of other outrages; and that the link was none other than the C.S.A.R. The purpose of an outrage like the rue de Presbourg explosion was obviously to create bewilderment and internal tension in France—such outrages might prove extremely useful in the midst of an acute international crisis.

If the C.S.A.R. did not revive the Front Populaire in a governmental sense, it certainly made an enormous impression on the country, and contributed to the success of the Left-Wing parties in the municipal elections in October. Though on a smaller scale, it acted on French minds much as La Rocque had acted on them in 1935 and perhaps delayed by a few weeks the final breakdown of the Front Populaire even in an ideological sense.

.   .   .   .

Except for the Cagoulard affair, everything went moderately smoothly until December when the Chautemps Government was faced with a particularly troublesome strike situation. The stay-in strike at the Goodrich tyre works at Colombes was the most unpleasant business of all; the Government thought at first of clearing the works with the help of the police, but the strikers were so defiant that, to prevent bloodshed, the police had to be withdrawn. The Right-Wing Press accused the Government of 'lack of authority'. In Paris the lorry-drivers struck, and the Christmas food supply had to be brought to the Halles in army lorries. The *Libertaire*, the Anarchist paper, chuckled over this 'strike-breaking by the Front Populaire Government'. Other strikes broke out, and on December 29, just as Paris was getting ready for the New Year *réveillon*, the buses and metros went on strike. The strike was fortunately settled twenty-four hours later. But it was a mischievous strike, and it created much ill-feeling; and it showed that the C.G.T. included certain unruly and irresponsible elements capable of taking grave decisions without asking the advice of the trade union leaders. M. Jouhaux

was as displeased with the strike as anybody else, and so were
the Communists—or, at any rate, their leaders.

If this strike was largely due to a lack of trade union discipline, there were other strikes where the strikers had genuine
grievances against the employers. It was clear that the labour
legislation of the last two years was not working smoothly, and
that it was necessary to supplement it by some new arrangements. M. Chautemps therefore decided, early in January,
to call together a conference of the Trade Unions and Employers' Federations with a view to agreeing on the terms of a
Labour Code, which would subsequently be approved by
Parliament, and so become law. The employers unfortunately
boycotted the conference; and this placed the Chautemps
Government in a difficult position. This boycott was accompanied by a new attack on the franc.

The behaviour of M. Chautemps in the days that followed
was truly bewildering. On January 13, at the instigation of
M. Bonnet, his Finance Minister, who said that he could not
'go on like this', he called a meeting of Parliament and demanded a vote explicitly rejecting exchange control. This
was asking a lot from the Socialists, many of whom had, since
the fall of the Blum Government, come to the conclusion that
only with exchange control could the Front Populaire programme be carried on. Even so, it was a rather academic point,
for in spite of their private views on the subject, they had
supported the Chautemps Government with the greatest
loyalty. M. Chautemps's strange move looked like a deliberate
attempt to break up the Front Populaire majority. What
strengthened this impression was that in the speech he made
that afternoon he violently attacked the working class, and
scarcely said anything of the sabotage of the Employers' Federation who had just wrecked his Industrial Peace Conference.

The Socialists nevertheless gave way, and agreed to vote his
motion against exchange control; but this did not suit M.
Chautemps. So, in order to break up the Government, he
violently attacked the Communists saying that 'he did not
desire their votes'. This was too much for the Socialists to
swallow; they declared that M. Chautemps had broken up the
Front Populaire majority, and the Socialist Ministers resigned
from the Cabinet. It was whispered that M. Chautemps was

bullied into this manœuvre by certain financial interests, who
had threatened to continue their offensive against the franc:
they (like M. Bonnet) were determined to break up the Front
Populaire majority, and also to turn M. Dormoy, the Socialist
Minister of the Interior, out of office; for they felt that he was
showing an excess of zeal in conducting his inquiry into the
Cagoulard case.

.   .   .   .

Be that as it may, it was the end of the Front Populaire
Government No. 2. Front Populaire Government No. 3, which
was not formed until nearly a week later—on January 18—
was a plain Radical Government under the same M. Chautemps, but no longer with Socialist participation. Parliamentary wits declared that if this went on much longer the
'Front Populaire Government No. 6' would be composed of
M. Tardieu, M. Laval and the Cagoulards. During the Cabinet
crisis, M. Blum, who was first asked to form the new Government, launched the idea of a 'National Government around the
Front Populaire—from Reynaud to Thorez'—that is, a
National Government comprising all the 'truly democratic
elements of the country'. He felt that this was warranted by the
grave international situation, and he also felt that the moment
was near when the opposition would try, in one way or another,
to turn the legal majority out of office, and form a National
Government dominated by the Right, after the manner of
1926 and 1934. He felt that if a National Government *must*
come, it should at least be a predominantly Left Government.
His idea was not accepted; but he hoped that it would make
headway, and would materialise sooner or later.

And so, M. Chautemps was back in office again at the head
of a much weaker combination. As expected, this Government
stayed in office only a short time. It had part of the Labour
Code passed by Parliament, but when on March 5 M. Chautemps asked the Socialists if they would support his request
for plenary powers and they said no, he suddenly resigned three
days later, without waiting for a Chamber vote. He said he
did not wish to 'break up the Front Populaire majority'—for
one ought to add that, since the formation of his second
Government, he had been all honey to the Left, even though
he had driven the Socialists out of his previous Government.

The subtleties of M. Chautemps during these two months took one's breath away.

As already said in the last chapter, there were some who wondered whether his real reason for resigning on March 8 was not a strong suspicion in his mind that something serious was about to happen in Austria. Chautemps, of course, denied this. But, in any case, on the day Hitler's troops marched into Austria, France was without a Government.

CHAPTER V

FRANCE AFTER THE ANSCHLUSS

THE SHORTLIVED BLUM GOVERNMENT

NEWS, more alarming every day, had been coming from Austria since the Berchtesgaden ultimatum. M. Delbos had said in the Chamber debate at the end of February that the independence of Austria was 'essential to the European balance of power'; others had lamented over the brutalities of Germany, and felt that Hitler was being greatly encouraged by the change in British foreign policy and by the 'neutral' attitude of Italy. Was there anything that could stop the Anschluss? Neither the Chamber debate at the end of February nor any newspaper in France during the ten days that followed were able to provide an answer. Clearly, there was nothing to stop Hitler.

And yet, somehow, nobody believed that Germany would *invade* Austria. Austria might be placed under Nazi control; Seiss-Inquart might play an increasingly large part; but the semblance of Austrian independence would somehow be observed. Hitler, it was believed, would be afraid of offending Mussolini too much if he invaded Austria. A *putsch*, perhaps; but not an invasion.

Almost every day I used to see at the Chamber a well-known liberal Austrian journalist. He was dejected after Berchtesgaden; not so much because Berchtesgaden had happened but because of the inferences that were drawn by everybody in France and England—'it really means the Anschluss in disguise'. 'Austria has still a lot of life in her,' he would say, 'just you wait and see.' And on that dramatic day when Schuschnigg announced the Freedom Plebiscite for the following Sunday, my Austrian friend was triumphant—'Didn't I tell you! Didn't I tell you!' he cried, almost weeping. 'You'll see, we'll get a seventy per cent majority against the Nazis on

Sunday! Monarchists, Catholics, Jews, Socialists, Communists
—everybody is behind Schuschnigg. The Socialist trade
unions are being revived—after the plebiscite we'll have a
real Democratic Austria! *Es ist ja wunderschön!'*

But the plebiscite was not to be. Two days before the
plebiscite, while Schuschnigg had become a national hero in
Vienna, the German troops moved across the frontier. It
created a fearful shock in France—even among the people who
had as good as accepted the Anschluss as inevitable. But the
people of France were still thinking of war as something remote
and abstract—in spite of Abyssinia and China and even Spain.
People somehow continued to think of Central Europe in
terms of German 'claims' and 'rights'; they did not visualise
armies crossing frontiers. It was something new and fearful.
The brutality of the whole thing, the cynical reasons given by
Germany for invading Austria, the atrocities that closely followed upon the invasion—all this was deeply disturbing to
the French. Austria had been subjected by violence—and no
Nazi plebiscite could contradict that. The invasion had been
precipitated in order to prevent a free plebiscite.

But while French opinion was shocked, and the French Press
was unanimous in proclaiming its indignation, the invasion
of Austria had, at the same time, a strange psychological effect
on the country. War, which had been an abstraction in most
Frenchmen's minds, had now become a reality. The Anschluss
was not merely the first territorial revision of the Treaty of
Versailles; it was worse—it was the first armed invasion that
Europe had seen since the last War. It created the vision of
marching armies, of enemy aeroplanes droning threateningly
over a large capital like Vienna. France lost nearly one and a
half million men in the last War; and rural and provincial
France especially, which is not accustomed to reasoning in big
international terms, is tired of war, and sick at the thought of
war. The invasion of Austria aroused indignation at first,
but also gave many 'that sinking feeling'. Was war becoming
a tangible reality once again? There had been Spain, of course
—but that was, after all, a 'civil war'.

And it was this 'sinking feeling' which was going to be
exploited to the full by the disciples of M. Flandin, and—by
Fascist and German propaganda. On February 21 and 22

Mr. Chamberlain proclaimed his lack of interest in Central Europe; but the effect of the Anschluss was to make not only England, but even the Chamberlain Government more Europe-minded. In France, significantly enough, the Anschluss had rather the opposite effect. M. Flandin's utterances which, before March, were treated as mischievous, but still rather absurd, paradoxes (the main purpose of which, it seemed, was to give M. Flandin a certain personal publicity —which he had never been able to achieve before; for he was always regarded as merely a ponderous bore)—now came to be regarded as something rather more important; and it is extremely curious that it was after the Anschluss, and not before, that France witnessed the first explosions of that defeatist campaign which was to gather such impetus during September.

The campaign was not continuous. For some time after the May 21 crisis it died down almost completely; but its first big display was in the weeks that immediately followed the invasion of Austria;—and it was certainly calculated to exploit the deep impression left in everybody's mind by the accounts of that lightning invasion. 'Let us keep out of all that.'

The campaign was at its height in March and April. It was conducted at that time almost solely by the Right-Wing Press.

'Will you fight for the Czechs?' *Gringoire* wrote on April 9 —the very *Gringoire* which had exclaimed three years earlier: 'Will you fight for the Negus?' Czechoslovakia was described as being 'not a country at all'; as 'the worst abortion that had come out of Woodrow Wilson's brain' (the writer of the article, incidentally, forgot that at the Peace Conference it was the French who insisted upon the 'strategic' Sudeten frontier, and that they were doing so against the advice of the Americans); the anti-Czech campaign conducted by *Candide* and *Gringoire* was also supported by the *Action Française*, by the *Jour*, and by a number of provincial papers like the *Petit Provençal*, the *Eclaireur de Nice* and others.

Thus, in the *Eclaireur de Nice* M. Léon Garibaldi wrote:

> The support that France might want to give to Czechoslovakia would, in any case, be totally ineffective; and let us also remember that the French people are not cannon fodder. No one has the right to drag the French people into a war which

does not affect our frontiers and our independence; and the bones of a little French soldier are worth more to us than all the Czechoslovaks in the world.

And the *Petit Provençal* protested against the idea of 'fighting for a country that looks rather like the Republic of San Marino'.

The *Action Française* had—it is only fair to say—always felt unsympathetic towards Czechoslovakia. For this great 'Nationalist' organ had always hated the League of Nations, and had identified Beneš with Geneva.

Why the League which could have become the best safeguard of French security if properly handled had always been an object of aversion and hostility to the French Right is something of a mystery—except that its basis was democratic, and so, distasteful; and it was also associated with the name of Briand and the French 'surrenders' to Republican Germany. And on many occasions in the past Léon Daudet attacked Philippe Berthelot for having favoured democratic and 'masonic' Czechoslovakia and his friend, 'Freemason Beneš', at the expense of Catholic Austria. And although the *Action Française* was not so emphatic about 'dropping' Czechoslovakia as, say, *Gringoire*, and was inclined to say that France could do nothing because she had gone all mouldy with Republicanism, it was still clear that Charles Maurras had made up his mind not to raise a finger for the Czechs. Such *nationalisme intégral* was surprising—except that in reality the *Action Française* had long ago ceased to be a Nationalist paper, still less a Royalist paper, and had become completely Fascist in mentality—an interesting point strongly emphasised by Georges Bidault, the Catholic writer, in the *Europe Nouvelle*. Beneš was also attacked in the *Jour* by M. Léon Bailby.

The anti-Czech campaign, though still limited to only a relatively small number of papers in March and April, was sufficiently violent to prompt M. de Kerillis in the *Epoque* to sound the alarm. '*Monsieur Hitler, ne vous gênez pas, prenez Prague!*' he wrote on April 17.

'Dear Mr. Hitler,' he wrote, 'France is the ally of Czechoslovakia, but she is determined not to keep her promise and her solemn undertaking to defend her. If you feel like leaping at Prague as you have already leaped at Vienna, you can be sure that France will be just as indifferent and just as resigned. So don't worry about us!'

Such is the meaning of the innumerable articles which have appeared for some time past in a certain pro-German and pro-Nazi Press in France—articles which the Berlin papers have been reproducing with wild enthusiasm. Such propaganda is also being carried out throughout the country with the help of enormous financial resources.

Here, for instance, is a Society, with headquarters in Marseilles, who have just sent me a sumptuous illustrated tract, and who tell me that they have sent this work to all the notables of the 2,800 communes of the nine departments of South Eastern France—'to all the mayors, assistant mayors, village councillors, priests, teachers, doctors, veterinary surgeons, hairdressers, stationmasters and tradesmen.' This tract has only one object; and that is to explain to the French that Czechoslovakia is an artificial country, unfit to live, and unfit to be defended, and which Germany can grab at a moment's notice. One can only wonder, with amazement and bewilderment, who is behind this propaganda, and who pays for it?

I am ready to admit that there may be certain French statesmen who in silence ponder over the enormous risks involved in a French intervention in Czechoslovakia's favour. I can even admit—though I disagree with such a point of view—that some may be saying to themselves: 'Let us try to the bitter end to save Czechoslovakia! Let us bluff! But let us not be dragged into a war which would be equal to suicide. At the last moment we shall leave her to her sad fate and repudiate our signature.'[1] But what are we to think of those who by word and deed coldly incite Germany to assassinate a small nation who has placed her trust in us?

And there followed the usual Kerillis tableau of Europe after the fall of Czechoslovakia:

Moreover, is it not wicked and criminal to conceal systematically from the French people, the incalculable consequences of a German conquest of Czechoslovakia? Bohemia and Slovakia are a bastion, a great junction that commands all the roads of Europe. With Czechoslovakia under her rule, Germany will be able to encircle Poland and Hungary, and gain an outlet to the reserves of oil and wheat in Rumania and Russia. If Hitler takes Prague, he will, in fact, have become master of Europe. With such an Empire next to it,

[1] One may wonder whom—if anybody—M. de Kerillis had in mind when he wrote this. The article was written as early as April 17, that is, barely a week after M. Daladier had become Premier and M. Bonnet Foreign Minister.

France will be only a small vassal state, subject to the whims and brutalities of the German colossus.

Are we to accept servitude and death? Is it to be a bad Frenchman, or a 'friend of Moscow' to remember that for the last thousand years our ancestors have struggled in order to prevent German hegemony over Europe—a hegemony which would mean the end of France?

M. de Kerillis, since 1936 Nationalist Deputy for Neuilly, a youngish-looking man with a peaky little face, was going to become the chief 'warmonger' of the Right during the September crisis. Kerillis was also the only deputy of the Right who, on October 4, 1938, refused to vote for Munich. The only others who voted 'against Munich' were—the Communists.

.   .   .   .

But to return to the anti-Czech campaign in March and April. This campaign, limited at first to the Fascist Press suddenly received most valuable support from some unexpected quarters. That respectable organ of old-fashioned Radicalism, the *Dépêche* of Toulouse, the organ of the Sarraut family, wrote one day in April:

> We are literally encircled and reduced to the bare possibility of strategic defence. We are on the defensive on our Continental frontier, on sea, and in our colonies. We are not professional pessimists; but it is no use denying facts.

And in a technical article in the *Journal des Débats* General Duval used arguments of the same sort.

But the greatest windfall of all came to the anti-Czechs from the *Temps*, in the form of an article signed by Professor Joseph Barthelémy, the leading authority on French constitutional law. This article created a storm.

Professor Barthelémy argued that since the Franco-Czech alliance was linked with the League Covenant, and formed part of the Locarno system of treaties, and that since the Locarno system had been repudiated by Germany, France was no longer under any legal obligation to go to the aid of Czechoslovakia.

And he concluded with the words:

> Is it worth while setting fire to the world simply in order to save the Czechoslovak State, a heap of different nationalities? Is it necessary that three million Frenchmen, all the youth of our universities, of our schools, our countryside and our

factories should be sacrificed in order to maintain three million Germans under Czech sovereignty?[1]

Coming from so responsible a writer and so responsible a paper, the article created an uproar not unlike the row that was caused in London by the famous *Times* leader at the beginning of September, advocating the cession of the Sudetenland to Germany. The Barthelémy article caused great alarm in Czechoslovakia; for thousands of copies of it, translated into German or bad Czech were distributed in pamphlet form throughout Czechoslovakia under the title: 'Czechs! France says: "Nothing Doing!"'

The day the article appeared, M. Osusky, the dapper Czech Minister, dashed in great agitation to the Quai d'Orsay, and a few days later the *Temps*, presumably at the urgent request of M. Bonnet, the new Foreign Minister, published an editorial in which it flatly contradicted all M. Barthelémy's legal arguments:

> The French Government (the *Temps* editorial wrote) always held the view that the Franco-Czech pact was binding irrespective of any Geneva procedure. If in the preamble to the said pact reference is made to the League of Nations, it is only as a reminder that the obligations arising from the League Covenant must be observed.

And, alluding to M. Barthelémy's reference to the Locarno Pact, the *Temps* went on to say that this was irrelevant for two reasons:

> First, because France has never considered her agreement with Czechoslovakia as being simply a little screw in the Locarno machine. Secondly, because the violation by Germany of the Locarno agreement on March 7, 1936 does not mean that the other signatories of the agreement are thereby freed of their obligations; and this point of view was definitely accepted in London on March 22, 1936, when the relations between France and Great Britain were rebuilt on the basis of Locarno.
>
> The other day a British M.P. asked whether the obligations arising from Locarno were still valid. Mr. Butler, Under-Secretary of the Foreign Office, replied in the name of the Government that Germany alone had repudiated the pact, and that all the other signatories continued to be bound by it. Whatever criticisms may be levelled against this official doctrine, the French Government holds that its obligations arising from the Franco-Czech agreement are sacred.

[1] *Le Temps*, April 12.

However, by the end of April the campaign began to sub-side—partly as a result of the Anglo-French meeting in London on April 29. Even *Gringoire* published a strong article by M. Tardieu upholding Czechoslovakia and expressing strong disapproval of the anti-Czech line taken by the paper during the previous weeks.

The great part of the Press—particularly the Left Press—had continued to uphold Czechoslovakia throughout March and April; the only important exception among the papers of the Left being *Syndicats*, the trade union weekly of strong pacifist tendencies, edited by M. René Belin, one of the 'moderate' leaders of the C.G.T.

But by the middle of May the anti-Czech campaign had died down completely, and even *Candide* almost apologised for its past brutality of language by saying that the Czechs were at last becoming reasonable and were going to enter into con-versations with their German minority; 'they are beginning to see at last that it can't go on like this'.

If the campaign subsided towards the end of April, it was partly for internal political reasons.

At first, it was partly started in order to embarrass and annoy the second Blum Government that had come into office im-mediately after the Anschluss. And its Foreign Minister was M. Paul-Boncour, a strong upholder of the League, and a per-son abhored by the Right.

.   .   .   .

There was something tragic and slightly absurd about this second Blum Government. The Chautemps Government, it will be remembered, resigned with great suddenness a few days before the German march into Austria. While this march was in progress, France was without a Government. The task of forming a Government was entrusted by the President to M. Léon Blum, who, as leader of the Socialist Party, was nominally responsible for the fall of the last Government, and so had first claim to the new Premiership. In January, with an eye on the international situation, he had already attempted to form a national Government 'around the Front Populaire' stretching 'from Reynaud to Thorez', that is, from the demo-cratically-minded elements of the Centre to the Communist Party who, though not strictly democratic, had on innumerable occasions proclaimed their loyalty to democracy 'in the present circumstances'.   One of M. Blum's motives in proposing such a National Government was to show that, if in emergencies in the past, a 'National Government' invariably meant a National Government controlled by the Right (e.g., the Poincaré Government of July 1926 and the Doumergue Government of February 1934)—and was so contrary to the verdict of the Electorate two years earlier—it was possible, for once, to form a 'National Government', two years after the election, which would not be in contradiction with the verdict of the Electorate.   It would, for once, be a predominantly Left 'National Government', and could still claim direct descent from the Front Populaire.   The plan failed; partly because the entry of M. Reynaud into such a Government was vetoed by the Alliance Démocratique, the party to which he belonged, but in which M. Flandin pulled the strings; and partly also because many of the Radicals were reluctant to be associated with the Communists; they thought it would not look respectable; their Front Populaire ardour had been damped by eighteen months of Front Populaire Government.   So the plan failed.   Instead, M. Chautemps formed his short-lived second Cabinet, which was to resign on the eve of the Anschluss.

French opinion had been deeply stirred by events in Austria, and M. Blum thought that the time was now *really* ripe for a National Government.   He was prepared to go to any length in trying to bring about such a National Government. While the German troops were marching into Austria, he called a meeting of the National Council of the Socialist Party, and implored them to authorise him to form a Government on an even wider basis than that which he had proposed in January.   It was no longer to be limited to the 'sincerely democratic' parties; it would include everybody.   Instead of '*de Reynaud à Thorez*', it would now be '*de Marin à Thorez*', and would so include even the die-hard Conservatives.   Only the outspoken Fascists would be left out.

> 'The moment has come,' he said, 'to make an appeal to the whole of France, to everybody, with one exception only: I mean those who have excluded themselves from the National community by conspiring against the republican institutions and by becoming agents of foreign Powers.

'It will not be the sacred union of 1914—the sacred union for making war. Ours will be a National Union which will save peace and defend the democratic institutions of this country. It will not be a "National Government" after the manner of the Doumergue and Poincaré Governments, which were directed against the working class. This will be a National Government around the working class, directed by the Socialists, with the participation of the Communists and the brotherly support of the C.G.T.'

The Socialists are the largest party in this country. And M. Blum asked that he be given a 'wider mandate, an unlimited mandate.' He was asking for it, 'in the interests of the party, of Socialism, of the country, and of peace'. If he dwelt so much on 'Socialism' and the 'Front Populaire', etc., it was because he was, after all, speaking to a Socialist audience.

He received full support from everybody—from Paul Faure, the Secretary General of the Party, and from the impetuous Zyromski, from the outset an enemy of Blum's non-intervention policy in Spain. Zyromski now cried:

'Spain and Europe are threatened by Fascist hegemony, while the working class are threatened with expulsion from the National Community! I beg you all to support Léon Blum.'

Only the revolutionary Pivertistes—a group closely akin to the Trotskyists, and who were to leave the Socialist Party a few months later—refused to accede to Blum's request. This was granted by 6,575 votes to 1,684—a remarkable demonstration of the public spirit of the Socialist Party.

But it came to nothing. The Right would not hear of M. Blum's proposal. On Saturday night, March 12, he called together the representatives of the Right Parties and addressed a warm appeal to them.

He tried to overcome their main objection—the presence of the Communists in the Government.

'Let me say this: in case of war you are going to mobilise the Communists as anybody else. The Communists, after all, represent 1,500,000 workers, peasants and small tradesmen. You have no right to throw them out. You will be in need of them when you will want to speed up armaments production. You will need their help as you will need the help of the C.G.T. What are you afraid of? Are you afraid that they will weigh heavily on foreign policy? But remember that, as the head of the Government, I preserved my complete independence on the question of Spain. Some of you have said that the presence of Communists in the French Government would have a bad effect abroad. It is an impious and abominable argument, for France cannot accept any veto from a foreign Power.'[1]

M. Blum admitted that it would be impossible for such a National Government to be in agreement on everything. But he was prepared to make the widest concessions. He said that the Right could choose the Finance Minister.

'My proposal is a good one, a necessary one. You might say that somebody else was better fitted for it than I am. Perhaps. But what is possible to-day [i.e. with the invasion of Austria in progress] may no longer be possible to-morrow. This morning the Socialists took a decision which was a great act of self-denial. Your refusal would leave a bad memory, and it would make it impossible for us to accept a similar offer from you once you had refused our offer. I beseech you to think hard. The country needs such a Government; the country wants such a Government. The country is waiting. I ask you to meditate on the gravity of my words.'

Many members of the Opposition were, in spite of themselves, moved and impressed. M. Paul Reynaud warmly supported M. Blum. The impetuous Henri de Kerillis rushed up to M. Blum, shook him by the hand and said: '*Monsieur Blum, vous êtes un grand Français.*' The Catholic *Démocrates Populaires*, profoundly shocked by events in Austria, passed a resolution saying that they would do nothing to hinder M. Blum in his task. But M. Marin, M. Flandin and M. Fabry carried the day. M. Flandin was particularly critical. No, the entry of the Communists into the French Government, however 'National', would deeply shock Mr. Chamberlain, and cause a breach with England. Germany and Italy would become openly hostile. He dwelt particularly on the deplorable impression it would create in England. He was followed by the great majority of the Right and Centre. The great French National Government, which was to be formed as an impressive retort to the Anschluss was 'off'.

The Radicals had been willing to enter the Government, in

[1] An interesting remark in the light of Hitler's veto against Mr. Churchill, Mr. Eden and Mr. Duff Cooper in his Saarbrücken speech ten days after Munich.

spite of strong objections raised by some Senators, particularly
M. Caillaux, to Communist participation.   But support for
M. Blum had been voted unanimously less twelve votes.   M.
Daladier was in favour of the plan.

If the Right sabotaged Blum's plan it was largely for internal
reasons.   They knew that the Front Populaire, left to itself,
would soon die a natural death, and that by agreeing to Blum's
National Government they would prolong the presence of the
Left Wing parties on the Government bench.   M. Flandin
and others were determined to drive, before long, the Communists and Socialists into Opposition.

Having failed in his 'National Government', Blum formed
a Government which was obviously unsuitable for the occasion.   It was a plain Socialist-Radical Government, almost the
very image of the first Front Populaire Government of June
1936.   It was an anachronism.   Blum himself felt it keenly
and repeated, perhaps a little too often—for it gave a handle
to his critics—that this was the wrong kind of Government in
the circumstances, but that it was prepared to resign immediately once a more representative Government was ready
to take its place.   It lived only three weeks—and an unhappy
life it was.   Encouraged by the presence of a Socialist at the
head of the Government, and provoked by the deliberately
uncompromising attitude of the big employers (who had their
own fingers in the political pie), the men in the Paris engineering industry went on strike; and for the first time since 1936
stay-in strikes broke out again on a very extensive scale.   At
one moment 150,000 men were on strike, and the unfortunate
French aeroplane industry was brought to a complete stand-
still.

Blum, though supported loyally by Daladier, the War
Minister, was in a desperate plight.   The Senate, which had
already thrown out his last Government, was determined to
turn this one out without delay.   It granted it grudgingly and
contemptuously an extra five milliards of inflation with which
it could carry on for a week or two; and then waited for M.
Blum's plenary powers bill.   For Blum was determined to die
fighting—or rather, his Socialist colleagues insisted that the
Senate's challenge be accepted.   They had the mistaken idea
that the overthrow of yet another Left Government by the

Senate could become the basis for a great anti-Senate campaign
in the country.

Blum's plenary powers bill was a bold enterprise, and was
intended, among other things, as a great financial sermon to
the country. It went on the assumption that France could not
go on living from hand to mouth as she had done for the last
seven years—with a little inflation here, and a little borrowing here, there and everywhere. In the process her public debt
had accumulated sky-high, and she was rolling down the slip-
pery slope towards complete bankruptcy. The reliance on
'confidence' had been overdone; Blum argued that even in
the most favourable conditions 'confidence'—that is, the
repatriation of exported capital estimated at eighty milliard
francs and the 'unfreezing' of the hoarded capital—could meet
only a small part of the Treasury's borrowing needs. France,
he said, would still have to continue borrowing forty or fifty
milliard francs a year, with immense rearmament bills accumulating. In fact, he was proposing to put France on what
might be called a semi-war basis, complete with a small capital
levy, a camouflaged form of exchange control (if it meant a
breach of the Tripartite agreement—one of the main causes
of the collapse of the Front Populaire programme—it couldn't
be helped), a large variety of taxes, and—this was to be Labour's
share in the 'all-round sacrifices'—a readjustment of the forty-
hour week. Trade and production would be revived by a
wide expansion of credit. Here was planned economy, an
economy reminiscent in some ways of German and Italian
methods.

The plan was accepted by a small majority of the Chamber,
but rejected by an enormous majority of the Senate. As in
June 1937 M. Caillaux made another scathing attack on
M. Blum and the Front Populaire, and accused M. Blum of
wanting to ruin the French peasantry with his capital levy.
M. Blum argued in vain that T. G. Barman in the *Times* had
described his plan as the first constructive financial programme
France had produced since Poincaré. M. Caillaux merely
snorted '*Diable!*' which might be translated 'like hell it is!'

That day—it was April 8—outside the Luxembourg Gardens, two or three thousand workmen—most of them Pivertistes, who were distributing leaflets in favour of the Spanish

POUM—demonstrated against the Senate; but it was a tame demonstration; it was too obvious that Blum was doomed to defeat. With the strike movement in full swing, the country was not behind Blum, and was waiting anxiously for more stable conditions.

.   .   .   .

M. Paul-Boncour was M. Blum's Foreign Minister, and his policy was intended to be a brake on 'Chamberlainism'. M. Paul-Boncour was a devotee of the League of Nations, and although he had always been considered rather a light-weight, the Left watched this resistance to Chamberlain with approval. As John Whitaker rather unkindly remarked at the time: 'Europe must have fallen pretty low if we have to pin our last hopes on Paul-Boncour!'

Like Blum, Paul-Boncour was fighting a losing battle.

The foreign policy of the Government was outlined in the Ministerial Declaration and in the speech M. Blum made immediately after it.

> 'We took office on the day after an event which created the deepest commotion throughout Europe, and which may engender some fearful new developments. It is our duty above all to avert the dangers arising from the international situation. France is unanimous in her passionate desire for peace.
>
> 'As regards peace in Europe, there is no initiative France will decline. She also wishes to safeguard her complete independence and her vital interests, preserve the safety of her frontiers and her communications, and honour fully the obligations bearing her signature. We shall increase France's armaments . . . and endeavour to strengthen our friendships and alliances. Our slogan is: peace with honour and liberty. International morality and solidarity are our principle. The *rapprochement* of all the forces of peace for the sake of collective security continues to be France's aim.'

And later, in his speech, M. Blum referred to Czechoslovakia:

> 'There is already a certain inequality between the democratic Governments and the others. For inhumanity is a great force—but it is not a force that we covet. . . . If Czechoslovakia is threatened—a hypothesis I reject—can we not best stave off this menace, in preparing to fulfil our obligations, by being in a position to utter our warning in the name of the entire French nation?'

M. Paul-Boncour was keenly aware of the menace to Czecho-slovakia. He did not think of Czechoslovakia in 'Runciman' terms; Czechoslovakia, to him, was still the Island of Democracy in the totalitarian sea of Central Europe, and a supremely valuable military ally of France. In the first week in April he summoned to Paris the French Ambassadors and Ministers in Bucharest, Warsaw, Moscow and Belgrade (as well as in Prague and Budapest), and instructed them to find out what military assistance, if any, could be obtained from the Govern-ments to which they were accredited in the event of a German attack of Czechoslovakia. He was making a last desperate attempt to revive mutual assistance and collective security in Central and Eastern Europe, and was ready to guarantee France's leadership in this revived collective security. This in itself was enough to infuriate the Press of the Right and to give impetus to the anti-Czech campaign of which I quoted earlier some significant examples.

M. Paul-Boncour took little notice of Mr. Chamberlain; and rather went on the assumption that England needed France as much as France needed England, and that, if it came to the worst, England could not stay out. But, if collective security could be achieved it would *not* come to the 'worst'. At the same time he was not above making advances to Italy, and as good as promised to recognise the Abyssinian conquest, and to send an Ambassador to Rome.

Apart from Central Europe, M. Paul-Boncour's great con-cern was Spain. Franco's troops were sweeping down the Ebro valley towards the sea; the outlook for the Spanish Govern-ment was grimmer than it had ever been. The fearful bomb-ing of Barcelona was threatening to break the moral of the civilian population.

Paul-Boncour 'relaxed' the frontier control to armaments, and large quantities of guns and machine-guns and munitions were sent across the Pyrénées. Paul-Boncour hardly made a secret of it; he considered it to be a matter of life and death for France. It was alleged in the Press of the Right that he was actually proposing to send several thousand French troops to Catalonia to stop the Franco advance; it was said that the French General Staff had turned the scheme down. Whether the proposal was actually made is difficult to discover; but

Paul-Boncour almost certainly considered it. He also considered the occupation of certain vital strategic points on the French sea route to North Africa—notably Cartagena and Minorca; but the British Government would not hear of it. For it was at that time that Mr. Chamberlain was busy preparing his famous Anglo-Italian agreement, and support for the Spanish Government was the last thing he wanted. What he was hoping for was an early Franco victory.

The British Government—though deeply shocked by Hitler's way of dealing with Austria—a shock which produced from Mr. Chamberlain the assurance on March 24 that Britain was not distinterested in the independence of Czechoslovakia (it was certainly an improvement on his speeches of February 21 and 22)—was, for a number of reasons, intensely disturbed by M. Paul-Boncour's activities, and there is good reason for saying that when the Blum Government fell on April 8, the British Government made it very plain to M. Daladier, the prospective new Premier, that it would consider the reappointment of M. Paul-Boncour to the Quai d'Orsay as eminently undesirable.

CHAPTER VI

ENTER DALADIER AND BONNET

O N Sunday, the 10th of April, two days after the defeat of the Blum Government at the Senate, the Daladier Government, which was to stay in office for a long time, was formed. Daladier! The name had been on everybody's lips for weeks; and there was something of a clamour for 'Daladier!' as the strike situation grew worse from day to day during the first week in April, and practically the whole metallurgical industry of the Paris area, with its 150,000 men, had come to a standstill. Not only people on the Right, but also many people on the Left wanted Daladier—though for a different reason. They felt that the man who had been War Minister for two years was the most desirable man to have at the head of the Government in the existing international situation. The 'strong-man' legend, the *'taureau de Vaucluse'* legend was being revived—and the most abject flattery was being poured down M. Daladier's throat by *Gringoire, Candide* and other pro-Fascist papers which in the past had treated him as *le fusilleur,* as the man who had 'shot down unarmed ex-servicemen' in the Paris riots of February 1934. Such flattery must have sickened M. Daladier himself. Why *Gringoire* and the rest were rejoicing so much was, of course, because the formation of the Daladier Government marked the end of 'Front Populaire' Government even in a diluted form, and finally killed the prospect of a National Government after the model advocated by M. Blum, and opened up prospects for an early change of majority. They thought that the Government would soon lose the parliamentary support of the Left, and be obliged to depend on the support of the Right; the change of majority which in 1926 and 1934 had resulted from a violent crisis two years after the Left election victory, they thought, would now come about peacefully.

It would be idle to pretend that the satisfaction caused by

the formation of the Daladier Government was confined to the Right-Wing extremists; the Radicals, and, in fact, the man-in-the-street, who had been profoundly disturbed by the strikes under the Blum Government, felt at heart that the Front Populaire experiment had come to an end.   They were inclined to say that it was 'nice to be back to normal at last'. They felt that 'strong man Daladier' was the best that could be got in the circumstances—though there were many who remembered one or two occasions when Daladier did not prove to be the 'strong man' he was reputed to be.

The Daladier Government—the Government which was destined to deal with the Czech crisis—was a predominantly Radical Government.   In spite of M. Blum's desire that the Socialists should participate, the Socialist rank and file, embittered by the indignities the last Blum Government had suffered at the hands of the Senate, would not hear of it. Instead, a number of men belonging nominally to the Opposition were included, among them M. Reynaud, M. Mandel and M. Champetier de Ribes.   It is worth noting that it was these 'Right Wing' members of the Government who, at the height of the Czech crisis, were to prove much more 'anti-Munich' than the Radicals; and that it was they, and not any Radicals, who were, on one memorable occasion in September, to rebel against the foreign policy of M. Bonnet.

The Government was composed as follows:

Premier and War Minister: M. DALADIER.
Vice-Premier and Minister of Co-ordination: M. CHAUTEMPS.
Minister of National Economy: M. PATENOTRE.
Minister of Justice: M. PAUL REYNAUD.
Minister of Interior: M. ALBERT SARRAUT.
Minister of Foreign Affairs: M. GEORGES BONNET.
Minister of Finance: M. MARCHANDEAU.
Minister of Marine: M. CAMPINCHI.
Minister of Air: M. GUY LA CHAMBRE.
Minister of Commerce: M. GENTIN.
Minister of Education: M. ZAY.
Minister of Agriculture: M. QUEUILLE.
Minister of the Post Office: M. JULIEN.
Minister of Public Works: M. FROSSARD.
Minister of Labour: M. RAMADIER.
Minister of Public Health: M. RUCART.
Minister of Pensions and Ex-servicemen: M. CHAMPETIER DE RIBES.
Minister of Colonies: M. MANDEL.

Of these M. Frossard and M. Ramadier, belonging to the small party, the Union Socialiste, half-way between the Socialists and Radicals, were to drop out in August as a protest against M. Daladier's broadcast attacking the forty-hour week—an attack which they considered ill-tempered, and liable to annoy the working class unnecessarily. They were replaced by M. de Monzie and M. Pomaret, nominally members of the same Party, though in reality much more 'capitalist' in their labour policy. M. Marchandeau, the Finance Minister, was a cautious and conservative financier, regarded for a long time as an understudy of M. Bonnet; it was not until November that he suddenly rebelled, and adopted ideas singularly reminiscent of those contained in the 'heretical' Blum plan of April 1938. He infuriated the banks, and was obliged to swop jobs with M. Reynaud. A question asked in April was why so brilliant a man as M. Reynaud was relegated to the relatively unimportant post of Minister of Justice, when he was obviously cut out to be either Finance Minister or Foreign Minister. It seems that his financial remedies were a little too harsh for the Left; and M. Daladier still wanted their parliamentary support—at least for a time; why he was not made Foreign Minister is rather more mysterious; perhaps he was too great a believer in collective security and other old-fashioned remedies to suit Mr. Chamberlain's taste; and in the Czech crisis he certainly proved to be the principal *belliciste* in the Government—equal to M. Mandel, the Minister of Colonies, who had been Clemenceau's right-hand man in 1917-18. In 1938, however, Mandel was violently abused in the 'Nationalist' Press, which attributed his 'warmongering' not to his past association with the Tiger, but to his Jewish descent.

.   .   .   .

But the two men who were to be the most in the public eye during 1938 were M. Daladier and M. Bonnet.

At the end of April I went over to London to report the important Anglo-French talks, which established the first direct contact between Mr. Chamberlain and Lord Halifax and the two 'new men' of France. One day, during the Conference, I was lunching at the Hyde Park Hotel—the headquarters of the French journalists—with Paul Nizan, and we were discussing Daladier and Bonnet. Nizan, who is not only a first--rate commentator on foreign affairs, but also one of France's leading young novelists, with a keen eye for human character, remarked: 'Daladier is made all of one piece—he is a bit of a rustic, and quite simple to understand. Bonnet is a much more intricate character, full of funny "complexes". *Il est caricatural,* and perhaps his physical appearance, with that enormous nose of his, accounts for a lot of these "complexes". He is extremely vain, extremely ambitious, very touchy, very susceptible to flattery; and can be very spiteful and resentful if you rub him the wrong way. He is a man who wants to be loved, and who suffers at the thought that he is not lovable. Laval who, politically, resembles him in many ways, was, with all his faults, a likeable kind of chap. Bonnet has very few friends and no end of enemies. Instead of friends, he has "contacts"; he is very intelligent, very ambitious—and thoroughly hard-boiled. His ambition is to be Prime Minister— and he may get there yet. It is also his wife's ambition, and Odette, who is a pretty woman, very well dressed, a niece of Camille Pelletan, and so a lady with great political "contacts", has been a great help to Georges in his political career. She is known as *soutien-Georges,'* Nizan laughed. 'But she is really a charming woman.'

Many months later I heard a strange story about Georges Bonnet from a man who did not like him. During the War Bonnet acted as counsel for the defence in the court-martial of a German officer. Bonnet considered the man to be innocent. He was nevertheless sentenced to death. And before the execution Bonnet stayed the whole night with him in his cell; and after the German had been shot, Bonnet smuggled his belongings to his old mother in Germany. A courageous thing to do in those days.

Bonnet, who started his Government career on the Conseil d'Etat, was one of the young politicians whom the Cartel des Gauches brought into prominence in 1925. With his Radical contacts, with his intelligence and ambition, he climbed the ladder that many Radical politicians have climbed. By 1932 —after another election victory of the Left—Bonnet had become one of the shining lights of the Radical Party, and was recognised to be one of the few able financial experts the Left had produced. He was Finance Minister in the Daladier

Cabinet of 1933, and, in that capacity went to the World
Economic Conference in London, where for the first time he
met his British opposite number, Mr. Neville Chamberlain,
Chancellor of the Exchequer. Mr. Chamberlain was not, however, well impressed by the French Finance Minister, whom
it was said at the time, he found cagey and lacking in frankness. M. Bonnet was then one of the founders of the 'gold
bloc'.

And then, in 1934, Bonnet's political progress, like the progress of several other Radical politicians, was savagely checked
by the *Affaire Stavisky*. Like Dalimier, who died soon afterwards a broken man, like Chautemps, and his brother-in-law
Pressard, Bonnet was selected as an object for an outrageous
Press campaign. *Gringoire, Candide*, and the rest, which in
1938 were to treat him as a great statesman, and as their
favourite Minister, drowned Bonnet in buckets of foul abuse.
He was a friend of Stavisky's, they said; he had lunched with
Stavisky at the Stresa Conference in 1932; and another friend
of Stavisky's, a M. Guibout-Ribaud, had been a member of
M. Bonnet's secretariat at the Ministry of Finance for nearly
a year and had acted as a link between the Ministry of Finance
and the crook. M. Bonnet was also attacked in Parliament;
and in the atmosphere of suspicion that the Stavisky Affair
had created, he cut a poor figure. He said he had not lunched
with Stavisky; but it was pointed out to him that he had; and
while his explanation that even if he did, he did not remember
Stavisky, and that one could not be responsible for anybody
one happened to meet at a lunch organised by a third party,
was reasonable enough, it did not satisfy the Right; as for
Guibout-Ribaud, Bonnet's explanations seemed even less satisfactory; for it so happened that although Guibout-Ribaud had,
from the start, been crossed off the list of members of the
Minister's secretariat, he still continued for a long time to
hang around the office in some vague capacity—though apparently without the Minister's knowledge. M. Bonnet's best
defence was that it was the Ministry of Finance, of which he
was chief, which in November 1933 vetoed Stavisky's new
issue of bonds—a veto which ruined the adventurer, and so
hastened the disclosure of the swindle; but the embarrassment
shown by M. Bonnet when he was questioned on two points

of detail was enough to give the reactionary Press a handle against him.[1] The Stavisky Affair seems to have had a profound effect on M. Bonnet's character.

Like many Radical victims of the Stavisky Affair and the 6th of February riots, Bonnet was restored to political life by the victory of the Front Populaire; so also was Daladier. Being a vain and sensitive man, he felt the injustice of it all very keenly; and, as a man who knows him well told me, it had the effect of making him cynical and hard-boiled. It is an explanation that may have an element of truth in it.

Yet already in 1936 Bonnet was one of the Radicals who were going to conspire against the Front Populaire; and he threatened to lead a Radical revolt against Blum as early as the autumn of that year. After a speech in which he severely criticised—and with some reason—M. Vincent Auriol's finance, Blum got him out of the way by appointing him Ambassador to Washington. During the decline of the Front Populaire in 1937 Chautemps brought him back in rather spectacular fashion from Washington, and appointed him Finance Minister. He arrived in Paris beaming with self-satisfaction, conscious of his indispensability and personal importance. His return marked the end of the Front Populaire in the financial and economic sense. On the night of his return a French journalist remarked: '*Ça ira mieux maintenant. C'est un malin. Et il a des belles relations dans la haute banque.*' At the Lille Congress in October 1937 he tried to force the Socialists out of the Government, and continued to plot against them; and it was also he who, indirectly, provoked the resignation of the Chautemps Cabinet in January 1938, which marked the end of Socialist participation.

. . . .

Daladier is a different kind of man. He is not the typical 'politician' that Bonnet is. A man of simple origin, the son of a baker in a small town in Provence, he is proud of his plebeian, but healthy rural origin—and is, in fact, rather snobbish about it. An unkind critic of Daladier once remarked: 'He always says "Je suis *sorti* du peuple"': meaning that he is

---

[1] The Stavisky Affair and the allegations against M. Bonnet are described in my earlier book, *France in Ferment* (London, 1934).

proud not to be there any longer.' Like many French Ministers, he rose from the small tradesman class to be an 'intellectual', and became shortly before the War a teacher of history.
He fought at Verdun and had a good War record. Like Bonnet,
he was brought into prominence by the Cartel des Gauches
election victory of 1924, and before very long he became a
leading light of the Radical Party—and, in fact, the leader of
its Left Wing. He led the anti-Government Opposition in
the Radical Party in the days when M. Herriot was co-
operating loyally in M. Poincaré's National Government of
1926-8. The two Edouards were for some years (1928-32) in
sharp competition for the real, if not nominal leadership of
the Radical Party. Daladier, cultivating the strong silent
manner—and silence is reckoned to be a sign of wisdom in
Provence, his exuberant native land—soon acquired the reputation of a true Jacobin, a man of steadfast democratic,
republican and anti-clerical principles—harder and more uncompromising than Herriot. On a public platform Daladier
looked grim and a trifle Napoleonic. In private, he could
be very charming, with a fund of quiet, almost English humour
—very different from the imaginative, almost Gargantuan
exuberance of the other Edouard.

He was War Minister in 1932, and was popular at the War
Office; and was Premier for the first time during nearly the
whole of 1933—until October when that parliamentary disintegration started, which three months later was to culminate
in the Stavisky Affair and the February riots. This disintegration was, in the first place, due to the pedantic and uncompromising attitude of M. Blum and the Socialists who refused
to appreciate the financial difficulties of the Daladier Government of 1933, and so broke up the *bloc des gauches*.

This Daladier Government was in office during the first year
of the Hitler régime, and the international atmosphere was
strained; and Daladier dealt with the situation with com-
mendable calm and level-headedness—though perhaps without any profound understanding of what was happening in
Germany.

There was, however, already then an empirical strain in
Daladier's character; unlike Paul-Boncour, he did not reason
according to certain set rules and principles; and although he

was nominally a 'League' supporter, he did not, in May 1933, reject the Four-Power Pact completely, which Ramsay MacDonald had brought back from Rome; and when, in October, Germany left the League, Daladier did not consider it wicked to attempt direct conversations with her; it was with his approval that M. Fernand de Brinon published in the *Matin* in November 1933, a sensational interview with a peace-loving and Francophil Hitler—an interview which was presumably intended as a preliminary to a possible Franco-German *rapprochement*.

The same empirical strain could be observed in his treatment of home problems. When, in the midst of the Stavisky scandal the Chautemps Government resigned on January 25, 1934, and M. Daladier was asked by the President to form the next Cabinet, he at first went completely off the beaten track of Cabinet-making, and attempted to form a Government of 'strong and honest men'—irrespective of their party labels. He hoped to bring into his Government even members of the extreme Right like M. Ybarnégaray; showed himself disgusted with Parliament and, not least, with the *République des Camarades*, and with his own Radical Party, whom he treated rather cavalierly on that occasion. His 'Government of strong men' failed—just as Blum's National Government of 1938 failed, and for similar reasons—and he had to fall back on the old Cabinet-making formulae. The result was the unfortunate one-week Daladier Government which was to be driven out of office by the 6th of February riots. I have described in an earlier book[1] the strange and rather incongruous behaviour of Strong Man Daladier during the days before the riots—the justified (but badly managed) sacking of Chiappe, the reactionary Prefect of Police, and the sacking of the Director of the Comédie Française, and his replacement by the head of the Sûreté Générale; and I shall not dwell on these unfortunate incidents again. The day of the February riots, in the course of which Daladier rather lost his head, must have been the blackest day in his life. He was not a *fusilleur*; if the rioters were fired at in the Place de la Concorde, it was because it was the only way of preventing an invasion of the Chamber—for the police had no tear gas in

[1] *France in Ferment*, Jarrolds, 1934.

those days. Overwhelmed by the tragic events, for which he was not responsible, but which he had provided with a pretext in sacking Chiappe, Daladier promptly resigned on the following day, and refused to listen to the 'republican' arguments of M. Blum, who said that no self-respecting Government should resign under the pressure of the Street, and that it must proclaim martial law, and must resist at any price in the name of democratic principles. But Daladier was a broken man, and retired into obscurity, only to see himself for months portrayed in the Press as *le fusilleur*, who had ordered 'unarmed ex-servicemen' to be shot down. The *Temps* boycotted his very name, and referred to him as *le député d'Orange*.

For a long time little was seen of Daladier—except scurrilous caricatures; and he did not make his *grande rentrée* into public life until the summer of 1935 as one of the leaders of the great Front Populaire movement. It was he who led the Radicals into the Front Populaire fold—rather against the wishes of the more cautious Herriot.

On July 14, 1935, in the Place de la Bastille, against the background of an immense banner displaying the texts of the Front Populaire Oath, Daladier was cheered by thousands of Socialists and Communists.[1]

The Front Populaire saved him, as it saved Chautemps and Bonnet, and many other victims of the reactionary offensive of 1934-5. But it was not until the Left Election victory of 1936 that Daladier found his way back to the Government bench. The Socialists were the largest Party in the new Chamber, and the Premiership went to Blum; but Daladier became War Minister and Vice-Premier; and, on the face of it, he remained loyal to Blum and to the Front Populaire until April 1938—though, at heart, he must have deplored the stay-in strikes and other Left-Wing excesses.

. . . .

In becoming Premier for the third time, he was received with enthusiasm by the men of the Right, and with much satisfaction by large sections of public opinion. For several days the Bourse soared, and the funds which had been leaving France at a disastrous rate during the previous Blum Government, began to rush back. What is more, M. Daladier

[1] See *The Destiny of France*, Chap. X.

promptly settled the strikes. For one thing, the strikers felt that the political atmosphere was no longer favourable; and secondly, the employers behaved more reasonably than they did while the Blum Government was still in office.

In his Ministerial declaration M. Daladier struck an appropriate martial note: 'My Government,' he said, 'is, first and foremost, a Government of National Defence.'

The Ministerial declaration was certainly well drafted, except for the extreme caution that marked the passages on foreign policy. It opened with the words 'A great and free country can only be saved by itself.'

> 'Most of its Ministers,' the declaration said, 'have taken part in the great popular movement [that is, the Front Populaire] which in time of danger saved French freedom and democracy. The Government now appeals to the whole nation to help it in its defence of freedom of the country and of peace. Europe is now in a state of change. Some countries are disappearing while new empires are coming into existence. In the circumstances national defence is no longer a matter of mere military technique.
>
> 'All problems, economic, financial, social, and political, are part of the single problem of security. France needs a healthy currency and a healthy rhythm of production, above all in the war industries. The Government therefore makes a patriotic appeal to both employers and workers. The workers must realise that stay-in strikes can create in France only a feeling of anxiety which may become a menace to the democratic régime. The employers, on the other hand, must apply loyally the labour code, which will, moreover, be completed by new provisions.'

Then came the important passage in which the Government said that,

> 'thinking only of the national intèrest, it would assure without delay the resumption of the manufacture of armaments indispensable to national security'

—a promise which was loudly cheered on most benches except on the extreme Left.

As regards foreign policy, the Government said that it was determined to defend France's interests everywhere, as well as the integrity of her Empire. Without referring to Spain, the declaration added that 'the Government would not tolerate any threat to France's frontiers, to her sea routes, or her colonies, and would deal firmly with all foreign agitators'.

'In all cases—in the case of strengthening our bonds with our friends *or in the case of proving our loyalty to all pacts and treaties we have signed*, or in the case of entering into equitable negotiations, it is indispensable that all the national energies be united.'

No specific reference was made to any single country, not even to Great Britain, and there was no specific reaffirmation of any particular pact or treaty. The phrase just quoted almost implied that these treaties could be properly observed only if France was united.

Never had a Ministerial declaration been so uncategorical in its statement on foreign policy—except in its references to France's own interests. It contained no reference to the League of Nations. This omission may be easy to understand, but deserves to be noted all the same. Some observers, in fact, wondered whether the earlier statement on the 'disappearance of some countries and the creation of great new empires' did not slightly savour of fatalism. In short, it was felt that M. Bonnet, the Foreign Minister, did not wish to have anything said which would alarm Mr. Chamberlain and Lord Halifax.

On the whole, however, the declaration created a good impression, and was approved almost unanimously—by 576 votes to four. Both the Communists and the Socialists (the latter rather reluctantly, it is true) voted for the Government—chiefly for the sake of preserving the semblance of the Front Populaire majority. About 100 members of the Right abstained. What added to the good impression made by the Government was the settlement, on the very day of the Ministerial declaration, of the strike in the aeroplane industry, and the prospect of an early settlement in the engineering industry. The Government had no difficulty in securing from both the Chamber and the Senate 'limited' financial powers.

As regards foreign policy, it is true that the Ministerial declaration was rather vaguer than it might have been; but it was known that M. Bonnet's first official act in becoming Foreign Minister was to invite M. Osusky, the Czechoslovak Minister, and to say to him:

'Contrary to certain rumours spread by a hostile newspaper

campaign, the position of the French Government in relation to
Central Europe has not undergone any change. If there are
people abroad who are surprised to find that our attitude is the
same as that of the last Government, it is because they do not
know France, and do not sufficiently appreciate the fact that
no French statesman worthy of the name can close his eyes on
the factors that must determine the attitude of French
diplomacy.'

That was plain enough. And, as already said, it was M.
Bonnet himself who was believed to have rapped the *Temps*
over the knuckles for the Barthelémy article and to have insisted on the publication of an editorial contradicting the
Professor's arguments in favour of abandoning Czechoslovakia.

.   .   .   .

One of M. Bonnet's first tasks, in arriving at the Quai
d'Orsay, was to try to make friends with Italy. The Anglo-
Italian agreement was on the point of being signed by Lord
Perth and Count Ciano, and M. Bonnet hoped to work out a
parallel agreement between France and Italy within a short
time. And although his Italian policy was to prove an interminable series of failures, he never ceased to hope.

Since the withdrawal of M. de Chambrun a year earlier,
there had been no French Ambassador in Rome; for the Italian
Government demanded that the credentials of M. de St. Quentin, M. de Chambrun's successor, be addressed to the 'King of
Italy and Emperor of Ethiopia'; and since the League Council
had not 'recognised' the conquest of Abyssinia, France had her
hands tied. The Italian Ambassador in Paris had, in turn,
been withdrawn on October 29, 1937. M. Bonnet was, however, determined to put an end to this anomaly; and it is true
to say that the greater part of French opinion was entirely
favourable to a *rapprochement* with Italy. It continued to
be assumed that the Anschluss had greatly shocked Italy, and
that the Berlin-Rome axis had already cracked; and it is certainly true that public feeling in Italy was, in the main, hostile
to Germany. A joke current in Rome at the time was that
Mussolini had exchanged the *Passo Brennero* for the *Passo
Romano* (the newly adopted goose-step).

One wonders when the idea first came to M. Bonnet that the
rapprochement with Italy might be 'worked' through Spain.

Now, March and April were the blackest months for the Spanish Government. In March, the Italian and German aeroplanes had performed their most hideous air raids on Barcelona, and on April 15, supported by Italian troops and a large Italo-German air force, Franco's army reached Viñaroz on the Mediterranean, south of the Ebro, and so cut Government Spain in two.

It was at this time that the Anglo-Italian agreement was signed. This agreement was, on the whole, well received by the French Government, which thought that it was not without direct interest to France. It accepted the *status quo* in the Mediterranean (and the French naturally thought that this applied to their possessions in the Mediterranean, as well as to the British possessions—a belief the Italians were later to contradict), and it promised to leave Spain to itself. But there were other points to clear up—particularly the *de jure* recognition of the Italian conquest of Abyssinia; and although in principle everything between France and Italy had already been settled by the 1935 agreement, it is certain that M. Bonnet was willing to pay a 'supplement', if Italy's friendship, or, at any rate, neutrality in case of war, could be firmly secured.

At any rate, two days after the signing of the Anglo-Italian agreement, M. Blondel, the French Chargé d'Affaires in Rome, had his first meetings with Count Ciano. The Italian Press, anticipating an early *de jure* recognition of the 'Emperor of Ethiopia', sounded very friendly. This friendliness may also perhaps have been dictated by Mussolini's desire to put himself in a stronger bargaining position in relation to Hitler during the latter's coming visit to Rome.

The Right and Official Press in French liked, however, to take this friendliness at its face value. On April 19, a Havas telegram from Rome said:

> The Fascist Government has received favourably the French suggestions, and these will be the object of early Franco-Italian talks,

while the *Temps* correspondent wrote:

> The contacts between Count Ciano and M. Blondel were marked by great cordiality and an excellent atmosphere.

He went on to say that France would aim at securing from

Italy assurances similar to those given to Britain. The technical questions would include the fixing of the exact frontier between Abyssinia and French Somaliland, everything concerning the Jibuti-Addis-Ababa railway, and similar matters.

It was hoped that the conversations would proceed rapidly and would be completed before May 9—that is, before the meeting of the League Council. In that case France would be able to associate herself with the British request to the League concerning the recognition of the 'Italian Empire'.[1]

.   .   .   .

A week later—on April 27—M. Daladier and M. Bonnet went to London to discuss the whole situation with Mr. Chamberlain and Lord Halifax. This French visit to London was the first since Lord Halifax had succeeded Mr. Eden at the Foreign Office. The Europe Britain and France were now facing was different from what it was during the visit to London of M. Chautemps and M. Delbos in November, and the foreign policy of Great Britain and France had also undergone considerable modifications. Since the last French visit Austria had disappeared; relations with Italy had greatly changed; the situation in Central Europe was infinitely more menacing; and in the Spanish civil war the position of the Government was now, thanks to 'non-intervention', incomparably worse than it was in November.

When I recently looked up my 'forecasts' of the Anglo-French conversation, I could not help chuckling—all the more so as I was then gently charged with cynicism by a friend at the French Foreign Office, who also said that I was very wrong to say that Daladier, like Chamberlain, 'would be only too pleased if the Czechs came to terms with Germany at any price'.

> 'The watchword of the present British Ministers' (I wrote at the time) 'appears to be "realism," and they no doubt trust that their French guests will be equally "realistic". On the whole they may be certain that they will find in M. Daladier and in M. Bonnet men who will answer "Yes" rather more readily than "No".
>
> 'The questions to be discussed are, as is officially stated, Spain, Central Europe, the Anglo-Italian agreement and the present Franco-Italian negotiations, the League Council and Abyssinia, and the Far East.

[1] *Manchester Guardian*, April 20.

'The first two are the most important, and on these, it would seem, France and England do not see completely eye to eye. The French Ministers, while not known—like their Socialist predecessors—to have any brotherly sympathies for the Spanish Government, are nevertheless alarmed for purely military and naval reasons by the recent developments in Spain. They will want to know the reasons for the extraordinary equanimity with which Mr. Chamberlain and other members of the British Cabinet appear to view a rebel victory, in spite of repeated threats to Gibraltar in the rebel Press, extravagant declarations of friendship to Germany, German activities along the Straits of Gibraltar, and the uncertainty as to the ultimate departure of the Italians from Spain.

'The French cannot share this British optimism and are particularly concerned by the threats to their sea communications with North Africa—which are of the most vital importance in case of war.

'Will the French firmly propose that something be done to safeguard these communications—for instance, through a "neutralisation" of the Balearic Islands, a measure which might, with British support, be proposed to Italy and be eventually incorporated in the Franco-Italian agreement? Further, the French are concerned by the activities of Germany in Spain, and particularly in Northern Spain. It is believed that a record of these German activities will be taken to London.

'In official quarters it is suggested that "nothing very sensational" will be decided about Spain, and that "things will have to take their course". *The French, in other words, are expected to agree with a statesmanlike air to stick to "non-intervention"*, even when it threatens to hit them straight on the head.

'Great concern is naturally also felt about Czecho-Slovakia, but it is not believed that Mr. Chamberlain will say any more than what he already said in his famous statement in the House of Commons on March 24—which was already more than most people expected. One has the impression that *while M. Daladier is prepared to take military action in the event of a direct German aggression against Czecho-Slovakia, he would, like the British Government, be only too pleased if the Czechs came to terms with Germany at any price*, and that the latest French assurances to Czecho-Slovakia do not cover the contingency of "internal aggression" covered by the assurances given to Czecho-Slovakia by the Blum Government a year ago.

'One suggestion is that *Great Britain and France may propose some form of mediation in the conflict between Czecho-Slovakia and the Sudeten Germans (in reality Germany)*.

'Partly with the help of German propaganda, *French opinion is becoming seriously divided on the necessity of "fighting for the Czechs."* A full-page article in *Gringoire* last week attacking Czecho-

Slovakia—an article which was joyfully reproduced under immense headlines in all the German papers—is an extreme but not altogether insignificant example of the state of mind existing among wide sections of French opinion. By way of apology many Frenchmen to-day say that Spain is of infinitely more vital importance to France than Czecho-Slovakia (not that they seriously propose to do anything about that either); while others say that instead of propping up Czecho-Slovakia, which is a "hybrid" country, it would be better to prop up Jugoslav and Hungarian resistance to the German advance.

'A common policy as far as possible in relation to Italy will be agreed upon, *though what the exact prospects of a Franco-Italian understanding are is still uncertain.* M. Blondel, the French chargé d'affaires in Rome, who has come to Paris to report on his talks to M. Bonnet, has (it is officially stated) brought back "a satisfactory impression", *but it seems probable that Italy is less in a hurry to come to terms with France than she was with England.* All she seems to desire at present is an "agreement of principle" which would enable France to join in the British request to the League concerning the recognition of the conquest of Abyssinia, while leaving for later discussion questions like Tunisia, Somaliland, and Franco-Italian relations in the Mediterranean generally.

'*In particular Italy seems at the present stage reluctant to give France any promises about Spain and the Balearics in addition to those already given to Britain.*' [1]

It was not too bad as a forecast, though a long-term, rather than short-term forecast; for in London, a lot of unpleasant points—particularly about Czechoslovakia—were nicely camouflaged. On the face of it, Britain had 'never yet taken such a firm stand in Central Europe'; *in reality, it was during these Anglo-French talks of April 29-30 that Lord Runciman was, if not born, at any rate, conceived.* And in return for this British 'firmness' in Central Europe, the French agreed to be as weak as they could possibly be about Spain.

The visit was not without solemnity. The French Ministers, who arrived at the French Embassy at Albert Gate on the Wednesday night, dined at Windsor Castle the next evening, and stayed the night there. Lord and Lady Halifax and the French Ambassador, M. Corbin, were also among the guests.

The band of the Grenadier Guards played during dinner,

[1] *Manchester Guardian*, April 26, 1938.

and afterwards gave a programme of music in the crimson drawing-room. M. Daladier and M. Bonnet were given suites in one of the towers in the guest wing, which are among the most sumptuous in the castle.

The dinner party took place in the State dining-hall, and the Windsor gold plate was used for the second time since the King's accession.

Before the French Ministers left the Castle in the morning the King personally conducted them over the State apartments.

M. Bonnet was so flattered at the thought of having stayed 'with the King and Queen' that (according to the French journalists at the Hyde Park Hotel) he could talk to them of nothing else all the next day.

As for M. Daladier, a little street incident occurred on the following afternoon which caused much amusement. As he drove up to the French Embassy in his car, he found an enormous crowd of people assembled in front of the Embassy door. He proceeded to wave his hat at them until it was explained to him that the people were only there to see a wedding party come out of the house on the opposite side of Albert Gate. M. Daladier seemed slightly disappointed.

The Anglo-French talks lasted nearly two whole days.

The most tangible result of the first day's talks—or so it seemed at the time, for since then very little has been heard of the arrangement—was an Anglo-French agreement to 'pool their resources'—which meant not only a close co-ordination between the armed forces of the two countries, but also various common arrangements for making purchases of aircraft and of the basic raw materials for purposes of rearmament, and also for accumulating food supplies.

But at that time Mr. Chamberlain and Lord Halifax did not wish the impression to gain ground that they had concluded an alliance with France.

While M. Daladier was rejoicing, the British Ministers were on the following day a little taken aback by the use of the word 'alliance' and of phrases like 'virtual alliance' and 'defensive alliance', not only in the French Press but also in a great many British papers, and it was strongly emphasised on the British side that the coming 'Staff contacts' were only a continuation of the contacts agreed upon in 1936 and that they did not constitute any new commitments or any change of British policy. On the Friday afternoon Lord Halifax actually hastened to give assurances to that effect to the German and Italian Ambassadors.

Apart from that the three main subjects were Spain, Czecho-slovakia and Italy.

'As regards Spain,' I wrote at the time, 'nothing of any value to the Spanish Government has been agreed upon. The French Ministers, aware of the response they would receive, do not even seem to have proposed any joint Anglo-French action which would tend to "neutralise" the Balearics and so protect the French sea route to North Africa, and it appears *that they were satisfied with the British argument that the Italians had pledged themselves to withdraw their troops from Spain and that they would "almost certainly do so", since it was in Italy's interest to remain on good terms with Britain!*

'Any danger, it was thought, might be counteracted by France from her newly constructed military aerodrome in Corsica. In the circumstances both the French and British Ministers cheerfully agreed on the full maintenance of non-intervention, and the French even agreed to restore the international frontier control along the Pyrénées as soon as the British plan providing for the proportional withdrawal of foreign troops began to be applied.

'Control apparently will come into force as soon as the international inspectors in charge of counting the volunteers have entered Spain, and may be terminated only if by the end of forty-five days the inspectors find that they cannot, owing to bad faith on either of the sides, succeed in their task. Considering Italy's avowed determination not to withdraw her troops before the end of the war, the whole scheme, with frontier control as its only effective measure, is another blow to the Spanish Government. Spain has again been betrayed.

'As for the activities of Germany in Spain—which M. Daladier stressed as hard as he could—it appears to have been agreed that nothing special could be done about it just now, *but that there would be no harm when the time came—and perhaps even sooner— in cultivating the good graces of General Franco. Britain (Mr. Chamberlain said) was looking forward to friendly relations with Franco after his victory.*

'*It almost looks as though the whole proposal were calculated to hasten a rebel victory* and to give pleasure to the Italians. M. Daladier was not at all keen on the scheme; but the British Ministers thought that if France hastened to make friends with Italy things would go better in Spain.'[1]

---

[1] *Manchester Guardian*, April 30.

It makes grim reading when one thinks of all that happened afterwards.

But it is hardly necessary to explain that Mr. Chamberlain was caring little for fair play in Spain, and that he was hoping desperately for an early Franco victory, which (so he thought) would completely 'normalise' relations with Italy. The French had similar illusions about Italy; a Havas note from London painted rosy pictures of a 'return to the Stresa Front', while the French Ministers

> warmly congratulated the British Ministers on the Anglo-Italian agreement. Unfortunately, they said, the Italians seemed to be less keen on coming to a similar arrangement with them. Not only were the Italians raising difficulties about Tunisia and native troops and also about the Jibuti railway, but it seemed doubtful whether even an 'agreement of principle' could be reached between France and Italy before the meeting of the League Council on May 9.
>
> The British Ministers said that they would do their very best to persuade the Italians not to be so 'difficult', and to tell them that it was essential from the British point of view that the Anglo-Italian agreement should be supplemented by an Italo-French agreement. In the circumstances the French Ministers are understood to have decided to join in the British action at Geneva even if no agreement at all was reached by that time— not even an 'agreement of principle'—between France and Italy, an action which would give the two countries freedom to recognise the conquest of Abyssinia if they felt like it.[1]

But the most urgent subject was Czechoslovakia. In the midst of the London meeting a Note came from the Czechoslovak Government indicating the extent to which Prague was prepared to go to meet Henlein's demands; and the document spoke of a very serious danger of war. It was earlier in the month that Henlein had formulated the eight points and the 'Karlsbad programme'—and this the Czech Government regarded as completely unacceptable. They were, in principle, prepared to grant the Sudetens a limited form of autonomy, but neither territorial, nor juridical, nor 'philosophical' autonomy, which would be contrary to the constitution, as well as the safety, of the Czechoslovak State.

The only way out of the difficulty was to bring pressure to

[1] *Manchester Guardian*, April 30.

bear on the Czechs. And that is what was in reality decided on April 29; and the pressure was already then called 'mediation'.

The British Ministers told the French that while they could not undertake any new obligations towards Czechoslovakia beyond the general statement made by Mr. Chamberlain on March 24, they said that they would endeavour to bring about through diplomatic contacts an agreement between the Czech Government, the German minority, and the German Government. Juridically, such a proposal already implied, as it were, the recognition of the Sudetens as a State within the State and of Germany as the third partner in the Czech-Sudeten quarrel. But the British Ministers felt that the situation was too serious to be put off by so fine a point.[1]

The 'solution' of April 29 was already essentially a 'Runciman' solution. And although France and Britain agreed that a solution must be found compatible with the security and the constitution of the Czechoslovak State, they more or less openly agreed that the phrase 'within the limits of the Czechoslovak Constitution' should be stretched to its utmost capacity. It was clear that what Hitler wanted was the Czech 'Maginot Line' much more than his three million fellow Germans (for what did he care for his Tyrolese brethren whom the Italians were treating very much worse than the Czechs were treating the Sudetens?); but this was difficult to explain to the general public. Hitler's and Henlein's case was perhaps a bad and dishonest case—but it was a case for all that; and that is why Czechoslovakia was difficult to handle as a technical question independently of its psychological implications. It was not enough to say that Hitler and Henlein were using democratic principles for undemocratic ends!

In London there were some further talks about developing British and French economic relations with Rumania, Hungary and Jugoslavia, and of propping up these countries economically; but the discussions did not go very far. Nor did the British Ministers show much interest in a number of financial questions raised by M. Bonnet.

.   .   .   .

For France, at that moment, was passing through another of her periodic financial crises. The formation of the Daladier

[1] *Manchester Guardian,* April 30.

Government had been well received by the business world; but a few days later the boom on the Bourse came to an end, and there was again heavy pressure on the franc. Except for borrowing ten milliard francs from the Bank of France, the Government was very slow in making any use of the 'limited' powers it had been given by Parliament, and there was a widespread impression that nothing drastic and spectacular would come out of its decrees. Moreover, there were continuous rumours that M. Reynaud was advocating a new devaluation—with the franc pegged to the £ at about 175. The rumours were not unfounded, and on the night of May 3—a day on which the franc had slipped to 170 to the £, M. Daladier made the sudden announcement on the wireless that it was necessary for France to make a fresh start; and that her anaemic economy must be placed on a solid financial basis at last—and he announced that the franc would be pegged to the £ and would not be allowed to fall below the rate of 179. This was the third devaluation since September 1936.

Although the first set of M. Daladier's decrees, which was published during the same week, was very unimpressive, and consisted of so many odds and ends, the effect of the devaluation was to bring in a short time about £100,000,000 of exported capital back to France. The motive behind this repatriation was profit-taking, rather than 'confidence', but it all looked good; and the devaluation was of great help to the Government. The defence loan of five milliard francs was subscribed without the least difficulty, and in the first half of May there was a wave of optimism in France.

．　　．　　．　　．　　．　　．　　．　　．

The London talks were followed up in different directions.

In Czechoslovakia the prospects for 'mediation' looked bad from the outset. On May Day Henlein made a violent speech in which, referring to his Karlsbad programme, he bluntly declared: 'I take nothing back.'

> 'No one,' he cried, 'has the right to call my recent speech a call to war. Our goal is equality of rights. This new order is of vital importance not for us alone but for the State and for all Europe. Every country which thinks that support of the Czech claim to overlordship serves the peace of Europe should note this. We will not accept the position of a minority.'

A renewed avowal of his party's allegiance to National Socialist principles was greeted everywhere with great applause. The celebrations staged by the Sudeten Germans were the biggest on record. Well over 1,000,000 persons, it was estimated, took part in the processions.[1]

On the other hand, in Prague and other purely Czech towns all the Czech parties united in common demonstrations of 'unity of the nation, defence of the Republic, democracy and peace'.

It was also on May Day that President Beneš sent a telegram to Hitler, which caused much interest, for it suggested that he was trying to improve the international atmosphere on the eve of the coming negotiations.

> 'On the occasion of the German national holiday I express to your Excellency my most sincere good wishes.'

I have not seen any record of Hitler's reply—if there was one.

The British and French 'mediation' began on May 7—ten days after the London meeting. The official statement issued in Prague said:

> The Minister of Foreign Affairs, M. Krofta, received the British Minister, Mr. B. C. Newton who assured M. Krofta of the friendly interest of the British Government and its disposition to help the Czecho-Slovak Government in its effort to solve the German question in Czecho-Slovakia by giving satisfaction to the reasonable demands of the German population in the spirit of the declaration of the Prime Minister, Mr. Chamberlain, on March 24.

A similar statement was made to M. Krofta by the French Minister in Prague, M. de Lacroix, who expressed himself, in the name of the French Government, in favour of a solution of the German question in Czechoslovakia which would be compatible with the safety of the State. The British and French Ministers expressed the expectations of their Governments that the Czechoslovak Government would go to the utmost possible limits within the framework indicated for a solution of the above question.

At the same time

the German Government was informed in the friendliest way of

[1] Reuter in *Manchester Guardian*, May 2, 1938.

this action and was asked to invite Herr Henlein to negotiate
with the Government at Prague on this matter.[1]

Competent observers clearly saw that the British and French
Governments were trying to square the circle; for they knew
that neither Hitler nor Henlein wanted 'concessions' which
would be 'compatible with the safety of the State', as the
French Minister in Prague had put it. Home rule compatible
with this safety was of no use to them.

But the French and British Governments did not see, or
did not like to see, this fundamental fact. It was hoped that,
rather than go to war, Hitler would, *at least for a time*, accept
some kind of home rule which would still keep Czechoslovakia
intact. And then, with much suddenness, came the crisis of
May 21.

During the previous days there had been rumours of German
troop movements along the Czech frontier—rumours similar
to those which had preceded the invasion of Austria. It is
curious that during that crisis of May 21-22, France kept
rather aloof from the diplomatic discussions. Trouble, it was
said at the time, was averted by the Czechs and—by the British.
On May 20, Sir Nevile Henderson, the British Ambassador in
Berlin, made his first inquiry at the German Foreign Office
about the alleged troop movements. He was informed by
Herr von Weissaecker that the troop movements were a matter
of routine and had nothing to do with the Czech elections.
At three o'clock on the following morning, a grave incident
occurred at Eger where two Sudeten motor cyclists, Hoffmann
and Böhm, on their way to Germany, refused to stop at the
Czech frontier, and were shot dead by Czech frontier guards.
Large quantities of anti-Czech leaflets—mostly reprints from
the French Press—were found in their possession. Early that
morning, the Czech War Minister called up several thousand
reservists, 'specialists', etc. Prague declared that this was not
a mobilisation—a step that could not have been taken by the
War Minister alone—but only a precautionary measure for
preventing any disturbances in the election areas.

That Saturday was a busy day for Sir Nevile Henderson.
He called, according to some accounts, four times, according

[1] Reuter, quoted in *Manchester Guardian*, May 9, 1938.

to others, six times, on the German Government, warning them that England would support France if Czechoslovakia were attacked. To prove that he meant business, the British Ambassador (it was said at the time) asked that a special train be placed at the disposal of the British Embassy on the following day; and it was claimed that this step was decisive in convincing the Germans that England was in earnest.

In any case, nothing serious happened. Germany, it was said, climbed down; partly perhaps because she realised that the Czech semi-mobilisation had rendered a surprise attack on Czechoslovakia impossible, and partly because she was impressed by Britain's firmness. Such was the interpretation currently given to the events of 'May 21'.

In the days that followed the crisis of May 21, France was full of praise for the British Government, and for its Ambassador in Berlin whose firmness had averted war. May 21, it was said, was a lesson: if France and England were firm on all similar occasions, war could be averted. Except that in certain circumstances, the combined firmness of the Powers might not be sufficient; and Pertinax, for example, wrote that in order to 'make May 21 work again' it was necessary to rebuild the 'French system', and, in the first place, to assure in advance the support of Russia in any future emergency of the same kind—a precaution the British and French Governments had deliberately failed to take, despite repeated Russian offers of staff talks.

> 'May 21,' Pertinax wrote, 'is a turning-point; but it is only a turning-point and not an end. The deliberations between Hitler and his men—his "moderates" and his "extremists"—will continue. And it is not certain that our British friends who saved peace by an act of firmness the other day, will not try, at some other critical moment, to save peace by an act of weakness. The end of the present crisis justifies the step taken by M. Blum and Paul-Boncour when, on March 15, they informed the British Government of France's firm resolution to defend Czechoslovakia. But British policy is empirical and has no fixed rules, and the internal disorder in France, if it is not stopped in time, may send off the "Chamberlain experiment" in a different direction.'[1]

Somehow, Pertinax did not, at the time, consider the

[1] *Europe Nouvelle*, May 28, 1938.

possibility that it was not only England, but also France, which might 'go off in a different direction'.

It must, however, be said, that certain members of the French Government—notably M. Bonnet—later claimed that the 'threatened invasion' of Czechoslovakia by Germany on May 21 was largely a show put up by the Czechs, for the purpose of testing the British and French reaction. And a man in close touch with M. Bonnet and M. Daladier later told me that the French Ministers 'could never quite forgive the Czechs their stunt of May 21'.

The Germans certainly declared it to be a stunt. Hitler said so in his Nuremberg speech. And already on May 24 the *Deutsche Allgemeine Zeitung* angrily wrote:

> A legend is spread around the world by the propaganda machine of the Entente. It is that Germany was about to disturb the peace and that only Great Britain's determined attitude saved the world at the last minute from a new catastrophe. Mr. Chamberlain is regarded as the saviour of peace. Paris congratulates Prague and London, and Prague and London congratulate one another. Peace was not menaced by Germany, therefore it could not be saved by Britain.

while the *Kölnische Zeitung* wrote:

> Of what does this British diplomatic success consist? Merely of having pretended to 'prevent' something which never was fact and never was intended.

In reality, the truth lay probably half-way. Even if Germany was not preparing to attack Czechoslovakia, it is still too simple to attribute the whole crisis of May 21 to a 'Czech stunt'. Whatever may have been the exact intentions of the Germans on May 20 and 21—and perhaps *they also* were curious to know what not only the British and French, but also the Czech reactions would be to their 'troop movements'— it may still be argued that the Czech semi-mobilisation was justified if only in view of the grave agitation in the Sudeten area, the frequent frontier incidents, and the numerous flights of German aeroplanes over Czech territory. There was a danger of a Sudeten *Putsch* which might have been supported from outside—but for the occupation of the Sudeten area by the newly called-up Czech troops. Allowance must also be made for the extraordinary atmosphere of tension that had been created by the election campaign.

.   .   .   .

In Paris the effect of the May 21 week-end was rather interesting.   The advocates of the surrender of Czechoslovakia were silenced for a time.   For some weeks M. Flandin made no speeches, and papers like *Candide* and *Gringoire* changed in tone, the former patting the Czechs patronisingly on the back for being good boys and for entering into negotiations with Henlein, and so trying to 'create for themselves a different kind of existence', and the latter allowing M. Tardieu to state on its front page his views why Czechoslovakia must not be abandoned.

The optimism in Paris lasted, in fact, longer than was justified by the facts.   It is true that M. Bonnet was not fully re-assured by the 'happy ending' of the 'May 21' crisis.   Speaking before the Foreign Affairs Committee of the Chamber on June 2 he said that while the British representations in Berlin on May 21 had averted immediate danger, he was not sure that all danger was over.   It is curious that at that time M. Bonnet still appeared to support—at least in speaking to the Chamber Committee—the Czechs against excessive German claims.   He thought it would be 'inadvisable for the Czech Government to grant minority rights to the Sudeten Germans which would be out of all proportion with their numerical importance.'[1] Nor did he *at that time* suggest that May 21 was only a 'Czech stunt'.

> The respective positions taken in the negotiations which were then in progress between Henlein and Dr. Hodza, M. Bonnet said, had not yet been sufficiently clearly defined.   It was therefore difficult to express an opinion on the chances of the negotiations. M. Bonnet said that he fervently hoped for a peaceful con-clusion of these talks, but until these were concluded and the Czech municipal elections were over the situation would remain 'rather menacing'.   In the course of his statement M. Bonnet emphasised several times the enormous importance of the close co-operation in all fields between England and France.[2]

The public rather lightly assumed that May 21 had taught Hitler a lesson and that in any case no startling new

[1] *Manchester Guardian,* June 4.
[2] *Ditto.*

developments were to be feared for a long time.   Most typical
of the attitude of the greater part of the French Press was this
headline in the *Intransigeant* of June 15:

> *Les négociations Hodza-Henlein qui vont s'ouvrir demain pourraient
> se prolonger jusqu'à l'automne.*

It is true that lower down, there was the sub-title '*Peu de
chances d'aboutir*'; but what mattered to the ordinary reader
was the *jusqu'à l'automne*.

But great uneasiness continued to be felt in Government
quarters; for while the pious hope continued to be entertained
that the Czechs would 'somehow' manage to come to terms
with the Sudeten Germans and get them—at least for a time—
to accept a form of home rule which would not be incompatible
with the independence and security of Czechoslovakia, this
presupposed a Sudeten retreat from the eight points of the
Karlsbad programme;[1] and such a retreat would have to be
agreed to by Germany.   In spite of the 'victory' of May 21,
nothing seemed less likely.   Under British and French pressure
the Czech Government agreed on June 10 to accept the Sudeten
Memorandum—(embodying in effect the Karlsbad programme)—as a 'basis of discussion', with the implication that
this was a 'maximum' demand, and that an agreement would
mean something half-way between what the Sudetens were
asking for and what they—the Czechs—were at that stage prepared to offer.   Such is the usual procedure in any kind of
negotiations; but with the Sudetens, backed by Hitler, it was
different.

A month after the negotiations 'on the basis of the Karlsbad

---

[1] The eight demands made by Henlein in his speech at Karlsbad on April 24,
were—
1. Full equality of status for Czechs and Germans.
2. This equality to be guaranteed by a recognition of the Sudeten Germans
   as a legal entity.
3. The determination and recognition of the German areas within the
   State.
4. Full self-government for these areas.
5. Legal protection for every citizen living outside the area of his own
   nationality.
6. Removal of injustices inflicted on the Sudeten Germans since 1918 and
   reparation for the damage caused.
7. Recognition and realisation of the principle 'German regions—German
   officials'.
8. Full liberty to profess German nationality and the German political
   philosophy.

programme' had begun, Herr Frank, the deputy leader of the Sudeten Party declared to the Prague Correspondent of the *Manchester Guardian* that

> the optimism expressed in Government quarters and voiced in the world Press about the negotiations was not justified and that he was on the contrary very pessimistic.
>
> It was an erroneous view to believe, he said, that there were any real negotiations between the Government and the Sudeten-German Party. The programme of the Party was laid down in Henlein's Karlsbad speech and the various demands in it had not in reality been taken as a basis for the negotiations. What had happened so far was just reconnoitring.
>
> The Government, he said, had communicated to the Sudeten-German Party leaders only a fraction of the contents of the Nationalities Statute, and though at that moment they were pledged to silence about the nature of the proposals he was pessimistic about their value.
>
> On the other hand, the leader of an important district in the Sudeten-German area said that probably the German population would accept the Government's proposals, but that they believed that if they were far-reaching enough Czech nationalist feeling would sweep away the present Czecho-Slovak Government. This German anxiety for the Czech Cabinet's position was not justified by facts.
>
> 'One cannot help feeling,' the *Manchester Guardian* correspondent concluded, 'that the Sudeten German problem could be reasonably solved if it were a purely internal problem. But the fate of the future relations of Czechs and Germans will not depend on either Herr Henlein or Herr Frank, but will ultimately be decided by the mood of the rulers in Berlin.'[1]

And *that* was just the trouble.

And so the negotiations between the Czechs and the Sudetens muddled along until the 20th of July or thereabout—and it was then that the British Government produced Lord Runciman.

Until that time French opinion had taken comparatively little notice of the Prague negotiations. French commentators protested from time to time against suggestions that continued to be put forward by various people in England for the 'neutralisation' of Czechoslovakia, or a plebiscite, or a 'cantonisation', 'after the model of Switzerland'. All this was silly, many Frenchmen thought. Either Czechoslovakia must remain

[1] *Manchester Guardian*, July 12, 1938.

territorially intact, with genuine sovereignty over her whole territory, or she would soon be destroyed by Germany. Too much amateurish thinking, they thought, was going on in England, particularly in the correspondence columns of the *Times*. Many other Frenchmen, however, did not think anything at all, and did not believe there was any need to worry *avant l'automne*.

CHAPTER VII

THE STRANGLING OF THE SPANISH REPUBLIC STARTS IN EARNEST

I F on the Czech 'diplomatic front' France scored, on May 21, something that looked like a victory, there were no victories on either the Italian or Spanish fronts.

The French Ministers returned from London with the illusion that the road was clear for a Franco-Italian *rapprochement,* and whatever happened in the interval to the Blondel-Ciano talks, which had started in the middle of April, they were determined to associate themselves with the British step at the Council Meeting at Geneva—a step as a result of which Britain and France would be free to recognise the conquest of Abyssinia.

In fact no advance at all was made in the Blondel-Ciano talks between May 1 and May 12—partly because it was during that time that Hitler went to Rome. Ciano, it was said, was otherwise engaged. But it was, at least, comforting to learn that the Italian papers were not attacking France. On May 12 the League Council met, and although M. Bonnet and Lord Halifax knew that they could not obtain any unanimous vote on the acceptance of the Italian conquest, they got nine members of the Council to declare that 'in their opinion each member of the League is free to decide for himself whether or not to recognise the Italian conquest of Abyssinia'.

The Emperor of Abyssinia was at Geneva, and had just paid part of Abyssinia's contribution to the League—it was all very awkward. Still, the declarations made by the nine members of the Council were exactly what the French and British Governments had been longing for. It was a little trick that M. Avenol had invented, after long consultations with the British and French Governments whom he had gone to see in London and

Paris.   Abyssinia officially remained a member of the League;
but the damage was done.[1]

> 'One need hardly say,' Mme Tabouis wrote, 'that this
> "freedom of appreciation" which a mere Secretary-General of
> the League had conferred on its members, is by no means
> compatible with the spirit of the League of Nations.   But the
> general situation is such that members of the League feel
> obliged to practise a certain opportunism, all the more so as in
> its present state the League provides nobody with collective
> security, and so obliges all nations to use their own wits in
> looking for the help they may need in case of unpleasant
> events.'[2]

Well, well.   Which, by the way, did not prevent Sir John
Simon from saying in the House of Commons on May 19:

> 'We now have, according to the strictest view of our League
> duties (!!!) the right to decide whether we shall recognise the
> Italian conquest of Abyssinia or not.'

And speaking of the 'settlement' of the Abyssinian question
by the League Council, the *Œuvre* pithily remarked: 'Liquid-
ation?   No—liquefaction.'

However, M. Bonnet returned to Paris, feeling very pleased
that the corpse of Abyssinia should have been cleared out of
the way.   There was nothing, he thought, to prevent a *rapprochement* with Italy at last, and the opening of discussions
similar to those that had led to the conclusion of the Anglo-
Italian agreement.

And he was particularly anxious to make friends with Italy,
especially as the situation in Czechoslovakia was threatening
to become nasty.   There was talk of troop movements, and of
some particularly important war council with Hitler in the
chair, which was supposed to have taken place immediately on Hitler's return from Rome to Berlin.   It was even
rumoured that Mussolini had encouraged Hitler to attack
Czechoslovakia.

Unfortunately it so happened—and there was nothing new
in this Italian technique—that no sooner had France helped
to dispose of the corpse of Abyssinia at Geneva than Mussolini
made his savage attack on France in his famous speech at

[1] *Manchester Guardian*, May 13.
[2] *Œuvre*, May 13, 1938.

Genoa on May 15. The speech was very polite to England, and was an obvious attempt either to drive a wedge between France and England, or else to compel France to yield on the question of Spain.

At that time the Spanish Government had, largely with the help of the French armaments, which had been sent there in the two previous months, succeeded in stopping the Aragon Offensive; and Mussolini and Mr. Chamberlain were both furious. Mr. Chamberlain's bitter disappointment at the Spanish Government's failure to allow itself to be defeated, was well reflected in the article by the Diplomatic correspondent of the *Times* on May 20, which I have already quoted.

And in his Genoa speech, Mussolini, after declaring that he would observe the Anglo-Italian agreement 'scrupulously', said:

> 'You will permit me to be cautious in what I say of the conversations with France, for they are still in progress. I do not know if we shall arrive at a conclusion for in one sphere which is much to the fore—I refer to the war in Spain—we are on the opposite sides of the barricade. They want the victory of Barcelona; we desire the victory of Franco.'

The speech was a bitter disappointment to the French Right, for in the course of it Mussolini also said that Stresa was 'dead and buried; and as far as we are concerned, it will never be resuscitated'. For these people had always refused to realise that Stresa had never been an Italo-Franco-British alliance, and was only an Italian manœuvre calculated to silence in advance any Anglo-French protests against the invasion of Abyssinia.

And the Genoa speech shattered another pleasant French illusion—namely that it was, as it were, by accident, that Mussolini had failed to counteract the Anschluss in 1938, as he had checked a Nazi advance on Vienna in 1934.

> 'To those people beyond the mountains who still have the melancholy ingenuousness to remind us of what we did in 1934, we reply once more before you and before the whole Italian people who are listening that from that year until March 1938, much water has flowed beneath the bridges of the Tiber, the Danube, the Spree, the Thames, and even the Seine.
> 'While this period was passing more or less tumultuously, Italy, engaged in a gigantic and bloody effort, saw those

sanctions, which we have not yet forgotten, applied to her. Meanwhile everything diplomatic and political which passed under the name of Stresa was dead and buried, and as far as we are concerned will never be resuscitated.

'Italy could not allow herself the luxury of mobilising regularly at the end of every four years to prevent the inevitable conclusion of a national revolution.'

(The reference was to the dispatch of Italian troops to the frontier in 1934 to prevent the Anschluss.)

French opinion was deeply shocked by the speech. A Cabinet meeting was held on the following Tuesday; and the Cabinet was divided. M. Daladier treated the speech as a piece of insolence. M. Bonnet, on the other hand, was much impressed by the phrase about the 'opposite sides of the barricade in Spain'; and felt that, especially with war threatening in Czechoslovakia, Italy must be bought off at any price. And he argued in favour of closing the Catalan frontier to armaments. He thought that that was also Mr. Chamberlain's desire. The Cabinet did not follow his advice, and he left the meeting in rather a bad mood. At the end of the week came the Czech crisis; and for a time little more was heard of Franco-Italian relations.

Only, there was one point on which M. Bonnet was quite right; and that was that Mussolini and Mr. Chamberlain were in complete agreement about the Catalan frontier. And in June, as we shall see, Mr. Chamberlain was going to ask the French to close it—which they did, on their 'own initiative', on June 13. Some interesting questions were to be asked on the subject in the House of Commons.

.   .   .   .

How anxious Mr. Chamberlain was to speed up a Franco victory could also be observed from the view he took of the bombing of British ships in Spanish waters.

And here we come to one of the most vital—or rather deadly —decisions taken by England and France: the deliberate strangulation of the Spanish Republic. It will be remembered that the advance of General Franco, whose troops had reached the Mediterranean in the middle of April, was checked; and although, during June and July, the Insurgents continued a slow advance towards Sagunto, on the Valencia road, it was clear that final victory, which seemed so near in April, had again escaped them.   The Nyon patrol set up in the autumn of 1937 had been of great help to the Spanish Government; for it put an end to the blockade that had been virtually put into operation by the systematic sinking of ships bound for Spanish Government ports.   The 'unknown submarines' guilty of this piracy were the great joke of the year; it was suggested in Paris that the Boulevard des Italiens be re-christened the Boulevard des Inconnus; and the comic papers would talk about the Unknown Ambassador who had called at the Quai d'Orsay, and of an Unknown Horse that had won the Grand Prix.

But Italy and Germany overcame the difficulties placed in their way by the Nyon agreement.   Instead of a naval blockade, they—and particularly Italy—gradually established a sort of air blockade over the Spanish Government ports.

The bombing was usually done while the ships—mostly British ships—were in harbour, that is, technically in terri-torial waters.   In January four ships were attacked, one by a submarine, and three from the air.

> On January 20, three planes dropped a number of bombs on the *Thorpeness* in the port of Tarragona.   The ship was seriously damaged and seven of the crew were killed and eight wounded.
> On January 27, the captain of the British ship *Dover Abbey* was killed by a bombardment.
> On January 31, the *Endymion* was sunk south of Cartagena by a submarine.
> On February 4, two seaplanes attacked and sank the *Alcira* when about twenty miles south-east of Badalona.

This new outbreak of piracy, however, led to new measures to stop it.   Mr. Eden, in the House of Commons, announced that the British Government had decided:

> That the time had come to let it be known once and for all that they cannot continue to deal with these attacks solely by protests or claims for compensation, which have failed to check the attacks or secure any material satisfaction for the damage done.

He added that if the attacks were repeated *the British Government reserved the right, without further notice, to take appropriate retaliatory action.*

For a time the warning had some effect, but once Mr. Eden had gone, the piracy started again, and in May and June, after the signing of the Anglo-Italian agreement it became almost a daily occurrence.

On March 15, the *Stanwell* was bombed and set on fire in the port of Tarragona. Three persons were killed and seventeen wounded, including the control observer on board.

On April 25, seven planes damaged the *Celtic Star* and *Stanland* in the port of Valencia. Two of the crew of the *Celtic Star* were seriously wounded

On April 29, the *Surrey Brook* was attacked by three planes when 25 miles from Barcelona. None of the six bombs hit the ship.

On April 30, the *Stancroft* was hit and seriously damaged in the port of Barcelona. One sailor was wounded. Other ships were slightly damaged.

On May 7, the *Greatend*, in the port of Valencia, was hit by a bomb which killed one sailor and wounded two.

On May 13, the *Greatend* was again hit by a bomb and caught fire.

On May 13, the *Euphorbia* was bombed when in the port of Barcelona. The captain and the first officer were wounded.

On May 22, the *Penthames* was hit by a bomb in Valencia harbour and two members of the crew were injured.

On May 25, while lying a mile and a half off Valencia the *Thorpehall* was bombed and sunk. Five of the crew were injured.

On May 29, the *Greatend* was sunk at Valencia.

On May 31, the *Penthames* was again hit in Valencia harbour and this time sunk.

On June 4, during a raid on Alicante the *Maryad* was set on fire. One member of the crew was killed and the non-intervention officer was injured.

On June 6, five planes raided Alicante and sank the *St. Winifred*. Five members of the crew were killed and several were injured.

At the end of May it was stated that twenty-seven British seamen had been killed and thirty-seven injured.

On June 7, six planes raided the harbour of Valencia and the *Thurston* was so badly damaged that she had to be dry-docked to prevent her sinking in the harbour.

On June 7, in a raid on Alicante the *Thorpehaven* was hit and damaged and the *English Tanker* was set on fire.

On June 8, a British dredger was sunk in the British-owned harbour of Gandia, about forty miles south of Valencia.

On June 9, the *Isadora* was bombed and put out of action at Castellon. In a raid on the French steamer *Brisbane* at Denia a British non-intervention observer on board and an Englishman who was the ship's agent were killed. The *Brisbane* was bombed again on two occasions.

On June 10, in raids on Alicante the *Thorpehaven* was sunk and the *St. Winifred* was again hit.

On June 10, the *Isadora* was again bombed at Castellon, and was also machine-gunned and she sank. At Valencia the British steamer *Stanray* was machine-gunned.

On June 15, in three raids on Valencia the *Thurston* was set on fire and the *Seapharer* was holed. Two French steamers were also sunk.

On June 16, the *Marconi* was attacked by insurgent planes while lying in Valencia harbour.

And so it went on. On June 22 alone two British ships were sunk. These were the *Thorpeness* owned by the Westcliff Shipping Company. She was bombed and sunk while at anchor three-quarters of a mile outside the port of Valencia.

The *Sunion* which was moored about a mile from the *Thorpeness*, was sunk some hours later.

In little less than a month Franco had sunk eight British ships; and had damaged several others.

Feeling was beginning to run high in England, and the House of Commons wanted to know what Mr. Chamberlain would do about it. On June 13, Mr. Chamberlain at last spoke. He announced in the House of Commons that no action would be taken to prevent the bombing.

'I do not think any action we can take is practicable in stopping these attacks if they persist.'

Mr. Chamberlain stressed his determination to preserve the Government's policy of 'non-intervention'. Protection of ships in port, he said, could only be afforded by stationing anti-aircraft guns on land or warships in or near the port. He continued:

'Since it is impossible to tell whether any aeroplane is intending to attack a British ship until the attack is delivered, and since to wait until the attack is delivered would be to deprive the defence of any useful effect, it follows that fire would have to be opened on all approaching aircraft. Action of this kind would obviously constitute participation in the defence of the port, and would amount to direct intervention in the civil war.'

The Government, he added, *had rejected any plan of retaliatory action.*

'The result of further and detailed examination made by his Majesty's Government,' Mr. Chamberlain said, 'has been to show that unless this country is prepared to take an active part in the hostilities effective protection cannot be guaranteed to ships trading with ports in the war zone while they are in territorial waters.

'In the opinion of his Majesty's Government they would not be justified in recommending such a course, *which might well result in the spread of the conflict far beyond its present limits.* They must therefore repeat the warning they have already given to British shipping on November 28 and 29 last, that, while they will continue to afford protection as hitherto to ships on the high seas, ships entering ports which are liable at any time to be the object of military operations must do so at their own risk.'

The speech, duly reported in Italy and Spain, had an immediate effect. On the following day two French ships were sunk and three British ships damaged.

But it left Mr. Chamberlain undeterred, except that, on June 23, he went so far as to say that the Government 'took a serious view of these attacks, and had instructed Sir Robert Hodgson, the British agent at Burgos, to ask the Burgos authorities to give an explanation of their action which on the face of it was entirely inconsistent with the assurances and promises they had made'.

For the rest, he repeated the old story—no protection for British ships could be afforded without risk of war, and ships must trade with Spain at their own risk.

The questions put to him by Mr. Attlee and Sir Archibald Sinclair may be summarised thus. Since British ships are trading legitimately with Spain according to the rules approved by the Non-Intervention Committee, why should they not be protected? For fear of what Franco might do? For fear of what another country might do? If so, what could be said for the merits of the Anglo-Italian agreement?

Mr. Chamberlain would not answer that question. He recognised a risk greater than was to be expected from Franco alone.

'If you start a war-like action against Franco,' said Mr. Chamberlain, 'or against some objective of which the ownership is doubtful, who can tell if you can stop your operations there without beginning another major war?'

During Mr. Chamberlain's speech there was a scene in the public gallery. Three men rose in different parts of the gallery and shouted remarks about 'the murdering of British seamen' and 'We demand protection!' They were ejected, one being carried out by two attendants.[1]

And in a speech a few days later Mr. Chamberlain ridiculed the Socialists who were showing so much concern for 'British property'.

Finally, following a suggestion made in the House by Mr. Churchill, Mr. Chamberlain instructed Lord Perth to go and see Ciano and ask him to use his influence with Franco against further air attacks on British ships. The fiction that they were 'Franco' planes was politely observed.

Clearly Mr. Chamberlain was becoming worried by the outcry in the country against his policy. An Exchange Telegraph message from Rome on June 28 said:

> It is understood that the Ambassador did not ask Italy to bring direct pressure to bear on the airmen who are responsible for the bombing of merchant ships off Government Spain. He merely pointed out that these incidents have made and are making a deep impression upon British public opinion and that it might be found difficult later to bring the Anglo-Italian agreement into force. He added that the Fascist Government's influence with the Burgos Government might usefully be brought into play in order to avoid a repetition of these tragic incidents.
>
> Lord Perth's visit to Count Ciano, unexpected as it was, made the deepest impression in Italian Government quarters, where the keenest desire has recently been expressed to see the Anglo-Italian agreement brought into force. It was thought this evening that the Italian Foreign Minister will again receive the British Ambassador within the next two or three days and that some useful results may then be reached.

It did a little good, but not much. On the day of Lord Perth's visit two more British ships were bombed by Franco, —one at Valencia, the other at Alicante—and three British seamen were killed.

However, on the following day Virginio Gayda announced in the *Giornale d'Italia* (with a nice ironical touch) that General Franco would not bomb British ships on the high seas, and would avoid bombing them in Spanish ports, as far as possible. 'Emphasis is placed in Rome,' Reuter added, 'on the exceptional treatment which is being offered to British shipping.'[2]

[1] *Manchester Guardian*, June 24.
[2] *Manchester Guardian*, June 30.

Gayda at the same time attacked the foreign Press for alleging that the bombing had been done on the responsibility of Italy, and again asserted that Italy's contribution to General Franco's forces was a small one.

Which, by the way, did not prevent an official statement from being published in Rome a few days later, saying that, since the beginning of the Spanish war, 120 Italian airmen had lost their lives in Spain. An impressive figure when account is taken of the shortage of aeroplanes and anti-aircraft guns on the Government side.

As for the bombing of British ships, there was a short respite, which reduced the pressure at home on Mr. Chamberlain. But by the middle of July the bombings of British ships started again. The *Stanland* was bombed at Valencia on July 18, by five planes and set on fire; eight dockers were killed; while the crew and the two non-intervention officers had a narrow escape. On July 28 the *Kellwyn* was bombed at Valencia, and Mr. A. Moyell, a Danish non-intervention officer, and a Chinese cook were killed, while the mate and three other sailors were wounded. Almost on the same day, on July 27, the *Kellwyn*'s sister ship the *Dellwyn* was sunk in the British-owned port of Gandia, south of Valencia, after having been attacked almost daily for a week.

Franco's plan for a 'free port' at Almeria came to nothing, as he demanded that even petrol should be treated as a war material, and could therefore not be unloaded in the 'free port'.

I quoted earlier in this book the passage in the *Times* of May 20 describing the alarm and anxiety caused in British Government quarters by the failure of the Spanish Government to be beaten in April; and everything tends to show that the British Government were extremely anxious for a rapid 'settlement' in Spain—that is, a Franco victory—without which the benefits of the Anglo-Italian agreement remained only theoretical. Mr. Chamberlain's excuse for not taking reprisals against Franco for the bombing of British ships on the ground that this might lead to a world war is totally unconvincing.

.   .   .   .

What also suggests that he welcomed, or was at any rate, pleased to condone the air blockade of the Government ports was the 'suggestion' he made to France early in June, that she close the Pyrénées frontier completely. No such 'suggestion', be it noted, was made to Portugal; the closing of the French frontier was to be 'unilateral;' and the reason given by the British Government for this suggestion to France was that it might improve the prospects of the plan for the withdrawal of volunteers which the Non-Intervention Committee was just then trying to put into operation. It is not clear, on the face of it, what connection there was between the arms that were going across the French frontier and the withdrawal of volunteers; except that it was hoped in London that a 'generous' French gesture would put Mussolini in a better mood for withdrawing his 'volunteers'. The frontier was effectively closed on June 13. Whether Mr. Chamberlain had any illusions that the Italian 'volunteers' would be withdrawn may be seriously doubted. At the same time it is noteworthy that neither then, nor later, did the British Government make any serious attempt to stop the deliveries of war material either to Spanish Insurgent ports or across the Portuguese frontier.

But the French frontier remained closed.

The matter was raised in the House of Commons on July 4. Miss Eleanore Rathbone asked whether the Government had used its influence to prevent the passage of arms into Spain over the Portuguese frontier. Mr. Butler, the Under-Secretary for Foreign Affairs, replied that up to the time of the withdrawal of British observers from the Portuguese frontier in June 1937, effective control had been maintained. Since then, Mr. Butler added, 'the Government has had no evidence to show that effective control is not being maintained'.

Miss Rathbone then wanted to know why it had been necessary to make strong representations to the French Government to keep its frontier closed, but no corresponding representations to Portugal. Mr. Lloyd George pressed this point, and drew from Mr. Butler the statement that no 'formal' representations or requests had been made to France by the British Government.

Mr. Attlee asked why it was always necessary to have affirmative evidence about the frontiers of the Spanish Government while a negative reply was good enough in the case of Franco's territory. This question, implying partiality on the part of the Government, was resented by Mr. Butler, who referred proudly to the achievements of the Non-Intervention Committee. Miss Rathbone was not impressed and gave notice that she would raise the matter again.[1]

On the following day Mr. George Strauss asked the Prime Minister whether the British Government had made any representations to the French Government suggesting the desirability of closing the Franco-Spanish frontier.

> *Mr. Chamberlain:* In the course of the normal interchanges of views with the French Government, his Majesty's Government has stressed the desirability of avoiding action which would interfere with the execution of the non-intervention plan, but has never suggested that the French Government in present circumstances, should take unilateral action in closing the frontier.
>
> *Mr. Strauss:* May we take it that the action taken by the French Government was quite independent and under no pressure or representation from the British Government?
>
> *Mr. Chamberlain:* Yes, it was an independent decision of the French Government.

As even the Paris Correspondent of the *Times* pointed out at the time, Mr. Chamberlain's reply was a quibble. The decision was, naturally, an 'independent' one, in so far as France is an independent and sovereign State; but the French certainly would not have closed the frontier without British pressure.

In the French Press of the Right there was at that time much quibbling over the phrase 'closing the frontier'. If the Left were protesting against the closing of the frontier on June 13 (the papers of the Right said), it meant that the frontier had been open until then. France, therefore, had been violating the non-intervention agreement, and nobody had the right to complain that Italy and Germany were violating it, too.

That was not the point. The French Pyrénées frontier was absolutely closed during the greater part of 1937. Until July,

[1] *Manchester Guardian*, July 5.

international observers were in charge of the control, and no armaments entered Spain. A great number of these observers —some of whom I happened to know personally—were violent 'anti-Reds', and certainly did their job well; and a Captain Lunn, their chief, paid a warm tribute to 'the most loyal co-operation' of the Gardes Mobiles. I am not so sure about the British control (for it was exclusively British and not international) on the Portuguese frontier; most of the inspectors were British residents from Lisbon, and were certainly on good terms with the Portuguese authorities, who themselves were working hand-in-hand with General Franco.

During 1937 the Spanish Government were certainly saved by the Russian armaments that reached them by sea; for hardly anything reached them by land, except during the last few months of the year—and not very much at that. The French frontier control was not properly 'relaxed' until March, when M. Blum became Premier and M. Paul-Boncour Foreign Minister; and under the Daladier Government the control remained 'relaxed'—until June 13. M. Daladier himself was much perturbed by the developments in Spain, and considered a Franco victory a menace to France; and although—as I already explained before—M. Bonnet considered about the middle of May the possibility of 'securing Italian neutrality' (for the situation in Central Europe was becoming dangerous) by closing the French frontier into Spain completely, M. Daladier would not have it. It took Mr. Chamberlain to persuade him to do so on June 13. The difference between 'control' and 'relaxed control', or between a 'closed' frontier and a 'hermetically sealed' frontier was explained by M. Blum in the *Populaire* on June 18 (before he knew of the decision of June 13—which was kept very secret for a time).

In his article he distinguished between the legal and the practical position of the French Government in relation to non-intervention.

'The non-intervention agreements,' he wrote, 'are legally still in force. As for the actual position, it is more delicate to define. One may say, however, that since the open admission of intervention made last September by Italy and Germany, and since the failure of the negotiations regarding the withdrawal of "volunteers", France has suspended the international frontier control and has ceased to play the gendarme on her own frontiers.

'She continues to respect the non-intervention agreement in so far as she is directly concerned—that is, she has always refused to authorise exports of armaments. But she no longer cares particularly whether this official refusal is being ignored.'

In conclusion M. Blum said that France was as determined as ever to respect non-intervention provided that it was, in M. Daladier's phrase—a phrase he had used only a few days earlier—just, reciprocal and effective. He regretted that the Communists should be clamouring for an official opening of the Spanish frontier, which he said, could do the Spanish Government more harm than good.

The Communists in reality, had good reason to be dissatisfied; for unlike M. Blum, they knew that the frontier had already been closed. On the same day as M. Blum's article appeared, the *Humanité* said that the strictest control had been set up on the Republican frontier 'in the last three days', and that this frontier was now 'hermetically sealed'. The *Humanité* alleged that *this measure was taken at the demand of the British Government and in spite of the failure to establish any sort of control in the Spanish rebel ports, or on the Portuguese frontier.* It further suggested that this French move constituted part of a new arrangement that Mr. Chamberlain might attempt to reach with Italy.

Already at that time Mr. Chamberlain had a valuable ally in M. Bonnet, not to mention M. Flandin.

First about M. Flandin. M. Flandin, who since February had been, as it were, impersonating the 'New Policy' of Mr. Chamberlain, made, very significantly, a violent speech against the Spanish Government on June 11, that is, two days before the frontier was closed at Mr. Chamberlain's request. 'After the experience one had of M. Flandin just before the Eden crisis,' said a Paris message in the *Manchester Guardian* of June 13, 'one cannot but wonder whether he has not again been "tipped off" in London and is not trying once again to anticipate British policy.'

'The greatest menace to the peace and security of France is the Spanish war,' he said. 'It is incredible that a political minority, more or less inspired by Moscow, should inflict upon France a policy contrary to her obvious interests.'

The 'political minority' M. Flandin meant was not only the Communists but all the Front Populaire parties, who, as it happened, represented the majority of the country. But that by the way. M. Flandin went on:

> 'Official France has not been neutral. She has been constantly sympathetic to the Reds and hostile to the Spanish Nationalists. The successive Front Populaire Governments have not ceased to tolerate an important transit of arms to Barcelona. Scandalous fortunes have been piled up through this traffic in the instruments of death.'

From what followed, it was clear that M. Flandin included the Daladier Government among the Front Populaire Governments and that he was trying to dictate a new Spanish policy to it:

> 'It is sheer hypocrisy to be indignant because so-called "merchant ships" are being bombed. They would not call at Spanish Government ports unless they were carrying suspect cargoes. We demand that an end be put to a policy which is prolonging the war in Spain and which is preventing us from co-operating with Italy in order to achieve an appeasement in the Mediterranean and in Central Europe, a policy which can only create for us the greatest difficulties in Spain, where we have so many commercial interests and whose raw materials we need.'

It was a very significant speech, which was loudly applauded in the Right Press, and which could almost have been dictated to M. Flandin from London.

And now for M. Bonnet.

M. Bonnet's greatest ambition was also to come to terms with Italy and to conclude a Franco-Italian agreement, and there is reason for saying that he pressed the French Government to accept Mr. Chamberlain's 'suggestion' about the closing of the frontier—not so much in order to give a chance to the plan for withdrawing volunteers—even the by no means 'pro-Red' *Paris-Soir* wrote that the Plan could achieve no practical results 'for two or three months, if at all'[1]—as in order to facilitate his negotiations with Italy. It was necessary that Mussolini should no longer be able to say that France and Italy were fighting 'on opposite sides of the barricade'.

. . . .

[1] *Paris-Soir*, July 7.

For since the middle of May when, at Geneva, France had got rid of all her obligations to the League on the question of Abyssinia, the Franco-Italian talks had got stuck. Three days after the lamentable session of the League Council, Mussolini had made his Genoa speech with the passage about the 'barricade'.

In Milan on June 2, Ciano made a speech which, from the French point of view, was no better than Mussolini's Genoa speech, and from the British point of view, considerably worse, for, unlike Mussolini's, Ciano's praise of the Anglo-Italian agreement was rather ambiguous.

> 'The Anglo-Italian agreement has the merit of having cleared the ground of the debris of the past and of having placed the relations between the two empires on a basis of clarity and loyalty, which is the only basis on which understanding between nations can rest firmly and solidly.
> 'Nothing is more dangerous than to conclude agreements which conceal beneath ephemeral compromises ambiguities and mental reservations. It is not in the style of Fascist Italy to enter into political combinations of this kind.'

Quite. Whereupon Ciano gave what might be called his interpretation of the Spanish clauses of the Anglo-Italian agreement. It was clear that in his view Spain was a matter that concerned the Berlin-Rome axis far more than it concerned England.

> 'Faithful to the conception of the Rome-Berlin axis, Fascist Italy will continue to pursue a policy of close collaboration and of intimate understanding with Nazi Germany. Italo-German solidarity made its first active manifestation when the two countries together took a definite stand against the attack which Bolshevism had launched on Spain.
> 'The fight, which still continues victoriously to-day, and in which much heroic Italian blood has been shed, will one day be recognised by all as one of the milestones in the historic resistance put up by Europe to the threat of disintegration. It will represent a new and high merit for our country that it has played so glorious a part in it.'

In the end there was a glowing reference to 'the strong and noble Japanese people' who were fighting Bolshevism— 'with which the Chinese Government have so unwisely associated themselves'. France was not even mentioned, except when Ciano spoke of Italo-Jugoslav relations, which, he said, were developing favourably 'without any unnecessary intermediaries'.

Even the most pro-Italian papers in France were much dissatisfied with Ciano's speech.

The *Temps* remarked that Count Ciano seemed to have overlooked two things—namely, that the Anglo-Italian agreement would remain meaningless so long as the conditions relating to Spain were not loyally fulfilled and so long as the agreement with England was not supplemented by one with France. In the view of French commentators Count Ciano's references to Spain clearly showed that no help whatsoever was to be expected from Italy in any attempt to mediate a peaceful settlement in the Spanish war.

M. Bonnet, speaking before the Foreign Affairs Committee of the Chamber on the same day, indicated that the Government would willingly appoint an Ambassador at Rome, but that it was anxious to see first whether anything good was likely to come out of the talks between Count Ciano and M. Blondel, the French Chargé d'Affaires in Rome. These, he said, had been suspended on May 17, and the Italian Government had not for the present shown any desire to resume them. M. Bonnet hoped, however, that they would be shortly resumed.

Of course, no good whatsoever came out of the talks between Blondel and Ciano, which were not in fact to be resumed until after Munich. During the whole summer Franco-Italian relations did not improve one whit—in spite of the fatal 'gesture' the French made on June 13—a gesture largely calculated to win over Italy's friendship—which was to close the Catalan frontier to armaments. It may be said without exaggeration that that was perhaps the most fatal day for the Spanish Government.

Mr. Chamberlain and M. Bonnet—who both hoped that all would be well again between Italy and England and France once Franco had won the war—are responsible for it. It is hard to believe that either of them were expecting the plan for the withdrawal of volunteers to be of any practical importance.

The French Government, for its part, did not wish Spain to be publicly discussed. On June 16 M. Cornavin, one of the

Communist deputies, twice attempted to force upon the Chamber a discussion on Spain and on 'the criminal scandal of non-intervention'. But on both occasions the Government evaded the discussion, and a few days later the Chamber was hastily sent on holiday. It is curious that M. Daladier should, on June 15, have made the following statement on Spain in his speech to the Executive Committee of the Radical Party:

> 'We remain faithful to the policy of non-intervention, but like all other international agreements it must be carried out loyally, reciprocally, and simultaneously. . . . We shall keep to the method of non-intervention, for we are determined that the destiny of Spain shall be settled by the Spaniards themselves.'

No doubt everybody agreed that the non-intervention agreement 'must' be carried out loyally. But how were Italy and Germany to be shown that they 'must' observe it? M. Daladier made no attempt to answer this question, and how could he with the British Government's attitude to all that was happening in Spain?

But it is curious that he should have spoken of the 'loyal, reciprocal and simultaneous' respect for the non-intervention agreement three days after his Government had agreed at the request of Mr. Chamberlain and at the instigation of M. Bonnet to the *unilateral* closing of the Catalan frontier. A unilateral action to which M. Daladier had firmly refused to agree a month earlier.

The trouble is, that, throughout 1938, Daladier was swayed by contradictory influences. There were moments when he spoke with grim energy and warlike determination; but these moments were followed by other moments when he meekly followed Bonnet.

But Bonnet, like Mr. Chamberlain, was perfectly consistent. His Spanish policy—closely dependent on his Italian policy— did not vary for a moment between May 1938 and the bitter end; and although it is difficult to say exactly at what moment he made up his mind to abandon Czechoslovakia, from that moment onwards he was perfectly consistent—in spite of his public utterances and his assurances to the Czech Minister— assurances which he *had* to give.

As regards Spain, it is not perhaps without significance that it was very soon after the closing of the Catalan frontier to armaments and while the bombing of British ships was in full swing that the Bank of France refused to hand over to the Bank of Spain the £7,500,000 of gold it had held for it since 1931, on the ground that if the Insurgents won, the Bank of France 'might have to pay twice'. The Spanish Government's claim was rejected by the first Chamber of the Paris Court of Appeal on July 6.

> The Court found that the Bank of Spain, being a company of shareholders, was not a State Bank, and therefore Spain as a State was not involved in the present case. The charter of the Bank of Spain had undergone changes 'owing to recent difficulties', the Court ruled.
>
> These changes were so serious that if the Bank of France were now to hand the gold to the Republican Government it might at some future date be compelled to make a similar payment to the other party. Therefore the Court refused the demand of the Bank of Spain that the gold should be handed over and ordered the Bank of Spain to pay costs. *Ruling that the matter was not within its competence and was too delicate to be judged summarily, the Court decided that the civil tribunal in Paris must settle the action. This meant a year's delay.*[1]

A year's delay! That is precisely what suited the enemies of the Spanish Government perfectly. The judgment was described in the Press of the Left as iniquitous, and was attributed to political wirepulling.

.   .   .   .

In spite of all this relations between Italy and France failed to improve. Far from it. On July 5 two French mountaineers who had in error crossed the Italian frontier were shot at without a word of warning by Italian frontier guards, and one of them, a young doctor, was gravely wounded; he was actually struck by a bullet after he had been pursued by the Italian guards a good long way into French territory.

Paris-Soir wrote that night:

> We shall not, until further notice, hold the Italian Government directly responsible for the incident. But one had the right to expect that in time of peace one could go for a walk in the mountains without the danger of being murdered.
>
> Perhaps the most serious thing of all is that the incident reveals a state of constant anger and an atmosphere of 'daggers drawn'.

[1] Reuter.

> Life is no longer respected. Instead of crying 'Hullo, who's there?, one now kills a man without further ado. This is a mentality of beasts and hooligans. Apologies are necessary, but to hope for an explanation would be to hope for too much.

The Quai d'Orsay protested. Presumably there was some kind of 'explanation' from the Italian Government; but nothing more was heard of the matter.

At the end of July the Italian Government made another show of bad temper by preventing Italian tourists from going to France. For this, no doubt, there were economic, as well as political reasons. The French Riviera, crowded as never before, was twice as cheap as the deserted Italian resorts— whose principal foreign customers were parsimonious German hikers. Better food and lower prices and the air of liberty in France were a great attraction to Italian holiday-makers. But on August 1 they were stopped from coming. The French Government retaliated as a matter of form.

CHAPTER VIII

ROYAL INTERLUDE

D URING that summer of 1938 there were days, and even
weeks when France seemed to be living in a fool's para-
dise. Or was it that everybody was, more or less, practising a
carpe diem philosophy? True, there were moments when
France was reminded of the danger surrounding her; thus
around July 10 news began to reach Paris of all kinds of war
preparations that were going on in Germany; and Germany's
silence at that time sounded more ominous even than all the
blustering of Mussolini and Ciano. On July 11 the Bourse
was acutely depressed.

But soon afterwards people forgot about it, and continued
their own preparations—for the *Fête Nationale* and for the
British royal visit. This visit was at first fixed for June 28,
but owing to the death of the Countess of Strathmore, the
Queen's mother, the visit was postponed until July 19. And
so the exciting atmosphere of preparation and anticipation
was extended over three extra weeks.

The political importance of the royal visit was obvious:
it was to be a glowing demonstration of the Franco-British
entente, 'the greatest safeguard of world peace'. It was somehow assumed that such a demonstration would even discourage
Germany against doing anything very rash to Czechoslovakia.

Here then is a 'diary' written during *la semaine inoubliable*.

June 13.

The postponement of the visit has caused a few inevitable changes
and alterations, but they are only matters of detail. For instance,
the school children, who have been looking forward to the royal
visit, and 10,000 of whom were to have greeted the King and Queen

in the Champs-Elysées during their drive from the station are now on holiday.   This is all the more regrettable as French children have taken an active interest in the royal visit.   They were taught in school to sing 'God Save the King', and a number of papers organised in June the dispatch of postcards from French children asking the little Princesses to come to Paris too.   Thousands of these invitations were handed to the British Ambassador a few days before the original date of the visit; Sir Eric Phipps thanked the children but said that the little Princesses much regretted to be unable to come 'this time'.   Another paper had organised the collection of school children's sous with which to buy dolls for the royal Princesses.

The postponement has also produced some changes in the street decorations of Paris.   Some of these had suffered from the rain and had to be 'refreshed'—particularly the umbrella-like objects in the Champs-Elysées; others were so strongly criticised that they were removed altogether—for instance, the large tricolour rosettes on the front of the Madeleine.   Looking like targets in a shooting booth, they were really rather absurd, and the red, white and blue draperies of the Madeleine and the Chamber of Deputies, hung not in front of the pillars but behind (which preserved the architectural outline of these buildings), are a great improvement.

But to come to the royal visit itself.   The truth is that nothing like it has ever been seen in Paris before.   Older people recall the splendours of the state visit to Paris of the Tsar and Tsarina in 1896 which marked, as it were, the honeymoon of the Franco-Russian alliance.   But people in authority say that it, as well as the British royal visit of 1914, was mere child's play compared with what Paris is going to see this time.

Paris—or the royal visitors?   For, to be quite truthful, it is not sure that the ordinary people of Paris will see quite as much as they would like to.   No doubt they will see the general setting and the street decorations—some admirable, as in the Place Vendôme or in the Avenue de l'Opéra, and others less so—and they will see the Eiffel Tower fly a Union Jack measuring 1,500 square yards, and they will admire the flood-lighting and other illuminations in Paris at night.   And Thursday the 21st will be a public holiday, and at almost every street corner the people of Paris will resume the dancing and rejoicing of the National Fête a week before.   As for *seeing* the King and Queen, most of them will be lucky if they catch a glimpse of them, during the fraction of a second, between two Garde Mobile helmets.

I mean the 'ordinary' people of Paris, not the people who are lucky enough to live in the Avenue Foch or the Champs-Elysées, or their friends whom they have invited for the Tuesday afternoon, or, lastly, those who can afford to rent a window in the Champs-Elysées for £10 or £15.

The precautions taken by the French authorities for the royal visit are truly totalitarian. Nothing is left to chance. Along the royal routes there will be on each side of the street double cordons of troops, and behind them a third cordon of police facing the crowd, and in addition to these cordons eight miles of wooden barriers— that is, four miles for each side. And in addition to these barriers (though this does not figure in the official programme) there will be in the crowd itself a rich sprinkling of detectives. Twenty thousand police and the whole Paris garrison and thousands of Gardes Mobiles will be on duty during the royal visit. Sixteen thousand officers and N.C.O.s of the Army Reserve will do special duty, which will consist in keeping an eye from inside the houses on the spectators at every window and balcony. To look at the royal procession, even from your own house, you must be able to show a special brown police pass, and your visitors must have blue passes; 250,000 such passes have been delivered. A number of applications have been refused. Compared with the ease with which royalty move about in England it seems over-fussy, but many ordinary Frenchmen to whom I have spoken thought it was 'just as well'. 'Certain foreign countries,' the man in my paper-shop said, 'would be only too glad to play some dirty trick on us and disgrace us in the eyes of the British. We shall not see much of the King and Queen, but it cannot be helped. I am sure they will like our Paris, and that's the main thing.'

The French like royalty, and above all, British royalty; some because they like royalty as such, others because the British Royal Family represents the head of a great democracy. Regarding those numerous Parisians who like royalty 'as such', La Fouchardière was scarcely exaggerating when he wrote the other day:

> 'It has been suggested that the public should be admitted to the royal apartments in the Quai d'Orsay after the royal visit; that ten francs should be charged at the door and the money be devoted to a charitable cause. I am sure it's a good idea, for our Parisians will pay ten francs to see empty royal apartments, even if they will not pay fifty centimes to see the President's apartments, complete with the President inside them.'

Needless to add, the British royal visit is altogether more important than any other royal visits; it has, in the eyes of Paris, the symbolic significance of the 'inseparability' of Britain and France in the Europe of to-day. The union of Britain and France is the best and the only solid hope in Europe to-day that peace may yet be saved. Not that many people in France are uncritical of the way the two great democracies have been 'saving peace' so far. Thus, while it is true that thousands and thousands of British flags are being bought by Parisians with complete spontaneity and without any official coaxing or compulsion, the *Canard Enchaîné* could not resist the temptation of producing a cartoon in which a Frenchman is shown putting up a Union Jack outside his window while another is seen looking at the sky and saying to him, 'The British flag—why you are crazy! Do you want Franco to come and bomb you?'

June 14.

The programme of the royal visit has been worked out in the minutest detail. Just an example. When the King and Queen arrive at the Bois de Boulogne Station on Tuesday afternoon, the President's car, outside the station, will not be facing Paris, but the Bois de Boulogne. Why? Well, because the King must sit to the right of the President; but he must also be the first to enter the car, and if he did that with the car facing Paris M. Lebrun would have to step over the King's legs, which would never do. Thus it is correct that the car should face the Bois de Boulogne and turn before entering Paris. The ceremonial at the station platform has been carefully worked out—literally—with a tape measure, so that everybody shall know exactly where he is to stand when the royal train steams in.

There is one town councillor who nearly tore all his hairs out when he suddenly realised that on his way to Versailles the King would pass through the 'zone'—that is, those little allotments on the outskirts of Paris where the poorest of the poor live in miserable hovels; he suggested that hoardings be put up with 'God Save the King' written on them in order to hide the offensive sight from the King's eyes. But it was decided that this application of the principle of 'Potemkin villages' would be excessive in the case of a democratic monarch.

The 'reception' of the King and Queen will begin even before they have landed in France. When they cross the Channel on their way to Boulogne in the Admiralty yacht *Enchantress* they will be met by an escort comprising many of the finest and newest vessels of the French Navy. Among them will be the battleship *Dunkerque*, four large cruisers of the *Georges Leygues* class, three destroyer divisions, three divisions of torpedo boats, and a squadron of submarines. After a brief reception at Boulogne, the royal train, drawn by a stream-lined engine, decorated with the Royal Arms will leave for Paris. The King and Queen will be accompanied by Lord Halifax and a suite of twenty other persons.

The finishing touches are being put to the royal apartments at the Quai d'Orsay, and one can speak of these at present only from hearsay. The taste with which these apartments have been arranged, the choice of the tapestries and other 'museum pieces' they will contain, the luxury of it all, with the bath of golden mosaic for the King and of silver mosaic for the Queen, both rather in the decorative style of the 1937 Exhibition, have been the talk of the town for some weeks. From these apartments the King and Queen will see, on the one side, the gardens of the Foreign Office and, on the other, the Seine, on whose embankments the last vestiges of the 1937 Exhibition have been carefully cleared away. As a special precaution the King and Queen will not be able to use the lift at the Quai d'Orsay, but will have to walk to their rooms on the first floor.

Soon after arriving at the Quai the King and Queen will drive to the Elysée to pay a visit to M. and Mme Lebrun.   The branches of the trees along the Avenue Marigny, along which they will now drive, have been cut in case they fall on the royal procession!   For no precaution is excessive in M. Sarraut's view.   M. Sarraut is a superstitious man and a week or two ago a tree in the Champs-Elysées was struck by lightning and killed a man.   Most of the members of the royal suite will not stay at the Quai d'Orsay, but at the Hotel Crillon, which is now connected with special telephone lines with the royal apartments.   Lord Halifax will stay at the Embassy.

June 15.

There is no end of talk in Paris to-day about the state banquet on Thursday in the famous Mirror Hall in the Palace of Versailles, the very hall where the Peace Treaty was signed nineteen years ago. What details and 'indiscretions' has one not already heard about this banquet!   The waiters will wear eighteenth-century dress— red coats and blue kneebreeches and powdered wigs; and M. Chautemps, the Vice-Premier, has taken a personal interest in the arrangements.   The waiters, he said, must not be too young, for they are apt to be inexperienced; nor too old, for they are apt to have the wrong waistline for such costumes; so 'slim and thirty' seems to be the principle on which they have been selected.   Ten chefs, with the most famous French chef-in-chief (if one may say so), are in charge of the kitchens; and some of the wines will be 'rarer than one can find in any Paris restaurant'.   The magnums of champagne will be of the same age as the King, and there will be a special Burgundy 'vintaged' in the year of the Queen's birth.   During the banquet the orchestra will play music by Lulli and Rameau, and after a short rest in their respective suites of rooms, specially arranged for the occasion but strictly after the model of the French kings and queens, King George and Queen Elizabeth will spend the afternoon in the Park of Versailles, where, to the music of Gluck, the ballet of the Paris Opéra will dance to them in the open air.

And there will be more dancing and singing and acting after the dinner that night, which M. Bonnet, the Foreign Minister, will give in honour of the King and Queen at the Quai d'Orsay.   Yvonne Printemps will be there, and Mlle Ozera, and M. Jouvet, the actor, and the little dancers of the Opéra.

On Friday, the King and Queen will take leave of Paris and travel to Villers-Bretonneux, where the King will unveil the war memorial to the Australians who fell in the War.   And then back home, without returning to Paris.

Their visit will give rise to innumerable activities *à propos* of the royal visit.   All the French wireless programmes will be crowded with accounts of the royal visit, and talks about English literature and the Entente Cordiale, and British art, and the cultural relations between France and England throughout the centuries, and broadcasts of Shakespeare; and I have just received the copy of a seven-page *Ode to England* to be broadcast on the first day of the royal visit.   A film called *Edward VII* will be shown.

Manufacturers of every variety of 'souvenirs' and handkerchiefs and handbags and what not are exercising their ingenuity in an effort to adapt the Union Jack and the tricolour to their wares to the best advantage.   The Paris shop windows are full of these novelties, while others are crowded with photographs of the King and Queen —and the Duke of Windsor.   And the French Post Office is bringing out a special 1.75 stamp with the Houses of Parliament on one side and the Arc de Triomphe on the other, and between the two, the hands across the Channel.

July 17.

Large crowds assembled in the Champs-Elysées this afternoon to see the new decorations—the golden garlands suspended from the trees and the new square columns which have been erected in the Place de l'Etoile in addition to the pyramid-like structures decorated with French and British flags which have been there for some time already.   The pyramids of mirrors in the Rond-Point are being scrubbed and polished and the display of British flags is multiplying at a fantastic speed.

Almost every shop window—even in parts of Paris remote from the actual scenes of the royal visit—is decorated with British flags and with portraits of the King and Queen; even in a chiropodist's window in the Boulevard Haussmann the plaster models of corns and bunions are displayed against a Union Jack back-ground; flags are flying from numerous windows, even in the working-class districts.   Every bus is decorated with French and British flags as well as every public building—even the entrance of the Santé Prison is now surmounted by a luxurious bouquet of Union Jacks.

Periscopes, with the help of which people will look at the royal procession over the heads of the police, are being sold by the thousand, and outside cafés street musicians are playing 'God Save the King' and 'Rule Britannia'.   New police precautions have been announced.   The Foreign Office will be completely isolated to strangers during the royal stay there, and the invitations to M. Bonnet's reception on Tuesday have been delivered by hand at the guests' houses lest they fall into the wrong hands.

Among the numerous presents to be made to the royal visitors there will be two dolls, said to be the most beautiful dolls in the world, each with a trousseau of forty-seven dresses.   These are to be given to Princess Elizabeth and Princess Margaret.

Another present is a collection of valuable pieces of Lyons silk, which will be presented personally to the Queen on behalf of the French silk manufacturers by M. Herriot, the Mayor of Lyons and

President of the Chamber of Deputies. The silks, as M. Herriot's letter to the Queen will say, have been specially woven for her.

July 18.

Paris is in a state of feverish excitement. The main streets to-day look as though the King and Queen had already arrived. Dense crowds can be seen in all parts of Paris associated in any way with the royal visit.

Most impressive of all perhaps is the Boulevard des Capucines, running from the Madeleine to the Opéra, with what looks almost like a red, white, and blue tunnel composed of canopies with their streamers and festoons spanning across the street—a 'tunnel' through which the King and Queen will drive to the Opéra on Wednesday night.

Thousands of people have come from the country and from the towns of France into Paris. Many of them can be easily identified by their quaintly old-fashioned clothes, never seen in Paris.

Almost as numerous are the visitors from England, who have greatly increased the proportion of grey flannel trousers in the Paris streets. The traffic on the boulevards and in the Champs-Elysées is denser than it ever seems to have been, and between the Madeleine and the Opéra the pedestrian moves faster than the motorist.

Great activity is to be seen in the shops, which are crowded with every variety of souvenir, and there was to-day a last-minute rush on grey and black top-hats and other equipment for the Bagatelle garden party and other receptions.

The newsboys were doing a booming trade in special editions of *Paris-Soir* with large splashes of red and blue on its front and back pages, and including such topical contributions as the actual music of 'God Save the King' with the English text accompanied by a French phonetic rendering of the words: 'Godd Saive aour Grechieuss Kinng,' and an article which claims that 'God Save the King' was composed by Lully in honour of Louis XIV.

The paper also contains articles by the inevitable M. Maurois and other celebrities, and details about life in Buckingham Palace, ('What does the King do when he wants a letter typed?') etc., and even fuller details of all that the King and Queen will eat (or at least be offered to eat) at the three great banquets during their stay in France.

The British Embassy, the Quai d'Orsay, the Elysée Palace, the Town Hall, and many other places are in a state of feverish activity. The Embassy, for instance, was busy handing out to Pressmen large envelopes full of documents which they will require during the royal visit—a whole collection of Press cards in different colours for the different occasions and dazzling red and blue leather armlets smelling to high heaven of some kind of varnish. Every journalist must wear one while on his job, even at the risk of being mistaken for a shoeblack or a railway porter.

A question debated among journalists was whether these armlets were compulsory at the garden party and how they would 'go' with the compulsory top hat and morning coat.   Fortunately, it seems that on these occasions the armlets may be hidden away.

The Faubourg St. Honoré is full of splashes of red and blue; so are many of the other streets around the Embassy, and if until recently the average Parisian was watching all these preparations with a touch of scepticism, ready at the least provocation to dismiss the decorations as 'ridiculous', Paris has now been seized by a sort of Coronation fever, and all the decorations—good, bad, and in-different—are accepted as part of the gay and festive atmosphere that has suddenly pervaded Paris in the last few days.

July 19.

And so the great day has come.   Punctually at ten minutes to five the royal train, drawn by its blue and gold stream-lined engine and with the Union Jack painted on its sides, steamed into the Bois de Boulogne station.

It is hard to believe that anything during the whole royal visit can be still more finely arranged than was the first contact with Paris of King George and Queen Elizabeth.   The small, almost derelict, Bois de Boulogne station had been transformed into a beautiful thing.   The platform, with a white canopy over it, was covered with a dark red carpet, and the walls, draped in white, were decorated with large bunches of flags and the golden emblems of France.   But to the station had been added a large hall the walls of which were hung with Gobelins tapestries, and the wide door under the red velvet draperies looked on to the large golden, almost Egyptian-like statue of France by Antoine Bourdelle.

By three o'clock in the afternoon Paris was ready to receive the King and Queen.   Hundreds of thousands of people were travelling in tightly packed carriages on the métro to the Champs-Elysées, the Etoile, and the Avenue Foch; in these streets police and guards were forming their cordons both in front and behind the three and a half miles of wooden barriers.

And at the station itself there was great activity.   Outside it troops were marching past, police cordons were being put up, and the guard of honour, consisting of several hundred Marine Fusiliers and naval cadets—the latter carrying halberds—were doing their final rehearsal, while women cleaners were giving a last brush to the carpets.   At the royal exit, under the cylindrical canopy sur-mounted by the Royal Arms, police inspectors were asking new arrivals not to walk on the carpet but 'just a little to the side'.   The hall and the passage to the platform were also finely decorated with rows of laurel trees in casks surrounded by pink and lilac hydrangeas.

Shortly after four o'clock the personalities began to assemble on the platform.   English civilians were wearing morning-coats and top-hats, and French civilians—a rather strange sight to unaccustomed English eyes—full evening dress.   Among the first to arrive was M. Daladier, the Premier.   He walked up and down the platform talking to M. Corbin, in his Ambassadorial uniform.

In the houses in the Boulevard Flandrin, looking straight on to the platform, people were leaning in bunches over the window-sills. Among them were many officers—these were there to keep an eye on the inhabitants of the houses.

At twenty to five cheering was heard from outside the station— it marked the arrival of the President of the Republic and Mme Lebrun.   The President was in evening dress with a wide red ribbon of the Legion of Honour across his chest; Mme Lebrun was wearing a summer dress of black and white trimmed with green and a pretty white and green hat to match.

In the next few minutes the platform was crowded.   Here were M. Herriot and M. Jeanneney, the presidents of the Chamber and of the Senate, and then there arrived in a crowd nearly all the members of the Government and members of the British Embassy in their full-dress Diplomatic, Army, Navy, and Air Force uni-forms.

Suddenly from out of the tunnel the engine with the French colours painted on its streamlined front emerged, and the train moved slowly along the platform and then stopped.   The door of the fourth carriage opened and the King and Queen stepped out. The King, wearing admiral's uniform, looked remarkably fit after his recent illness.   He warmly shook hands with President Lebrun and with Mme Lebrun.   M. Lebrun kissed the Queen's hand, and Mme Lebrun curtsied to her.   The President then presented to the King and Queen M. Herriot and M. Jeanneney and the members of the Government.

The Queen, who was wearing a pale cream two-piece costume trimmed with silver-fox fur and a hat to match turned up in front and trimmed with sprays of grey feathers, looked charming and slightly flushed with excitement.

After the presentation the Queen took M. Lebrun's arm and Mme Lebrun the King's, and they moved slowly up the steps towards the Gobelins Hall.   Here the King reviewed the guard of honour, and the staff of the British Embassy and other personalities were presented to him and to the Queen.

What an excellent first contact with Paris!   French art—old and new.   The fine tapestries had by this time been delicately floodlit, and outside, Bourdelle's statue, standing on its high white pedestal and decorated with tricoloured streamers, looked dazzlingly bright when looked at from the dark hall.   Moreover, after a dull morning and afternoon the sun had suddenly come out.   At the foot of the statue large crowds of school children, many in pretty pale blue frocks and white bonnets, were waving British flags, and as the King and Queen came out into the open from the Gobelins Hall the military band struck up 'God Save the King'.   At that moment the

Union Jack was hoisted up the high mast beside Bourdelle's statue, and when a minute later the band struck up the 'Marseillaise' 10,000 white pigeons concealed behind the statue were suddenly released, and rising in a wonderful fan-like movement disappeared into the trees of the Bois de Boulogne.

The King and Queen were not only delighted; they were visibly moved by the charm and beauty of this first reception that Paris had given them.

The King and President Lebrun then boarded one of the two royal cars and the Queen and Mme Lebrun accompanied by Lord Cavan the other. The procession was headed by a detachment of mounted Republican Guards, with their Brass helmets and red plumes. Two generals on horseback and a party of motor-cyclists escorted the two royal cars. They were followed by a whole cavalcade of more Republican Guards and of Moorish horsemen, with their white cloaks waving in the wind. Then the other official cars followed.

And then on this sunny afternoon the royal cavalcade sped down the Avenue Foch and past the Etoile and down the Champs-Elysées. What a reception Paris gave them! The enthusiasm of the several hundred thousand people who must have been there to see the King and Queen drive past was enormous—and spontaneous. Over the three and a half miles of the royal route like a large ocean wave the cry of '*Vive le Roi!*' sped down Paris. Paris was welcoming the King and Queen and the head of the great sister democracy. Along the route salutes were fired and bands played 'God Save the King' and the 'Marseillaise'.

By half-past five the great entry into Paris was over. Accompanied by M. Lebrun the King and Queen had arrived at the Quai d'Orsay, where they were received by M. Bonnet and were shown into their beautiful rooms on the first floor. The people in the streets slowly dispersed feeling well rewarded for their long wait and commenting on the brilliance of the ceremony, on the smart looks of the King and the charming manner of Queen Elizabeth. And everybody said what a pity it was that the little Princesses had not come. 'They would have enjoyed it so much.'

The enthusiasm is general and is not confined to the 'West End' by any means. A large part of the public in the Champs-Elysées had come from the working-class districts. M. Blum in the *Populaire* warmly welcomed to-day the head of 'British democracy,' and the Communist *Humanité* was altogether enthusiastic about the King and Queen.

The King and Queen had only a short rest after they arrived in their apartments in the Quai d'Orsay this afternoon, as shortly afterwards they returned the visit by calling on the President at the Elysée Palace. It was here that the President conferred upon the Queen the Grand Cross of the Legion of Honour, while the King conferred on President Lebrun the G.C.B. The President also received the collar of the G.C.B., which, according to tradition, is to be returned by his heirs.

The King and Queen then returned to the Quai d'Orsay, but only to change, and at eight o'clock they were back at the Elysée for the great state banquet.

The King was wearing the uniform of a Marshal of the Royal Air Force. The Queen wore a white dress glittering with diamanté, low at the neck with short sleeves and a hooped skirt. Impressive against the glittering white was the scarlet ribbon of the Legion of Honour. The Queen wore diamond drop earrings and her tiara of Maltese crosses and fleur-de-lys, with the Koh-i-noor in the centre. She also wore the Garter in diamonds on her left sleeve and a magnificent corsage ornament.

There were 270 guests at the banquet, and at the top table M. Lebrun and the King sat together, with the Queen on M. Lebrun's left and Mme Lebrun on the King's right.

The tables were decorated with candelabra with live candles and wicker-work baskets arranged like rose trees in full bloom. Towards the end of the banquet the King and M. Lebrun exchanged toasts; the King, who spoke in French (an attention that was greatly appreciated), in a slow but firm and clear voice, said:

'I rise with pleasure and gratitude to reply to the very cordial and moving words of welcome which you have addressed to the Queen and myself. We are no strangers to your beautiful city. It is a source of great satisfaction to us that our first visit abroad since the beginning of our reign should be to Paris, the noble capital of this friendly country to which Great Britain is united by so many common memories and sacrifices.

'The Queen and I have been deeply touched by the welcome which you have given to us to-day. In spite of the strip of sea which separates us, our two countries have seen their destinies inevitably drawn together with the passage of the centuries, and it would now be impossible to recall a period in which our relations were more intimate.

'In the past the great men of both our countries have been somewhat slow at times to appreciate each other's qualities. This is no longer the case to-day. A long and close collaboration has succeeded in proving that we are inspired by the same ideal. Our peoples have the same attachment to the democratic principles which are best suited to their natural genius, and we have the same belief in the benefits of individual liberty. We are proud of this political faith which we share with other great nations, but we fully realise that it carries with it heavy responsibilities, and in the period in which we live it demands from us all to a high degree the noble qualities of courage, wisdom, and determination.

'At the same time, as you, M. le Président, have said, there is nothing exclusive in the understanding between us; our friendship is directed against no other Power.   On the contrary, it is the ardent desire of our Governments to find, by means of international agreements, a solution of those political problems which threaten the peace of the world, and of those economic difficulties which restrict human well-being.   The action of our Governments is thus directed towards a common goal— that of assuring the happiness of the peoples of the world by means of true co-operation. . . .'

After the banquet there was an artistic soirée to which many other guests were invited.

It was a brilliant affair, even though many thought the programme a trifle long.   The King and the Queen, sitting in the front row, seemed, however, to be enjoying it.   The programme consisted of a sketch by Sacha Guitry, with the famous actor in the part of Louis XIV; five songs sung by Mme Valerin, of the Opéra, with M. Hahn, the well-known composer, at the piano; and a one-act play by Musset, played by actors of the Comédie Française.

Outside, the lovely gardens of the Elysée Palace were floodlit. The Place de la Concorde and the Quais were crowded with people until the early hours of the morning.   They had come to see the fireworks from the Eiffel Tower; and in the Boulevard, teeming with people, worse traffic jams occurred than any seen even during the rush hours on ordinary days, and continued until two in the morning.   Paris was enjoying itself.

July 20.

Glorious summer weather marked the second day of the royal visit in Paris.   It has been a busy day for the King and Queen—so busy that many have been wondering whether the programme for to-day had not been rather overcrowded.   Not that their good humour ever abandoned either the King or Queen, who were clearly enjoying it all, even though they must certainly have felt tired by the end of the day.   During the day the Queen wore four different dresses.

Although the soirée at the Elysée last night went on until well after midnight, the King and Queen were up by eight o'clock this morning, and the King, again wearing admiral's uniform and accompanied by the Duke of Beaufort and Lord Birdwood, the military, naval, and air attachés of the Embassy, and others, began the day with a pilgrimage to the tomb of the Unknown Soldier under the Arc de Triomphe.   On his arrival the military bands played 'God Save the King' and the 'Marseillaise'.   He was received here by M. Champetier de Ribes, the Minister of Pensions, who presented to him General Gamelin, Vice-Admiral Darlan, and General Vuillemin, the heads of the General Staffs of the Army, Navy, and Air Force.

Delegations from French ex-servicemen's associations, with their banners, and of the Paris branch of the British Legion were assembled round the arch.   The wreath of Flanders poppies the King laid on the tomb was inscribed 'From King George VI and Queen Elizabeth.' During the time when the King was laying the wreath on the tomb the people around the arch, who until then had been loudly cheering, fell into complete silence. It was an impressive moment. Going round the arch, the King then shook hands with the heads of all the delegations, and after signing the Golden Book he returned by car to the Quai d'Orsay.

Shortly afterwards President Lebrun and Mme Lebrun arrived there. And now began one of the most pleasant episodes of the royal visit—the sail down the Seine to the Paris Town Hall, past the Louvre and the Ile de la Cité and Notre-Dame. In this glorious summer weather Paris was looking its best.

A landing stage, decorated with flags, had been built outside the Foreign Office, and after reviewing the guard of honour composed of French marines the royal party sailed down the Seine in a little white launch manned with bluejackets, some of them carrying halberds. No precaution being excessive, it is said that shortly before the royal sail everybody on board was searched. The launch, white and streamlined and decorated with golden ornaments and with a cabin of mica sides in front, from which the King and Queen could get a perfect view, was a pretty sight as it sailed down the Seine escorted by several blue motor-boats belonging to the French Atlantic Fleet. The people on the banks were cheering loudly.

At the Pont Neuf a delightful and amusing sight awaited the King and Queen. Here was a touch of fairy-tale fantasy.

Imagine a French garden—say a fragment of the park of Versailles— with clipped trees and shrubs half-submerged under water, and among these trees and shrubs every kind of sea monster spouting water;—two creatures with interminably long giraffe-like necks, and looking like pictures of the Loch Ness Monster, and around them other strange beasts—a seven-headed hydra and animals that looked half fish and half frog, and others that were half fish and half snail with golden wings and golden fins, and all spouting water.

Later in the day I walked across the same Pont des Arts from which thousands of pictures have been painted by good, bad, and indifferent artists of the famous view of the Pont Neuf and the towers of Notre-Dame beyond; the artists were now producing the same familiar picture, but this time with all the spouting monsters as part of it. An old artist in a velvet cap seemed to be having a great struggle with the correct shape of the 'Loch Ness Monster's' ears.

The greater part of the Place de l'Hôtel de Ville, the scene of so many historical events of the past, had been cordoned off by ten o'clock, but behind the barriers large crowds had gathered to see the King and Queen arrive. Here were the proletariat of Paris—and they cheered as spontaneously as anyone in the West End.

The reception in the Town Hall was brilliant and impressive, though inevitably a trifle commonplace—at least as far as the public ceremony went. The Grande Salle des Fêtes, where the King and

Queen were received, is not one of the architectural successes of Paris. Its windows look onto a dark street, and the heavy candelabra were all ablaze even on this sunny morning. The ceiling is gilded and painted in the gaudy and over-ornate style of 1880 or so. The rooms leading up to the Grande Salle were lined with a guard of honour consisting of municipal guards with their red plumes and Republican Guards with their brass helmets and sabres drawn.

Before the King and Queen arrived the hall was crowded with two thousand people, including the representatives of almost every branch of Paris activity. There were also present a large number of deputies and senators and nearly all the town councillors. Among those on the platform was the Negro deputy for Guadeloupe.

The appearance of the King and Queen accompanied by President and Mme Lebrun was greeted with loud cheering. The King, wearing the admiral's uniform, was looking remarkably young. The Queen was again dressed in white with a double string of pearls. They were welcomed by M. Prévôt du Launay, the President of the Paris Town Council (roughly the equivalent of the Lord Mayor), and M. Villey, the Prefect of the Seine.

After their speeches of welcome the King replied slowly, but in good French:

'It was with deep feeling that I crossed the threshold of this Paris Hôtel de Ville, which calls forth for me so many memories of our common past. My grandfather came here in 1903 and helped to lay the foundations of the entente between France and Great Britain. My father came here in April 1914 to confirm this entente, which soon after received its baptism of fire. To-day I in my turn have come, and I find that our entente has lost nothing of its strength or its vitality.

'I ask you, gentlemen, to tell the City of Paris on our behalf how much the Queen and I have been moved by your welcome. We appreciate enormously the grace and beauty of our reception, the friendly character of which has specially touched us. Therefore, gentlemen, I express to you all my warm and grateful thanks.'

After the King's speech the wives of town councillors and other persons were presented to the King and Queen. After that the King and Queen were taken into a more private room of the Town Hall, and it was here that they were presented with several gifts by the city of Paris—a gold cigarette case which greatly pleased the King, for he promised always to use it; a set of Lalique glass for the Queen; and several presents for the little Princesses—including a number of finely illustrated books for Princess Elizabeth and a doll's flower-shop for Princess Margaret.

The King and Queen then returned to their launch, and on the Seine they were saluted by a crowd of French boys and girls in blue athletic costumes who were standing in their canoes and waving their paddles in a rhythmic movement.

After their visit to the Paris town councillors the King and Queen arrived at the Embassy for lunch shortly before one o'clock. The King had changed into a morning coat. It was an all-British luncheon, and before it, in the Embassy gardens, where the band of the Grenadier Guards played 'God Save the King' the King and Queen 'reviewed' the 200 men of the Paris branch of the British Legion. On the veranda of the Embassy they then received the representatives of the British organisations in Paris and the Dominion offices and consulates, as well as the clerical staff of the Embassy.

All this took a long time, and the visit to the British Exhibition at the Louvre was an inevitably short one, for the garden party at Bagatelle had been fixed for four o'clock. The rural setting of the little palace at Bagatelle, on the fringe of the Bois de Boulogne, is one of the loveliest spots in the neighbourhood of Paris. The famous Bagatelle rose gardens were no longer in bloom, but the lawns and trees in their different shades of green looked beautifully fresh in the sun. Bright touches of colour were added by the large sprays of red and salmon-pink gladioli on the open-air buffets.

The centre of the garden party was on the slopes of a small hillock at the foot of which there was a pond grown over with water-lilies. Across this pond a sort of pontoon had been built. This was the 'stage'. Heralded by music from an orchestra on the other side of the pond, the King and Queen arrived soon after four o'clock. Like most of the men present, the King was wearing a morning coat and a grey top-hat, and the Queen a white crinoline dress and a large picture-hat trimmed with ospreys. In this open-air setting, with the soothing landscape of the Ile de France on all sides, the dancing —or rather the rhythmical movements—that a bevy of young girls in pale-blue tunics were performing on the bridge of the pond to the soft music of Debussy was particularly lovely.

In a different way, but equally pleasant, was a sort of 'fashion show' organised by Mme Lanvin, that also took place on the bridge with gentle music coming from behind the trees. And there was more dancing and music later.

As the streets along which the King and Queen travelled were cleared of traffic it took a long time for ordinary people to return from Bagatelle, for drivers were obliged to devise all kinds of roundabout ways of entering into Paris, and in many places there were some bewildering traffic jams.

It was not until six o'clock that the King and Queen returned to the Quai d'Orsay, only to change again (the King into full uniform) and to drive to the banquet they were giving in honour of M. and Mme Lebrun at the British Embassy. About sixty guests were invited. The Embassy produced for the occasion the famous service of gold plates and the golden candelabra and table urn which Napoleon had given as a wedding present to his sister Pauline Borghese, the owner of the present Embassy until it was bought for the British Government by the Duke of Wellington about 120 years ago.

And at night there was the gala at the Grand Opéra with
'Salammbô' on the programme.

Surrounded by cavalry, the King and Queen arrived at ten
o'clock. When they entered the whole audience stood up and
turned towards them, and there were prolonged shouts of '*Vive le Roi,
Vive la Reine!*'

July 21.

This morning for the first time since their arrival the King and
Queen had separate engagements. The Queen visited the Hert-
ford British Hospital, in the suburb of Levallois and opened a new
ward called the 'Coronation Ward'. The hospital has, during its
long history, held an important place in the life of the British colony
of Paris, a colony which in recent years has fluctuated between
10,000 and 30,000 and which, in spite of the popular French
conception of the invariably rich Englishman—at least when he is
abroad—has known much poverty and hardship.

In the meantime the King had left by train for Versailles to
attend the great military review.

The royal train carrying the King, the President, Lord Halifax,
members of the French Government, and other personalities left
the Gare des Invalides after the usual ceremonial at 10.40 and
arrived at Versailles twenty-five minutes later. In eight cars the
party then travelled to the official stand near the Town Hall in the
wide Avenue de Paris which runs towards the enormous Place des
Armes in front of the Palace of Versailles.

The town of Versailles was gaily decorated, and there were large
crowds estimated at 100,000 along the pavements of the Avenue de
Paris and of the street along which the royal procession, headed by
a party of Algerian Spahis, travelled from the station. At the
corner of the two streets there were several hundred children who
cheered and waved British flags as the King passed.

The King, wearing the 'Field Marshal's khaki uniform, took his
seat in the grandstand decorated with evergreens and gladioli. By
his side were the President of the Republic; the 82-year-old Marshal
Pétain of Verdun fame, looking, with his almost youthful complexion
and white moustache, remarkably fit for his age; General Gamelin,
Admiral Darlan, and General Vuillemin (all three newly-created
Knights Grand Cross of the Royal Victorian Order), and other
generals and admirals. Among the civilians were M. Daladier,
M. Chautemps, M. Herriot, M. Jeanneney, and M. Henri Haye, the
Mayor of Versailles, who had come in the King's car from the station.

In spite of the dull weather the review, which lasted no less than
seventy minutes, was a brilliant affair, and not only brilliant but
strikingly competent in every detail. Salutes were fired, and after
a bugle-call, battalion after battalion marched or rode past in perfect
step to the sound of military music. First came several cavalry
battalions; then, in their stiff, black, gold-embroidered uniforms and
with their swords drawn came the studious-looking cadets of the

Polytechnique, many of them with spectacles on their noses; these were closely followed by the St. Cyriens with their picturesque tricolour plumes and carrying bayonets. Next came the sprightly Chasseurs Alpins—first a battalion wearing field helmets and then other battalions wearing the familiar large blue beret and carrying with their rifles either alpenstocks or pairs of skis.

And then in the distance, far down the Avenue de Paris, one saw from the royal stand a whole forest of bayonets approaching. Less colourful than the rest, no doubt, these thousands and thousands of 'ordinary' French infantry dressed in khaki were deeply impressive as they marched in brisk and perfect step past the King. There were some twenty to twenty-five thousand of them, a fraction of France's conscript army—the successors of the *poilus* of Verdun, the flesh and blood of the people of France. Thousands and more thousands marched past—each man with his own mind and his own personality, but perfectly disciplined when performing his soldier's duty.

The *poilus* were followed by another ten minutes of 'pageantry'. Zouaves wearing tall red fezzes rode past, then some black Senegalese warriors, their band beating drums and twirling trumpets and trombones in the air; Algerian Fusiliers in broad blue plus-four-like breeches and blue tunics with splashes of yellow; and several battalions of the Algerian and Moroccan Spahis in their white fluttering cloaks.

All this looked romantic; what followed was less so. It was the motorised and mechanised units, ordinary armoured cars, and armoured cars on caterpillar wheels drawing 75-m.m. field guns; then some specimens of long anti-aircraft guns followed by larger 6-inch guns, their carriages inscribed with the useful motto: 'A well-kept gun is worth two.'

Next came a whole swarm of motor-cycles with armoured side-cars carrying automatic rifles, and more armoured cars carrying the famous Hotchkiss machine-gun which can fire some 500 rounds a minute.

The review closed with an overwhelming display of tanks—whole crowds of small ones looking like monstrous little brothers of the Baby Austin and running almost as fast; then larger and larger and larger tanks, the largest of all being the 50-ton tanks which, like battleships, are not numbered but known by their names—mostly names of French towns and provinces. The largest of all the French tanks—those weighing 80 tons—were not shown as they would have damaged the street.

It was a dull morning and the air display was postponed until the afternoon. It was then that the King watched the air display from the gardens of Versailles. Several hundred aeroplanes in group formation, and mostly flying very low, droned over the city of the French kings. Here were the Dewoitine bombers and the beautiful (for in spite of grim associations they were beautiful, Bloch bombers, looking like so many giant dragonflies, and most remarkable of all, the new Morane pursuit planes, flying at over 360 miles an hour. The Morane planes are among the first serially produced planes, and the French Government is making every effort to increase their serial production.

The royal visit to the Opéra last night is still the talk of Paris, and will no doubt continue to be so for some time. With perhaps a slight touch of snobbishness, one of to-day's papers says that 'for once' the public was brilliant even in the gallery, for with only two thousand seats' available 'even many distinguished members of Parliament' were only too glad to get a seat in the 'gods'.

'Dazzling' and 'radiant' are the adjectives used to describe the appearance of the King and Queen in the President's box, which was decorated with bunches of hydrangeas, and fashion specialists are wondering whether the crinoline—a number of which were already seen at the Elysée Palace on Tuesday night—will become the keynote of this year's women's fashions as a result of the Queen's visit to Paris.

If those who were inside the theatre are more than delighted with all they saw and heard, the many thousands of people who were behind the police cordons in the Place de l'Opéra and who clamoured for the King and Queen for hours on end are less pleased; they are disappointed that the King and Queen should not have appeared on the balcony during the interval, and rightly or wrongly, they are blaming M. Sarraut, the Minister of the Interior, for being 'overfussy'.

But such occasional grumbling against the Government has not detracted from the genuine enthusiasm that has been aroused in all French quarters by the royal visit. Everybody feels that it consecrates, as it were, the entente between the two countries which has become more and more inevitable, both for their own sakes and for the sake of European peace generally. Moreover, in spite of the great difficulty that the ordinary Parisian has had in seeing the King and Queen, he has been genuinely touched by many things they have said and done, not least by the King's generous gift of 100,000 francs for the poor of Paris.

The King and Queen, with M. Lebrun, spent the whole afternoon to-day in the palace grounds at Versailles. The famous fountains were playing in the park, and the banquet in the Mirror Hall was the most elaborate masterpiece of gastronomical art. Three hundred guests were present. The waiters, all carefully selected for their competence and good figures, wore eighteenth-century dress and periwigs, and the menu was both delicate and gargantuan—if one may use the two adjectives together.

The Army review, which occupied the morning, being over, the King and Queen were taken for a time away from unpleasant realities and given for a few hours the illusion of living in a happier world, a world of art and music and beautiful things. A short concert of old French chamber music was given in the chapel of the Palace, and later the King and Queen walked about the gardens of Versailles and attended a carefully reconstructed *fête-champêtre*, complete with shepherds and shepherdesses dancing on the lawns around Apollo's bower, and listened to a nymph—in reality a well-known actress—recite to them Molière's *Compliment au Roi*.

Soon after five o'clock the King and Queen left Versailles for Paris, and on this last night of their visit M. Bonnet, the Foreign Minister, gave a banquet in their honour at the French Foreign Office, followed by a large reception.

July 21 (Midnight).

There was only one flaw in the otherwise perfect atmosphere of the royal visit, and that was the absence of any really direct contact between the King and Queen and the ordinary people of Paris. And this flaw was corrected on their own initiative by the King and Queen when, shortly before midnight, they appeared on the floodlit balcony of their apartments of the Quai d'Orsay and waved to the thousands of people who had been waiting all evening outside and calling for the King and Queen. The enthusiasm of the crowd was such that several people who witnessed the scene said they had never seen anything like it in Paris since Armistice Day in 1918.

The reception at the Quai d'Orsay to-night, with its lovely floodlit gardens thrown open to the guests, was particularly successful. So also was the musical programme, which included Yvonne Printemps and Maurice Chevalier.

Many of the guests commented on the conversation in the gardens between Lord Halifax and M. Flandin, the advocate of the policy of retreat, all the more so as the talk continued for well over half an hour.

It is announced that President Lebrun will visit London next year.

It was the personal wish of the King and Queen that the news of the President's acceptance issued while they are still in France.

In the morning the King and Queen leave for Villers-Bretonneux, on the Somme, where the King will unveil the Australian war memorial. They will return to England later in the day, arriving in London at 9.15.

Villers-Bretonneux, July 22.

King George did for Australia to-day what his brother, King Edward VIII did for Canada almost exactly two years ago. It was on July 26, 1936, that King Edward unveiled the Canadian war memorial at Vimy Ridge. To-day, not very many miles away from Vimy, King George unveiled the memorial of Villers-Bretonneux standing on the hill behind the war cemetery with its two thousand graves. Many of the simple white tombstones are nameless, and say only: 'A soldier of the Great War (an Australian regiment),' and below it: 'Known unto God.'

At the end of this cemetery is an open grass lawn, and here the new memorial has been built with its tower overlooking the wide northern plain of France. Around the memorial rich fields of corn stretch over many miles; it is hard to imagine that this country was once the scene of some of the deadliest fighting in the War. Villers-Bretonneux, a village entirely rebuilt since the War, is a 'godchild' of Melbourne, and the school and other buildings have been built with money mostly collected by Australian school children.

The memorial, forming the three sides of a quadrangle, has in the centre a tower 105 feet high. It is simple in design, and the two pavilions on either side, as well as the small colonnade at the top of the tower, strike a classical note. The three walls connecting the tower with the pavilions are inscribed in large lettering with the names of the principal military operations on the western front where Australians fought—the Somme, Albert, Pozières, Menin Gate, Passchendale—and below in smaller lettering, the 10,892 names of Australians who died in the War but have no known grave—that is, nearly one in four of all the Australian dead. It is to all the Australian dead, but more particularly to these, that the Villers-Bretonneux memorial is dedicated.

The King and Queen, who left Paris at 10.30 this morning, arrived at Villers-Bretonneux by train shortly after one o'clock. Since the Australian memorial stands on 'British soil', it was for the King to receive President Lebrun, who arrived a few minutes later accompanied by several Cabinet Ministers and other personalities. With the King and Queen were Lord Halifax and members of the British Embassy in Paris, while Mr. Hore-Belisha, Mr. Stanley Bruce (the Australian High Commissioner), and Sir Earle Page (the Deputy Premier of Australia) had arrived from London at Villers-Bretonneux some time earlier.

The King, wearing a morning coat, and the Queen, dressed in white, walked through the cemetery beautifully decorated with flowers and then inspected the guard of honour, consisting of some 250 Australian ex-servicemen wearing their war medals.

The lower part of the memorial, with its small iron gate, was concealed under a large blue Union Jack with the two white stars—the flag of Australia. To the left was a band of Grenadier Guards in their bearskins and red uniforms and to the right a French military band, and behind both of these rows of French cavalry in khaki.

The unveiling ceremony was much less elaborate and generally on a smaller scale than the ceremony at Vimy Ridge two years ago.

After Sir Earle Page (the Deputy Prime Minister of Australia) had invited the King to unveil the memorial, the King spoke. After three days in Paris it must have been a relief to him to speak publicly again in English, and he spoke with great fluency and ease.

In concluding the speech, the King pressed a button, a bell rang, and at the same moment the blue flag covering the lower part of the tower of the monument dropped softly to the ground. President Lebrun then spoke and after him Sir Earle Page. Sir Earle Page's

speech was followed by a dedication service conducted by the Rev.
George Green, a former chaplain with the Australian forces. He
prayed for Australia and for all ex-servicemen. The 'Last Post'
was sounded by the Grenadier Guards, there was a minute's silence,
and a prayer was then said by Mgr. Martin, the Bishop of Amiens.

President Lebrun in his speech said;

'Our nations still stand shoulder to shoulder for the maintenance of the ideals for which so many of our people laid down
their lives.'

President Lebrun, who made a reference to the King's own
experience 'amidst the shot and shell and the din of battle,' said that
the affirmation of friendship between Great Britain and France
retained in the present troubled times actuality and force.

After the benediction a hymn was sung, and then the military
bands played the 'Marseillaise' and 'God Save the King'. A wreath
of Flanders poppies was then laid on the memorial by the King and
Queen and another wreath by the President of the Republic. While
the King and Queen slowly moved down the steps of the memorial
and down the cemetery the band played 'Land of Hope and Glory'.

A few minutes later the King and Queen left by car for Villers-
Bretonneux Station, where they took the train for Calais.

It may seem a trivial detail when one writes about it, but it was
an inescapable and most unpleasant detail to those who attended the
ceremony. For some unknown reason—perhaps it was the presence
of so many cavalry horses or it may have been something else—the
whole neighbourhood of the war memorial was swarming with
clouds of tiny insects not much larger than specks of dust. Were
they tiny midges or what?—I don't know. They looked more like
miniature caterpillars. But whatever they were they had sharp
little stings, and the temptation to sweep them off one's hands and
face was irresistible. The King was observed once or twice discreetly rubbing the little pests off his hands and face. Others could
be seen going almost into contortions, and the only two persons who
seemed entirely unperturbed and unaware of the insects were M.
Lebrun and the Queen. I may testify that it was an extremely hard
endurance test.

And so the royal visit ended on a note of pious remembrance. It
was a visit which has been not only a masterpiece of French genius
in its numerous aspects but an act of statesmanship.

The brilliance and the beauty of the reception was equalled only
by the graciousness of the King and Queen themselves—and by
their endurance, for however delightful it all was, it was still hard
work for them.

And, after all the banquets and dinners, there may be at least a
grain of truth in the prophecy made by the *Canard Enchaîné* that for
the next week the daily menu at Buckingham Palace will consist of

Vegetable Soup.
Boiled Noodles à la Westminster.

Bicarbonate of Soda à la Windsor.
Filtered Water.
Camomile Tea à la St. James.

The people of France will keep a happy and grateful memory of these four days—and their pleasure will be all the greater when they read to-morrow morning the message the King sent to President Lebrun before leaving French territory this evening.

He said:

> 'On leaving the shores of France the Queen and I desire to express to you, M. le Président and Mme Lebrun, as well as to the members of the French Government, our heartiest thanks for the great kindness and hospitality shown us during our visit. We appreciate more than we can say the infinite care taken on every side to ensure our pleasure and comfort.
>
> Never, we feel, can your beautiful capital have been shown to greater advantage by the ingenuity and labour of her citizens, and the charm and variety of the displays, in which French genius has once again shown itself unsurpassed, made a lasting impression on us.
>
> Nor, M. le Président, shall we ever forget the warm and affectionate welcome given us by the men and women of your country, for it has touched us deeply, and we are truly grateful. I regard it as yet another proof of those ties of cordial friendship and mutual esteem which have so long bound our two countries together, a friendship based on common ideals and common sacrifices and directed solely to the maintenance of a just and lasting peace.
>
> The Queen and I bid au revoir to the people of France, and thank them from our hearts.'

The message, which was drafted by the King himself, is a perfect summary of the true significance of the royal visit to France.

It was really a most successful week—though perhaps a little tiring for those directly concerned. It was hard work for us journalists. What a bore to put on a morning coat and top hat every morning—only to change into tails at night. And to remember all the time about the various passes and badges and invitation cards. The genuine enthusiasm did not prevent the comic papers from producing a few good *blagues* that week.

The *Canard* had some amusing cartoons—of the King and Queen looking stealthily—like true British imperialists—for oil in the cellars of the Quai d'Orsay (a joke which the French at any rate found excruciatingly funny); of the French detective with bowler hat and moustache popping his head out of the King's breakfast egg; of the detective's legs showing below the picture of Queen Victoria in the Queen's drawing-room at the Quai d'Orsay. A week or two before the visit, it showed a picture of General Branconnier giving English lessons to President Lebrun: 'Now, please translate: "The joy of receiving Your Gracious Majesties is greater than the hat of my aunt's gardener." ' Mme Lebrun's curtsy to the Queen was described as a *génuflexion catastrophique*, and there was some speculation on what the Queen and Mme Lebrun talked about in driving down the Champs-Elysées. The *Canard's* suggestion was: 'It is just as well that Your Majesties have arrived on a Tuesday; because on Mondays all the butchers' shops are shut.'

In spite of these *blagues*, it may be said that the royal visit had the effect of greatly increasing the popularity of M. Lebrun. *'Lui et sa dame se sont fort bien débrouillés,'* was the general verdict.

.   .   .   .

It was during the royal visit that a decision of the utmost importance was taken. It was when Lord Halifax informed the French Ministers of the British Government's proposal to send Lord Runciman to Prague. The French agreed. Captain Wiedemann had, during the previous week, visited London.

The decision to send Lord Runciman to Prague was kept dark for several days. At the reception at the Quai d'Orsay on the last night of the royal visit to Paris, while Lord Halifax was talking at great length to M. Flandin among the floodlit emerald trees I met M. Osusky, the Czech Minister. 'Quite satisfactory, quite satisfactory, the talks about Czechoslovakia. *Really* quite satisfactory,' he said. 'Any new developments?' 'No, no, nothing new, everything *quite* satisfactory.' One could see he was hiding something, and that he was not so sure that it was all *quite* so satisfactory.

At length, M. Flandin left Lord Halifax, and departed, with a great big smirk on his face. Had Halifax told him about Runciman? What was he so pleased about? Flandin had, a month earlier, violently attacked Daladier for supporting the Spanish Government. Now he seemed to be *persona grata* at the Quai d'Orsay. Bonnet had by that time persuaded Daladier to follow Chamberlain's advice about the Catalan frontier;

and, as for Czechoslovakia, Bonnet and Flandin were already seeing, more or less, eye to eye.

Even though, exactly a week before the royal visit, Daladier had said: 'The solemn undertakings we have given to Czechoslovakia are sacred and cannot be evaded.'[1]

[1] Speech in Paris, on July 12.

CHAPTER IX

AUGUST: THE RUNCIMAN RESPITE

N OBODY had any serious illusions that Lord Runciman
would bring about a lasting settlement of the Czech
problem. The view taken in British Foreign Office quarters
was well summarised by the Diplomatic Correspondent of the
Manchester Guardian on August 2:

> It is not believed here that the gulf between what Prague
> can offer and what the Sudeten German party can accept (or
> will be allowed to accept) can be bridged. But one thing
> would seem to be quite certain—that only the friendly mediation
> of the Western Powers can now avert a Central European war.
> Naturally Czechoslovakia, as by far the weaker Power, does not
> want a war.
> The hope entertained here is that Germany will not want the
> war either, and that even if she is not satisfied by whatever
> agreement may be negotiated between her protégés, the Sudeten
> German party, and the Czechoslovak Government she will
> accept a temporary accommodation that will at least represent a
> kind of armistice in the conflict between herself and Czecho-
> slovakia. If Lord Runciman and his staff can help to bring
> about an accommodation of that kind his mission will have been
> a success.
> It is believed that if any accommodation, however patchy,
> can be reached by the end of October the situation will at least
> have been saved until the spring.

In France, opinion on the Runciman Mission was divided.
Those who desired, above all, to preserve an extremely valuable ally in Central Europe, were greatly alarmed; those who
wanted, above all, to avoid the danger of war looked hopefully
to the Runciman Mission for at least a 'temporary' easing of
the situation. In the Government itself these two opinions
were held—the former by M. Reynaud and M. Mandel, the
latter by M. Bonnet, M. de Monzie and others. M. Daladier
was not quite sure what to think of it; for he knew that his

military advisers were greatly perturbed at the thought of all
that the Runciman Mission might eventually produce. A
number of papers raised objections to Lord Runciman personally; the *Humanité* said that he was 'notoriously pro-German', and added that, in any case, he understood nothing
about the complexities of the Czech situation. Pertinax, representing the old Nationalist tradition, and voicing the
opinion of French military experts, observed that in Anglo-
French policy the lead had, up till then, been in the hands
of France.

> 'The *primary fact* has, so far, been France's determination not
> to allow Czechoslovakia to be invaded. Now the lead has been
> taken out of France's hands, and the *primary fact* is now no
> longer the Franco-Czech alliance, but the results of the Runci-
> man Mission; that is, the "Runciman Report".'
> He went on to argue that whether this report was regarded as
> official or unofficial, it would in any case have the support of
> British opinion and of the British Government, whatever its
> conclusions; and it would, in practice, be binding on the Czech
> Government, and the French would, willy-nilly, be obliged to
> follow. 'At the same time,' Pertinax said, 'it will not be in
> any way binding for Germany—with the result that Czecho-
> slovakia has from the outset been placed at a disadvantage.
> Lord Runciman's responsibility is overwhelming. For
> although his role will not be officially one of arbitration, it
> will be so in fact. *And unless he is extremely careful he may
> easily open the dikes to the rapid absorption of Central Europe by
> Germany.*'

As seen by most Frenchmen at that time, complete territorial
autonomy was 'completely out of the question', because
it would mean, in effect, the transfer to Germany of the
whole fortified fringe of Czechoslovakia. If Czechoslovakia
and the Franco-Czech alliance were to be saved, it was necessary
to secure an agreement between the Czechs and Sudetens which
would still leave the military authority of the Czechoslovakian
State unimpaired over its whole territory. The Sudetens, left
to themselves, could certainly come to such terms with the
Czech Government; but then the trouble was that they were
not left to themselves, and that all the wires were being pulled
by Germany, to whom a continued Czech military control of
the Sudeten areas was the very thing that was not acceptable.
The Sudeten 'rights' were only a pretext; for what did Germany

care for the 'rights' of say, the Germans in the Italian Tyrol?
But the only way of demanding from Germany that she accept
a settlement compatible with the sovereignty of Czechoslovakia
was to threaten her with war; and neither the French nor the
British Government were prepared to do so.

.   .   .   .

The preservation of the military mechanism of the Franco-
Czech alliance—of 'the Bohemian bastion'—was, psychologically, a bad slogan for convincing not only British but even
French public opinion.   It was not enough to say that the
Sudeten agitation for complete autonomy (for the question of
the transfer of territory had not yet arisen at the time) had
been artificially worked up by Nazi propaganda; the man-in-
the-street was becoming gradually convinced that the Sudeten
Germans were entitled to their claim; and the fact that the
Czech crisis was, as it were, spread over a period of many
months gave Germany the opportunity to impress gradually on
the minds of the British and French people that the Sudetens
had a good case for national autonomy; and once this had sunk
into British and French minds, the next step was to impress
upon them the fact that even with autonomy Czechoslovakia
would still be a mess, and that it might be just as well to accept
a clean cut—that is, the transfer of territory.   Where persua-
sion—through the Press and in other ways—did not work,
intimidation was resorted to.

The slow process by which French opinion was gradually demoralised was a masterpiece of tactics and propaganda.
The Germans rightly guessed that, in spite of all the official
assurances given to Czechoslovakia, there was, both in French
political quarters, and among the French people themselves,
a soil rich in war-weary pacifism.   M. Bonnet, the French
Foreign Minister, a man with a great influence both inside the
Cabinet and with the Press, was himself strongly inclined towards this pacifist view which, he perhaps sincerely believed,
represented the innermost feelings of the greater part of the
French people, and who—as subsequent events were to show—
did everything to discourage the revival of patriotic or
militarist sentiments.   But that did not become fully apparent
until later.

.   .   .   .

August was, in spite of everything, a holiday month in France. I went first, to Brittany which was packed with English tourists, and later down to the French Alps and the Riviera. Nobody seemed to be greatly worried. A widespread feeling was: 'Nothing much is likely to happen as long as Runciman is in Prague. *Qu'ils se débrouillent.'*

At politically-minded Geneva Runciman was treated with great suspicion, and the general feeling there was that if only France and England and Czechoslovakia acted again as energetically as they did on May 21, trouble could be avoided. Only would they?

In the south, *la province* was living its pleasant, slow, epicurean life, eating lovely food and drinking lovely wine. Runciman and Czechoslovakia seemed a million miles away. Hitch-hiking was the great sport during that beautiful summer of 1938. Holidays with pay were in full swing. The Mediterranean coast, from Mentone to Marseilles, was swarming with people. 'We have never had such a wonderful season before.' Thousands of English cars, hundreds of Swiss and American cars, cars from Egypt and India and South America could be seen all over the place. Montparnasse had migrated to St. Tropez. 'You see,' a hotel-keeper explained, 'the international situation is doing us a world of good. People who used to go to Austria no longer like to go there since the Anschluss; Spain is closed to tourists, Switzerland is expensive, in Italy the food is bad, and a lot of people don't like the Fascists—so where are tourists to go except to *la belle France*— with 175 francs to the £? It is true that the Italians are not allowed to come here any more; but we can well afford to manage without them.' During the French equivalent of the bank holiday week-end around August 15, the shortage of rooms was such that in a great many places people simply slept on the beach. Bathrooms were turned into bedrooms and the proverbial billiard tables into beds. 'I couldn't sleep a wink on your blasted billiard table,' the *Canard Enchaîné* reported a visitor as saying. 'So sorry,' said the maid, 'but before putting down the mattress I forgot to remove the billiard balls.' With jokes about billiard tables life seemed superbly normal.

.   .   .   .

And yet anyone lying on the beach at Juan-les-Pins would

only have had to open any newspaper to see that the world was not faring well. Relations with Italy were as strained as ever. M. Blondel, the French Chargé d'Affaires in Rome arrived in Paris on August 3 only to report to M. Bonnet that 'there was no question at present of a resumption of the negotiations' which had been suspended in April. M. Bonnet thought the Italians ungrateful. Had France not done everything to please them? Had she not even closed the Catalan frontier to armaments? Asked by the Press on his return to Rome if he had anything to say, M. Blondel replied that the leading article of the *Temps* on the previous day had 'amply described the present state of Franco-Italian relations'. This article stated that

> since the closing by France of the Pyrenees frontier the responsibility for making a gesture towards reopening negotiations had devolved upon Italy.[1]

The closing of the frontier had been 'suggested' to France by Mr. Chamberlain on the ground that it would give a better chance to the Non-Intervention Committee's attempts to put into operation its plan for the withdrawal of volunteers. This plan, as was to be expected, came to nothing. After keeping everybody waiting for seven weeks, Franco, while accepting it in principle, rejected it in practice. Nevertheless the Catalan frontier remained closed, both officially and unofficially, because M. Bonnet was still hoping to make friends with Italy. And it remained closed till the bitter end.

. . . .

Since the beginning of August the news from Germany was going daily from bad to worse. By the middle of the month there was no longer any doubt that at least 500,000 reservists had been called up; Germany had now 1,500,000 men under arms; civilian property was being commandeered on such a vast scale, on the eve of the great manœuvres on the Czechoslovak and French frontiers, that the public in Germany was becoming increasingly nervous every day, and talking more and more openly of war. A tremendous rush was being made to complete the fortifications in the west, and particularly along the Rhine. The Berlin correspondent of the *Times* reported

[1] Reuter from Rome, August 5.

that something like 300,000 men were working on these fortifications day and night. So many men had been taken away from
work (one report said) that the Munich underground had
almost stopped. There was a heavy slump on the Berlin
Bourse.

And even yet, French opinion was not unduly perturbed.
On August 17, M. Blum wrote in the *Populaire*:

> We cannot close our eyes to the unusual character of the
> German manœuvres. It is natural for the Army to hold
> manœuvres at this time of year. What is not natural is the
> importance given to these manœuvres, their duration, the scope
> of the mobilisation, and the requisitioning. What is still less
> natural is their co-existence in time and their continuity in
> space with events in Czecho-Slovakia. Nevertheless, French
> opinion remains calm, serious, and perfectly self-assured. The
> Government shows neither nervousness, emotion, nor pre-
> cipitateness.
>
> In my view, this is right in all respects. I believe that
> reflection and critical analysis of the facts lead to the dismissal
> of the hypothesis of an act of sudden aggression by Hitler
> against Czecho-Slovakia—even during the weeks when he will
> have ready in his hand an army whose exact strength is un-
> known. The most plausible conjecture is that Hitler is em-
> ploying this menace to settle the Sudeten question peacefully
> but nevertheless in his own way.
>
> The menace is suspended over France and England more than
> over Czecho-Slovakia. By making French and British opinion,
> which desire peace, aware of the war danger, Hitler reckons
> without doubt upon making London and Paris put a new turn
> of the screw upon Prague. Perhaps he feels that the Runciman
> Mission is taking a bad turn for the Sudeten case. Perhaps
> impatience is gaining ground and he wishes to hurry matters.
> The immediate danger is that this calculation should succeed.
> Nevertheless I remain confident that neither London nor Paris
> will consent to be the instruments of Hitler's manœuvre.

In the *Figaro* M. d'Ormesson did not think it mattered.
Hitler, he thought, needed a little excitement for his own
prestige.

> The partial mobilisation appears to be a sort of moral revenge
> for the 21st of May. 'You thought you were able to intimidate
> us,' declare the masters of the Third Reich. 'Very good, here is
> our reply. You may consider yourselves as being warned.'
>
> The explanation is the German need for prestige. People are
> ignorant of Hitler's policy, if they forget that periodically the
> régime needs excitement.

Henri de Kerillis took the threat more seriously, but thought that it could be checked, as it was on May 21, by a counter-threat, provided—he added significantly—'the nerve and the moral of our people are solidly forged'.

.   .   .   .

It was at that time that the United States Government, unwilling to see matters drift any further, gave Germany a discreet first warning.

On August 16 Mr. Cordell Hull said on the wireless:

> 'To-day invasion of territory of sovereign States, destruction of lawfully constituted Governments, and forcible seizure of hitherto independent political entities and interference in the internal affairs of other nations, wholesale violation of established treaty obligations, attempts to adjust international differences by armed force—all these appalling manifestations of disintegration seriously threaten the very foundations of our civilisation. . . .
>
> 'Whatever may be our own wishes and hopes we cannot when there is trouble elsewhere expect to remain unaffected. When destruction, impoverishment, and starvation afflict other areas we cannot, no matter how hard we try, escape impairment of our own economic wellbeing. When freedom is destroyed over increasing areas elsewhere our ideals of individual liberty, our most cherished political and social institutions are jeopardised.'

And he concluded:

> 'When the dignity of the human soul is denied in great parts of the world and when that denial is made a slogan under which propaganda is set in motion and armies take the field no one of us can be sure that his country, or even his home, is safe.'

And two days later, on August 18, Mr. Roosevelt said at Kingston, Ontario:

> 'We in the Americas are no longer a far-away continent to which eddies of controversy beyond the seas could bring no interest or harm. Instead, we in the Americas have become a consideration to every propaganda office and to every general staff beyond the seas. The vast amount of our resources, the vigour of our commerce, and the strength of our men have made us vital factors in world peace, whether we choose or not.'

The two speeches created a big impression in France. M. Béranger, President of the Foreign Affairs Committee of the Senate, and former French Ambassador in Washington, wrote:

The United States will be alongside Britain and France on the day when the great decision must be made.   To ask more of America would show a lack of intelligence and would be unseemly.   It is necessary to understand one's friends if one wishes to be able to count upon them.

M. Blum, no doubt smelling a rat at the Quai d'Orsay, thought that Mr. Cordell Hull's speech contained not only a warning to Germany but also one to England and France which, he said, 'must not acquiesce in a new defeat to the democratic cause without discouraging United States opinion and running the risk of alienating it'.

The Quai d'Orsay-ridden the *Temps* was much more cautious:

It would be yielding to dangerous illusions to assume that at present the American people have rallied to a policy of active intervention in Europe. . . .

And so on.   As if *that* was the point!   But throughout the September crisis M. Bonnet consistently minimised the part America was playing; by declaring her material role in European affairs to be nil, he also implied that her moral role was of no importance.   To the Foreign Affairs Committee and at other gatherings he would always say: 'You know, I spent a long time in Washington; and I know how isolationist they all are at heart.'. . . No doubt in his public speech at the Pointe de Grave on September 4 he went to the other extreme; but that is another story—and a curious one at that—which I shall mention later.

.   .   .   .

The Czech affair, in the meantime, still continued to be in British hands, and the French were, more or less, standing aloof, except that, now and then, their Minister in Prague would be instructed to lend a hand in giving another turn to the British screw.

But in spite of more and more Czech concessions, the atmosphere in Central Europe was not improving, and a 'settlement' between the Czechs and the Sudetens was as little in sight as ever.   On Saturday, August 27, Lord Runciman sent an urgent request to Henlein to call on him at Prince Clery's castle in Bohemia where he was spending the week-end.   The meeting between Henlein, Lord Runciman and Mr. Newton, the

British Minister in Prague, lasted for two hours, but without any appreciable development for the better.

On that same day Sir John Simon made his Lanark speech— a speech for which the French had been waiting impatiently; for *at that stage* the view popularly taken in France was that if only Britain took a firm stand, Germany would be frightened to go too far. Sir John Simon's speech was, the French thought, fairly satisfactory, but not perhaps quite tough enough. Still, it was sufficiently tough to produce an angry outcry in the German Press, which declared it to be an encouragement to 'Czech arrogance' and to the Prague 'warmongers'. It said that the speech showed no appreciation of the position of the Sudeten Germans.

In his speech Sir John Simon reaffirmed Mr. Chamberlain's declaration of March 24 on the position of Great Britain in regard to Czechoslovakia. 'That declaration holds good to-day,' he said. 'There is nothing to add or to vary in its contents.' (That declaration, it will be recalled, was a warning that if war broke out 'it would be quite impossible to say where it would end and what Governments might become involved'.) Sir John added:

> 'To find a solution for the controversy in Czecho-Slovakia contributions from all concerned are needed. We are convinced that, given goodwill on both sides, it should be possible to find a solution which is just to all legitimate interests. And there is no need to emphasise the importance of finding a peaceful solution. For in the modern world there is no limit to the reactions of war.'

.   .   .   .

A serious shock to France came two days later—on August 29, a day on which there were important conversations on Czechoslovakia. Sir Nevile Henderson had specially come from Berlin to report to Mr. Chamberlain and Lord Halifax. That afternoon the startling news reached Paris that Hitler had just paid a surprise visit to the Rhineland. Accompanied by eight Generals of the General Staff, including General Von Brauschitsch and General Keitel he had visited Kehl, exactly opposite Strasbourg that morning. He had arrived at Kehl by road at 9 a.m.

'A quarter of an hour previously,' Reuter wrote from Strasbourg, 'the French police had been informed by the German authorities that the Chancellor was on his way, and both the French and German ends of the international bridge over the Rhine were closed.

'As soon as Herr Hitler arrived all the Kehl S.S. men were mobilised. There was no official reception. At 10 a.m. Herr Hitler's inspection ended and he and his suite left Kehl in the direction of Offenburg, ten miles to the south-east.

'Shortly after the party had left the frontier was reopened and traffic between the two banks was resumed. Herr Hitler also inspected the frontier almost as far as Switzerland. Herr Hitler's visit appears to have come as a surprise at Kehl, and there were no flags to greet him.

'In Strasbourg the tour was taken very philosophically by the inhabitants, the majority of whom were unaware of the Chancellor's presence until after he had left. Only a few persons who were turned back at the bridge heard that Herr Hitler was on the opposite bank. Others only learned of the tour in the noon news broadcast.

'The inhabitants of Strasbourg recall that Field Marshal Goering has also inspected the frontier fortifications.'

One is not so sure that the people of Strasbourg took it as 'philosophically' as all that; for it was soon after this 'surprise visit' to Kehl that the people of Strasbourg began to take their money out of the savings banks, and prepare to move farther inland.

In any case, the visit to Kehl on August 29 was, as it were, an ominous prelude to the great historical month of September 1938.

Book II

SEPTEMBER

CHAPTER X

WAS MUNICH INEVITABLE?

IN any attempt to assess the proportion of blame due to France and Great Britain in the handling of the Czech crisis, one important fact should always be borne in mind: and that is that while France was an ally of Czechoslovakia, Great Britain was not. This fact was often forgotten—by the French themselves. As we have seen from the preceding chapters, the lead in the handling of the Czech affair had since April been passing more and more into British hands—and the French Government was relinquishing this lead with surprisingly great ease. On the face of it, this leadership was not abandoned until the dispatch to Prague of the Runciman Mission which, in the words of Pertinax, became 'fact number 1', whereas until then 'fact number 1' had been the Franco-Czech alliance. But in reality, the lead had already passed into British hands some time earlier; the principle of British mediation had already been agreed to at the end of April; and I remember how in London, after the conclusion of the Anglo-French talks, I remarked to one of the shrewdest French journalists: 'Well, there is going to be one victim of these talks—and that is Spain,' to which my *confrère* replied: 'You are wrong. There are going to be two victims; and the other one is Czechoslovakia.'

The firm Franco-British stand was successful on May 21; and that kept up the illusion for some time that a 'firm stand' might work again; but was not May 21 something of a fluke? There were German troop movements along the Czech border, and Germany may have been up to some mischief, provided she discovered that she could get away with a 'localised' war; but it is certain that her military preparations had not gone very far, that she was not ready for a major war, and that she could not even *pretend* that she was ready for such a war. She

decided therefore to do better next time. It is noteworthy
that in May France and Britain had not been subjected to that
intimidation which was to be practised on them so successfully
in September.

But no sooner had the effects of May 21 worn off, than
Britain, supported by France, continued her pressure on
Prague (which was, in effect, the form that her 'mediation'
took at that time). But at that time France, at any rate, still
assumed that a settlement would be reached and 'must' be
reached in a manner compatible with the integrity of Czechoslovakia; and, after the appointment of the Runciman Mission, M. Bonnet instructed M. Corbin to tell the British
Government that only a settlement within the present borders
of Czechoslovakia and compatible with the continued sovereignty of the Czechoslovak State over all its territory, was
acceptable to France. But it was really little good informing
the British Government about it; such a statement was
obviously only the expression of a pious hope, and no more,
since Lord Runciman had already in effect been given *carte
blanche*.

Then came August, and the great German mobilisation.
For a good long time France did *nothing* about that mobi-
lisation. She was just waiting. The Government, and
particularly M. Bonnet, kept on suggesting that France
could do nothing without being certain of British support.
The French Left Press begged England to say something.
Sir John Simon spoke sufficiently clearly at Lanark on
August 27. But still France did nothing—or next to nothing.
It was not until September 5 that the Maginot Line was
properly manned. About 100,000 'specialists' were called up.
After that France sat back and waited for the Nuremberg
Congress and Hitler's speech. It is not in the least surprising
that, in the circumstances, the Nuremberg Congress should
have produced what it did produce. It was all very well for
Sir Nevile Henderson to 'warn' the Germans about Britain's
attitude; the Germans did not believe that the French would
'march'.

And then, after Hitler's speech, came the French Cabinet
meeting of September 13, which was a complete climb-down.
In spite of everything, in spite of the firm 'authoritative state-

ment' published in London two days earlier, it decided against mobilisation; and Mr. Chamberlain was expected to settle matters somehow. Mr. Chamberlain went off to Berchtesgaden. After what had happened in Paris, one can well imagine Hitler's self-assurance.

By that time Mr. Chamberlain was, obviously, willing to accept almost any 'compromise'. For Mr. Chamberlain, as the French should have known, was in any case not a man particularly well suited for defending the interests of France's ally. But they did not care. They wanted him to shoulder the responsibility for the surrender of Czechoslovakia, and then be able to say that 'it was England's fault'.

Incidentally, it is curious that it was not until Berchtesgaden that Germany first demanded the cession of the Sudeten territory. Almost right up to the middle of September Germany had still spoken of Sudeten 'rights'; i.e., she still spoke in terms of a settlement *within* the limits of the Czechoslovak State—even though the rights demanded were no longer compatible with the integrity of that State. Even in his Nuremberg speech on September 12 Hitler still spoke as though he were ready to accept a settlement at least nominally *within* Czech limits, and his allusion to a plebiscite was left deliberately vague. It was not until the day when Mr. Chamberlain flew to Berchtesgaden that Hitler realised the extent to which Britain and France were frightened; and it was while Mr. Chamberlain was flying to Berchtesgaden that Henlein published his famous proclamation saying *for the first time* that the Sudetens wished to be incorporated within the German Reich. Until that day the Sudetens had—albeit extravagantly —asked only for autonomy within the framework of the Czech State. It was during Chamberlain's flight to Berchtesgaden that the autonomists became rebels.

And soon after Berchtesgaden Hitler confessed that he did not think Chamberlain would accept 'self-determination', and that it was a pleasant surprise to him to find that he had done so.

Berchtesgaden really meant the end of Czechoslovakia; and France's responsibility for Berchtesgaden is immense.

After everything was over, a close associate of M. Daladier's told me:

'Notre erreur fatale, c'est de ne pas avoir pris position au bon moment.'

Prendre position: it was easily said. And the question arises whether Munich could have been avoided.

What could *prendre position* have meant? It could have meant this. Since France was Czechoslovakia's ally, it was for her to warn Germany *as early as possible* that, while willing to support the minority claims of the Sudeten Germans, compatible with the sovereignty of the Czechoslovak State, she could not consent to a *territorial* change, or to a form of Sudeten autonomy which would in practice have amounted to the same thing.

If this warning alone failed to achieve the desired effect, France could have gone a step farther. During the great German mobilisation in August, she could *also* have mobilised in the same proportion. The whole atmosphere at the Nuremberg Congress would have been entirely different. Would Britain have opposed the French mobilisation in such circumstances? It is, to say the least, extremely doubtful. Even before France had done anything Sir John Simon virtually promised France full British support if she felt obliged to go to war, and the authorised statement on September 11 made this pledge even more precise. But still the French would not budge. But when on the 12th Hitler spoke, he was clearly convinced that since France had assumed an attitude of non-resistance, and had not even said: 'The Czech Plan No. 4 is even more than we could have expected from the Czechs; and we shall not urge them to yield another inch,' Germany could go on asking for more and more. But the French Government was unenterprising and did not want even to *risk* a war, and kept on saying that no support was to be expected from England, and that it was better to let England arrange things 'somehow'. Even on September 13, the day after Hitler's Nuremberg speech, France failed to mobilise, and hoped that Mr. Chamberlain would 'arrange things' at Berchtesgaden.

September was marked in France by an intense conflict between the 'pacifists' and the 'warmongers'. In reality the warmongers were the men who were trying to 'bluff' Hitler into moderation, into the acceptance of a solution acceptable to Czechoslovakia, and who in the last resort, were inevitably prepared to risk a war. They might have yielded in the end if Hitler had still demanded annexation, but at least they *tried* to dissuade him, in the only language he understood, from doing so. And the chances are that if they had taken a strong stand in time, and had rallied to France many of the other countries threatened by German hegemony, *it is not their bluff, but Hitler's which would have been called. But their readiness to bluff and to take a risk came to nothing, because the 'pacifists' kept on proclaiming that France would neither bluff, nor take any risks;* and that if only Hitler was patient enough to wait a little, he would get everything, or almost everything, without fighting. For if in July M. Bonnet still told M. Corbin that Lord Runciman's proposals must be compatible with the integrity and sovereignty of Czechoslovakia, he no longer cared very much. Since France was not going to risk a war, it was obvious that her concessions were going to increase in the same proportion as Hitler's demands.

One of the most astonishing things of all is that, *on the whole, the French Government was more 'pacifist' than the British Government. That is to say that, given the fact that France was Czechoslovakia's ally, she was, relatively, much softer than was England as a non-ally of Czechoslovakia.* That is even truer if one compares not the two Governments, but the Press of the two countries, and in this case not only relatively but absolutely. If at any time in the first two weeks of September France had taken a strong lead in firmly opposing Germany's deliberate intention to destroy Czechoslovakia, the British Government and British opinion would have supported her. The British Foreign Office was clearly opposed to a surrender of Czechoslovakia; so also were certain members of the French Foreign Office;—but only to be violently abused as warmongers in *Gringoire* and other papers of the same sort— and that *with M. Bonnet's approval.* For immediately after Munich two of the three high officials attacked in *Gringoire* were got rid of by M. Bonnet. M. Pierre Comert, the head of the Press Department, was appointed to a much more obscure post, while M. Massigli was sent as Ambassador to Ankara. M. Léger alone was left where he was: *le morceau était trop gros,* somebody remarked.

The British Foreign Office would, in the main, have welcomed a firm French stand in the first half of September, and so would have a very large part of British opinion; there was a moment early in September when an energetic French lead could in a large measure have revived collective security in Europe. Turkey, Jugoslavia, Rumania, and even Poland—though not perhaps M. Beck—were showing signs of anger and anxiety at the sight of Germany's immense war preparations; and Russia was, to all appearances, ready to support a policy of resistance. As for Italy, she was obviously wobbling. A bold French lead at that moment would probably have received support from England and the chief Eastern European States; and collective security might in a large measure have been restored. But this brief psychological moment—it lasted only a few days—was missed. No attempt of any sort was made in that direction, while Russia was deliberately discouraged from doing or saying anything. Mr. Duff Cooper's criticism of the British Government for its failure to mobilise the fleet or give Germany some other equally tangible warning long before the crisis had come to a head *could have been addressed even more effectively to the French Government.*

Instead, the French Government preferred to leave the fate of her ally in the hands of Mr. Chamberlain who certainly did not think of Czechoslovakia in terms of France's treaty obligations. For, perhaps, long before anybody else, Mr. Chamberlain had got the idea that the Czechs and the Sudetens could not live together much longer. He did not reason in general European terms. And the French *must* have known of Mr. Chamberlain's personal opinion on Czechoslovakia. His opinion had, in fact, been given considerable publicity in the American Press.

According to Joseph Driscoll in the *New York Herald Tribune* of May 14, Mr. Chamberlain had, in the first week in May, discussed the Czech situation at a private luncheon given by Lady Astor to a group of American correspondents. The Prime Minister then apparently already believed that Czechoslovakia could not survive in its existing form. He was convinced that, to avoid resort to force, the Czech Government should promptly make concessions to Germany, and already thought that frontier revision might be preferable to cantonal autonomy. The revision he envisaged was the cession of a 'fringe' of territory to Germany which, according to him, would transform Czechoslovakia into a smaller but sounder State.

Whether this New York story was not only an indiscretion, but also a slight exaggeration, it sounds extremely plausible. As for the Prime Minister's belief that, after partition, Czechoslovakia would be a 'smaller but sounder' State, it is conceivable that with the illusions he then still entertained on the possibilities of loyal co-operation with the Dictators, he *did* (perhaps sincerely) hold such a belief.

And so it was Mr. Chamberlain who, with the blessings of the French Government, was to handle the Czech crisis. One of the most remarkable features of French conduct was the discouragement given by M. Bonnet to any energetic move in Czechoslovakia's favour coming, not only from France, but also *from Britain*. Throughout September, M. Bonnet privately told everybody that *no* firm stand was to be expected from Britain; and when, at the height of the crisis Lord Halifax and the Foreign Office *did* take a strong stand, M. Bonnet did everything to suggest that it meant nothing. I shall deal later with the remarkable case of the Foreign Office *communiqué* of September 26, and of the treatment it received in France. In effect, M. Bonnet spent his time suggesting to the British Ambassador that France would not 'march', and suggesting to the French that the British could not be relied upon. As for the Russians, he claimed that they were no good at all— another point I shall discuss later. M. Bonnet *wanted* Munich; and he was not alone in wanting it. To the unfortunate Czechs alone he would not at first admit it, but on the contrary continued to assure them as late as the first week of September of French support. But the Germans knew what he really felt, and they acted accordingly.

So the policy of firmness was being consistently rejected by the French Government.

A 'firm stand' could have been taken, and Munich might have been avoided; only there were formidable psychological obstacles in the way. In spite of all the arguments about the Czech Maginot Line and the Bohemian Bastion, France and Britain (and, in a large measure, French and British opinion) were led away by the ethnical argument used with such tremendous effect by German propaganda. But it was an ethnical

argument the futility of which was terribly difficult to demon-
strate—until the day when the Germans demonstrated it themselves by walking into Prague.   The most that could be
said against it in September was what Low said.   He
hit the nail on the head with his cartoon on the 'Procession
of Nightmares'—the Nightmares being: Germans in Czechoslovakia, Germans in Rumania, Germans in Hungary,
Germans in Alsace, German-speaking Swiss, Germans in
America, and so on.   *Nevertheless the case for defending the integrity of Czechoslovakia was, if not exactly an
unconvincing one, at least not a sufficiently clear one;* and the
French Press—whether in some cases bribed by Germany, or,
in others, simply reflecting a weary isolationist mood—had
made every effort for months to confuse the issues in the
French mind.   It was somehow bad style to talk about the
Czech Maginot Line; just as it was bad style to quote *Mein
Kampf*; people replied: 'That's all very well, but——'; and
*the fact that three million Germans 'wanted to be German',
was difficult to explain away by strategic arguments.*   It was
not until the last week of September that a large part of
French opinion *fully* realised that in wishing to destroy Czechoslovakia, Germany was striving to dominate Europe by the
threat of its force.   It was Hitler's bellowing on the wireless
that convinced hundreds of thousands of Frenchmen of Hitler's
evil intentions—Frenchmen whom no arguments about the
'Bohemian Bastion' or even the sacredness of France's signature
could convince.   Hitler made them angry.   But there were
millions of others who still did not see it, or who preferred
to take a chance on it.

These introductory remarks on September 1938 will, I hope,
help to understand the more chronologically arranged record
of events that is to follow.   A point worth remembering is that
pacifist, Flandinist, and German-paid propaganda always made
a special point of saying that *whoever favoured a policy of
'firmness' in relation to Germany was a belliciste—a warmonger—and wanted war with Germany.*   That was Bonnet's
argument, and early in December (though not before that) it
became Daladier's argument: *'La politique de fermeté, c'était
la politique de guerre.'*

CHAPTER XI

THE PARIS PRESS IN SEPTEMBER

BEFORE coming to the more chronological story of September, I might add for the reader's convenience, a description of the principal Paris papers in their attitude towards the Czech crisis during September. The policy of 'no surrender' was advocated with great vigour by only five dailies and two of the important weeklies. These papers naturally criticised with great violence the Daladier Government, and in particular M. Bonnet.

The great *belliciste*[1] paper was the Communist *Humanité*, with its closely reasoned and unusually well documented foreign editorials by Gabriel Péri, the Communist deputy for Argenteuil, a man of great culture and with a fine polemical pen. *Belliciste* was also the evening paper, *Ce Soir*.

Next, the Nationalist *Epoque*. Henri de Kerillis, the impetuous Nationalist deputy for Neuilly, described as the Cassandra of France by some, and as an 'hysterical woman' by others, represented what might be called the old traditional policy of French nationalism, to which the 'Eastern Alliance' was an unanswerable dogma. M. de Kerillis's articles abound in references to François Ier and his alliance with the Great Turk, to Cardinal Richelieu and his alliance with the Protestant princes, to Napoleon's fatal error in quarrelling with Russia in 1811; to the double error of Napoleon III who gave Germany a free hand in the East in 1866 (hence the famous phrase: 'After Sadowa Sedan'), and who failed to achieve an alliance with Russia which would have made all the difference in 1870; and, naturally, to Poincaré and to the classical nationalism of Maurice Barrès. Kerillis has no anti-Fascist

---

[1] Here and everywhere I use the words *belliciste* and *warmonger* for convenience, and ironically. Anybody who stood for a policy of firmness, and resistance was branded a *belliciste*.

prejudices; to him Germany, always striving for European hegemony, is simply France's hereditary enemy; *any* alliance —even with the hated Bolsheviks—is good if it can keep Germany in check. Apart from Germany, Kerillis is not hostile to Fascism; he was rapturously pro-Italian during the Abyssinian conflict, and wailed over sanctions which had made an enemy of Italy; but later he lost his long-cherished illusions about the fragility of the Berlin-Rome axis, and no longer even blamed sanctions for it; but admitted that Italy had, unfortunately, become Germany's satellite. In the early days of the Spanish war Kerillis was passionately pro-Franco, but later complained bitterly because France had allowed Franco to be snatched away by Italy and Germany, and wished France had backed him from the start—overlooking the fact that Franco was already *then* being backed by Berlin and Rome.

The *Ordre*, nominally a Right-Wing paper, is edited by M. Emile Buré, also a nationalist of the Barrès or rather, Clemenceau school. It consistently supported the Franco-Soviet Pact, and the maintenance of as many Eastern alliances as possible. 'After Sadowa Sedan', was, as it were, its slogan. M. Buré, married to a Rumanian, has close personal contacts with Rumania. Since the end of the *Echo de Paris* which died in June 1938, Pertinax has been a regular contributor to the *Ordre*. He differs from Kerillis (with whom he seemed to be in perpetual conflict on the *Echo de Paris* over the Abyssinian crisis) by a far wider knowledge of international affairs and by a clearer and less emotional presentation of his facts and arguments.

The weekly, the *Europe Nouvelle*, pursues the same policy as the *Ordre*. The editor is Pertinax. It has specialised in devastating 'revelations' about M. Georges Bonnet.

The *Aube*, edited by a brilliant writer, M. Georges Bidault, may also be classified among the 'warmonger' papers. It is the organ of liberal Catholicism, strongly opposed to Fascism on both religious and political grounds. Its views closely reflect those of Cardinal Verdier, the Archbishop of Paris. More ambiguous during the September crisis was the attitude of the other Catholic paper, *La Croix*.

An important weekly advocating the policy of firmness and

'no surrender' was the *Lumière*, edited by M. Georges Boris.
The *Lumière* presented, as it were, in an undiluted form the
anti-Fascist substance of the Left-Wing and Front Populaire
outlook. Its contributors are mainly Socialists and Left-Wing
Radicals like M. Albert Bayet. In the view of the *Lumière*,
it is useless closing one's eyes to the fact that the battle in
Europe—where the international battle is full of internal repercussions—is above all an ideological battle. M. Flandin's
mentality has closer affinities with that of a German Nazi than
with that of a true French democrat. A victory for Hitler
means a victory for the French Fascists or *fascisants*. The
Lumière, like some of the other 'warmonger' papers, foresaw
in the betrayal of Czechoslovakia a deadly blow to the democratic cause.

The Socialist *Populaire* like the trade union paper, the
Peuple, were both anti-Fascist and were intensely revolted by
Germany's bullying of Czechoslovakia, which they treated as
a sister-democracy. But both papers showed some hesitation
on the best way of dealing with the Czech crisis. M. Blum,
though begging England to show 'firmness', himself showed
considerable hesitation in advocating a 'firm' policy. This
self-consciousness has been attributed to a number of causes:
first, to the knowledge that there was a large body of ultra-
pacifist opinion in the Socialist Party, and that a breach within
the Socialist Party could only be avoided by a cautious handling of the Czech situation; secondly, to Blum's own innate
pacifism and the reluctance to take any war risks (cf. his
handling of the Spanish problem), and lastly, perhaps, to a
certain self-consciousness created by the propaganda which
consisted in saying that 'the Jews want war, because they hope
to destroy Hitler'. Although he wanted to see Czechoslovakia
saved, Blum praised Mr. Chamberlain for his 'noble audacity
in his will for peace' when the British Premier took the aeroplane for Berchtesgaden; and when after Berchtesgaden, the
dismemberment of Czechoslovakia was decided upon, Blum
said that he had received the news with 'mixed feelings of
cowardly relief and shame'. But Blum's cautious and somewhat uneasy 'firmness' was offset in the *Populaire* by the altogether outspokenly pacifist articles of Paul Faure, whose
argument was that 'war was, in any case, not a solution'.

Conflicting tendencies of the same kind were to be found in the *Peuple*, the organ of the C.G.T., except that its Communist members were more outspokenly 'firm' than the hesitating 'warmongers' of the Populaire. One hundred per cent 'pacifist' as *Syndicats*, the weekly organ of the syndicalist and anti-Communist section of the C.G.T. (Belin, Delmas, etc.).

It is curious to note that that great anti-Fascist satirical weekly, the *Canard Enchaîné* became, at least as far as M. Bénard's 'leaders' were concerned, almost rabidly pacifist in September, one of its principal arguments being: 'What do we care if 3,000,000 Germans want to be German?' A similar line was taken by M. Bergery in the *Flèche*.

The rest of the Paris Press, as we shall see, ranged from the half-hearted semi-official outlook (strongly inspired by M. Bonnet) to the plainly defeatist outlook which, in practice, was not very different. During the first week or ten days of September most of these papers were still moderately 'firm'. But by the middle of September, if not before, all these officially inspired papers were ready to accept 'any settlement of the Czech crisis short of an invasion.' In the *Œuvre*, the 'warmongering' articles of Mme Tabouis were cancelled out, as it were, by the 'pacifist' editorials of Jean Piot, the editor of the paper and an ex-serviceman who loathed the very thought of another war; and even Mme Tabouis, who regarded the loss of Czechoslovakia and 'consequently', the loss of the whole of Eastern Europe as disastrous to France, actually said less than she would no doubt have liked to say; for the *Œuvre*, which had changed hands some months earlier, was now much less the great independent organ of militant Radicalism than it had been. Although the change-over was not brutal, the *Œuvre* tended more and more to reflect the views of M. Bonnet than those of M. Herriot. The two other Paris papers, which were at least nominally Radical, the *Ere Nouvelle* and the *République*, reflecting the views of men like M. Caillaux, were among the most 'defeatist' of all.

The conservative *Figaro* reflected a certain variety of views: while M. d'Ormesson was essentially *bonnetiste*, M. Romier took a rather longer view, while writers like M. Mauriac and M. Duhamel were, chiefly for moral and intellectual reasons, deeply perturbed by the deadly spread of the Nazi Anti-Civilisation in Europe.

The two popular evening papers in Paris, *L'Intransigeant* and *Paris-Soir* were 'pro-Munich'. Very notable in this respect were the articles of M. Sauerwein in *Paris-Soir*.

The *Temps* was even more *officieux* than usual, and in the first half of September it did not hesitate to criticise openly the 'dilatory tactics' of Dr. Beneš. Later it shed crocodile's tears over the fate of Czechoslovakia. Much the same line was also taken by the *Petit Parisien*. However, it is only fair to say that both the *Temps* and the *Petit Parisien* refrained from the grosser forms of misrepresentation practised by certain papers of the Right, such as the *Jour*, the *Journal*, the *Matin* and the *Action Française*. Although M. Bailby in the *Jour* and M. Maurras in the *Action Française* betrayed brief moments of hesitation at the prospect of Germany's immense bloodless victory, all these papers, as well as the pro-Fascist weeklies like *Gringoire* and *Candide*—not to mention a plainly Nazi sheet like *Je Suis Partout*—were ideologically hostile to Czechoslovakia, even if not openly friendly to Germany, and, on the whole, fully prepared to abandon Eastern Europe to its fate. They were also keenly looking forward to the political consequences in France itself of the surrender of Czechoslovakia. The *Matin* in particular, was always playing on the 'anti-Comintern' string, and seemed to favour the destruction of 'Bolshevism' by Hitler. All these papers, more or less believed in the virtues of the Four-Power Pact policy.

So also did the *Information*, the leading Paris financial paper. Controlled by a bank which is known to be in close contact with M. Bonnet, the Foreign Minister, the *Information* counted among its principal contributors M. Fernand de Brinon, a leading light on the Comité France-Allemagne—a body working for the 'cultural' *rapprochement* between France and Nazi Germany. M. de Brinon had for many years advocated a *direct* understanding between France and Germany, had stood for Four-Power Pact politics, and for the surrender of the whole of Central and Eastern Europe to German 'influence'. As long ago as 1933 he went to Germany to interview Hitler, and produced (with the approval of M. Daladier, the then War Minister) a sensational interview in the *Matin* with an almost extravagantly pacifist Hitler. M. de Brinon concluded the article by expressing his profound belief in Hitler's sincere desire to make friends with France. M. de Brinon, who writes numerous and regular articles on Franco-German relations in the German Press, wrote, shortly after Munich, a sensational article demonstrating the virtues of 'self-determination' which since Munich, he said, had been accepted as an 'unchallengeable' principle. M. Ybarnégaray and others have publicly, in the Chamber of Deputies, referred to M. de Brinon with great contempt. The papers of M. Doriot, the *Liberté* and the *Emanicipation Nationale* were also entirely defeatist; the *Liberté* being the only paper that printed M. Flandin's poster on September 26, virtually inviting the people of France to resist against mobilisation. Like the poster, the *Liberté* was seized by the police.

As for Colonel de la Rocque who from a budding and almost blossoming dictator in 1935 had now degenerated into a not very competent newspaper editor, he was, during some days in September, altogether incoherent. On the day after the Anglo-French acceptance of Hitler's Berchtesgaden plan, La Rocque proclaimed in his paper, the *Petit Journal*, that the authority and prestige of France had never yet stood so high!

The proportion of papers which advocated 'any old settlement' of the Czech conflict or a complete betrayal of Czechoslovakia was, it will have been noted, extraordinarily high. To say that this Press reflected accurately the feelings of the French people would be untrue; it reflected, above all, the influence of certain big financial and big business interests (not that big business in France was unanimous in its defeatism —thus the *Journée Industrielle* reflecting the views of a large part of the big employers, including some who had big interests in Czechoslovakia was by no means whole-heartedly pro-Munich). Further, it reflected the views of M. Bonnet and many other leading politicians, many of whom were sincerely convinced that French opinion was not 'marching', and that, in any case, it was not worth while risking a war for Czechoslovakia. It also reflected the views of the *fascisant* elements who looked upon the Czech crisis as being, above all, an internal French issue: the betrayal of Czechoslovakia, they were convinced, *would completely discredit democracy in*

Europe, and would enable them to gain greatly in influence, first, by stamping out Communism in France, and then Socialism, and then the democratic régime altogether.   The *Gleichschaltung*, or even the vassalisation of France did not unduly terrify these people.   Kerillis has quoted a number of letters from people who said in effect that 'they would sooner be ruled by Hitler than by the Front Populaire'.   The deterioration of the older *national* standards of France was very apparent from the Paris Press of September 1938.   Naturally a favourite 'defeatist' argument, especially during the later stages of the crisis, was also the 'non-existence' of the French Air Force and of A.R.P. in France.

So there was a large variety of factors in France working in favour of the Munich surrender.   Some respectable, others less so.

Only for a day or two after the partial mobilisation was anything like national unanimity restored in the Press but even then not for long.

At the same time, as has been rightly remarked, the French people were, in reality, far better than either their Press or their politicians.   The readiness with which all the recruits joined their regiments, the absence of any 'incidents' during that day—and that in spite of weeks and months of 'defeatist' propaganda—was a surprise to those who were convinced that the French people would not 'march for Czechoslovakia'.   A very high proportion of the French people felt instinctively, and in spite of everything, that it was not simply a case of marching 'for Czechoslovakia', and that far greater issues were at stake.

Another point that will have been noticed from the above discussion on the Press is that there was no sharp division into Left and Right over the question of Czechoslovakia.   It could not be said that all the people on the Right were 'defeatists' and all the people on the Left 'warmongers'.   As there were 'warmongers' among the Catholics (and their party the *Démocrates Populaires*) and among the Nationalists (Pertinax, Buré, Kerillis, etc.—and Kerillis's influence was in fact far greater than is suggested by his isolated position in Parliament and the relatively small circulation of the *Epoque*), so there were also 'pacifists', and advocates of 'peace at any price' on the Left,

above all among the Socialists and the Trade Unionists.
As for the Radicals—if they may be classed as a 'Left' party—
probably eighty per cent of them were 'pro-Munich'.   Except for the Communists, who, on the face of it, at any rate,
were completely unanimous in their policy of 'firmness'
(though one would hesitate to vouch for the complete unanimity of their rank and file), all the parties without exception
were divided, whether Left, Centre or Right.   The Radical
Party's feelings were, on the whole, well reflected in the hesitations and uncertainties and quarrels within the Daladier
Government.   Oddly enough, as has been already noted, the
two outstanding 'warmongers', that is, men who took an extremely grave view of the consequences of a surrender of
Czechoslovakia, were not Radicals, but two Centre Members
of the Cabinet—M. Mandel and M. Paul Reynaud.

As for M. Daladier he was, as somebody remarked at the
Chamber at the time of the crisis, the Mystery Man of France
—'*bonnetiste* one day and *belliciste* the next'.   But, in reality,
the *bonnetisme* was the stronger and the more lasting feeling
of the two.

CHAPTER XII

SEPTEMBER: BEFORE BERCHTESGADEN

F RANCE was Czechoslovakia's ally; but nearly all that was happening during that first half of September was happening—outside France. In Prague, at Nuremberg, in the Sudeten country, and in London. In France, there were only 'reactions'. But little action. M. Bonnet alone was very active.

I must mention here a curious little episode that occurred a few days before September. On August 24, Mr. Chamberlain, Lord Halifax and Sir John Simon held an important conference at the end of which it was decided to give a strong warning to Germany on the eve of the Nuremberg Congress—a warning to the effect that England would support France if the latter went to the aid of Czechoslovakia. Sir Nevile Henderson was instructed to convey this warning to the various Nazi leaders at Nuremberg. On August 25, the D.N.B., the German news agency, in a message from London denied 'on official authority' that any such British step was contemplated. Naturally, no such official denial had been given to the German agency. But, curiously enough, the Agence Havas published on the same day a message corroborating the German story:

> Surprise is shown in well-informed quarters at the news published in the British Press this morning according to which at their meeting yesterday, Mr. Chamberlain, Lord Halifax and Sir John Simon had decided to make shortly a statement to the effect that Britain would support France should the latter go to the aid of Czechoslovakia. M. Georges Bonnet to-day telephoned to M. Roger Cambon, the French chargé d'affaires in London. M. Cambon had seen Lord Halifax this morning. The Foreign Minister obtained no confirmation, and the news appears to be unfounded.

In spite of this message, which was obviously 'officially inspired', Sir John Simon made his speech at Lanark two days

later, and Sir Nevile Henderson soon afterwards communicated the British Government's warning to the Nazi
leaders.[1]

It was on September 1 that Sir Nevile Henderson saw Ribbentrop. The story goes that, as on one or two subsequent
occasions, Ribbentrop simply laughed in reply to the British
Ambassador's warnings; but if so, did he not laugh because
he was certain, not so much about Britain's determination to
do nothing, as about France's extreme reluctance to 'march'
for her ally? For if France was not going to 'march', obviously
Britain was not going to 'march' either.

On September 2 Paris was talking of a *détente*. Why? It
sounds funny; on the previous day Lord Runciman had decided no longer to keep up the pretence of 'mediating' between
the Czechs and the Sudetens, and had openly made Hitler
a partner in the negotiations. He had sent Henlein to see
Hitler (or such at least was the official version of Henlein's
journey to Berchtesgaden). Hitler had rejected the Czech
Plan No. 3 but had accepted to continue negotiations. Whereupon Lord Runciman naturally pressed the Czech Government to produce Plan No. 4. That day, M. Bernus, in the
Journal des Débats, had the sense to say that it was no use
talking of *détente* because the German Press was a trifle less
offensive than usual; anything might happen to-morrow. *On
ne peut rien prévoir.*

Nothing so gloomy in the *Figaro*, where M. d'Ormesson,
after referring to Germany's war preparations and to the atmosphere of exasperation that was being created round the
German-Czech crisis, was happy to state that

> France had seldom been so calm and so full of goodwill.
> Whatever may be the interests and the passions, which are
> anxious to exaggerate their own importance, we must at any
> price demonstrate this one vital fact—the peaceful solidity of
> our country. Otherwise the risks will grow week after week.

In other words, it was no use demonstrating any kind of
strength, or to warn Germany; it was enough to impress her
with France's 'peaceful solidity'—whatever that meant. On
the following day—September 3—the Press was a little more

[1] *Les Volontaires*, January 1939.

alarmed. In the same *Figaro,* the more clearsighted M.
Romier wrote:

> There are three possibilities—Hitler may (1) intervene in
> order to 'protect' a possible Sudeten rebellion, (2) demand a
> plebiscite, which would break up the territorial unity of Czecho-
> slovakia, or (3) propose an eleventh-hour compromise which
> would not leave the Czechs with too much bitterness. The
> Nuremberg Congress will show which course Hitler has chosen.
> *His choice will largely depend on the news he receives from abroad.*

Precisely. But no news was coming from France to impress
him. The following day, Sunday, September 4, was, however,
marked by an important event. That afternoon Mr. William
Bullitt, the United States Ambassador, and M. Georges Bonnet 'celebrated' Franco-American friendship at the unveiling
of the monument at the Pointe de Grave commemorating the
landing in France in 1917 of the American troops.

The attitude of the United States during those weeks was
admirable. Reference has already been made to the speeches
made two weeks earlier by Mr. Roosevelt and Mr. Cordell
Hull. Now it was Mr. Bullitt's turn to give a new American
warning to Germany. Apart from speeches, the United States
had shortly before concentrated a naval squadron in the
Atlantic.

After exalting the ideals of freedom and democracy that
were common to France and the United States, and recalling
President Roosevelt's recent speech, Mr. Bullitt said:

> 'World peace is essential to us, for we know that a general
> war to-day would mean the destruction for a certain time of all
> the values of civilisation accumulated with so much labour
> during the course of centuries.
> 'The people of France and of the United States ardently
> desire peace, and we pray that we may be able to remain in
> peace with all other nations.
> 'But if war breaks out in Europe once again *no man can say or
> predict whether or not the United States would be involved in such a war.*'

Referring to Mr. Cordell Hull's plea for international collaboration, Mr. Bullitt deplored the fact that there were certain parts of the world where this spirit of collaboration 'shone
by its absence'. The Ambassador concluded:

> 'The colours under which Lafayette fought are the colours of
> liberty. These colours are those of France and the United

States and several other countries; they are the old, old colours
of common sense and human decency, of Christian charity and
tolerance; they are the colours of freedom and peace.'

For a cold and calculating man like M. Bonnet and for one
who claimed to know America so well and to be so certain
of her fundamental 'isolationism' the speech he made on that
occasion seemed extravagant and almost irresponsible:

> 'One is inclined to say that it is the fate of France's arms and
> America's arms to be assembled under the same banners when-
> ever they are called upon to defend those principles [liberty
> etc.] which our two nations consider to be the most precious
> heritage of mankind.   The one friend is irresistibly compelled
> to rush to the help of the other friend who is in danger.'

Passionate opponents of M. Bonnet have gone so far as to
suggest that this extravagant indiscretion was deliberate, and
was calculated, in the most Machiavellian manner, to produce
an isolationist outburst in America; an outburst which would
discourage the British and French advocates of a 'firm' policy—
that is, all those people who were certainly looking hopefully
to America for strong moral and economic, if not military,
support.   Whether Mr. Roosevelt's Hyde Park statement on
September 11, when he declared the interpretations of his
European policy to be 'about one hundred per cent wrong'
was intended as a direct reply to M. Bonnet is not certain;
but it may well have referred to certain articles published in
America on the strength of M. Bonnet's extraordinary statement.   In any case, it was a surprising statement—and a dangerous one—to make.

In the course of his speech, M. Bonnet referred to the Czech
crisis.   He placed Prague and Berlin on the same level, treating them as two equally naughty boys:

> 'We are not underestimating the gravity of the Czech problem.
> But we hope that, thanks to the love of peace that must inspire
> all nations, thanks to the sense of grave responsibility that must
> be felt by the Governments of Prague and Berlin, and thanks
> also to the loyal and close co-operation between Great Britain
> and France, the grave menace to European peace will be
> averted.'

But his speech contained no warning to Germany, except
for an assurance that 'France would faithfully carry out the
pacts she had signed'.

A writer in the *Europe Nouvelle* later made the following remarkable allegation:

The British Government had by this time discovered that it had been pretty well left alone to carry the Czech baby; and it was becoming more and more puzzled by the extraordinary 'reticence' of the French Government. The British Foreign Office therefore specially asked M. Bonnet to include in his Pointe de Grave speech a declaration of loyalty to Czechoslovakia.

The semi-official *Intransigeant* wrote that evening:

> One hopes that these elevated words may be heard and understood in Berlin. The two orators were careful not to utter any warning, and appealed, on the contrary, for conciliation. Mr. Bullitt even referred to the limitation of armaments and to an economic understanding among nations. As for M. Bonnet, in a speech full of elevated thoughts, he displayed the most sincere desire for conciliation. He declared, however, that France would remain loyal to the agreements she had signed. Germany knows this well, even though some of Herr Hitler's advisers have tried to cast doubts on our loyalty and our resolution.

'*De quoi se marrer,*' as the *Canard Enchaîné* would say. The *Humanité* was rather less pleased:

> M. Bonnet yesterday declared that France would be loyal to the treaties she had signed. Very good. But not good enough. It was necessary in the present circumstances to dot the i's. M. Bonnet would have served peace better had he proclaimed that the integrity of Czechoslovakia and her independence were essential to France's security.

. . . .

In the meantime things were going from bad to worse in Czechoslovakia. After being informed of the Hitler-Henlein talks, Lord Runciman told London that he had 'not lost all hope'. At the same time Henlein was saying that there could be no compromise. 'The eight points of the Karlsbad programme are a minimum.' Clearly he was going to ask for more before long.

While he was saying this, all the bells of Nuremberg were announcing Hitler's entry into the town. The Congress started with a gala performance of the *Meistersinger*; in French, *les*

maîtres chanteurs, the Blackmailers. An easy pun, but a singularly appropriate one.

It was during that same afternoon that the French Government at last published a *communiqué* saying that certain
reservists had been called up to man the Maginot Line.

> Because of the international situation and the large re-
> inforcements in both men and material sent by Germany to our
> north-east frontier, the Government has had to take a certain
> number of measures of security.
>
> The principal measure is to recall a certain number of reservists
> to the colours in order to maintain at their full complement
> the troops of the Maginot Line and other garrisons. Officers
> and men on leave have also received the order to return to their
> garrisons.
>
> These measures should not disquieten the public, whose calm
> is one of the essential elements of peace.
>
> Moreover, according to the latest news, the general situation
> seems to be developing towards a settlement.

What the last paragraph was based on was a complete mystery. The speeches made by Goebbels and the Sudeten leaders
on the previous day suggested anything in the world except
that 'the general situation seemed to be developing towards a
settlement'. Was the French public being deliberately doped
into complacency and passivity?

The Diplomatic Correspondent of the *Manchester Guardian*
wrote that night from London: 'The crisis, according to the
view taken here, would seem to be approaching its most critical
stage.'

M. Blum's comments in the *Populaire* on the military precautions are characteristic of the cautious and pacifist mood
of the Socialist leader.

> On the other side of the Rhine operations have for the last
> fortnight been in progress—operations which are called
> 'manœuvres'. But these manœuvres are accompanied by a
> mobilisation and extensive requisitions—and no one knows
> how long all this is to go on. Corresponding and 'adequate'
> measures in France would have been the calling up of all the
> immediately available reservists, *(les classes disponibles)*. *The
> Government has signed no such order, and in my opinion is right.* It
> has done nothing that would have looked like the beginning
> of a mobilisation. It has confined itself to a few justified
> precautions. Was it right or wrong to have made these

measures public? One may argue on this point. They are of so small a volume that they could have passed unnoticed both here and abroad. But, after all, why hide anything from the nation when there is nothing to hide?

Needless to say, Henri de Kerillis, boiling with Clemencist indignation, took a different view. He wrote in the *Epoque* on September 9:

> The German game is successful beyond all Hitler's hopes. France and England failed to learn a lesson from their great victory of May 21. Impressed by Germany's military display, they have been trying to keep her quiet with concessions. The Czechs are being constantly asked to capitulate; and our statesmen fail to realise that each new retreat by Prague is a new defeat for London and Paris, and a new cause for German exultation. Paris and London are frightened to answer Germany's military preparations by equal preparations. They are frightened to call up ten classes of reservists, to build three lines of retreat behind the Maginot Line, to begin the evacuation of Paris, to concentrate the British and French navies in the North Sea. The moral side of the drama is being neglected, and mischievous campaigns have made disastrous progress on both sides of the Channel.
>
> If this goes on Germany will believe that she can do everything. She will no longer be satisfied with a moral victory: she will want a material triumph. She will no longer be content with a Sudeten statute in Czechoslovakia; she will want to annex the Sudetenland. . . . Before it is too late, we must warn Hitler.

He concluded by saying that the defeatists were 'not France'.

Much has been written about the famous *Times* editorial of September 7, which, in suggesting the transfer of the Sudeten territory to Germany, acted as a tremendous encouragement to Hitler. It was wicked, and ill-advised, and all that, and Mr. Kennedy more than deserved the Government's *démenti* that afternoon.

But, actually, it was probably excessive to blame the British Government for Mr. Kennedy's thoughtlessness—which is, apparently, all that it was. Perhaps the pretty sentence with which he wound up his leader was only a sudden and unfortunate recollection of an argument he had at some time heard from somebody—who knows? But I have reason to believe

that there was no sinister plot behind that *Times* editorial—
though, I admit, it did look rather like it.

But although the *Times* is a famous paper, while the *République*, is not, the article the latter published *not on the 7th, but on the 6th of September*, was in some ways more significant than the *Times* leader.   M. Emile Roche, the president of the Radical Federation of the Nord, and the leader of the extreme Right Wing of the Radical Party, is a very close associate of M. Caillaux, and—of M. Bonnet.   And this is what M. Roche wrote in the *République* on September 6:

> Will the Sudetens refuse the offers Prague is making them?
> Do they want a form of autonomy that Prague cannot grant
> them?   Is that a reason why we should gradually accept the
> idea of an inevitable war?   It seems insane to me.
>   No!   The talks between Prague and Karlsbad, and the
> talks between Paris, London and Berlin must continue.   And
> a peaceful solution *must* be found.
>   *Can Prague still persist in counting 3,200,000 Germans among its
> loyal subjects?   If so, all will be well.*
>   *But, if not, then the two races which cannot agree to live together
> within the framework of the centralised Czech State must be separated.*
> Neither of them would die as a result, nor would Central
> Europe.   We do not believe that they would like one another
> any better after millions of people had been killed in a war.

The phrase 'centralised Czech State' was perhaps calculated to 'cover' M. Roche, in case of trouble; but the meaning of his article was perfectly clear.   It said exactly what the *Times* was going to say *twenty-four hours later*.

And that was the day on which the Czech Government, almost squeezed to death by Lord Runciman, produced its Plan No. 4.   Did the French Government declare publicly, as it might well have done, that Czechoslovakia had now gone to the utmost limit of concessions, having almost accepted the entire Karlsbad programme, and that no more concession would be demanded from it by France?   No, the French Government said nothing of the kind.   As we shall see, in the days that followed,·France actually lent a hand in giving the Czechs another turn of the screw.

'Plan No. 4' of the Czech Government provided the Sudetens with a far wider autonomy than that enjoyed by any minority in Europe.   Without German pressure, the Sudetens should

have been more than satisfied.[1]   Only two points of the Karlsbad programme were rejected by the Czechs—the two points
that were essential to Hitler—namely point 3, which demanded
the legal recognition of the German regions in one unit,
whereas the Czech Plan proposed to divide them into three
departments, and point 8, which demanded full liberty for
German ideology, which would have meant the establishment
of a totalitarian State within a democratic republic.

'With the publication of this plan'—the Prague Correspondent of the *Manchester Guardian* wrote on September 7, 'the
Government has shown its willingness to make a far-reaching
contribution to the maintenance of the peace of the world.
Now similar sacrifices are demanded from the Sudeten Germans and from the Great Powers.

'The Czech population, which had been watching events

---

[1] The following is a comparison between the Karlsbad programme and the
'final' Czech offer of September 6:

KARLSBAD DEMANDS	CZECH OFFER
I	**I**
Full equality of status between Czechs and Germans.	Proportional employment of officials according to population.
II	**II**
Guarantee of equality by recognition of the Sudeten Germans as a legal entity.	Employment of officials in the districts of their nationality.
III	**III**
Determination and legal recognition of the German regions within the State.	Local regions to have police of their own nationality.
IV	**IV**
Full self-government for those German regions.	New language law based on complete equality.
V	**V**
Legal protection for every citizen living outside his own national region.	Assistance to depressed Sudeten industrial areas.
VI	**VI**
Removal of injustices inflicted on Germans since 1918 and reparation for the damages caused thereby.	Self-government for the national minorities in the areas in which they show a majority. All questions not dealing with national unity to be dealt with locally.
VII	**VII**
Recognition and realisation of the principle 'German regions—German officials.'	Departments for minorities in central administrations.
VIII	**VIII**
Full liberty to profess German nationhood and German political philosophy.	Protection for citizens against denationalisation.
	IX
	The plan to be put in force as soon as possible.

with a certain optimism, is now filled with gloom and bitterness. The concession which admits the German local police has especially embittered the non-Henlein minority in the Sudeten part. It is feared that the handing over of the police to the Germans will cause an enormous exodus of Czech and Jewish manufacturers and merchants from the Sudeten parts and from the mixed territories.

'It is curious that to-day incidents are being reported by which apparently the Sudeten Germans want to prove that it is impossible for them to live if the Czech State Police remain in their areas. The Czech-German problem is getting more and more complicated day by day instead of taking a turn for the better.'

Paris was, perhaps for the first time, becoming aware of the full gravity of the situation. That night groups of ten or twenty people could be seen at various points discussing events in Czechoslovakia—an unmistakable sign of altogether unusual nervousness.

There was also great excitement in the Chamber lobbies; which in the last few days, had begun to fill up, even though Parliament was not sitting. People were wondering whether the Czechs had not gone *too* far, whether the Czechs would be able to keep full control over the districts controlled by German police, and whether these districts were not likely to become hotbeds of Nazi rebellion. M. Frossard, M. Daladier's former Minister of Public Works (he had resigned from the Government a fortnight earlier after Daladier's broadcast on the forty-hour week), wrote in the *Homme Libre* on September 9:

> This is not a capitulation; it is a heroic sacrifice. . . . Lord Runciman had hitherto been able to exercise his pressure and influence only on the Czechs while the Germans and the Sudetens have not yielded one inch and have in practice not taken the slightest notice of Lord Runciman's 'mediation'.

And M. Blum, in the *Populaire* wrote:

> British and French pressure in Prague cannot be driven any further. Paris must no longer act in Prague but in London, and London must no longer act in Prague but in Berlin.

But all eyes were turned to Nuremberg: would Hitler accept or not? There was an uneasy feeling that he would not.

On the previous day Geneviève Tabouis had reported in the *Œuvre* that

> Hitler had solemnly asked Ribbentrop to tell him whether England would march, if France marched; Ribbentrop replied that she would not; and that Germany could 'go ahead'.

No doubt, M. Bailby was angry with Geneviève:

> How does she know what Hitler said in private to Ribbentrop? She wasn't there.

But there was a growing feeling that neither England nor France was doing their job properly in impressing Hitler.

On the following day, after the Morawska-Ostrawa incidents and the rejection by the Sudetens of the 'final' Czech plan, M. Blum wrote, in the *Populaire*, with a characteristic opening sentence:

> To act means, for the present, to speak. But we must speak clearly, dotting all the i's, and leaving no room for any error or misunderstanding or doubt in the minds of the German leaders regarding the real position of France and Great Britain. What is at stake is not the future of the Sudeten Germans, but the future of Europe, the future of Britain and France. If the great democracies express sufficiently strongly what they feel, they may yet save themselves, Europe and peace.

What was the French Government hoping for? It seems that two things were still hoped for: one, that England would 'warn' Hitler; another, that the Czechs would allow themselves to be squeezed still more.

Here are the highly characteristic headlines of the officially-inspired *Paris-Midi* of September 8:

> *Hitler, Goering and Ribbentrop are examining Plan No. 4 which, in their view, can, at most, serve as a basis for negotiations. But since the Czechs have reached the limit of concessions, what will be plan No. 5? Will it be Runciman's plan or Hitler's plan?*

Just like that.

And on September 9, when the Slovaks, Hungarians and Poles began to cause trouble, *Paris-Midi* came out with the superbly fatuous headline:

'VERS UNE SUISSE DANUBIENNE?'

while in the *Journal*, M. Alphonse de Chateaubriand was
going into raptures over the Nuremberg Congress:

> German youth! With what fervour they surround the master
> of Germany! How he feels what these young people want!
> An unforgettable sight, when, on his arrival, they saw him
> appear on the top of the station stair. There is a fixed look
> in his eyes. He looks at the cheering crowd, which surrounds
> him like a surging ocean. There is a grave look on his face. . . .
> War. . . . Peace. . . .
> The Germans say: 'Prague will decide.' Many Frenchmen
> think: 'He cannot avoid a war.' While others still say: 'He
> will go step by step.'
> 'No!' repeat unceasingly those who know him. 'He will
> place his genius at the service of the world, and he will give it
> Peace.'
> If only one could be sure. . . .

But that by the way—as an example of French Hitler-
worship.

The important question between the 8th and 10th of September when the crisis was rapidly coming to a head, was
whether England would speak. For in French official quarters
they were still shrugging their shoulders, saying that it was
'all very difficult' so long as England had not made her position sufficiently clear.

On the 8th the British Home Fleet assembled for naval
manœuvres in the North Sea.

On the 9th the Sudetens proclaimed a state of emergency,
and apparently waiting for Hitler's speech, suspended their
talks with the Czechs, who, they said, were no longer capable
of keeping law and order.

The French called up a number of naval reservists, and
there was said to be great activity at Brest and Toulon, where
the Atlantic and Mediterranean fleets were assembled.

On the 10th there were important ministerial consultations
in London. The situation was becoming so serious that the
Opposition leaders were summoned to No. 10. At the Foreign
Office on the previous day Lord Halifax had already seen
Mr. Eden; and Mr. Chamberlain had decided to send a note
of warning to Hitler.

But nothing much was happening in Paris. The *Petit
Parisien* warned Germany that if she invaded Czechoslovakia

'la riposte serait foudroyante'. England, the United States, everybody would be against Germany. Whereupon, however, it hastened to add:

> If, on the contrary, the Reich does not depart from the road of peace, and collaborates sincerely at a friendly settlement which England and France are doing all they can to reach, then such a settlement will be reached before long. The two Western Powers are ready to redouble their efforts so that these delicate negotiations may succeed.

Redouble their efforts—after Prague had already reached the 'limit of concessions'!

Others, however, were clamouring for a British declaration.

The declaration came on September 11. It was the famous 'authorised statement' which, as was generally known, had been made to the Press by Mr. Chamberlain himself.

After recalling that Lord Runciman had already settled a great number of difficulties in the past, the statement said that there might be some new difficulties and some new deadlocks; but so long as Lord Runciman remained in Prague, there was no reason why a solution should not be found.

After commenting on Sir John Simon's Lanark speech, and saying that its meaning was perfectly clear, the statement continued:

> Great Britain could not remain aloof if there were a general conflict in which the integrity of France was threatened. . . . It is of the utmost importance that Germany should make no mistake about it: she cannot with impunity carry out a rapid and successful military campaign against Czechoslovakia without the fear of intervention by France and even Great Britain.

It was good enough. It was as good as the French could have expected. And it was a particularly useful warning after Goering's speech on the previous day.

On that Saturday night of September 10 Paris was in a state of jitters. The morning papers had said that, since Hitler was not going to speak until the Tuesday, it would be a *week-end d'attente*. It was a fine evening, and the Champs-Élysées were crowded with people, most of them looking healthy and tanned after their summer holidays.

'*Paris-Soir! Paris-Soir!*' the newsboys were shouting. '*Discours sensationnel de Goering!*' The papers were being

snatched up. The result was—long, gloomy, anxious faces.
In two-inch letters *Paris-Soir* announced:

VIOLENT DISCOURS
DU MARECHAL GOERING

and, as sub-headings:

'We await the events that are inevitable. . . .'

'No army can enter German soil, and we are ready to
make the last sacrifice.'

'The idea of frightening us is laughable.'

'It is intolerable that a nation of miserable pigmies—one
scarcely knows where they have come from—should behave as
it is behaving towards a great civilised nation. . . .'

'Instead of discoursing on peace, the British would do better
to take care of their little Jewish State, of which they are in
charge, and which is torn by civil war. . . .'

'We have never been so powerful. A blockade against us has
become impossible.'

All in large letters on the front page. One can imagine the
effect. Many a Parisian spent a bad night—the first of many
to come.

On the Sunday, M. Bonnet went to Geneva where he conferred with M. Litvinov and M. Comnene, the Rumanian
Foreign Minister. He was going on the following day, to
report his impressions to the Cabinet.

.   .   .   .

Hitler was to speak at Nuremberg at seven o'clock on
Monday.

That afternoon the French Cabinet met; I went down to
the War Office to see the Ministers arrive. They all looked
very grim and important. Two hours later they started coming out, one by one. As usual, the journalists wanted to know
what had happened. But all were very reluctant to talk. Only
M. Sarraut, looking mysterious, said that a great many things
had been discussed—but mostly 'on a hypothetical basis—for
we still do not know what Hitler is going to decide to-night'.
I asked M. Sarraut what he thought of the British 'authorised
statement' of the previous night. 'Are you satisfied, *M. le
Président?*' '*Oui, je suis très, très, très satisfait,*' he declared,

with a rattling *crescendo*. 'So you can't complain any more of insufficient British support?' 'Certainly not,' M. Sarraut replied.

A point worth noting. At the Foreign Office, in the Chamber lobbies and elsewhere, a lot of them had been saying: 'Oh, if only we could be sure of British support. . . .'

We waited for some of the other Ministers, but not all of them came out. After the Cabinet meeting, M. Daladier had retained M. Bonnet, M. Chautemps, M. Pomaret and M. de Monzie. A curious assortment: for these four were the principal advocates of an 'easy-going' policy. What were they talking about?

That Cabinet meeting was 'hypothetical'. All kinds of measures were discussed that would be taken if war broke out. Finishing touches were given to the mobilisation plans; emergency measures of an economic and financial order were also discussed, including a possible moratorium on commercial payments, foreign exchange restrictions, and so on.

A strangely-worded *communiqué* was published after the meeting:

> The cabinet meeting at the Ministry of War under the presidency of M. Daladier studied recent diplomatic documents and political events abroad, regarding which M. Bonnet made a statement.
>
> The Cabinet paid tribute to the patriotism, calm, and *sang-froid* of the nation. It also received from North Africa and our colonial Empire the most moving testimony of fidelity to France.
>
> This dignified and reasonable attitude of the country is of particular value for the defence of peace.

The tribute to the calm and self-assurance of the French people was well deserved. France had certainly kept remarkably calm—except for Goering's speech that Saturday afternoon. But on the following day already the speech had been watered down in the morning papers.

Internal quarrels had become less noticeable; and the patriotic sense of responsibility was apparent from the remarkable fact that there had been little or no export of capital during the previous week; and—except in Alsace— no run on the banks and savings banks. At least not yet. Important also was the reference to the French overseas territories—a warning to Italy and Germany not to count on trouble in the French colonies.

What did M. Bonnet tell the Cabinet after his talks with M. Litvinov and M. Comnene? The Russian Foreign Minister had assured him at Geneva on the previous day that the U.S.S.R. would come to the aid of Czechoslovakia in the event of war, and after a decision by the League Council declaring Czechoslovakia to be the victim of aggression. This formality was provided in the Russo-Czech Pact, and was understandable, since Russia had no common frontier with Czechoslovakia; and it was necessary to give Rumania the legal right under Article 16 of the Covenant to allow Russian troops to pass through her territory. Although at that stage Rumania, naturally, did not wish to commit herself openly to allowing free passage to Russian troops and planes, there was no doubt that she would not deny Russia this right if it came to the point.

But M. Bonnet does not appear to have given quite that impression to the Cabinet, and, according to reports published both about this and subsequent Cabinet meetings, to have said in effect that the Russians and Rumanians had wrapped themselves up in League procedure, and, generally, to have shown little eagerness to help. Moreover, he is understood to have made the most of the 'decapitation' of the Red Army, and to have expressed great doubts as to its efficiency.

After the Cabinet meeting, and M. Daladier's talks with M. de Monzie, M. Bonnet, and the rest, the Premier held another conference with General Gamelin, the Head of the General Staff, General Georges and General Billotte, the Military Governor of Paris. He discussed with them the final mobilisation arrangements, the evacuation of Paris and of the Paris suburbs, active and passive air defence, and so on. It all looked very earnest and sinister. What was Hitler going to say?

I had an hour before Hitler's speech, and dropped in at the Chamber. As I was leaving the War Ministry I saw M. Mistler arrive. The handsome young president of the Foreign Affairs Committee of the Chamber, who spends his spare moments writing plays for the Odéon, was, during those days, one of the most active 'pacifists' in Paris. He and M. Flandin and M.

Caillaux were pulling wires as hard as they could go. The first thing that must be prevented, they thought, was a mobilisation.

In the Chamber lobbies that evening 'pacifist' propaganda was in full swing. One deputy was vociferating about *la jeunesse française*; France had no lives to spare for the sake of Czechoslovakia. *On sera tranquille derrière la ligne Maginot.* He spoke with conviction. He probably meant what he was saying. 'Only twenty years' respite since the last war—no it isn't long enough. We must gain strength. If *la jeunesse française* is killed off it'll mean the end of France and French civilisation. *Il n'y aura que des vieillards en France.*' Others were arguing about the French Air Force. 'How the devil can we go to war? Flandin has just been saying that we have only 600 aeroplanes which are any good at all.'

'Six hundred! He didn't say six hundred; he said sixty!'

I saw a reporter from the *Jour*. 'Well, are you dropping Czechoslovakia?'

'*La Tchécoslovaquie—croyez-moi, on s'en fout éperdument. Beneš—il nous emmerde.*'

I went home and turned on the wireless. There he was, already bellowing. Die Niederträchtige something or other. Howls, howls, howls. Der Herr Beneš—More howls. Gott der allmächtige has not created 3,000,000 Germans to be placed under the niederträchtige tutelage of 7,000,000 Tschechen. I shall not tolerate—Ich werde es nicht dulden—howls, howls, howls—that 3,000,000 unhappy Kreaturen shall be oppressed, and I ask the foreign Staatsmänner—pfui! pfui! pfui!—to note that this is not an empty phrase. Howls, howls, howls. The Cathedral of Strasbourg (*con dolore*) means much to us Germans; but we have crossed it out, so that we may once and for all put an end to our eternal feud with France. May 21 was an unerhörte Lüge—'But this will never happen again,' I said to myself at the end of May, and since that day Herr Chef-Ingenieur Todt and hundreds of thousands of German hands have been building fortifications on our western frontier. We are now invincible. More howls. Oh! the cannibal feast! And when the speech was over, the howls became deafening, and the Sieg heil! Sieg heil! Sieg heil! went

on interminably. And then the trumpets and drums played
a sort of cannibal march—Siegfried motif—tum—tururum—
tum tum—Siegfried motif—tum—tururum—tum tum. Wag-
ner gone cannibal. Oh! turn off the bloody thing!

I went out into the street. Mme Bousquet, my concierge,
looked out of her lodge. 'What's wrong with him?' she said.
'He must be off his chump. *Est-ce qu'on gueule comme ça?*
They *must* be a lot of savages. I had to turn it off, because
Guy and Monique began to cry.'

The silence in the street was almost uncanny. At the
tabac a couple of drunks were quarrelling about something
quite unpolitical.

I went back to the War Ministry. No, there was no Cabinet
meeting; and there wasn't going to be one to-night. Three
or four reporters were hanging about the entrance. 'Pretty
bad, Hitler's speech, don't you think? Smells of war.' '*Pen-
sez-vous,*' one of the reporters said. 'They're going to get a
plebiscite, and that'll settle it.' 'Is that what the Government
says? Didn't look like it this afternoon.' 'Of course, the
Government will accept a plebiscite.' 'What about Reynaud?'
'Oh, he doesn't count.'

I went on to the Quai d'Orsay. Just my luck—here was
Mistler again. He had seen Bonnet. 'What's he saying?'
'He hasn't had time to study the speech properly; but the
first impression is that the door for further negotiations has
not been closed. The speech hasn't improved the outlook, but
hasn't made it any worse either.'

'What do you make of the story about the Rhineland fortifications?'

'Oh, there's a lot of bluff in that. We know what the fortifications cost us, and how long it took us to build them. Besides,
cement needs a good long time to harden. I don't think
the German generals would support Hitler's claim that
the fortifications are impregnable. Still, we might have
thought of all that on 7th of March 1936,' he added philosophically.

The telephone to London was a bother that night. The
whole Continent seemed to be talking to London via Paris.
Especially Prague, which had only one or two direct lines to
London—and these were constantly engaged by the British

Legation and by Lord Runciman. It took an hour and a half
to get through.

.   .   .   .

The day after Hitler's speech was in a sense the most decisive
moment in the whole Czech crisis. The French Cabinet met;
and it was clear that if a firm stand was to be taken, if a final
attempt was to be made to stop Hitler from attacking or dis-
membering Czechoslovakia, it was now or never. Lord Runciman was still in Prague, and trying to 'continue negotiations';
but more and more 'incidents', involving bloodshed and loss
of life were being reported from the Sudeten country. These
were, as somebody remarked in Paris, 'the first results of
Hitler's speech.'

In spite of it, the greater part of the Paris Press, partly
under official influence, tried to take the rosiest possible view
of the Nuremberg harangue.

> 'It is in the general interest of Europe,' M. Bourguès wrote
> in the *Petit Parisien*, 'that the negotiations that are continuing
> in Prague under the guidance of Lord Runciman should go on
> uninterruptedly. So grave a matter must be treated without dila-
> tory tactics. The Beneš plan is really very liberal, and should lead
> to an agreement satisfactory to both the Czechs and the Sude-
> tens, on condition that confidence is restored on both sides,
> and that questions of detail are settled in a broadminded
> spirit.'

As if the Czech 'Plan No. 4' was not broadminded enough!

M. d'Ormesson in the *Figaro* thought that 'a door had been
left open' for further negotiations.

M. Guérin, in the *Œuvre*, was less optimistic. 'One has to
cling on to the last hope,' he wrote. And he saw the last hope
in the fact that Hitler had mentioned the word 'settlement'
and had not mentioned the word 'Anschluss'.

As for the *Matin* it said quite candidly that France had no
reason to make war if the Sudetens wanted a plebiscite.

The two great pessimists were, as usual, Kerillis and Péri.

> 'The end of it all,' Péri wrote, 'will be a settling of accounts
> with France; and this settlement will be all the easier if, drugged
> by Hitler's protestations of love, we allow our system of security
> to be destroyed.'

The French Government had now come to the crossroads.
Resist or yield? Two men, M. Paul Reynaud, the Minister

of Justice, and M. Mandel, the Minister of Colonies and old Clemenceau's disciple, were all for resistance; that is, for an immediate partial mobilisation, which, they thought, could alone convince Hitler that France was meaning business, and would oblige him (since he obviously did not want war with France, England, Czechoslovakia and Russia) to accept a settlement which would leave the integrity of Czechoslovakia intact. Clearly, what interested him far more than the welfare of the Sudeten Germans (for what did he care for the Tyrolese?) was the destruction of Czechoslovakia as a military power, as an ally of France, as that platform near the heart of Germany from which (as Kerillis so often recalled) Berlin could be bombed—which it could not be from France or England.

M. Mandel and M. Reynaud knew that if France failed to react, Hitler's next step would be to ask for a plebiscite or an annexation of the Sudetenland. He had already made a veiled reference to the plebiscite in his speech on the previous night. These two Ministers were, in some measure, supported by M. Champetier de Ribes, the Minister of Pensions, M. Campinchi, the Minister of Marine, and, to a lesser degree, by M. Zay, the Minister of Education, and M. Queuille, the Minister of Agriculture.

But the 'pacifists' were in the majority. The principal 'pacifists', who made no longer any secret of their belief that it was not worth while risking a war for Czechoslovakia, and who perhaps did not believe that Hitler could be intimidated, were M. Bonnet, the Foreign Minister, M. de Monzie, the Minister of Public Works, M. Pomaret, the Minister of Labour, and M. Chautemps, the Vice-Premier. Their views were not greatly dissimilar from those held by M. Flandin, M. Caillaux, M. Mistler, and others who had been pulling wires as hard as they could during the previous days.

Here is one of their arguments:

France is a war-weary country with a low birthrate, and provincial opinion is not prepared for a war over Czechoslovakia. It is not without significance that all the principal 'pacifists' represented rural constituencies in the Centre or West of France: M. de Monzie and M. Pomaret represented the Lot; M. Caillaux the Sarthe; M. Bonnet, the Dordogne; M. Flandin the Yonne; M. Chautemps the Loire-et-Cher. In and outside the Cabinet they spoke, as it were, 'in the name of the French peasantry'; that peasantry which had always supplied the greater part of the army recruits.

Needless to say, at that Cabinet meeting of September 13, other arguments were also used by the 'pacifists': the numerical and qualitative inferiority of the French Air Force, and the complete inadequacy of A.R.P. in Paris and other French centres.

The story goes that M. Bonnet—or was it M. Daladier?—produced General Gamelin's report on France's military possibilities in case of war; and read out to the Cabinet General Gamelin's enumeration of France's weak points—particularly her inferiority in the air; but omitted his conclusions which were to the effect that Czechoslovakia must not be abandoned, and that, if unfortunately war could not be avoided, France could be sure of victory.

It has often been argued that France, as an ally of Czechoslovakia, could have been of little immediate use to the Czechs; for since the French Army, with its Maginot Line was adapted to defence and not to aggression, and since the Siegfried Line had rendered an invasion of Germany practically impossible, France could only rely on a successful long war, at the end of which Germany would have been brought to her knees by a blockade. The principal military operations against Germany would have been done by the Czechs and Russians (whose support, M. Bonnet claimed, should not be relied upon). Actually, General Gamelin did not visualise the war as a motionless concentration of French and German troops on the two sides of the Rhine frontier; a French invasion of the Saar was contemplated; and it is remarkable that in his speech at Saarbrucken on October 11—that is, *after* Munich—Hitler admitted that two zones of the German frontier still remained to be fortified—the zone of Aachen (Aix-la-Chapelle) and the Saar zone.

But, in speaking to the Cabinet, M. Bonnet is understood to have dwelt on France's weak points, and not on her strong points—or on Germany's weak points. And again he emphasised that the Russians were too far away, and their army was, in any case, in a mess. At most, their air force could be of some nuisance value; but Czechoslovakia would be destroyed in a short time, and then the Russian Air Force would not be much good either. And it is reasonable to suppose that he also declared that Great Britain was neither ready nor willing to 'march'; and that a mere 'bluff' would not achieve the desired result.

M. Daladier wavered. He tried to weigh up all the pros and cons; France's military obligations, the possibility of a German climb-down, and, on the other hand, the millions of lives that might be lost if the bluff did not come off. He must have thought of his native Provence, of his two sons, of the quiet pleasant life under the olive trees. Was Czechoslovakia *absolutely* essential to the continued existence of France? Was it certain that if Czechoslovakia fell, Germany would automatically become the unchallengeable mistress of Europe? He wavered and hesitated, and in the end decided that there should be no mobilisation—not yet. M. Chautemps was of the same mind; he also had two sons of military age. He had often said he would not let them die 'for Spain'; why should he let them die for Czechoslovakia? If Hitler had to be 'warned', he should have been warned before Nuremberg; now it was too late; Hitler had committed himself too far. Why nothing had been done sooner, was another matter.

After the Cabinet meeting it was declared that more reservists 'may be called up'; a decree was signed by the President prohibiting the export of a long list of raw materials—notably iron, steel, scrap iron, raw wool, raw shrunk cloth, and skins and hides. M. Marchandeau, the Finance Minister, said that a number of financial and economic decrees had been prepared which would come into force in case of war. But under these arrangements, he said, everybody would retain the free and complete disposal of his deposits, whether in savings or other banks. And M. Patenôtre, the Minister of National Economy, added:

> 'In 1914 we had to improvise, but if by an unfortunate chance the catastrophe of war should occur we shall not now be taken by surprise. We have foreseen all the economic and financial consequences which a conflict would involve, and I have taken account of the measures which are required, including a moratorium and a suspension of payments.'

But none of these measures was sufficient to impress Germany.

Clearly, France was not 'marching'. Another rather more important decision was, however, taken by the Cabinet that day; and that was to prohibit all public meetings dealing with international questions. It seemed important to the Government not to allow the Communists, with their 'warmongering', to excite the populace, which in 1936 had given M. Blum so much trouble with its clamour for 'aeroplanes for Spain'.

During that day M. Daladier had two meetings with the British Ambassador, Sir Eric Phipps. It is said that after their first meeting that afternoon, Sir Eric reported to London on the great bewilderment he had found among the French Ministers.

That night Sir Eric Phipps was at the Opéra-Comique when he received a message from M. Daladier asking him to see him at once. The Ambassador jumped into a taxi and drove to the War Office. The situation in Czechoslovakia was growing worse every hour. At 5.30 p.m. the Sudetens had sent an ultimatum to the Czech Government demanding the revocation within six hours of the martial law measures that had been enforced in a number of Sudeten areas. What happened during M. Daladier's and Sir Eric Phipps's meeting that evening? Nobody quite knows; except that, in leaving the War Office, Sir Eric dropped the enigmatic phrase: '*Il faut que cette chamaillerie cesse.*' I rang up C——, and repeated to him the historic phrase.

'Ho-ho! Wonder if he's been told by London to pull his socks up?'

'So do I. Do you think they are going to stand up to Hitler?'

'Maybe—unless they propose to give hell to the Czechs instead.'

(It should be added that we did not know at that time what exactly had happened at the Cabinet meeting earlier in the day.) Later that night it was clear that it was again the Czechs and not Hitler who were going to be 'given hell'. A number of messages from Lord Runciman had been communicated to the French Government. The view expressed on the British side was that Runciman still remained 'the last hope'. And that night M. Daladier, taking the view that the *chamaillerie* was still an 'internal' Czech affair, sent another message to Prague urging the Czech Government in 'a firm and friendly manner', to use the utmost moderation. The appeal was, clearly, being sent to the wrong address.

Il faut que cette chamaillerie cesse. Was it during that meeting on the night of September 13 that the 'direct contact' with Hitler was discussed? It is probable. M. Daladier had, in the past, often believed in the virtue of direct talks with Germany. And when, twenty-four hours later, the sensational announcement was made that Mr. Chamberlain was going to fly to Berchtesgaden in the morning, M. Daladier made the following statement:

> 'At the end of yesterday afternoon, in view of the rapid development of events in Czecho-Slovakia which rendered negotiations on the spot very difficult, I took the initiative to establish a personal and direct contact with Mr. Chamberlain with the object of examining with him *the possibility of adopting an exceptional procedure* which would allow for the examination with Germany of the most effective measures to assure a friendly solution of the differences which separate the Sudeten Germans and the Prague Government, and in consequence to maintain the peace of Europe. I am therefore particularly happy that the two Governments should see eye to eye.'

It was said that M. Daladier had himself been surprised and rather taken aback by the announcement of Mr. Chamberlain's solo flight to Berchtesgaden; because he had imagined that he would take part in these discussions. But now Mr. Chamberlain was in exclusive charge of Czechoslovakia's fate. However—if one is to judge from Munich—it would probably not have made much difference even if M. Daladier had gone to Berchtesgaden, together with Mr. Chamberlain.

One can well imagine Mr. Chamberlain's reasons for going alone. After what had happened on the previous day, it was clear to him that the French were not 'marching'; yet if he took Daladier with him, the French Premier would have felt obliged to ride the high horse, and speak of France's honour and treaty obligations—which might have made Hitler lose his temper and might have spoilt everything. Actually it is more probable that Daladier was only too glad that Mr. Chamberlain should have relieved him of all responsibility.

Be that as it may, the French had again, largely through their own fault, dropped out; and the lead was again exclusively in British hands.

CHAPTER XIII

BERCHTESGADEN TO GODESBERG

UNTIL late in the evening, when wireless listeners learned with amazement that Mr. Chamberlain was going to Berchtesgaden (many at first refused to believe it—so fantastic did it seem) Wednesday, September 14, was a day of uneasy tension in Paris. Prague had failed to call off the martial law, and Henlein had refused to negotiate, saying that 'since the Sudeten ultimatum had not been complied with, any further talks with the Czech Government were without object'. Prague was awaiting from hour to hour the mobilisation of ten classes of reservists. In Berlin, it was said that if any disorders broke out in the Sudetenland, Germany would intervene. The Press in Paris was either frankly pessimistic or frankly defeatist. M. Stéphane Lauzanne, in the *Matin*, was advocating a plebiscite.

> Ireland and Macedonia in the past, and Palestine to-day show that when two nations cannot live together any longer, they must be separated.

M. Blum, in the *Populaire*, had a brainwave—a Franco-British police force in the Sudeten areas. In a manner slightly reminiscent of the late Dr. Coué, he wrote:

> The Sudeten question can be peacefully settled: therefore it must be peacefully settled. It must and it can be settled in such a way that the settlement reached will not engender immediate iniquities and new dangers. Even to-day, especially to-day, it is a question of wisdom and courage. If we have the will, peace will prevail.

M. de Kerillis was dramatic:

> I consider it my sacred duty to say that we have reached a point where we cannot yield another inch; and Germany must be told this. We are in the presence of a diplomatic Verdun.

We must restore within ourselves the heroic souls of the defenders of Verdun. Without heroism, without risk, there is
no way out of the present situation. Yes—war may break out
if the fanaticised Sudetens burst into open rebellion. But
there is a good chance that there will be no war so long as we
form a solid block, ready to face anything.

A diplomatic Verdun! The French Government let Mr.
Chamberlain fight the battle for them.

That Wednesday—the day on which the flight to Berchtesgaden was announced—will be well remembered in Paris; for
it was on that day that the municipal carts began to deposit
little piles of sand in front of the doors. Without warning,
or almost without warning. Many concierges complained:
'They are just making a filthy mess of the pavement—what are
we supposed to do with it?' Some were funny about it, saying
it would be nice for the children; or nice for the cats. Some
concierges took the sand down the cellar, saying they had no
room for it upstairs, and that they weren't paid to trail buckets
of sand up five flights of stairs. Instructions were issued to the
effect that if a two-inch layer of sand was put on the floor of
the garret, or the top storey if there was no garret, incendiary
bombs falling into the sand would go out automatically. If
not, they would, within four minutes, melt metal over a radius
of thirty yards. It all sounded too gruesome to be true. And
anyway, what guarantee was there that the bomb would not
miss the patch of sand on the top floor? Few people took it
seriously and in the street people could be heard saying that
it was all eyewash—the Government was trying to show it was
doing something about A.R.P.—and others said it was just
another municipal racket by the Topazes. A few days later,
the papers said that the price of sand had gone up four times.
'Of course, it's just a racket.'

But somehow, at that stage, nobody was *convinced* that war
was imminent; and the sand was treated as a bad joke. 'If
they had provided masks instead, it might have done more
good.'

And so, that night, a startled Paris learned that Mr. Chamberlain was going to see Hitler the next day. '*Un espoir se
lève sur l'Europe*,' *Paris-Midi* announced the next morning.
And, probably reflecting official views, it added:

> Two questions will be discussed by Mr. Chamberlain and Hitler: (1) the liquidation of the Sudeten problems, on the basis of a plebiscite. (2) More general problems concerning Europe and the Third Reich.

Nothing about the integrity of Czechoslovakia, or the Bohemian Bastion. The Paris public was being asked to accept the plebiscite idea, that is, the transfer of territory.

M. Bourguès in the equally inspired *Petit Parisien* used exactly the same words: 'a settlement on the basis of a free plebiscite, after the manner of the Saar plebiscite.' M. Bourguès went on to explain why M. Daladier was not going to Berchtesgaden.

> There was a danger that if he had gone it would have developed into an international conference. Other Powers would have wanted to be represented too, and this would not have simplified matters.

That day the Chamberlain legend was born. The *Matin* and *Excelsior* thanked Mr. Chamberlain on behalf of France's mothers and France's children; M. Frossard in the *Homme Libre,* wrote:

> This move, unprecedented in the history of the world, points to the tragic gravity of the situation, and earns for the grand old man the respectful admiration of the civilised world. I am now convinced that war has been rendered impossible.

M. Blum was also full of admiration, and even gave a share of his admiration to M. Daladier:

> Mr. Chamberlain's resolution will stir the imagination of the world—and that means a great deal. In his will for peace he is showing a noble audacity.

The only discordant notes came from the *Ordre,* the *Epoque,* the *Humanité,* and from the *Peuple,* the trade union paper, which was not in one of its pacifist moods that day. M. Harmel promised 'to eat his hat if any good came out of the Chamberlain visit'.

> Mr. Chamberlain is a cross between Machiavelli and Mr. Micawber; and when he goes on a mission of this kind, there is nothing to look forward to. His journey will be another defeat to the cause of peace.

It is characteristic of the division in the French trade union movement that on the following day even before anything definite was known of the results of the Berchtesgaden talks, the *Peuple* published an article by M. Belin, the 'moderate' trade union leader, which was in flat contradiction with M. Harmel's piece on the previous day:

> I am grateful for the respite, even if it is only one of a few days. And I should welcome a settlement, even one with a great many drawbacks. A mediocre and even a bad settlement is better than even a victorious war. I am convinced that the damage caused by a war will be greater and more irreparable than that caused by even a bad settlement of the minorities problem of Czechoslovakia.

Paris spent the 15th and 16th in a state of hopeful but uneasy expectation. The news from Czechoslovakia was bad. Henlein and other Sudeten deputies had fled to Germany. What were they preparing? Many people remembered the Austrian Legion; was there now going to be a Sudeten Legion? In the meantime order was being restored in the Sudeten territories by the Czech authorities; but in the disturbances since September 12, twenty-nine people had been killed, most of them Czechs, and seventy-five wounded; among them sixty-one Czechs. While Mr. Chamberlain was seeing Hitler, Prague, according to the papers, was 'very calm' and was 'calmly and firmly' rejecting any idea of a plebiscite.

News from Berchtesgaden was scanty at first. Blurred telephotos showed Mr. Chamberlain and Hitler and Ribbentrop and the British Ambassador sitting with blank faces round a tea table decorated with flowers. Then, later in the evening, it was learned that Mr. Chamberlain was returning to London the next morning. Had the talks broken down? No, not exactly; but soon it was clear that Mr. Chamberlain was bringing back nothing better than an ultimatum. The officially inspired Press in Paris was almost cheerful. '*Détente. Ultimatum.*' *Paris-Midi* wrote:

> The *détente* in Europe has been created by Hitler's ultimatum. We had reached such a point of tension that the ultimatum has almost created a feeling of relief. For 'ultimatum' means 'delay'.

And the semi-official *Petit Parisien* was for the first time openly advocating the annexation of the Sudetenland by Germany:

> The Czechs have for centuries been accustomed to struggling with the Germans, and they are not easily upset by German insolence. But they are experienced and practically-minded people, who know how to obey their interests and to silence their feelings. They may, therefore, reasonably wonder whether, at the pass that has been reached, it would not be more advantageous, *if their country is to remain strong and solid* [a pretty argument!]   that the disloyal citizen should be detached from it and be allowed to go and share the bitter lot of the Austrians.

This was no longer the *République,* a paper with no readers; this was the *Petit Parisien* speaking, the most widely read morning paper in France.   One cannot help laughing when in his speech at the Chamber on October 4, M. Daladier described the 'anguish' with which he and M. Bonnet learned from Mr. Chamberlain in London on September 18 of Lord Runciman's conclusion that the Czechs and the Sudetens could no longer live together.

'*Avec quelle émotion!*'   Until that time, he said, the French Government had always thought of a settlement 'within the framework of the Czech State'.   Yet the inspired *République* (not to mention the *Matin*) had openly advocated the transfer of territory as early as September 6, while the even more semi-official *Petit Parisien* had proposed it on September 17.   '*Avec quelle émotion!*'

And, in the meantime, M. Flandin was doing his little best not only in Paris, but also in London.   In the *Evening Standard* of September 16 he warned England that the French people would 'refuse to fight a war to save peace'.

.   .   .   .

There was a feeling in Paris during those two days after Berchtesgaden that Mr. Chamberlain was snubbing the French Ministers.   On the day of Berchtesgaden the papers already announced that M. Daladier and M. Bonnet would probably travel to London at once to discuss the 'ultimatum'. It was not until two days later, after the British Cabinet meeting on Saturday that an official invitation was received.

On Sunday morning, September 18, the two French Ministers flew to London.   The great majority of the French Press

had by this time already impressed on its readers that the
transfer of the Sudeten territory was the only solution. There
were still some, like the *Œuvre,* which spoke of an international conference, which would include Mr. Roosevelt and
Stalin—a conference at which the Czech conflict and other
matters might be settled; others, like the *Peuple,* called for
the union of all the peaceful nations, who would 'enforce their
will' on Hitler; but few had any illusion left. M. de Kerillis
broke into lamentations:

> Oh, that voyage! That voyage! And to think that M.
> Daladier claimed the authorship of the idea! As if anybody
> could imagine that it would change the face of things! But
> alas! We are not living in the age of Corneille. . . . We are
> living in a hard, savage, barbarous age. Old England and
> Old France understand nothing about young Germany.

M. Péri in the *Humanité* was speaking of the coming betrayal, and of *the suicidal policy which consisted in buying
a short respite at a colossal price.* But M. Lauzanne in the
Matin was saying that if an invasion of Czechoslovakia was
a crime, a refusal, at the risk of war, to hand the Sudetens
over to Germany would be an equally great crime.

.   .   .   .

The conversation at Downing Street on Sunday, the 18th,
lasted all day long. What took a long time was the French
effort to persuade Britain to guarantee the new frontiers of
Czechoslovakia. On their return to Paris the French Ministers
claimed that it had been terribly difficult to get the British
Ministers to agree to this. Maybe; *but were not the French
asking for that guarantee simply in order to salve their conscience, or rather to whitewash themselves in the eyes of French
opinion; and was not the reluctance of the British to give this
guarantee due to their knowledge that the guarantee would
inevitably prove a scrap of paper and so lower—even in advance (for nobody would take such a guarantee seriously)—
the value of Britain's signature?*
There is little to suggest that the French put up any
resistance against accepting the Berchtesgaden ultimatum,
which now came to be known as the 'Anglo-French Plan'.
Back in Paris, they claimed that they had been unable to
resist, as Mr. Chamberlain was very firm in demanding their

prompt acceptance; but it was later claimed by some critics of MM. Daladier and Bonnet that that was not exactly the case; that Sir Robert Vansittart and even Lord Halifax were by no means pleased with the plan, and that there were 'considerable possibilities of resistance'. M. Péri in the *Humanité* was particularly emphatic on this point.

. . . .

The French Ministers returned to Paris early on Monday morning, and a Ministerial Council met at the Elysée at 10.30 to endorse the London Plan, before its dispatch to Prague. The majority of the Cabinet accepted this plan; but reservations were made, particularly by M. Mandel, M. Reynaud and M. Champetier de Ribes. M. Reynaud asked M. Bonnet to pledge himself not to bring any pressure to bear on the Czech Government; the Czech Government must be free to decide for itself. M. Bonnet agreed to this.

Taking a long view of it, it is amazing to think with what ease, and almost eagerness, the majority of the French Cabinet accepted the dismemberment of Czechoslovakia which meant, in effect, the breakdown of France's system of Eastern alliances and the loss of her best-organised ally with 40 divisions.

After the Cabinet meeting M. Bonnet had an hour's conversation with M. Osusky, the Czech Minister in Paris, and submitted to him the Anglo-French Plan. Why he needed a whole hour is not clear; for all the French Foreign Minister said in effect was one word: *acceptez*.

In leaving the French Foreign Office M. Osusky looked profoundly perturbed, and bitterly remarked to the journalists outside: 'Here you see the condemned man. He has been sentenced without even being heard.' M. Osusky's bitterness was understandable, it was he who in the previous two years had assembled the most impressive collection of French assurances of support, assistance, and loyalty to the Franco-Czech Pact.

'Sentenced without even being heard.' It had been the same in London on the previous day. M. Masaryk, the Czech Minister, had not been allowed to join in the Anglo-French talks.

How was the Anglo-French Plan received in Paris? By Péri, Pertinax, Kerillis and other *'bellicistes'* it was naturally treated as folly and as a betrayal both of Czechoslovakia and of France's vital interests. The Communist Party published a manifesto, a good deal of which to-day sounds prophetic:

> Obeying the injunctions of Hitler, Mr. Chamberlain has got the British and French Ministers to agree to a dismemberment of Czechoslovakia, the integrity of which is inseparable from France's security and the peace of Europe.
>
> Repudiating the treaties bearing the signature of France and the undertaking they solemnly renewed only a few days ago, the Daladier Government have agreed to this new capitulation to international Fascism.
>
> After that Hitler will be able to demand French colonies and Alsace Lorraine, while Mussolini will ask for Tunisia, Corsica, Nice and Savoy.

The manifesto protested against the prohibition of public meetings and also against the Government's failure to consult Parliament on the grave decisions it was taking.

M. Blum, as he openly admitted, was much more divided.

> I do not know Czechoslovakia's answer yet. . . . But whatever happens, the consequences of the London Plan will be far-reaching both for Europe and France. War has probably been averted. But it has been averted in such conditions . . . that I cannot feel any joy, and am merely filled *with mixed feelings of cowardly relief and shame.*

But the semi-official Press no longer worried about the moral aspect of the affair; and demanded only one thing—Prague's immediate acceptance. The crocodile's tears were mingled with threats. The implication of most of the comments was that it was all the fault of the Czechs, anyway.

M. Sauerwein, in *Paris-Soir,* accused the Czechs of *aveuglement surprenant*, since they did not realise long ago that all this was inevitable.

M. Bailby in the *Jour* was even more explicit:

> M. Hodza yesterday made a completely useless speech.[1] In the presence of facts, it is no use talking. No Frenchman will deny that the sacrifices demanded from Prague are atrocious, and there is no Frenchman who is not feeling profoundly sorry for the Czechs. But if Czech opinion was not informed sooner, and if the Prague Ministers did not make the necessary concessions in time, if, after the publication of the Karlsbad programme, they failed to accept the Sudeten terms, whose fault is it?

[1] The Czech Premier had said that the Czechs would fight rather than accept plebiscite.

It was all pretty low. For, in fact, it was the fault of the French. Karlsbad programme? That dated back to April. Had not the French Government reaffirmed until the first week in September that they would support Czechoslovakia; had not M. Bonnet declared to the Foreign Affairs Committee of the Chamber two months after the Karlsbad programme, and to M. Corbin, nearly four months after the Karlsbad programme that the settlement of the Sudeten problem must be compatible with the integrity and sovereignty of Czechoslovakia—which the Karlsbad programme was certainly not? If the Czechs were blind, it was because they had been blinded by French assurances and promises.

M. Roche, in the *République*, reflecting the views of M. Bonnet, went even further:

> If the Czechs reject the London Plan, it will be their own lookout. There is no treaty that we know of which would compel us to intervene.

There followed an enumeration of all the Czech sins since 1919:

> Since all the advice we gave the Czechs was ignored [what, advice—except the advice to accept the Runciman mission? —and this advice was followed] every Frenchman is entitled to say that Prague has no claim on him; for Prague refused to see the dangers for which it was heading.

In short, France had foreseen everything; but the Czechs had been blind, and therefore they could blame themselves.

As for the *Petit Parisien* it dwelt on the British guarantee, which, it said, should make the London Plan much more palatable to the Czechs; and it urged the Czechs to accept: eighteen German divisions, it said ominously, were ready to attack Czechoslovakia.

The only comic relief that day was provided by our *confrère*, ex-would-be-Dictator, Colonel de la Rocque, who wrote in the *Petit Journal*:[1]

---

[1] The decline of Colonel de la Rocque was as rapid as his rise to fame in 1934-5. His failure to run candidates in the 1936 election was a serious error, and the dissolution of the Croix de Feu in June of that year was another blow to the Colonel's prestige. The P.S.F. (*Parti Social Français*) which was formed after the dissolution of the Croix de Feu and its affiliated groupings, lacked the authority of the old party, and had, moreover, a serious new competitor in M. Doriot's

The role our country has played in these last weeks will have been one of the wonders of our history. In spite of the pressure of the revolutionary warmongers, and of the pacifist climbers [?] our Ministers have known how to defend both our national honour and the peace of the world. . . . Eternal France alone was qualified for such an act of arbitration. Such is the noble tradition, the great destiny, the magnificent fortune of our country.

The Colonel was not joking; he was in dead earnest.

.   .   .   .

On Tuesday, the Czech Government, after many hours of deliberation, virtually rejected the Anglo-French Plan, and proposed that the dispute be submitted to arbitration, in accordance with the German-Czech arbitration treaty. Mr.

P.P.F.   It is true that the P.S.F. continued to claim two million *adhérents*, but the figure seemed exaggerated.   But the worst was yet to come.   In the summer of 1937 Colonel de la Rocque was negotiating the purchase of the *Petit Journal*, a nondescript paper that had often changed hands, and continued to be in financial difficulties, with a view of turning it into the daily organ of the P.S.F.   The *Jour*, the *Action Français* and other papers of the Right which were catering to the very public La Rocque was hoping to conquer, started a campaign against the Colonel, and this campaign culminated in two spectacular libel actions in the course of which M. Tardieu, the former Premier, who had been won over by M. Bailby of the *Jour*, struck a devastating blow at La Rocque, who had in his writings and speeches never failed to denounce with a great display of *ancien combattant* righteousness the graft and corruption of the parliamentary régime.   M. Tardieu claimed that when he was Premier he used to subsidise Colonel de la Rocque heavily and regularly out of the secret funds, and that he passed his 'good servant' on to his successor, M. Laval.   The Colonel, though flatly denying the charge, cut a rather poor figure in court.   But the 'sinking' of the Colonel, (who, for all one knows, may have thought it perfectly legitimate to receive financial help for his reactionary movement from a reactionary premier,) was done in an ugly and almost sadistic manner, amid loud rejoicing from all the French Fascist elements.   In a sense, the attack may be regarded as one by the French Section of the Fascist International (with their open worship of Mussolini and Franco and their sneaking admiration for Hitler) against the muddle-headed, but mainly French Nationalism of Colonel de la Rocque. The reason why M. Tardieu (who for instance in the case of Czechoslovakia did not at all see eye to eye with the *Jour*, *Gringoire*, etc.,) gave the Fascists this terrific support—was largely a personal vendetta between him and La Rocque—a vendetta which M. Bailby succeeded in exploiting.

Though looking much smaller after his law court experiences Colonel de la Rocque nevertheless remained at the head of the P.S.F., and also remained editor of the *Petit Journal*, a new *métier* at which he hardly excelled.   Actually, a great deal of sympathy was felt for La Rocque over the scurrilous treatment he had suffered at the hands of his enemies ; and if the *affaire* did some harm to his prestige, it did not increase the authority or popularity of M. Tardieu. A person handing out secret funds is, after all, an accomplice in a shady business, and has no business to impersonate virtue and integrity and to denounce those he has paid as crooks and thieves.   Or, if he was denouncing La Rocque, he should have given the list of all the people he had subsidised;—otherwise it was merely a personal vengeance.

Chamberlain was in a hurry to fly to Godesberg, and the invocation of an old treaty, which Germany certainly regarded as a scrap of paper, struck him as fatuous and mischievous. Among the 'pacifists' in Paris there was the outcry that the Czechs were 'sabotaging peace'.

What followed was to be one of the most vital episodes in the Czech crisis. Paris that evening was in a state of great uncertainty. In London the Inner Cabinet met, and sat till 10.30 p.m. There were telephone conversations between London and Paris. Conversations with M. Bonnet alone, or also with M. Daladier? It is one of the obscure points in the story of the Czech crisis. All that is certain is that a couple of hours later, M. de Lacroix, the French Minister in Prague, who had already seen M. Krofta and other members of the Czech Government during the day, was instructed by M. Bonnet to call on President Beneš, together with Mr. Newton, the British Minister, and to inform him that if the Czech Government did not accept the Anglo-French Plan, it must do so at its own risk. France would not go to war if, following this refusal, Germany attacked Czechoslovakia. M. de Lacroix who on the previous day had already carried out the painful task of handing the Berchtesgaden ultimatum to M. Krofta reluctantly obeyed his chief's orders. At 2.15 a.m. on September 21 the British and French Ministers drove up at the President's palace, and informed him of their Governments' decision.

To justify M. Bonnet's step, the *République* later made the extraordinary claim that M. Beneš had *asked* the French Government to threaten Czechoslovakia with non-support if she failed to accept the Anglo-French Plan. That alone, the *République* claimed, would have enabled Beneš to get the Czech people to accept the Plan. In reality this is a complete distortion of the facts. Dr. Beneš had simply asked for a *written* confirmation of France's decision not to abide any longer by the Czech alliance.[1]

On the French Right it was later claimed that if, during the two previous days the Czechs were so 'difficult', it was because they were hoping for a Cabinet crisis in Paris. One

[1] This whole extraordinary episode is discussed in detail in the *Nineteenth Century*, February 1939, pp. 174-84

of the stories told was that M. Mandel had urged M. Beneš to resist; and that he promised to do his best to bring about a change of Government, with Herriot as Premier. It was even said that at Godesberg Hitler had triumphantly announced to Mr. Chamberlain that he had gramophone records of the telephone conversations between Prague and London, and between Prague and Paris—conversations between Lord Runciman and the British Government, talks between Beneš and the French 'warmongers'.

Is it only gossip? In any case the French 'pacifists' tried to make political capital out of the stories that the French 'warmongers' had urged Beneš not to accept the London Plan, i.e., the Berchtesgaden ultimatum.

In Prague the acceptance of the ultimatum under French and British pressure aroused intense anger. There were violent anti-French demonstrations in the streets; and General Faucher, the head of the French Military Mission in Prague, resigned his post and placed himself at the service of the Czech Army. He returned all his French military decorations to the French Government. The story of this one and only French *beau geste* during the whole of the Czech crisis was virtually suppressed by the officially-inspired papers. Some dismissed it as quixotic and theatrical.

On Wednesday, September 21, it was learned that M. Paul Reynaud, M. Mandel and M. Champetier de Ribes had 'offered' to resign from the Cabinet; or rather, that they had resigned, but that they had left it to M. Daladier to choose his time for making their resignations official. (M. Daladier had apparently asked them not to resign officially as it would create complications just on the eve of Mr. Chamberlain's voyage to Godesberg.) If they wanted to resign it was because M. Bonnet, they said, had broken the pledge he had given to the Cabinet on the Monday; which was that he would not bring any pressure to bear on the Czech Government, and would not try to bully them into accepting the Anglo-French Plan. According to the *Canard Enchaîné of* September 28 M. Bonnet already *then* said, in reply to these accusations, that Beneš had 'asked' for this pressure; but the three 'warmongering' Ministers can hardly have believed it. It is curious that it was not until after Beneš's resignation from the Presidency that such an explanation was openly produced by the *République*.[1]

Needless to say, the pro-Fascist Press—the *Jour, Gringoire*, the *Action Française* and the rest of them did not fail to attack the three Ministers, whom they also accused of plotting against the Government.

. . . .

In the meantime Mr. Chamberlain was preparing to fly to Godesberg. The French papers were full of 'colourful' stuff about the beauties of the Rhine, and of the riot of flags that was decorating the two hotels at which Hitler and Mr. Chamberlain were going to stay; they also gave the readers historical explanations of why, of all places, Hitler had chosen Godesberg as a meeting place. There were anecdotes about Mr. Chamberlain's umbrella, and photographs of Mr. and Mrs. Chamberlain returning to Downing Street after a walk in St. James's Park. On the morning of the departure *Paris-Midi* announced:

> Mr. Chamberlain is leaving for Germany with a plan in his pocket. Let Germany make no mistake about it: this plan provides for certain limits beyond which England will not allow Germany to go.

For there was an uneasy feeling that Godesberg was not going to be a mere ceremony at which Mr. Chamberlain would announce to Hitler Czechoslovakia's acceptance of his ultimatum, while Hitler would accept the 'modalities of execution' prepared by the British and French. For in the interval between Berchtesgaden and Godesberg Hungary and Poland had put forward their own claims; and this was threatening to complicate matters. M. Litvinov's solemn announcement at Geneva on the day Mr. Chamberlain flew to Godesberg that Russia would fulfil her obligations to Czechoslovakia, if France did the same, was more or less ignored by the Great Powers, not least by England and France.

In Paris they were waiting for the results of Godesberg. I went to the Chamber that afternoon. Outside I met N. 'Come

[1] The story of how Beneš had 'asked' for the French ultimatum was to be denounced as a fabrication in a letter published in the *Europe Nouvelle* of October 29. The letter was written by M. Hubert Beuve-Méry, the *Temps* correspondent in Prague, who had by that time resigned from the paper.

on to the café instead,' he said. *'A la Chambre, ça pue le cadavre. Cette boîte me dégoûte.'* They were all, he said, so damned pleased about the way Bonnet had got the Czechs to surrender and had foiled the *bellicistes*. There was some talk of the disruption of the Cabinet in a day or two; some people were pushing hard for an Herriot Government; but Daladier did not wish to call Parliament; and it did not look as though there were going to be a change of Government. 'It's all pretty sickening,' N. said. 'If only we had a few faces like this in our Government,' he went on, pointing to the picture in the evening paper of General Sirovy, the leader of the Czech legionaries, with a black patch over one eye, who had just become Premier of Czechoslovakia in her 'supreme hour'. *'Une bonne gueule,* don't you think?' N. was a reserve officer and thought he might be called up at any moment. 'For Godesberg is not going to be such a simple business as all that.'

For the next twenty-four hours Paris waited for the results of Godesberg. The news from there was puzzling and disquieting, with successions of stories that the conversations had broken down; that Mr. Chamberlain had sent a letter to Hitler across the Rhine and was waiting for a written reply. One thing seemed clear—and that was that Hitler, satisfied with the way in which his methods had worked so far was now asking for more. Part of the French Press tried at first to show that the prospects were not at all unsatisfactory. On September 23 *Paris-Midi* tried to suggest that if the Godesberg conversations were dragging on, it was because 'the subject of the conversations had been extended'. And it is curious that, on that morning—it was the second day of Godesberg—the correspondent of *Paris-Midi* at Godesberg should have written that the talks between Mr. Chamberlain and Herr Hitler, and, on the other hand, the technical talks between Sir Horace Wilson, Sir William Strang and Ribbentrop were in reality preparatory conversations calculated, if possible, *to prepare the ground for a conference to which at least France and Italy would be invited.*

Was it only a wild guess by a French journalist who did not know how to fill up his column? Or was 'Munich', complete with Mussolini, already 'in the air' on the day of Godesberg? Or, lastly, was such a Four-Power conference the expression of the secret wishes of the French Ministers who up till then had been excluded (largely through their own fault) from all the talks with Hitler?

.   .   .   .

I shall not attempt to seek an explanation for that singular phrase in *Paris-Midi*. It is conceivable that, before everything had gone wrong at Godesberg during the afternoon of the second day, the possibility of 'Munich' *was* considered, and that after the breakdown of the talks, 'Munich' was no longer mentioned.

The other possible explanation is the 'fake theory'—namely, the theory that Munich was—regardless of the final 'breakdown'—firmly decided upon at Godesberg, and that the French mobilisation, the mobilisation of the British Navy, and Mr. Chamberlain's tragic broadcast of September 27 which was to send a cold shiver down millions of spines were part and parcel of a put-up show—the purpose of which was to get a panic-stricken world to accept the Munich settlement with gratitude and relief. No! Such a theory seems rather too Machiavellian for a man like Mr. Chamberlain—even though it *has* been put forward.

This theory received some support even from M. Fabre-Luce, an ardent admirer of Mr. Chamberlain and M. Bonnet. He had the indiscretion of describing the *coup de théâtre* in the House of Commons on September 28 as *une bonne farce!*[1] He may, however, have meant that Munich was in reality agreed upon a few hours before, and not five days before Mr. Chamberlain's House of Commons speech. Some sinister significance has also been attached to Mr. Chamberlain's words before leaving for Munich: 'It will be all right this time.' Supporters of the 'fake' theory have further said that since the fate of Czechoslovakia was sealed at Berchtesgaden, it was surely 'unnatural' to mobilise and threaten war over some 'points of detail', which, according to this theory, were all that the Godesberg conflict amounted to. This theory, though perhaps plausible on the face of it, minimises three points:

(1) The great guiding principle in the Anglo-French attitude to the Czech crisis was that almost any settlement would do, so long as there was no armed attack on Czechoslovakia, which Hitler now wanted for military prestige. If there had been

[1] *Histoire secrète de la négociation de Munich.*

an actual act of aggression, France, in spite of everything, would have found it extremely difficult to remain aloof.

(2) It is possible that Mr. Chamberlain did believe—or at least tried to believe—that Czechoslovakia could continue a more or less independent existence under the Anglo-French Plan; while the Godesberg Plan clearly provided for the complete economic vassalisation of Czechoslovakia with all her essential railways cut by German *enclaves*, etc.

(3) If the substance of the Godesberg Plan was accepted at Munich it was because after the *coup de théâtre* of September 28 war had become psychologically almost impossible, especially in England.

So, while there were some arguments in favour of the 'fake' theory, one still finds it difficult to accept—especially when the charge of 'faking' is made against Mr. Chamberlain. Such a 'fake' could have been only the work of a political chessplayer of real genius—and unlimited cynicism.

It is, therefore, in the belief that there was no 'faking' that I shall complete the story of France's part in the Czech crisis.

CHAPTER XIV

FRENCH MOBILISATION AND THE SCARE DAYS IN PARIS

I T will have been noticed that, up till the moment we have reached—that is, Friday, September 23—France's part in this vast conflict over the fate of her most reliable ally in Central Europe had been almost exclusively passive, except for minor mobilisation measures, the distribution of sand to Paris householders, and M. Bonnet's 'ultimatum' to Dr. Beneš. The rest, to use newspaper phraseology, was little more than 'reactions'. Reactions to what Mr. Chamberlain was doing, and Hitler was doing and the Czechs were doing. What the Czechs were doing was, in fact, of only secondary importance to the French. Not a single speech was made between September 4 and Munich by either M. Daladier or M. Bonnet.

France's role as a dumb witness came to an end on Friday night, September 23. That evening, while Mr. Chamberlain was still at Godesberg, the French Government, in agreement with London (i.e., Lord Halifax and the Foreign Office) released the Czechoslovak Government from its undertaking not to mobilise. French 'pacifist 'writers like Pierre Dominique and Fabre-Luce, later claimed that both in London and Paris that day the 'warmongers' had gained the upper hand.

One good piece of news reached Paris that day; and that was Russia's threat to denounce her non-aggression pact with Poland, if Poland invaded Czechoslovakia. Though cold-shouldered by French and British alike, the Russians, it seemed, were doing their best. There were some people in Paris that day who thought that this Russian warning might prove a turning-point in the whole crisis, and a signal to all the democratic countries to pull themselves together, and to stop

the rot.   It was certainly the first gesture of 'firmness' coming
from any potential enemy of Germany.   And more gestures
were to come.

That night a number of us were dining at the *Petit Riche*
with a British army man, who was explaining to us the technical difficulties of giving military assistance to Czechoslovakia.
The atmosphere in Paris that night was one of depression and
vague anxiety, but there was nothing unusual in the streets.
We did not know yet about the coming Czech mobilisation.
People at the corner table were discussing the relative virtues
of the old stock and the present stock of the *Petit Riche's*
Santenay.

We later dropped in at Reuter's office.   We met Gordon
Waterfield on the stair.   'I am going home—anyone coming
my way?'   'Going home already?'   'Yes, I am going home to
get a pillow and a blanket.   I have got to stay the night in
the office.   Anything may happen.   They are expecting a
French mobilisation.   Daladier is conferring with the Generals.
The news has just come through that the Czechs have mobilised.   And Godesberg is a washout.   Chamberlain is coming
back to-morrow morning.'

Here was a mouthful.   In the Place de la Bourse all was quiet.
Nothing startling anywhere.   Café de la Paix crowded as usual.
At the French War Office alone there was much coming and
going.   *'Alors, on mobilise?'* I asked a French reporter, who
was taking notes of the arrivals and departures.

'Il paraît,' said he, adding facetiously: *'Mais la mobilisation
n'est pas la guerre.'*

It was what they said in 1914.

    .   .   .   .

Inside the War Ministry important talks were in progress
Earlier that night Sir Eric Phipps had informed M. Daladier
of the breakdown at Godesberg; and now M. Daladier was
conferring with the Generals.   General Gamelin had felt all
along that France's diplomacy during the last months *had
been completely out of proportion with her military strength*;
and it was reported that he greatly resented the account given
of his report both to the French Cabinet and to the British
Government; an account which had over-emphasised the weak
points and suppressed the favourable conclusions.   General

Gamelin now insisted on at least a partial mobilisation of the French Army; and M. Daladier agreed.

Early next morning the *affiches blanches* were displayed on the *mairies* and other public buildings throughout France. The *affiche blanche* is associated in the popular mind with general mobilisation; the use of the same poster for a partial mobilisation was no doubt calculated to create a psychological effect in the country. This it certainly did—much more than had been done by the mobilisation orders sent out to reservists individually earlier in the month.

Categories 2 and 3 were called up. The system of mobilisation had been changed in France in 1936 (after the old system had shown itself to be too unwieldy at the time of the Rhineland *coup*); and these two 'categories', which represented about 600,000 reservists, did not correspond to any 'classes'. The categories (*echelons*) into which the French Army reserve is now divided comprise people of different ages, each *echelon* representing, as it were, a useful 'assortment' of all kinds of reservists. It is part of what is called 'vertical' mobilisation, as distinct from the 'horizontal' mobilisation, by classes.

The *affiche blanche* caused great commotion in Paris that morning. Although it was announced by the Government that this partial mobilisation must not be considered as a first step towards general mobilisation, everybody felt that it was singularly reminiscent of it. In food-shops, around underground stations, and in the streets generally people assembled to discuss the partial mobilisation order. Altogether it was accepted as something inevitable, and there were no protests and no attacks on the Government; on the contrary, the Government, many people felt, could not have done anything else. If there was any anger at all it was reserved for Hitler. In the Place Denfert, the old woman at a flower-stall looked wretched, but went on with her work as usual. Three of her four sons had been called up that morning. My landlord and his three brothers, all reserve officers, left for the eastern frontier that night. The only complaint—especially by the women—was that 'they don't give them much time to say good-bye to the family'.

The centre of life in Paris was the Gare de l'Est. Immense crowds had gathered there in the afternoon to see the reservists off. And with all the streets around the station blocked with people traffic in that busy part of Paris was almost at a stand-still. In front of the station a wooden barricade had been erected with a notice painted in green saying: 'Entrance for reservists,' and opposite it a notice-board on which was written in chalk: 'Last train for Strasbourg to-day 4 p.m. Last train for Metz to-day 4.30 p.m.'

Over the heads of the large crowds handkerchiefs were being waved to the reservists as they were disappearing inside the station. These were mostly young fellows—some well dressed, some poorly dressed, some still wearing the blue cotton trousers of the Paris mechanic. All were carrying little suitcases with their personal belongings. A number of reservists had already been put into field uniform in Paris.

Many were being seen off by women carrying babies and by young girls. Many of the women were weeping. The reservists looked earnest and a little grim, conscious of doing a painful but necessary duty. A few of the younger fellows smiled and even laughed as they waved good-bye, but these were rather forced, artificial smiles. One felt an undercurrent of anger against Germany. A lot of these people had heard Hitler bellowing on the wireless; they did not care much about Czechoslovakia, but they felt that Germany was throwing about her weight in an ugly, menacing manner. There was no singing and shouting, no 'Marseillaise' or 'Madelon'; no 'enthusiasm', no illusions about the glorious panoply of war, but only a feeling of bitter necessity. Only here and there a few working-class lads were singing the 'Internationale'.

From time to time a little crowd of pacifists of the Marceau Pivert school would shout 'Down with war,' but they were coaxed rather than ordered by the police to disperse. An old woman with an alcoholic face perched on a bench was screaming in a shrill voice, '*La guere est une saloperie!* War is a filthy business. The profiteers are sending you to the front.' But nobody took much notice of her.

An elderly man shaking his head said he remembered 1914 when at the same Gare de l'Est people shouted '*à Berlin*'. Of course he was imagining these things more than remembering them. In 1914 there were also plenty of weeping women at the Gare de l'Est. Nobody shouted '*à Berlin*' this time. It was rather sad and solemn, and nobody had any illusions about the romance of modern warfare.

The cafés all around the station were crowded with soldiers and reservists being seen off by their friends and families. Here was a middle-class family—a lad of twenty in a tweed suit, with heavily-rouged mamma who looked sulky and growled when a crowd of Communists marched past, singing the 'Internationale', a pretty sister who said nothing, and a father with a white moustache and a heavy gold watch-chain who handed a bundle of notes to the boy and clicked glasses with him silently, and with his cheeks twitching.

Obviously, nobody was *enjoying* it; but there was no terrible gloom and depression at the Gare de l'Est. Nor was there anything to indicate that the French people 'did not know (as was later maintained by some "pacifists") what it was all about.' At the Gare de l'Est that day nearly everybody spoke of *les Boches.*

The editor of the leading Paris evening paper sent his reporter to the Gare de l'Est that day, and told him to give as depressing an account as possible of the reservists' state of mind. The reporter returned to the office with his *papier*: 'I assure you they aren't in such a state of gloom and funk at all. Go and look for yourself.'

From the Gare de l'Est I walked down the Boulevard Sébastopol. There were crowds everywhere, strangely silent crowds. In cafés people sat sipping their drinks but saying very little to each other. All the shops were open—shoe- and hat- and fur-shops and stationery-shops advertising notebooks for the opening of the schools next week; but wherever I looked in, there was not a single customer anywhere. The crowds outside were not thinking of shopping—though this was one of the great shopping streets of Paris.

As one walked through Paris that day and looked at the earnest and almost grim expression written on all faces, one was impressed by the deep unity of the French people in a moment of danger. The people were certainly showing an infinitely better spirit than either the newspapers or the politicians. On Saturday night the Paris building trade, who had been on strike—and they had good reasons for striking—sent a delegation to the Minister of Public Works and another to the Prefect of the Seine saying they would resume work at once and unconditionally for the sake of national defence and for the air defence of Paris.

And on the Sunday morning a similar announcement was made by the miners who had been on strike in the north of France.

.   .   .   .

In addition to the partial mobilisation, a number of other measures were taken. Motor transport was requisitioned in different parts of the country, and in Paris motorists served with the requisition order were told that they must not leave town in their cars. Priority was given to troop trains on the railways.

The distribution of sand against incendiary bombs continued in Paris and the distribution of gas masks was announced in some parts of town—though there was some uncertainty about this. Plans for the evacuation of over a million people within two or three days were said to be ready to be carried out at any moment.

On that Saturday evening I met a friend who had just come from the German Embassy. This, he said, was guarded by heavy polices forces, and he found that the Embassy staff had been profoundly impressed by the change that had come over Paris in the last days—not least by the mobilisation and the spirit of the people.

This hardening of the French attitude was regarded by many to be of decisive importance in averting a German attack on Czechoslovakia during the next few days. The French mobilisation had at least the effect of reducing the possibility of a 'localised' war—which Hitler would have welcomed.

And then came the four Scare Days.

It may however be said at once that during these four days—that is, until the Wednesday afternoon when Munich was announced—there were few people in Paris who regarded war as a certainty; to many it was a fifty-fifty chance. A great many others said knowingly that there would be no war. Only was it to be avoided by a German climb-down or another Anglo-French climb-down?

Two characteristic opinions are worth quoting; one from

my friend, the one-eyed plumber in the rue de la Glacière, a
good type of French artisan, chock-full of common sense and
very independent-minded. For three months in the year he
abandons all work and goes home to fish. The plumber was
convinced there would be no war, because, 'once you show
the Boche that you are not frightened of him, he will inevitably give way'.

The very opposite view was held by my French bank
manager, and in fact by all the clerks in the bank (i.e. those
among them who had not yet been mobilised)—and that was
that the French and British Governments were determined
to yield, if Hitler did not give way.

These two opinions, roughly, correspond to those held in
France during the danger week in September by (*a*) the optimists among the *peuple* and (*b*) the optimists in business.

But to most people it was fifty-fifty. That, of course, was
sufficiently bad to warrant anyone who had the slightest
chance of doing it, of sending at least the children out of
Paris.

The schools were to open on October 1, and many children
had already returned from the holidays. In many cases, however, children who were still in the country were told to 'stay
on'.

Paris has one peculiarity which London lacks. Nearly the
whole *petite bourgeoisie* and the upper strata of the working
class have still some connections with rural or provincial
France. It automatically provides a piece of A.R.P.—and
this was very evident during the four 'scare' days in September.

During those days Paris was cleared of a large part of its
child population. *On ira chez grand'mère dans la Creuse*, or
chez ma belle-sœur du côté de Rouen, or *chez ma cousine dans
la Sarthe*.

The large-scale exodus, as we shall see, did not, however,
begin until Monday, September 26.

.   .   .   .

On the day of the partial mobilisation M. Daladier worked
all day at the War Office examining 'the indispensable measures of security demanded by the international situation'.
Among these measures was the Government control of the

news service on all the wireless stations, both State and private. In leaving the War Office he said that the measures

> 'had been received and carried out throughout France with the *sang-froid* and the resolution that the Government had expected from the Nation.
> 'Our country,' M. Daladier added, 'will thus be in a position to pursue with calm and dignity the diplomatic talks on which the maintenance of peace depends.'

M. Pierre Dominique later wrote that about that time M. Daladier had gone 'warmongerish'; and one certainly has the impression that during that day M. Daladier was beginning seriously to regret the weakness that France had, until then, displayed. Gossip-writers recorded that for some days afterwards he was hardly on speaking terms with M. Bonnet. During the previous week relations had already been slightly strained between the Premier and the Foreign Minister.

> After the Cabinet meeting of September 13 (the *Canard Enchaîné* related) M. Daladier wondered whether he shouldn't give a broadcast address to the nation; but, on second thoughts, he decided not to say anything: since he had no mobilisation to announce, there was not much point in announcing a non-mobilisation.
> It was then that M. Bonnet coolly declared:
> 'If you are not going to talk, I'll talk.'
> Edouard bit his nose off:
> 'If the Prime Minister has got nothing to say, the Foreign Minister has got to keep his mouth shut.'
> Feeling much annoyed, M. Bonnet locked himself up in his study at the Quai d'Orsay.
> Half an hour later, M. Stéphane Lauzanne joined him.
> There were some who later insinuated that the famous article in the *Matin* demanding the transfer of the Sudeten territory to Germany, was written by M. Georges Bonnet himself. . . . As if M. Stéphane Lauzanne could have allowed that![1]

And another bit of *Canard* gossip which I report, of course, *sous toutes réserves*, told the following story about the Anglo-French meeting in London on September 25 and 26:

> On Sunday and Monday M. Bonnet wanted, on two or

---

[1] *Canard Enchaîné*, September 21. Let it not be objected that I am using a frivolous source of information. The *Canard* is frivolous in form but not in substance and its political notes are written by some of France's best journalists such as André Guérin.

three occasions, to speak. But each time he was cut short by
M. Edouard Daladier. For Edouard was feeling a bit sick.
For had not Mr. Chamberlain in person said to him:
  'Wasn't the Gamelin Report your Foreign Office sent us a
bit incomplete?'
  With a mischievous twinkle M. Daladier replied:
  'Oh, that was nothing, Mr. Chamberlain. Our Foreign
Office sent us, during one of our last Cabinet meetings, a
British Admiralty report.'
  And, after a pause:
  'And it, also, was incomplete.'
  M. Daladier, of course, is making no secret of the fact that
he is fed to the back teeth with his Foreign Minister.
  Which is also the feeling of M. Mandel, and M. Paul Rey-
naud, and M. Champetier de Ribes, and M. Gentin, and M.
Queuille.
  And sometimes M. Campinchi and M. Zay feel that way too.
And, now and then, even M. Lebrun, especially after having
had a talk with General Gamelin.[1]

It is significant that although M. Daladier was feeling
energetic and rather defiant, and had regained much confidence from the good spirit shown by the reservists, and the
successful manner in which the partial mobilisation had been
carried out, the Bonnet-inspired Press continued to preach
moderation to—the Czechs, and to ask them for more sacrifices
—namely to accept the Godesberg ultimatum as well.

  'Having accepted the sacrifice of the Sudeten territories,'
  M. Bourguès wrote in the *Petit Parisien* on Sunday, September
  25, 'one cannot imagine our Czechoslovakian friends (!) en-
  dangering the British Premier's efforts at appeasement merely
  over some questions of procedure. Faithful to her promises (!)
  France is ready to defend the integrity (?) of Czechoslovakia
  against an armed attack. England would certainly follow, and
  so would Russia. But, etc.'

It is curious that Russian help should have been mentioned
for the first time in the officially-inspired Press.
  On the whole, however, the mobilisation had not been without effect. Even M. Roche in the *République* wrote on
September 25:

  England and France are trying to avoid a conflict; they are
  doing it in a spirit of self-denial rare in the history of the world.

[1] *Canard Enchaîné*, September 28.

But if Germany believes that she can take advantages of this, and make us accept her own terms by sheer bullying, the risk of war will increase, and the idea of war will be accepted by all, British and French alike.

In this paper we have been indefatigable in defending peace. But peace with honour and dignity.

Before leaving for London M. Daladier and M. Bonnet attended a Cabinet meeting at which greater unanimity was shown than at any of the previous meetings. The Anglo-French meeting in London was, in reality, a war council. When Mr. Chamberlain and Lord Halifax met the French Premier and Foreign Minister on the Sunday afternoon, they were in possession of a message from the Czechs concerning Hitler's latest demands. The Czech Government had found the terms unacceptable.

The British and French Ministers began their discussions at 9.20 p.m., and were still in conference at 11.25, when the British Cabinet, which had sat for four and a half hours in the morning and afternoon was reassembled.

After seventy minutes the Cabinet rose at 12.35 a.m. and the Anglo-Italian discussions were resumed.

A few minutes later the French Ministers left Downing Street and it was announced that the discussions would be resumed at 10.30 on the following morning.

The last decision taken on the Sunday night was to summon General Gamelin to London early the next morning.

In the meantime the Czechs were preparing to resist *à outrance*; French 'pacifists' later accused the Czech Government of having wished to profit from the Godesberg ultimatum in order to go back on their acceptance, under British and French pressure, of the Anglo-French Plan of the previous week. The charge is silly; for if there was to be a war, the Czechs were obviously not going to abandon their line of fortifications *before* the war had broken out.

.   .   .   .

During that Sunday there were a number of other important developments. One was Mr. Roosevelt's first message. President Roosevelt telegraphed to Germany, Czechoslovakia, Great Britain, France, Poland, and Hungary urging that negotiations should continue, recalling the Kellogg Pact, and emphasising the incalculable dangers of war to the social structure of every country.

It is curious how the Right in France, and even part of the officially-inspired Press had constantly minimised Mr. Roosevelt's influence, and how even at the peak of the crisis, they preferred to see Mussolini come to Europe's rescue rather than Mr. Roosevelt.

These papers were, naturally, polite about Roosevelt; but no more. Thus, in its Press review on September 25 *Paris-Midi* said ironically that that morning's *Peuple* (the trade union paper) was 'back at its hobby (*sa marotte*) again—another periodic appeal to Mr. Roosevelt!' But that was only the Press; and M. Daladier and Mr. Chamberlain replied at once, welcoming the President's move. In Germany the President's appeal was ignored. No mention of it was allowed on the wireless or in the newspapers, and it was not until twenty-four hours later that Hitler deigned to reply, putting in advance the blame on Beneš if war were to break out. Hitler cabled:

> The possibilities for a just settlement, are exhausted with the proposals of the German [Godesberg] memorandum.

Mussolini did not refer to it in his speech. In Prague on the other hand, it was immediately broadcast.

Poland, in the meantime, was becoming increasingly agitated and aggressive—and that in spite of Russia's threat to denounce the Russo-Polish non-aggressive pact if Poland were to attack Czechoslovakia. Poland and Czechoslovakia were both France's allies; and now that one was preparing to attack the other, it was clear how low France's authority had fallen in Central Europe. The *Humanité* was fulminating against M. Bonnet for having failed to warn Poland that if she attacked the Czechs, the French would denounce the Franco-Polish alliance: Russia had set a good example; why was not France following it?

As for Mussolini, he made a speech at Verona in which he urged Britain and France to abandon the Czechs before war became inevitable.

. . . .

In London the British and French Ministers, while no

doubt leaving themselves some loopholes, decided in effect that they would stick to the Anglo-French proposals.

> 'These proposals,' the Diplomatic Correspondent of the *Manchester Guardian* wrote on September 26, 'might be carried out more quickly than was originally intended, in which case Germany would occupy those regions of Czechoslovakia where the Sudeten Germans are in the majority sooner than was planned; indeed, almost at once, but this is the limit beyond which the French and British Governments will make no further concessions.
>
> 'Hitler's essential demand, which amounts to immediate control of Czechoslovakia and the seizure of her main strategic points, of her main railway system, of many of her industrial centres and armament factories, is rejected, no matter what form it takes. The Czechoslovak Government has been left in no doubt in this respect, while Germany has been informed that if she conducts unprovoked war against Czechoslovakia France and Great Britain will immediately go to war with her.
>
> 'All hope of peace has not yet been abandoned. If Hitler were willing to engage in further negotiations war might still be averted. If he were to give way now and revert to the Anglo-French proposals he would still have won a prodigious diplomatic victory.'[1]

It is fairly clear that M. Daladier and Mr. Chamberlain and Lord Halifax were feeling quite 'firm' on that Monday morning, after their talks with General Gamelin. As for M. Bonnet, he did not play an active part in the talks, and was being kept rather in the background by the Premier. He seems to have felt rather sore about it, for, if one is to trust a writer in the (usually reliable) *Europe Nouvelle*, he was so much impressed by British firmness, that he thought it—almost excessive. Therefore, to cool the unexpected British ardour, he instructed M. Corbin to explain to the British Government that if war broke out, France would expect Britain (1) to introduce conscription immediately and (2) undertake to pay half the cost of the war.

General Gamelin stayed on in London after the French Ministers had left, and saw Lord Gort, Chief of the Imperial General Staff, and also consulted with French military experts at the French Embassy. The British Ministers were impressed by General Gamelin and by his account of the French Army;

---

[1] *Manchester Guardian*, September 27.

the weak point was the French Air Force; while the French, for their part, were sorry to find that, to begin with, England had no more than two divisions immediately available for France. The French wanted at least twelve; though General Gamelin, it appears, did not doubt that he could hold the Maginot Line almost indefinitely even without early British help on land, and even invade the Saar which had not yet been fortified. Later in the day he returned to Paris.

. . . .

That night Hitler spoke at the Sportpalast in Berlin—if it may be called speaking. The parts of the speech dealing with Beneš were like one long-drawn out paroxysm of rage.

> The question which has been agitating these last few months is not named Czecho-Slovakia; its real name is Herr Beneš.
>
> We were prepared to renounce all armaments if the other nations were prepared to do the same.
>
> We have carried out a rearmament *such as the world has never seen.*
>
> Germany and France are two great nations who both want to live and work, and they both will do that best if they co-operate. Czecho-Slovakia is the last territorial claim I have to make in Europe. *But it is one I will not renounce.*
>
> I offered my hand to Great Britain. I renounced building more than a given number of ships to give England a feeling of security and give both nations peace.
>
> I naturally feel for the Slovaks, Hungarians and Poles, but I am only the speaker for my Germans.
>
> The friendly attitude adopted by the Italian nation in the hour of Germany's need will never be forgotten, and if ever an occasion should arise when Italy stands in need of a similar service we shall come to her assistance.
>
> Now I have for the first time stated that the self-determination of *the 3,500,000 Sudetens at last must come into force, and that we won't wait any longer. I am not willing any more to stand by calmly without acting and see these madmen, who believe they can mishandle 3,500,000 people, and I have no doubt German patience is at last at an end.*
>
> The memorandum which I wrote and which is my last and final word for the British Government contained only the method of execution. The German territories in Czecho-Slovakia now become part of the German Reich. They will not become part of it when Herr Beneš has succeeded in expelling one or two million Germans, *but now and right away.*
>
> I have chosen this frontier, which, on the basis of ethno-graphic knowledge, is the German frontier. *I said that this*

territory will become German and that the final delimitation of the exact frontier line would be left to a plebiscite. I made the Saar Statute the model for this plebiscite. I said to Mr. Chamberlain 'If you only want plebiscites in special areas, very well.'

If the Czechs solve the problem of their other nationalities in a decent manner, *then the Czech nation does not interest me any more and I, as far as I am concerned, will guarantee it.*

England and France made the only possible demand—namely, that Czechoslovakia should cede the Germans. We know what Herr Beneš said. Faced with British and French threats that they would no longer help him, he found a way out. He said, 'Yes, these territories must be ceded.' *What did he do? He did not cede these territories, but expelled the Germans. Here the game ends.*

I left no doubt with Mr. Chamberlain that our patience was nearing its end. *Now our patience is at an end.*

Herr Beneš will have to surrender his territory to us on October 1. Herr Beneš now concentrates his hopes on the world. He hopes that Mr. Chamberlain will be turned out of office and M. Daladier too. He still hopes to be able to avoid the fruits of his madness.

Beneš will have to surrender this region on October 1. He thinks he can evade his duty. I can only say this: Two men confront each other—there is Beneš and here am I.

I am grateful to Mr. Chamberlain for his endeavours, and I think he is convinced that Germany wants peace, but there are limits. I assured Mr. Chamberlain that after this there would be no more international problems. I promised afterwards that if Herr Beneš would settle peacefully his problems with the other minorities I *would even guarantee the new Czech State.*

We do not want any Czechs. Our demand for the Sudetens is irrevocable.

Now for Dr. Beneš. He has it in his hands to choose either peace or war. He will accept my demands or we shall go and liberate our Germans.

Know this, my German people. After four years of war and in the fifteen years of my political struggle nobody can reproach me for ever having been a coward. In the same way I now step ahead of my people. I shall be the first soldier right in front of them, and behind me, let the world know it, the people marches in step.

We are decided. We are ready. Let Beneš choose.

It makes absurdly tame reading.

As F. A. Voigt wrote that night:

He spoke under the stress of terrible emotion. At times his words came slowly and with long intervals between them. But when he spoke of democracy, of Czecho-Slovakia, and Dr.

Beneš, he worked himself into a passion of fury. At times he roared like a wild animal, and his audience—evidently a huge crowd—roared with him. . . . It is very difficult not to regard his speech as a war speech.[1]

The 'animal roaring' is feebly rendered in italics in the above quotation. An outstanding feature of his speech was that at no moment did he give his audience the least suggestion that what he was threatening to produce was not a mere German march into Czechoslovakia, but a European war. Only on the following day did it begin to dawn on a large part of the German people how great the danger was.

But the speech was not made for internal consumption only. Hitler knew that millions of people all over the world were hearing him. Was not the 'animal roaring', at least to some extent, deliberate; was it not, like the insane outburst of rage with which he is said to have welcomed Sir Horace Wilson, Mr. Chamberlain's emissary, on the following day, calculated to create the impression, perhaps not least in the mind of Mr. Chamberlain, that *Hitler was mad*; and that he would go to war even though he knew that Germany would be ultimately crushed by the Franco-Anglo-Russo-Czech coalition? Was not this simulation of madness the supreme bluff? Herr Abetz, one of the Germans who, on December 6, accompanied Herr von Ribbentrop to Paris, related, with a great display of joviality, how, on September 28, the day the British Fleet was mobilised, Hitler was 'literally in a blue funk', and was wondering 'how the devil he was going to get out of the mess without loss of face'. The French gentlemen of the Comité France-Allemagne to whom Herr Abetz told the story, laughed themselves nearly sick.

The moral of the story is that if no desperate appeal had been addressed from London to Rome on the 28th, Mussolini would, if it had come to the worst, have undertaken to 'save peace' on his own initiative—in order to get Hitler out of the 'mess'. There is, in fact, reason to believe that Hitler had already told Mussolini of his worries on the 28th, and even before.

But the great achievement was, of course, to wait until England asked and begged for this intervention. As we shall

[1] *Manchester Guardian*, September 27.

later see, M. Bonnet later made serious efforts to show that it
was really *he* who first thought of Munich.

· · · · · · · · ·

On the night of Hitler's speech, the British Foreign Office
issued its famous authorised statement—a statement the like
of which had never been made by Britain in time of peace
before. The British Government was, clearly, anxious to
avoid the charge made against Sir Edward Grey who, had he
spoken sooner, would probably have averted the War in 1914.

> During the last week Mr. Chamberlain has tried with the
> German Chancellor to find a way of settling peacefully the
> Czecho-Slovak question. It is still possible to do so by negotia-
> tion . . .
> The German claim to the transfer of the Sudeten areas has
> already been conceded by the French, British, and Czecho-
> Slovak Governments. But if, in spite of all efforts made by the
> British Prime Minister, a German attack is made upon Czecho-
> Slovakia *the immediate result must be that France will be bound to come
> to her assistance and Great Britain and Russia will certainly stand by
> France.*
> It is still not too late to stop this great tragedy and for the
> peoples of all nations to insist on settlement by free negotiation.

This brings us to the *fausses nouvelles* episode in Paris,
which marked, as it were, the climax in the battle between the
'pacifists' and the *'bellicistes'*. The 'pacifists', as we have seen,
were the people who did not want anything to happen that
would encourage France to take a firm stand; and in those last
days of September, when the choice seemed to lie between
a firm stand against Germany even at the risk of war and a
complete surrender without such immediate risk, they did not
want anything to happen which would act as an argument
against such a complete surrender—that is, a perfectly free
hand for Germany in Czechoslovakia, if the latter persisted in
rejecting the Godesberg memorandum.

Incredible as it may sound, the British *communiqué*, which
would have aroused boundless gratitude and enthusiasm in
France in 1914, was treated by a part of the Press as a forgery
or a semi-forgery; while M. Bonnet allowed it to be under-

stood that the British *communiqué* was of no vital importance.

The *communiqué*, as I happen to know on the best authority, was written by Lord Halifax in person, and was to have been broadcast that night by the B.B.C. in German in such a manner that it would reach a very large number of German listeners; unfortunately, for some technical reasons, the broadcast did not quite 'come off'. But think of the impression it would have made in Germany on the very night Hitler was suggesting that France and England were 'against Beneš'!

But that by the way.

I cannot improve on Hamilton Fish Armstrong's account of how the British *communiqué* was treated as a *fausse nouvelle* in the French Press. This is what he writes in *Foreign Affairs* of January 1939:

> The Havas agency in London received a typewritten copy of the *communiqué* from the Press Bureau of the British Foreign Office at 9.15 p.m. It transmitted the text to Paris, describing it as a 'declaration of the Foreign Office'. The *Action Française*, whose former devotion to monarchism has largely given way to interest in Fascism, reported that when news of the British *communiqué* reached Paris several deputies called on M. Bonnet at the Quai d'Orsay and asked him if he could guarantee its authenticity. Reply: 'We have not received any confirmation.' M. Leon Bailby's *Jour*, though the *communiqué* was being printed as a matter of course in all the British papers, and on front pages in America, called it 'most suspect'.[1] Emile Roche, in the *République*, asked if it were not being circulated in order to heighten the tension with Germany by bringing in Soviet Russia. The *Liberté*, a paper of openly Fascist tendencies, on September 30 reported an interview with Daladier. Question: 'What was the origin of the unbelievable dispatch

[1] Here were Bailby's exact words:
'La note ajoutait que "la Grande-Bretagne et la Russie seraient certainement aux côtés de la France."
'Rien de plus insolite et de plus suspect qu'une pareille communication dont ni le ton, ni les termes ne sont dans les habitudes du Foreign Office. Au point qu'on a pu, à Paris, elever des doutes sur l'authenticité de ce document.
'Le mot "la Russie" n'est plus jamais employé dans la langue officielle. On dit: l'U.R.S.S. Comment, d'autre part, savait-on à Londres, au Foreign Office, au point de s'en porter garant, que "la Russie" se battrait aux côtés de l'Angleterre, alors qu'aucun représentant attitré du gouvernement des Soviets n'a été officiellement consulté sur cette éventualité? . . .'
(It might be added that in a broadcast, for which the *communiqué* was intended, the word obviously to use was 'Russia' and not the 'U.S.S.R.').

speaking of the aid which England and Russia would give France?' Answer: 'From an official of no importance.' The *Matin* on October 2, continuing the campaign, referred to the 'soi-disant *communiqué*' of the Foreign Office as 'a clever lie'.

As a matter of fact these and other French papers which labelled anyone accepting the *communiqué* as 'war-mongers' went further than was necessary in their efforts to protect M. Bonnet's course from criticism. The French Foreign Minister did not himself call the British Foreign Office *communiqué* a lie; he simply is reported to have said *it lacked confirmation*. He may have been as firmly determined now to execute the terms of the French treaty with Czechoslovakia as he presumably had been earlier in the summer, and may have been glad at heart to hear both from Chamberlain personally and from the Foreign Office that Britain would help if necessity arose. The quotations given here from the French Press may have reported Bonnet and Daladier incorrectly. There have been previous occasions when French papers did that. *What is of prime importance is the lack of enthusiasm with which Bonnet received a public statement of British policy regarding what has always been considered the essential touchstone in Anglo-French relations,* and the further fact that defeatist rumours calling the statement untrue were permitted to circulate through large sections of the French Press *without, so far as can be found, adequate contradiction.*

Later, after Munich had produced the result which MM. Daladier and Bonnet had become persuaded was advisable, the truth about the *communiqué* came out. Already on September 28 Chamberlain had publicly confirmed the accuracy of the British position stated in the *communiqué* when he said that on September 26 'we told them (Daladier and Bonnet) that if as a result of these obligations (to Czechoslovakia) French forces became actively engaged in hostilities against Germany, we should feel obliged to support them'. In other words, two days before the *Liberté* reported Daladier as saying that the Foreign Office *communiqué* came from 'an official of no importance,' Chamberlain had given Daladier a similar statement of the British position. And the *Matin* spoke of the *communiqué* as 'a clever lie' four days after Chamberlain had made a public declaration of a policy identical with the one which the *communiqué* announced. On September 30 the British Foreign Office re-affirmed the accuracy of the *communiqué*, with an expression of surprise (according to the *Petit Parisien* of October 1) that such confirmation should be needed for an official British statement. On October 3, speaking in the House of Commons, Anthony Eden referred to the *communiqué*, approvingly as one of the factors which had helped avert hostilities. And finally, on October 4, in his official governmental declaration, M. Daladier said: 'On the evening of September 26, in an official information to the Press, it was stated in London that if Germany attacked Czechoslovakia, France would go to her aid and that "Great Britain and Russia would certainly be on the side of France".'

I may add two points, both equally remarkable, and the first of which pretty well deprives M. Bonnet even of that slight benefit of the doubt that Armstrong gave him. M. Pierre Comert, the Press Chief of the Quai d'Orsay, after being attacked for months by *Gringoire*, the *Action Française*, etc., was deprived of his post by M. Bonnet soon after Munich and transferred to a much less prominent post—though a better one than the obscure sinecure that had been prepared for him in the first place. In paying a tribute to M. Comert's past services as Press Chief on October 24 (for M. Comert was too big and too popular a man to be simply fired, in accordance with *Gringoire's* advice) M. Bonnet said:

'I wish to put an end to the absurd legends that have been spread about the Press Service of the Ministry of Foreign Affairs. At no moment was this service in any way responsible for what was called *fausses nouvelles*. These did not come from the Ministry; and, in any case, most of them proved, subsequently, to be true.' (*Et dont la plupart d'ailleurs, se trouvèrent confirmées par la suite.*)

Par la suite was lovely! Why did not M. Bonnet publicly declare that the British *communiqué* was true the very moment its authenticity was queried, instead of allowing the 'absurd legend' to spread?

But that is not all. M. Pierre Dominique, one of the great 'pacifists' of M. Roche's *République* published a book, several months after Munich, in which he denounced both the French and the British 'warmongers'. And in spite of all the official confirmation of the authenticity of the British *communiqué*, he glibly declared that these confirmations had to be made simply because Lord Halifax was a gentleman:

There were many of us who on first seeing the British *communiqué* treated it as a forgery. No—it was *not* a forgery. But the *communiqué* was drawn up by Sir Robert Vansittart, the chief of the War Party at the Foreign Office, and was endorsed by an obscure underling. Out of sheer gentlemanliness (*délicatesse d'âme*), Lord Halifax did not wish to repudiate the document. In short, it was an act of bad faith.[1]

[1] Pierre Dominique: *Après Munich: Veux-tu vivre ou mourir?* (Paris, Stock.)

Chief among the other *fausses nouvelles* which was once again to arouse the fury of the 'pacifists', was the Havas telegram from Berlin on Tuesday, September 27 saying that there would be general mobilisation in Germany at 2 p.m. on the following day.   Already that morning (according to Mr. Chamberlain's subsequent statements) Sir Horace Wilson was informed of the coming 'action'.   The only possible query was whether by 'action' was meant an attack on Czechoslovakia, or 'merely' a general mobilisation.   Most of the Foreign Correspondents in Berlin took it to mean general mobilisation. Reuter and the *Times* both reported it as such.   At *that time* the news was perfectly correct; if it was contradicted by the D.N.B. (the German official news agency) at 2.40 a.m. on the next day, *it was probably because in the interval Berlin had learned of the mobilisation of the British Navy.*   The 'general mobilisation story reported by Havas in rather milder terms than those used by the British Press, did not fail to arouse the fury of the 'pacifists', i.e., the advocates of unconditional surrender to Germany; they thought it would produce a sharp 'militarist' and patriotic reaction among the French people. The *Action Française, organe du Nationalisme Intégral* produced the following piece from M. Léon Daudet:

> The scoundrel (*le misérable*), who is obviously affiliated with the war gang, and who launched this alarming piece of news, must be discovered, arrested and tried.   Such a crime deserves merciless punishment.   It shows up the war plot that is being hatched in the obscene darkness.   The Sudeten affair (Hitler said so the other night in a speech that was extremely violent in relation to Beneš, and very restrained in relation to France and England) is a local affair which must be circumscribed and settled locally.

Léon Daudet was reacting to Hitler's speech in exactly the manner in which Hitler was hoping France to react.   And this was the man who had written endless panegyrics in honour of Clemenceau!   It was enough to make the Tiger pirouette in his grave.   For here was the supreme synthesis of cold feet and frantic pro-Fascism—a pro-Fascism that had become completely blind to all that *nationalisme intégral* stood for.   If such an attitude was understandable in the case of Bonnet and many other people, it was plainly indecent in the case of the *Nationalistes Intégraux.*

Daudet, however, tried to whitewash Clemenceau by implication. Clemenceau created the Czechoslovakia of 1919—complete with the Sudeten country—but the treaty of alliance was drafted by Philippe Berthelot and Dr. Beneš. And Philippe Berthelot was *un gredin vendu.*

> Some day we may know how much Beneš paid him. We already know that Rumania paid him 250,000 francs. Without a sou in the world this scoundrel (*scélerat*) had the most beautiful collection of obscene Japanese objects and drawings in the world.

All of which presumably meant that the great Clemenceau would never have signed an alliance with the Czechoslovakia he had made. But that by the way.

A number of other papers also thundered against the *fausse nouvelle* concerning the German mobilisation.

What did Paris look like during the great Scare of September 25 to 28?

.   .   .   .

REGARDING PARISIAN A.R.P.

I may as well begin by saying that air-raid precautions in Paris were negligible—or rather the 'passive defence of Paris', as distinct from its 'active defence'.

Regarding 'active' defence, there were said to be seventy-two anti-aircraft batteries around Paris, representing several hundred guns; and a prominent member of the War Office assured me at the end of September that 'not one aeroplane in fifteen' would get as far as Paris. Which did not prevent 'pacifists' like M. Pierre Dominique from later claiming that there was not around Paris any 'active defence' worth mentioning, and that at the height of the crisis several anti-aircraft batteries had to be rushed to Paris from Toulon—which (he claimed) left the great French naval base in the Mediterranean as good as defenceless.[1] Probably the truth lay somewhere half-way between the two assertions. There were, naturally, also some anti-aircraft batteries on the Maginot Line and at various points between the frontier and Paris. The other form of 'active defence' was the French Air Force—but that

---

[1] Pierre Dominique, *op. cit.*

is a matter which will be dealt with later. Although some
£200,000,000 had been spent on the air force between 1928 and
1938, the 'pacifists' claimed, at the time of the crisis, that
the French Air Force was 'as good as non-existent'. Which
was, of course, an absurd exaggeration.

'Non-existent' was an adjective that could more reasonably
have been applied to 'passive defence', or what we call A.R.P.
This adjective was actually used by General Mordacq in a book
published at the end of 1937; and between then and the September crisis certainly no appreciable progress had been made.
The system—if it may be called a system—was in a complete
muddle. The A.R.P. services were divided up in some arbitrary
way between three Government departments—the War Office,
the Air Ministry and the Ministry of the Interior; and this lack
of 'single command' was disastrous. There were constant
squabbles between the Prefects under the orders of the
Minister of the Interior, and the local authorities who were, for
financial and other reasons, unwilling to carry out the
Prefects' instructions; and it was not until the end of July
that a Government decree attempted to unify and co-ordinate
the services dealing with 'passive defence'. At long intervals—
roughly once a year—there had been various air-raid 'rehear-
sals' in Paris, and once, in 1937 a complete blackout was tried
out; but experts did not consider it a success. Large crowds
assembled in the Place de l'Opéra and along the Boulevards
to see it; the public treated it rather as a joke, and for several
days afterwards the comic papers told no end of stories about
all that pickpockets and other enterprising young and old men
managed to do during the blackout.

For some months before the crisis, official A.R.P. booklets
were available, free of charge, at every Paris police station;
but that was the most tangible piece of A.R.P. as far as the
man-in-the-street was concerned. No doubt, there were some
impressive bomb-proof shelters in Paris; at the Bank of France,
at the Foreign Office, and several other Government departments, at the Hôtel de Ville, at the Préfecture de Police and
so on. There were also a few good public shelters, such as the
underground station at the Place des Fêtes in the East End
of Paris; and there was, of course, the *métro* itself—though,
being much nearer the surface than the London tube, it pro-

vided insufficient protection against direct hits and none
against gas. Apart from that, A.R.P. was confined to 'private'
shelters and—to the evacuation of Paris.

Regarding these 'private' shelters, the police had made a
complete survey of all the cellars of Paris that could be used
as shelters in an air raid; and it was stated that there were
no fewer than 27,000 such shelters, providing enough room for
1,720,000 people or about half the population of Paris. In
every house a notice had been put up a long time ago, saying:
'Your nearest shelter is at——.' In the suburbs, there were
caves to shelter 600,000 people—a considerably smaller proportion of people than in Paris; for the houses in the suburbs
are smaller and less solidly built, and some have no *caves* at
all or at least none fit to act as shelters. Only—there was a
snag. The vision of a *cave*-dwelling Paris living safely through
a hundred bombardments was largely theoretical. And that
was made amply plain by the free booklet distributed at the
police stations. On the eve of the September crisis few people,
as far as one knows, had taken a single one of the 'preliminary
precautions' strongly recommended in the booklet—such as
the various ways of 'reinforcing' the cellars, the sandbags for
protecting the exits of the cellars, and so on.

> 'Without much cost,' the booklet said, 'the roofs of the cellars
> may be strengthened by means of wooden props which would
> give the roof a resistance to a 'static burden' of four to five tons
> per square metre representing the average weight of building
> material liable to be accumulated should the five- or six-floor
> building collapse.'

Only there seemed to be some divergence of opinion as to
what constituted a 'static' burden. Did the term include the
weight of a 'crash'?

Iron and concrete reinforcements were declared to 'last
longer' than wooden reinforcements.

The book contained a large number of other instructions—
hatchets and pick-axes must be provided in each shelter against
the danger of being buried alive.

> 'Special attention must also be paid to incendiary bombs, as
> in the middle of the din caused by the anti-aircraft guns their
> appearance is apt to pass unnoticed.'

Further:

> 'inhabitants are warned that poison gas contaminates both food and water, and they are advised to store certain quantities of these in hermetically sealed containers.
>
> 'The alarm being sounded ten or fifteen minutes before the bombing begins, people are invited not to lose their heads but to turn off the gas and light, to put on their gas masks, and descend into their cellars without undue hurry'.   The advice went on to say:'And even when the house collapses over your head do not lose your self-control; the roof of the shelter having stood the collapse there is no immediate danger.'

The instructions made rather depressing reading, but the reader was, after all, warned from the outset that:

> 'The people who have remained in Paris must not consider the measures as absolute.   They must become used to the idea that war involves risks, and that all they will have a right to expect from the authorities is that these risks be reduced in the greatest possible measure, but not abolished.'

If half the population could, if it came to the worst, seek refuge in the registered cellars, the other half—or possibly more—was expected to leave Paris immediately on the outbreak of war.   The persons to be evacuated fell into two categories—the *dispersés*, who were to be removed far away from Paris (these were people who had no particular reason for staying in the capital) and the *éloignés*, that is, those who were going to have one or more members of their family working in Paris, and whom they could, therefore, go and see from time to time with comparative ease.

The booklet declared that the plans for this 'dispersal' were far advanced, and that provisions had been made for the train and road services that would do the 'dispersing', if possible within a couple of days.   This did not, however, mean that the registration of inhabitants with the indication of the exact bus, car, or train they must take was by any means advanced.

The system had been worked out in its general lines rather than in detail.

And the phrase in the booklet which described the exact moment when 'you must be sure to put on your gas mask' sounded—during the September crisis—even sillier than the instructions about propping up the cellars and making them gas-proof.

For, in fact, all these instructions were theoretical, and none of them had been carried out by the time the danger came. Except for some privileged services, which had been provided with gas masks, no gas masks were to be obtained in Paris for love or money.

All that had been done shortly before the scare week was to distribute sand against incendiary bombs. How the general evacuation would have been carried out, if it had come to the point, is hard to say. It was claimed that 'everything was ready', but was it?

So, generally speaking, when the scare week began, there were plenty of *caves* in Paris but hardly any of them either bomb-proof or gas-proof; there was some sand for extinguishing (with luck) incendiary bombs; extra trains were run to facilitate the 'voluntary evacuation' of Paris; there were no gas masks, and none of the cellars had been propped up. Perhaps the 'active defence' would have chased away the enemy aeroplanes; but no one could tell.

The truth is that Paris felt pretty helpless.

The best solution was—to escape. If you could not escape, then—I shall here quote the reflections of Teffi, the well-known Russian *émigré* writer, whom life had taught to take things calmly.

'Well, Paris is pretty calm,' she wrote. 'There is no panic. The police booklets have told us not to run about wildly and not to scream. Where are we to run away to, and at whom are we to scream?

'We know exactly how to behave. The moment the sirens go off, we must buy a house in the South and fill it with foodstuffs. If that is impossible, we must without a moment's delay make friends with somebody owning a château in the Touraine country. But if we fail in this, then the only thing to do is to buy a gas mask. Or, better still, several gas masks, one for each kind of gas. But if we find that there aren't any gas masks, we'll just have to do without. . . . As regards incendiary bombs, we know that it is enough to sprinkle a little sand on them: Usually you can't put out a fire with sand, but with an incendiary bomb it's automatic.

'And if you are bored with sitting inside your own *cave*, you have only got to follow the instructions: get some sandwiches and a thermos flask and an electric torch, and a wet blanket and a *vase de nuit* and go out for a walk in search of another shelter.

'And so, armed to the teeth with sandwiches, we are waiting.

The one bright spot on the horizon is the idea that we may not
have to pay our next rent.'

.   .   .   .

Exactly. 'Armed to the teeth with sandwiches,' we were
waiting. Or at least those of us were waiting who had not
departed to the country, or to their, or somebody else's château in Touraine. The exodus from Paris began on Saturday,
reaching its peak on Tuesday night and Wednesday morning.
During those days a large part of the child population of Paris
was 'voluntarily' evacuated. By Monday night some 300,000
people had left Paris; by Wednesday, twice that number.

It started on the Sunday. Thousands of cars were speeding
West and South. The rich were, naturally, the first to go.
On the great main roads to Dijon and Nevers and Rennes the
hotels were beginning to profiteer on a big scale. A room
that cost twenty francs fetched 100, which the motorists gladly
paid. By Tuesday the price went up to 200. On and on they
would drive away from the danger zone, and rent bungalows
and cottages for a year on the Breton coast, and pay an exorbitant amount of rent in advance, and stuff up the cottage with
food. Soldiers on the road would jeer at them as they drove
past. *Embusqué, va!*

Children were a different matter. Many mothers would, on
Sunday or Monday, take their children *chez grand-mère* in
the Creuse, and come back to Paris on Wednesday morning.
On the Tuesday the opening of schools was postponed from
October 1 to October 10 ('October 10,' the pessimists reflected,
'wonder what Paris will look like on October 10!'). There was
no longer any excuse for leaving the children in Paris. Train
services were doubled and trebled; immense crowds were assembled at the railway stations, with people arriving two or
three hours before the departure time of the trains. How
reminiscent the stations were of the great holiday exodus at
the beginning of August—and yet how different! The traffic
in Paris, largely consisting of taxis loaded with luggage,
seemed faster than usual. Everybody seemed to be hurrying
somewhere, either to leave town or to make some last-minute
arrangement. There were long, and at times, impatient
queues outside the savings banks. The lights in the streets
were being dimmed and at night the streets were almost com-

pletely dark. On Monday, all house painters were conscripted, and were busy camouflaging factories and railway stations. Trenches were being dug in the Parc Montsouris. In the Underground on Tuesday night I witnessed a strange scene in which a woman with a child was upbraided as 'inhuman' by the rest of the passengers for not having sent her child out of Paris. She explained apologetically that she was sending it the next morning.

.   .   .   .

How clearly I remember those last three days of the Great Scare. On Monday things still looked fairly normal. Mme Bousquet, my concierge, wondered whether she should take away the children to their aunt in the country, and in the end decided to wait for 'just another day'. She was more worried lest her husband should be mobilised. 'Like to look at the *cave*?' she asked. 'It's a good *cave,* and was used during the last War. Mme L., the propriétaire, has given strict instructions that only the *locataires* are to use it; she doesn't want any strangers dropping in from the street. Mme L. is going to the country to-morrow.'

The P——s dropped in on their way to the railway station, and gave up the keys of their little house at Sceaux. Old P. is a retired French lecturer at Glasgow University; but *Madame* is a Scotswoman, and she was determined to be 'at home' if it came to any trouble. They said it was quite a job getting tickets for the Boulogne train. If we wanted to stay at Sceaux, we could do so. I said I thought I'd rather not. There was a military aerodrome near by, and no *cave*.

Mme Fayolle, in the paper-shop, said I could buy my papers somewhere else for all she cared; *she* wasn't going to stay in Paris; she had already sent her little daughter away, and was going to follow. It was quite bad enough to have a son on the Maginot Line; the poor boy had sent a card saying he had had to spend two nights in a barn, and he had caught a bad cold. 'And you know how delicate he is.'

My greatest fear was to be without tobacco, and I bought five packets that morning—to begin with. Ensor had come over from London that morning to 'have a look' at Paris. He thought war was a pretty safe bet, but 'not before Thursday'. We lunched at the Petit Riche, which was crowded.

Went to the Gare de Lyon to look at the departing crowds, and also to recover an overcoat I had left in the train the week before. There was no coat, but plenty of crowds. But they were very conscientious at the *objets trouvés*, and went to no end of trouble to find my coat, and nobody suggested that there were more important matters to think about. Their job was to look for lost coats, and they stuck to their job. Later I joined some *confrères* at the Hotel Jacob, to see Hubert Ripka who had just arrived from Prague. Ripka was the editor of the *Lidovy Novini*, and a close friend of Beneš. He looked worn out. 'Whatever happens, we are not going to abandon our fortifications,' he said with a desperate note in his voice. 'But you accepted the Anglo-French Plan.' *'Je m'en fous.* The Anglo-French Plan was cancelled by the Godesberg ultimatum.' He called the French Ministers a lot of names.

Edgar, who was also there, said triumphantly that he had discovered a firm that agreed to sell him three gas masks. Perhaps they didn't do much good; but they acted like a mascot— gave you self-confidence. David thought gas masks were a lot of British eyewash; you couldn't swamp the whole of Paris with gas. At the Deux Magots met Jacques G., an engineer who was going to be mobilised the next day. 'I hope to God we have the war *now* and get it over. It'll be far worse if we wait.' Frank dropped in at night, bringing with him another Czech refugee who had just come from Prague and was 'so glad to be in Paris. Everything in Paris,' he said, was 'so quiet and normal.' Naturally they wanted to hear Hitler's speech. I turned on the wireless. Hitler bellowed: *'Beneš und ich, Beneš und ich.'* The Czech decided that there wasn't much to choose between Paris and Prague.

.   .   .   .

Tuesday. Called on old G. He and Mrs. were going to the station to book tickets for Thursday. They had some friends staying at Bagnoles de l'Orne, and had been offered a room. Mrs. G. was crying and packing up blankets and pillows and winter clothes. 'The house at Bagnoles is damp and cold— damn these Czechs,' old G. grumbled. 'It's no fun leaving home—heaven knows for how long. I don't mind so much myself, but my poor wife is desperate. Leaving the little nest to be blown to bits. You've got to understand women.'

Met Barsalou of the *Depêche* and C., a member of Sarraut's *cabinet* for lunch in the place des Victoires.   Mme Barsalou had just returned from Arles, where she had dumped the children.   Had a very good lunch, in spite of C.'s pessimism. He thought the wheels of war were already turning; people had accepted the idea of war; and that was fatal.   We went on to the broadcasting station where C. was working; he produced some telegrams from Rome suggesting that Mussolini was up to something.   In the Boulevard Haussmann saw whole family standing on the pavement with hampers and suitcases, waving desperately at 'engaged' taxis, as they dashed past.   Taxis were making pots of money that day.   Shops— except those selling trunks—were empty, and many assistants were mobilised.   At the Parc Montsouris they were digging trenches of sorts, and at the Louvre pictures were being packed up.   Went to the bank to take out enough money to last a couple of months—just in case.   Monsieur S., the cashier, thought it was foolish of me.   *'Vous aller voir,'* he said knowingly.   He seemed genuinely unperturbed.

Some excitement in the Boulevards that afternoon.   Two posters: one by Flandin, the other—a large yellow poster—by the Postmen's and Teachers' Trade Unions.   Both pacifist *à outrance*.

M. Flandin's poster said:

ON VOUS TROMPE

and denounced the ideological war that was being prepared by the politicians of the Front Populaire.   He also denounced the *fausses nouvelles* spread by the warmongers, and went on to say that all the quarrel with Hitler was now over a question of procedure.

There must therefore be no mobilisation, which would only lead to the massacre of millions of Frenchmen.   Parliament must be called and there must be an 'objective discussion' of the situation.   *Pas de chantage au patriotisme!*   All Frenchmen must unite in their determination to defend peace.

It was interpreted by some as a call to Frenchmen not to obey the general mobilisation order, were it to come.   The police tore down the posters, and the *Liberté* which had printed it that night on its front page, was confiscated.   On the next

day the *Action Française* spoke highly of the poster the ideas
of which, it said, had been borrowed from the A.F. and protested against its laceration by *le gorille* Sarraut. The *Lumière*
later claimed that the poster was printed *with the approval of
at least two members of the Government,* and in February,
M. Flandin claimed that *throughout September he had worked
in the closest co-operation with the Government.*

And the postmen's and schoolteachers' posters said:

> We do not want war.
> In these grave hours we are certain of expressing the wish of
> the immense majority of the French people by saying that we
> wish a peaceful settlement of the present international crisis.
> Only a few days ago a settlement was considered possible,
> and agreement had been reached on the principle of the dispute.
> How can we now tolerate that for reasons of procedure, amour-
> propre or prestige, the statesmen should break off the negotia-
> tions which have gone on for weeks, and plunge the whole of
> Europe into the most frightful of wars.
> We ask the French Government to persevere and not to be
> discouraged by new difficulties. We ask it in its negotiations to
> give expression to the ardent love of peace of the people of
> France who have lost so many victims on the battlefields of
> Europe.
> We ask that the rational message of President Roosevelt be
> listened to: 'It is better to make peace before the war than after
> the war. Armed force provides no solution for the future, nor
> for the good of humanity.'

Dropped in at the *Times* office. B. said he heard of a place
where one might be able to get gas masks to-morrow. Question
arose what we journalists were going to do. Our suggestion
was: British Press headquarters at St. Germain. Good views
of Paris during air raids from Pavillon Henri IV. Within
easy reach of Paris, too. Could go and look at the wreckage
next morning. C., living on top of enormous block of flats
at St. Cloud—a magnificent target, and dangerously close to
the Renault works—thought he'd stay and see *at least* the first
big bombing. Anyway, nothing was settled; it was better to
find out first where the Government was going to go. Berlin
Times Correspondent had been instructed to leave Berlin next
day. Paris correspondents were to go to London at the end of
the week to confer on war-time organisation.

At the Chamber people were in a blue funk; Flandin was

asking that Parliament be called; he claimed that Parliament would never allow France to declare war on Germany because of Czechoslovakia.

That night listened to German broadcast from the B.B.C. about mobilisation of British Navy, A.R.P., trenches, gas masks, evacuation of children, and what not. Then Chamberlain spoke. It was a tragic speech by an old man who seemed to have broken down:

> To-morrow Parliament will meet and I shall be making a full statement of the events which have led up to the present anxious and critical situation.
>
> An earlier statement would not have been possible when I was flying backwards and forwards across Europe and the position was changing from hour to hour, but to-day there is a lull for a brief time, and I want to say a few words to you, men and women of Britain and the Empire, and perhaps to others as well. First of all, I must say something to those who have written to my wife or myself in these last weeks to tell us of their gratitude for my efforts and to assure us of their prayers for my success. Most of these letters have come from women— mothers or sisters of our own countrymen. But there are countless others besides—from France, from Belgium, from Italy, and even from Germany—and it has been heartbreaking to read of the growing anxiety they reveal and their anxious relief when they thought, too soon, that the danger of war was passed.
>
> If I felt my responsibility heavy before, to read such letters has made it seem almost overwhelming.

He now spoke with tragic sincerity—though it was not perhaps the best way of staying Hitler's hand:

> How horrible, fantastic, incredible it is that we should be digging trenches and trying on gas masks here because of a quarrel in a far-away country between people of whom we know nothing. It seems still more impossible that a quarrel which has already been settled in principle should be the subject of war.

'People of whom we know nothing!' What a sudden insight into Chamberlain's fundamental provincialism!

> I can well understand the reasons why the Czech Government have felt unable to accept the terms which have been put before them in the German memorandum. Yet I believe from my talks with Herr Hitler that if only time were allowed it ought to be possible for arrangements for transferring the territory the Czech Government have agreed to give to Germany to be

settled by agreement under conditions which would assure fair treatment to the populations concerned.

You know already that I have done all that one man can do to compose this quarrel.

After my visits to Germany I realised vividly how Herr Hitler feels that he must champion other Germans and his indignation that grievances have not been met before this.

He told me privately, and last night he repeated publicly, that *after this Sudeten German question is settled that is the end of Germany's territorial claims in Europe.*

After my first visit to Berchtesgaden I did get the consent of the Czech Government to proposals which gave the substance of what Herr Hitler wanted, and I was taken completely by surprise when I got back to Germany and found that he insisted that the territory should be handed over to him immediately, and immediately occupied by German troops without previous arrangements for safeguarding the people within the territory who are not Germans or who do not want to join the German Reich.

I am afraid I must say I find this attitude unreasonable.

'Unreasonable', what a superb understatement!

If it arises out of any doubts Herr Hitler feels about the intentions of the Czech Government to carry out their promises and hand over the territory, I offered on behalf of the British Government to guarantee their word, and I am sure the value of our promises will not be under-rated anywhere. I shall not give up the hope of a peaceful solution or abandon my efforts for peace as long as any chance for peace remains. I would not hesitate to pay even a third visit to Germany if I thought it would do any good. *But at this moment I can see nothing further I can usefully do in the way of mediation.*

(Uttered in a tone of hopelessness. The phrase sounded like a death sentence.)

Meanwhile there are certain things we can and should do at home. Volunteers are still needed for air-raid precautions, fire brigade and police services and for Territorial units. I know that all of you, men and women alike, are ready to play your part in the defence of the country, and I ask you all to offer your services, if you have not already done so, to the local authorities, who will tell you if you are wanted and in what capacity.

Do not be alarmed if you hear of men being called up to man the anti-aircraft defences or ships. These are only precautionary measures such as a Government must take in times like this.

But they do not necessarily mean that we have determined on war or that war is imminent.

And then came the famous conclusion:

> *However much we may sympathise with a small nation confronted by a big, powerful neighbour we cannot in all circumstances undertake to involve the whole British Empire in war simply on her account. If we have to fight it must be on larger issues than that. I am myself a man of peace to the depths of my soul. Armed conflict between nations is a nightmare to me, but if I were convinced that any nation had made up its mind to dominate the world by fear of its force I should feel that it must be resisted. Under such a domination the life of people who believe in liberty would not be worth living.*
>
> *But war is a fearful thing and we must be very clear before we embark upon it that it is really the great issues that are at stake and that the call to risk everything in their defence when all the consequences are weighed is irresistible.*
>
> For the present I ask you to wait as calmly as you can the events of the next few days. As long as war has not begun there is always hope that it may be prevented, and you know that I am going to work for peace to the last moment. Good night.

The telephone rang. It was A., a French journalist. 'What do you make of it?' 'I couldn't swear to it, but it sounds to me like the beginning of a *dégonflage*. "People we know nothing about", and "not sure whether the Germans really want to dominate the world", and Hitler's assurance that "he won't ask for any more".' But it was a moving speech for all that—it was tragic and human—and how different from Hitler's horrible bellowing the night before. As somebody remarked that night, it showed the whole world the difference between dictatorship and democracy.

And that night, how many people must have gone to bed wondering if it wasn't going to be their last restful night.

And then—Wednesday.

.   .   .   .

Wednesday. 'Black Wednesday.' Mme Bousquet, the concierge, went off with the children early in the morning. She came to say good-bye and said she would be back at the end of the week, if her husband wasn't mobilised in the interval. In the meantime an old woman, whose sister had a shop in the rue de la Glacière and who was staying in Paris 'for the present' would look after the house. Of course, if war broke out, she'd probably leave, too; 'but then you are not going to stay here either, will you?' I said I didn't know.

There was talk of the wholesale evacuation of Paris; but nobody quite knew when or where or how; people were preferring to go off on their own.

Things had been happening at the Foreign Office and at the Quai, and in Berlin, and in Rome during the night. And Washington had been active. Roosevelt had addressed his 'final appeal' to Hitler. The British Navy had been mobilised. There was a suspicion in Paris that morning that not all was over—and that something was happening. The German ultimatum to Prague was going to expire at 2 p.m. Somebody was going to climb down—only, would it be Hitler or *us*? There were many who felt that Chamberlain's broadcast had, in effect, prepared the ground for a climb-down. Only—one couldn't be certain of anything.

The papers that morning were—if anything—less gloomy than on the Tuesday morning.

'La Paix ne veut pas encore être vaincue. . . .' *Paris-Midi* wrote.

And, below it:

'The two last chances of peace: Roosevelt, Mussolini?'

They put Roosevelt first. Only Roosevelt was proposing an immediate conference in a neutral country of the Powers concerned in the Czech Problem. Smelt too 'democratic'—too League of Nationish; what if the Russians decided to come? It all might not suit Hitler and Mussolini. On page three of the same paper there was a much more emphatic and explicit headline:

THE DUCE MAY YET SAVE EVERYTHING
BY PROPOSING HIS MEDIATION
(1) a 15 days' truce
(2) a conference of the European 'chiefs'.

However, that morning several of the people to whom I talked did not take it seriously: 'the papers are just trying to prevent a panic'.

Took a bus to the Place de l'Opéra. The traffic seemed crazy. Everybody seemed in a desperate hurry. Terrific traffic jams around the Gare St. Lazare. People were fighting for seats on the trains. Walked up the rue Lafayette; met a Russian *émigré* friend who worked in some kind of business. His *patron* had decided to close it down. 'I'll be all right—I'm too lame to go into the army; but they'll be only too glad to take me on in a munition factory at Asnières. Make quite a lot of money there.' He had already gone to inquire. Painters were busy camouflaging the works. Went into a shop to buy some toothpaste. Solitary assistant greeted me like a long-lost brother. 'It's twelve o'clock—and I swear you are the first customer to-day. If only I were selling suitcases—or gas masks!' Met Frank at the Rotonde for lunch. The place looked completely deserted—only two more customers besides us. The waiters looked *distraits*. 'Hell, I wish I was home in Omaha,' said Frank. I offered him the P——s' 'quiet little country house' at Sceaux; 'it's not far from the military aero-drome, but it's not too bad.' No, Frank didn't like the idea, and said he'd sooner be in Omaha.

Went home to find that Peter had rung up—'What's wrong?' 'We are going to have a Press conference at my office at three. Z. from the Quai d'Orsay is coming to talk to us about Press arrangements during the war.' 'Is it as bad as all that?' 'Nothing like being on the safe side. Thomas and David are coming too.'

Rang up Richard Mowrer. 'What are you going to do?' 'I'm going to buy a bicycle.' 'A bicycle?' 'Sure. It ain't going to be much use living *in* Paris; so I'm going to find a place some ten kilometres out of town, and come in every day whenever necessary.' 'What about your car?' 'You never know about the gasolene. There mayn't be any, and they may also commandeer the car.'

I then went to Peter's 'Press conference'. Monsieur Z. of the Quai was there. In opening the proceedings Peter announced that he had a good idea. We ought to have a jour-nalists' colony—not too near, and not too far from Paris. So that we could get into Paris by car—just about an hour's run. He had discovered a lovely little country inn just off the Pon-toise road; Mme Dulac, the *patronne*, cooked the most deli-cious meals. He pointed to it on the map; 'This,' he said, 'is what the Paris region will look like to the airmen.' Couldn't the Government, he said, commandeer the place for the British Press? And couldn't it guarantee that there would be enough

petrol for the two cars? And couldn't we have a special telephone line put in by the P.T.T.? Monsieur Z. a little doubt-
fully, said he would inquire. 'But aren't you in too great a
hurry to make such arrangements?' he said. 'Still, there's no
harm in discussing all the possibilities,' said Peter. 'Are
the Government offices to stay in Paris in case of war?' 'Yes,'
said Monsieur Z. 'The Foreign Office and the Presidence du
Conseil are certainly not going to move; I don't know about
the rest. Some of them may be moved.' 'You are lucky,' said
Peter a little enviously. 'You've got the best shelter in Paris.'
'*Oh, moi, vous savez,*' said Monsieur Z., '*je suis mobilisable.*'

And then we asked questions about the Censorship and
about telephoning to London, and gathered that there would
be a censorship, and that, in all probability, it would not be
possible to telephone London.

And while we were talking, a Frenchman from next door
came dashing in:

'Hitler and Chamberlain and Mussolini and Daladier are
meeting at twelve at Mulhouse to-morrow.' *Coup de théâtre*;
but—followed by a moment of doubt. 'Don't be absurd—why
should they meet at Mulhouse? Are the French giving away
Alsace-Lorraine?' 'Hell, I don't mean Mulhouse, I mean
Munich.' That sounded more like it.

And Herr Goldberg, a German *émigré*, came in from next
door and said: 'Isn't it wonderful to think of the money Hitler
could make on the Bourse if he wanted to!'

'I told you you were in too great a hurry,' said Monsieur Z.

'No, no,' said Peter, 'it is just as well; and we may as well
go on considering the arrangements. You will inquire about
the petrol, won't you? Very, very kind of you to have come.'

In the street outside the traffic seemed to have slowed down.
Was it just imagination? In the Place de l'Opéra people were
snatching up *Paris-Soirs* with giant headlines. But the feeling
that afternoon was not one of exuberance. In the Café des
Capucines I overheard two men talking:

'*Tout de même, quel soulagement!*'

'*Hm, oui, enfin. . . . C'est le soulagement qu'on éprouve
le moment où on a fait dans sa culotte.*'

On my way home I saw a taxi laden with pillows and mat-
tresses and wicker baskets driving up to a house. The people

had *returned* from the station. They and the people on the first floor were waving frantically. '*Pas de guerre! Pas de guerre!*'

La mère Thiébaud was standing outside her house in the rue Broca. 'Have you heard?' I asked. 'Yes, of course,' she said, not sounding much impressed. 'All right if it's put off for a long time—but if it's only for a few months it's hardly worth it. *On l'aura dans des pires conditions.*'

La mère Thiébaud was an old peasant woman with a fund of common sense; and although she read the *Journal* every morning, she had worked it all out for herself.

. . . .

That night Daladier spoke on the wireless. His voice sounded firm and authoritative:

> I announced that I would make a statement this evening to the country on the international situation; but early this afternoon I received an invitation from the German Government to meet Chancellor Hitler, Signor Mussolini and Mr. Chamberlain in Munich to-morrow. I have accepted the invitation.
>
> You will understand that on the eve of such an important negotiation, I must postpone the explanations I was going to give you. But before leaving, I wish to address my thanks to the people of France for its attitude, so full of courage and dignity.
>
> I thank particularly the men who were called to the colours for their calm and their resolution.
>
> My task is a hard one. Since the beginning of the difficulties through which we are passing, I never ceased for a day to work with all my strength for the safeguard of peace and for the vital interests of France. I shall continue this effort to-morrow, with the thought that I am in complete agreement with the whole nation.

M. Daladier had remained all morning at the War Office, and had conferred with M. Langeron, the Prefect of Police, M. Bonnet, M. Marchandeau, the Finance Minister, General Gamelin, and M. Mistler, the President of the Foreign Affairs Committee of the Chamber—and an ardent *Munichois*.

At the Quai M. Bonnet had received two visits from Sir Eric Phipps, and had also seen the Russian, Polish and United States Ambassadors. These, apparently, had simply come to 'inquire'.

. . . .

What was it that had happened at the Quai d'Orsay on the night from Tuesday to Wednesday? It was later claimed that if Bonnet was not alone in 'saving peace', he certainly played a 'decisive part' that night. It was even vaguely suggested that it was on his initiative that Munich was arranged.

There are several 'Bonnetiste' accounts of that night at the Quai d'Orsay; some of them were published soon after Daladier's 'triumphal' entry into Paris.

On October 8 the *Intransigeant* claimed that it was M. Bonnet's two messages on the night of September 27-28, one to M. François-Poncet, the Ambassador in Berlin, the other to M. Corbin, the Ambassador in London, 'which were to spare the lives of millions of Europeans'. Mr. Chamberlain was not even mentioned—it looked as though Munich was the work of M. Bonnet alone. This is what M. Thouvenin, one of M. Bonnet's *hommes de confiance* wrote:

> On September 27 one did not yet want to believe in the imminence of the catastrophe. During the whole afternoon Paris and London were examining compromise proposals tending to authorise the entry to German troops into territories *outside* the Czechoslovak fortifications. At 5.45 p.m. Sir Eric Phipps came to confer with M. Bonnet. It was then that M. Bonnet learned that if by 2 p.m. on the following day the Czech Government had not sent plenipotentiaries to Berlin or had not accepted the terms of the German (Godesberg) memorandum, mobilisation measures would be taken by Germany and followed by military action.
>
> That same evening at 10 o'clock Mr. Chamberlain gave his famous broadcast. . . .
>
> At 11 o'clock the British Government ordered the mobilisation of the British Navy. The situation seemed to become more and more critical. M. Georges Bonnet declared to the British Ambassador, who again came to see him, that one must not lose heart, that one must persevere to the end and that peace could yet be saved.
>
> The minister was now alone in his office. He was thinking hard. The telephone rang. It was M. Léger, the Secretary-General of the Foreign Office, who was giving him the latest news which M. Bonnet thereupon transmitted by private wire to M. Daladier who also was 'standing on guard'. M. Daladier had just received the United States Ambassador and had told him that Europe was hoping for a new message from President Roosevelt. Outside the window, the garden of the Quai d'Orsay was dark. How calm it was! And yet . . .

Alone in his office, M. Bonnet reflected, weighing up possible decisions. After mature reflection, at 1 o'clock in the morning, he took a decision: he was going, at this hour of supreme effort to take a double step to save peace. He sent M. François-Poncet an urgent telegram in which he requested him to ask Chancellor Hitler immediately for an audience so that he could submit to him a compromise proposal. M. François-Poncet was instructed to recall to the Führer that the cession of the Sudeten territory to Germany had already been officially granted to the German Government, with the double guarantee of France and Britain, and that this guarantee was sufficient to dispel the doubts the Chancellor had expressed as to whether the Czechs would fulfil the agreement entered into in principle.

It now depended on the Reichsführer—and on him alone— whether peace was to be saved without Germany's losing the advantages that had already been agreed to.

A little later, at 2.50 a.m. M. Bonnet telegraphed to M. Corbin in London: the idea of a conference had been suggested; it was important that Signor Mussolini should be associated with it, and that Italy should urge Herr Hitler to support this proposal.

And so, two official telegrams left the Minister's office at the Quai d'Orsay on that historic night; and they were to spare the lives of millions of Europeans.

.   .   .   .

M. Thouvenin then continued:

These supreme efforts were going to succeed. On the following morning September 28, Signor Mussolini obtained from Herr Hitler the extension by twenty-four hours of the German ultimatum; and in the end Herr Hitler agreed to the conference.

In Berlin M. François-Poncet called on Herr Hitler. The conversation had scarcely begun when the telephone rang: it was Signor Mussolini calling the Führer. This telephone converstaion was going to modify the course of the Franco-German talk. No sooner had he left Herr Hitler and returned to the Embassy than M. François-Poncet was called up by Herr von Ribbentrop who was going to announce the Munich conference to him. . . .[1]

One can only hope that Mr. Chamberlain will, some day, express an opinion on this extraordinary account of how 'peace was saved'.

But here is still a better account of the 'historical night' by another 'pacifist', M. Paul Allard; for according to M. Allard,

[1] *Intransigeant*, October 8.

peace was saved in the last resort not by M. Bonnet but by—
M. Piétri, not even a member of the Government!

> At 10 p.m. on the night of September 27-28 M. Bonnet
> expressed to Sir Eric Philipps (*sic*) the hope that on the following
> day Mr. Chamberlain would make another supreme effort; at
> 11 p.m. M. Bonnet sent M. François-Poncet a cyphered tele-
> gram [nothing here about 1 o'clock and the trees in the garden!]
> instructing him to see Chancellor Hitler the next morning and
> to propose to him a practical plan for the occupation of the
> Sudeten country—a plan which he had personally elaborated,
> during the day, with Mr. Daladier. [M. Allard's Daladier is
> rather more active than M. Thouvenin's.] At 2 a.m. M.
> Bonnet sent a telegram to M. Corbin inviting him to bring
> about a British *démarche* in Rome.
> It is established that at that moment the Duce alone was in a
> position to assume the role of a friendly mediator—and he
> proved to be a decisive factor in the calling of the Four-Power
> Conference.

It is disappointing to find that M. Thouvenin's moving
tableau of the calm trees and of M. Bonnet thinking in soli-
tude is completely lacking in M. Allard's account—which goes
on as follows:

> It is not without interest to know that at that historical hour—
> it was a little before 2 a.m.—M. Bonnet received a reply from
> London to his telegram of 11 p.m. With him, in his office,
> were M. Jules Henry and M. Piétri, deputy and former Minister.
> It was then that M. Piétri suggested to M. Bonnet that the
> idea be followed up of associating Signor Mussolini directly
> with an immediate conference. At the same moment M.
> Frossard (who had at the Chamber, on the same day,
> advocated a Four-Power Conference) telephoned to M. Bonnet,
> and a sort of three-men colloquy took place. Whereupon, M.
> Bonnet wrote out his telegram [to whom? to Chamberlain, or to
> Corbin, to whom he had already telegraphed at 11 p.m.?].
> Mr. Chamberlain appealed to Signor Mussolini. The Duce
> immediately telephoned Herr Hitler and threw, it is said (!),
> Italo-German friendship into the balance. . . . Peace was
> saved.[1]

These stories, the first of which at any rate was certainly
written *ad maiorem gloriam* of Georges Bonnet—call for two
remarks. Mr. Chamberlain, in his House of Commons speech
on September 28 made no reference whatsoever to any part

[1] Paul Allard. *Le Quai d'Orsay*, pp. 165-6.

played that night by M. Bonnet in the calling of the Munich Conference.

Secondly, it would seem from these stories that the final surrender was decided upon by the French rather than by the British; and that at the very moment when, as a result of the mobilisation of the British Navy, Hitler was beginning to wonder how he was going to get out of a hopeless mess without loss of prestige. The moral of these French stories about the 'historic night' is that it was M. François-Poncet's communication to Hitler, rather than any British move which saved Hitler from a plight that was becoming desperate. It is true that the François-Poncet démarche ran parellel with Mr. Chamberlain's 'final' letter to Hitler, but this letter is not as obvious a surrender as the François-Poncet communication. This letter read as follows:

> After reading your letter I feel certain that you can get all essentials without war and without delay. I am ready to come to Berlin myself at once to discuss arrangements for transfers with you and representatives of the Czech Government, together with representatives of France and Italy if you desire. I feel convinced that we can reach agreement in a week.
>
> However much you distrust the Prague Government's intentions, you cannot doubt the power of the British and French Governments to see that the promises are carried out fully and carefully and forthwith. As you know, I have stated publicly that we are prepared to undertake that they shall be so carried out.
>
> I cannot believe that you will take the responsibility of starting a world war which may end civilisation for the sake of a few days' delay in settling this long-standing problem.

Mr. Chamberlain asked for 'a week' and asked that the Czechs be included in the talks. The French however accepted Hitler's date of October 1. If only they had waited a few hours longer, Hitler who, after denying the German mobilisation order upon hearing of the mobilisation of the British Fleet, was now obviously scared, might easily have accepted a Conference on Roosevelt lines, instead of a 'Munich'. The French démarche, much more than Chamberlain's 'last letter' saved him from the unpleasant necessity of yielding. However, M. Bonnet's friends are very proud of it all, and claim for M. Bonnet the glory of Munich—a glory to which, they say, he is more entitled than are the British.

 · · · · · · · · ·

On September 29 the Press published a Havas message from Berlin describing as follows M. François-Poncet's historical visit to Hitler on the previous morning.

> M. François-Poncet was received by Herr Hitler this morning. The conversations lasted about an hour.
> It is said that the French Ambassador submitted to him some new suggestions from the French Government with the view to a peaceful settlement of the German-Czech conflict. According to well-informed sources, it is understood that the proposals provide for the occupation of the Sudeten country by German troops.
> Immediately after M. François-Poncet had left Herr Hitler also received Sir Nevile Henderson, the British Ambassador.
> It is further claimed that Signor Attolico, the Italian Ambassador was also received by the Führer, and it is said that he asked the Chancellor to prolong until October 1 the time given to the Czechs to evacuate the Sudeten country.

Although the exact meaning of the 'Sudeten country' is left vague, it is fairly clear from all this that it was already in Berlin on September 28, and not on the following day at Munich, that the substance of the Godesberg Plan was virtually accepted. And accepted by the French sooner than by the British. For the French 'new suggestions' certainly went beyond the Anglo-French Plan—a plan which, at least on the face of it, was still the basis of Chamberlain's 'last letter' to Hitler.

CHAPTER XV

THE MUNICH TRIUMPH

M. DALADIER went to Munich alone, leaving M. Bonnet behind. Was he hoping to impress the Germans and Italians by his strong-man manner, and try to save what wreckage could still be saved? On the face of it Mr. Chamberlain and M. Daladier were in a very strong position when they left for Munich. The British Navy was mobilised; France had close on 1,500,000 men under arms, and it was known that German opinion was intensely perturbed at the discovery that the 'localised' war against the Czechs had in the two or three previous days threatened to develop into a war against a large European coalition.

Hitler himself seems to have wondered on the night of September 27-28 when he heard of the British naval mobilisation how he could get out of the hole. Mussolini came to his rescue; but, in addition to that M. François-Poncet already informed him on the morning of September 28 that the French were prepared to accept almost anything—with the result that he had nothing to fear from Munich. On the face of it, and but for the French *démarche* of September 28, France and England could have insisted at Munich on Germany's acceptance of the Anglo-French Plan of September 18, and could have rejected Godesberg.

But in reality this was no longer practicable. The substance of Godesberg had already been accepted by M. François-Poncet, and, after the psychological 'no-war' shock on the afternoon of September 28, it was difficult for Mr. Chamberlain and M. Daladier even to bluff at Munich. British opinion, in particular, after being worked up to the realisation that war was inevitable and after suddenly collapsing with relief, could not possibly be expected to face war 'over Czechoslovakia' once again. So, technically, Britain and France were in an extremely strong position at Munich; psychologically, they were in a very weak one. Especially England; for France, where the 'scare' had not been so great as in England, and where, consequently, the 'collapse' of Wednesday afternoon was not so devastating, could still put up some kind of resistance at Munich.

And M. Daladier actually tried to do so at first; but received little support from Mr. Chamberlain.

It is said that he went to Munich with the firm intention of 'standing up to the Dictators', and that he 'stood up' to Hitler fairly well for the first couple of hours, though what he was 'fighting' for could, obviously, only have been details. Czechoslovakia had been sacrificed at Berchtesgaden, and England and France never even thought of going back on the 'Anglo-French Plan'. But after lunch Daladier's resistance weakened. Perhaps it was Mr. Chamberlain's fault. It may also be that Goering managed to fascinate him. Goering behaved with a kind of coarse, loud joviality, slapping Daladier on the back, and saying that he liked and admired the French—'what fine chaps they were during the War!'—and that it was absurd for two great nations, which could be good friends, to quarrel over silly things like Czechoslovakia. Goering must have touched on one of Daladier's soft spots—which was his profound belief that France and Germany ought *somehow* to make friends and never go to war again. Later that day the Havas Correspondent asked Goering what he though of Daladier: 'The very kind of chap I like,' Goering replied; and then added, *'und er ist so elastisch'*. The story goes that while Daladier 'passed' the message, though not without making a face, Bonnet in Paris stopped it from appearing.

The 'inside' story of the Munich Conference still remains to be written; and only snatches of information suggest the strange atmosphere in which it was conducted. It seems that if, during the morning meeting, Daladier put up a good fight, and demanded that the Czechs be given time to carry out an orderly evacuation, and even argued about the area to be transferred, he more or less broke down later in the day.

An insight into Daladier's state of mind at the end of the Munich Conference is provided by the following account of how the Czechs were treated at Munich. This account, published in summary form in the *New Statesman and Nation* and published in full in the Paris *Ordre* was based on first-hand information.

Dr. Hubert Masarik and Mr. Mastny were summoned to Munich to receive the Dictators' ultimatum about the future of their country. They arrived at Munich by aeroplane soon after three o'clock on September 29, were met at the aerodrome by a police car and, accompanied by members of the Gestapo, driven to the Hotel Regina, where the British delegation was staying. The conference was already in session and it was only at seven o'clock that they were able to obtain some conversation with Mr. Gwatkin. They tried to press certain economic and other problems on his attention. He was personally sympathetic but said they scarcely seemed to realise how painful it was to negotiate with Hitler, and made it clear that the plan under discussion was much worse than the terms of the Anglo-French Plan. At about ten o'clock the Czech delegates went into Sir Horace Wilson's room, where the plan was briefly explained to them but no serious attention paid to their objections. They were warned that if the Czechs did not accept promptly they would be left to make their own terms with Germany and that the French might sound very sorry, and all that, but that they would certainly do nothing to help them. At 1.30 a.m. they were shown into the conference room. Hitler and Mussolini had gone, leaving Mr. Chamberlain, M. Daladier, Sir Horace Wilson, M. Léger and Mr. Gwatkin to inform them that the agreement had been signed. The French were obviously embarrassed; the agreement was read, but their protests and doubts about the definition of areas of 'preponderantly German character' and about the absence of safeguards for their vital economic and strategic interests, were brushed aside. Questions about proposals for supervision of the 'plebiscites' by international or British troops were referred to the International Commission. Mr. Chamberlain was tired out and yawned repeatedly, *while M. Daladier was too embarrassed to answer when they wanted to know whether the Czech Government was to have the opportunity of making any statement or giving any reply to the proposals. It was left to M. Léger to explain bluntly that no reply was expected from the Czechs* and that the agreement was regarded as already accepted. A Czech delegate was to be in Berlin not later than 5 p.m. on the same day to meet the International Commission, and an officer to go to Berlin to discuss the details of the evacuation of the first zone.

. . . .

It is certain that at Munich Daladier felt intensely unhappy about the result of the conference. Several correspondents who saw the statesmen emerge from the conference room have described their faces. Demaree Bess (*Saturday Evening Post*, December 3) said Daladier seemed 'sunk in the depths of despair', Chamberlain had 'his usual poker face', while Mussolini had a 'broad smile' and Hitler was 'walking on air'.[1] 'Depths of despair' seems to have been the impression Daladier gave everybody that night. When he returned to his hotel, a number of French journalists were waiting for him, and naturally went up to him to ask questions. There was a wild, vacant look in his eyes, he opened his mouth to say something, then changed his mind, and hastily walked to the lift.

Still, on the following morning, he tried to make the best of a bad job. Before leaving Munich he said to the correspondent of the D.N.B., the official German news agency:

> I think the Munich meeting may prove to be an historical date in the life of Europe. Thanks to the great comprehension shown by the representatives of the four great Western Powers war has been avoided, and a peace with honour assured for all nations.
>
> It was a great pleasure to me to find that there was no feeling of hatred or hostility towards France in Germany. I can assure you that there is no feeling of hostility towards Germany in my country; and that was true even during this last period of diplomatic tension and military preparations. The two nations must come to an agreement, and I am happy to devote all my strength to this necessary and faithful understanding. I have already thanked the Führer and Marshal Goering, as well as Herr von Ribbentrop for the cordiality of their reception. Also please convey my best thanks to the people of Munich.

According to Havas, 'M. Daladier left the Hotel Vierjahreszeiten at one o'clock accompanied by Herr von Ribbentrop.

[1] Quoted by Hamilton Fish Armstrong, *Foreign Affairs*, January 1939.

Shortly before Marshal Goering had gone up to M. Daladier's room and they had a cordial talk which lasted about ten minutes. Outside the hotel there was a guard of honour composed of SS men, and behind them a large crowd who loudly cheered the representative of France. All along the way from the hotel to the aerodrome M. Daladier was the object of warm ovations. At the aerodrome, where he was received by General von Epp, the Statthalter of Bavaria, he reviewed a guard of honour, while the band was playing national anthems. Standing for a long time on the gangway of the aeroplane M. Daladier waved greetings to the cheering crowds.'

In the aeroplane, however, his good humour must have left him. He now keenly felt the humiliation of all that had happened; and, moreover, he had left Mr. Chamberlain *en tête-à-tête* with Hitler. It didn't look nice. One can imagine Daladier—who has always suffered from a slight form of provincial *méfiance*—saying to himself, as he was flying across the Black Forest: '*Ils se sont peut-être tous un peu foutus de moi*' —even Mr. Chamberlain, who was now talking to Hitler about heaven knows what.

When the aeroplane was in sight of Le Bourget an extraordinary thing happened. M. Daladier saw large crowds assembled near the aerodrome. He felt intensely uncomfortable. *How* were they going to receive him? But he soon realised that the people were cheering and waving. Well, since the people were pleased, it was no use looking unhappy. So in coming out of the aeroplane, M. Daladier, looking rather red in the face, waved as cheerfully as he could.

With the usual exceptions, the Paris Press that day had described Munich as an unspeakably happy event. And at one o'clock the French radio announced the exact route along which M. Daladier would travel from Le Bourget to the War Office. It was M. Bonnet's idea. Since Mussolini and Hitler and Chamberlain were going to make triumphal entries into their respective capitals, there was no reason why M. Daladier should not receive equal treatment. Otherwise Munich might look like a French defeat, like the Diplomatic Sedan the warmongering Kerillis had announced in the *Epoque* that morning. A story told in Paris at the time is that Bonnet actually wanted all the churches to ring their bells during Daladier's entry into Paris; but that Cardinal Verdier, the Archbishop of Paris, would not hear of it. There were, no doubt, some who thought it would have been best for Daladier to sneak into Paris by *métro* with his hat well over his face; but it really would not have done.

I had forgotten all about the triumphal homecoming—it seemed so unimportant—when, about four o'clock in the Boulevard Haussmann, I saw a large crowd lining the pavements outside the Galeries Lafayette, and on the opposite side of the street, as well as all down the rue Lafayette. Several houses were decorated with flags, including some Union Jacks (probably a remnant of the royal visit). Shop-girls were standing on the balcony of the Galeries Lafayette holding tri-colour flags, and a facetious-looking street-sweeper waved a broom with a handkerchief tied to it—which caused much amusement in the crowd.

Some cried *'Vive la Paix!'* and others cried *'Vive la France!'* Nobody mentioned Czechoslovakia. A workman next to me remarked rather ironically, *'Vive la France malgré tout,'* and a messenger boy with a bicycle said that since the Boulevard Haussmann has been closed to traffic half an hour earlier there was now a terrible traffic jam higher up the avenue where it runs into the Grands Boulevards, and the drivers were all 'cursing like blazes'. A grimmer touch of irony was added a few minutes before M. Daladier's car drove down the rue Lafayette by the appearance of a brewer's lorry labelled *'La Sedan, Bières Extra-Fines'*.

And then at last came a small open car, with Daladier standing up in it and looking rather red and bewildered. Next to him, with a self-satisfied smirk on his face, sat M. Bonnet. *'Vive Daladier!'* *'Vive la Paix!'* *'Vive la France!'* And the girls on the balcony of the Galeries Lafayette waved their little flags.

In spite of the cheering, in spite of the profound relief that war had been averted, there was an undercurrent of uneasiness in Paris and the cheering itself had a rather conventional quality. And one doubted whether the leading article in the *Paris-Soir* that night really reflected the feelings of the man in the street.

As a result of this terrible crisis (it said) France could have died or might have come out much reduced in authority. She has come out of it with her head erect, with her friendships strengthened, with the Anglo-French friendship definitely sealed, and with new friendships in prospect.

And, illustrating this article, was a photograph showing Hitler and Goering looking on patronisingly as Daladier was signing the Munich agreement. One wondered how many people in Paris looked at this photograph that afternoon with any sense of historical perspective.

There was, altogether, much nonsense in that issue of *Paris-Soir* they were selling on the afternoon of M. Daladier's return from Munich. That day it opened a public subscription for a villa in France to be presented to Mr. Chamberlain, *'le Seigneur de la Paix'*. The villa was to be near some river where the Premier could fish. It also announced that a Paris town councillor had already proposed that an avenue in Paris be named after 'September 30'. There were other suggestions for an avenue Chamberlain and an avenue Daladier, and even an avenue Mussolini; however, nobody went so far as to propose an avenue Hitler—not even M. Flandin. Two days later *Paris-Soir* announced:

> *Dans un élan magnifique*
> *nos lecteurs*
> *continuent de nous adresser des dons pour*
> *'La Maison de la Paix'*,
> *qui sera offerte à M. Chamberlain.*

In twenty-four hours, it said, the subscription had exceeded 100,000 francs (£550). The subscription was open for a month; £1,500 was all that they managed to collect. In the end, the money was handed over by Mr. Chamberlain himself to some ex-servicemen's organisation, when he came to Paris at the end of November.

Although at the Bon Marché and the Printemps and in other shops they continued for some weeks to sell 'lucky umbrellas' in the form of clips and brooches it was soon found that the supply was greatly in excess of the demand. And in my working-class district I dropped, several weeks later, into a paper-shop, and the old woman asked me appealingly to buy a photograph of Mr. Chamberlain. 'I have had it for two

months, and nobody will buy it—I'll give it you for one franc
instead of 2.50.'

.   .   .   .

And it may be said at once that the Anglo-German declaration which came immediately on top of Munich created an extremely unpleasant impression in Paris, and damped what
Chamberlain enthusiasm may have existed in the country.
Even the Right, who, for ideological reasons, had been looking forward to a 'Four-Power Pact' Europe, were annoyed; it
looked as though both Chamberlain and Hitler were beginning to treat post-Munich France as a negligible quantity.
Although, in reality, there was nothing so very sinister in the
Chamberlain-Hitler declaration (for Chamberlain was particularly anxious to get some such declaration in view of the
two veiled threats Hitler had uttered in September to denounce the Anglo-German Naval Treaty) the French felt
cheated. England had got something concrete out of the
Munich meeting, while France had nothing to show. They
thought the Germans were already busy driving a wedge between France and England, with a view to isolating France, in
accordance with the recipes of *Mein Kampf*.

And Henri de Kerillis, on October 2, quoted the words said
to him some time earlier by a prominent Englishman (his
description suggested that it was Mr. Churchill):

> The Czecho-Slovak affair may have much graver con-
> sequences than is imagined. For three centuries British policy
> has been based on the balance of power in Europe. We have
> always fought against the hegemony of any one Power. But
> this policy was possible only because we always had a strong
> point of support which we used as our basis. In reading your
> papers, in looking at your reactions, we are for the first time
> beginning to wonder whether such a point of support exists any
> longer. It is therefore possible that the time will come when we
> may be obliged to break away from our traditional policy, and
> instead of resisting against the dominating Power in Europe we
> shall endeavour to come to terms with it.

M. de Kerillis added to this:

> It is only fair to say that he did not add 'at your expense'.
> But nevertheless his words have worried me greatly; and I also
> remembered *Mein Kampf* with the isolation and destruction
> of France as Hitler's ultimate aim.

.   .   .   .

A stranger demonstration even than Daladier's entry into Paris on the day of the Munich agreement took place in the Champs-Elysées on the following night, when, at the suggestion of the Paris Association of Ex-Soldiers M. Daladier rekindled the flame on the grave of the Unknown Soldier. Enormous crowds gathered around the Etoile that night, and the traffic was held up for over an hour. As on Armistice Day, the Arc de Triomphe was decorated with a large tricolour banner, illuminated by a searchlight rising high into the sky. And with strange fervour thousands of people that night sang the 'Marseillaise': *'Le jour de gloire est arrivé.'*

To those who, like Pertinax, felt that 'France had retroactively lost the world war at Munich' the ceremony seemed sacrilegious; to many it was a rather personal thanksgiving ceremony; to some it was a political demonstration. The Champs-Elysées crowd—as readers of my last book will remember—is predominantly a '6th of February' crowd; and on that night, when Munich was celebrated round the Arch that had been built to commemorate the battle of Austerlitz (in what was still remaining of Czechoslovakia!), hundreds of young men stretched out their right arms in the Fascist salute. Daladier, their villain of the 6th of February, had now become their hero of the 30th of September.

And, there is something ironical in the thought that in both cases it just happened—without Daladier having desired it. He did not desire the 6th of February riots; nor did he, at heart, desire Munich. In spite of himself he became first, *le fusilleur,* and now the Man of the Munich Peace.

. . . .

The Chamber met on Tuesday, the 4th of October, to hear M. Daladier's statement on Munich.

Parliament was called for a brief 'exceptional' session on October 4. The whole debate on Munich lasted barely six hours; and technically it was only a discussion on the motion of adjournment approved by the Government. The rest of the first day and the whole of the second day was concerned with the new plenary powers bill. Once this was passed, Parliament was sent on holiday again.

Although it was one of the *grandes journées* of Parliament, and the Chamber was crowded, everybody felt that the calling

of Parliament was, to the Government, little more than an
unpleasant formality.   The whole crisis had occurred without
Parliament having been consulted at any moment—in spite
of numerous requests that Parliament be called.   These requests, incidentally, came chiefly from the 'pacifists' who were
convinced that the majority of the Chamber and Senate was
'pacifist' like themselves.   M. Flandin was particularly firm
on this point; and one of the principal arguments used against
a 'firm' policy was that the Chamber would in no circumstances consent to declare war on Germany even if Czechoslovakia were invaded.   The argument certainly reflected
to some extent the state of mind in French Parliamentary
quarters at the end of September, that is, *before* the guns had
gone off; what Parliament would have done once the war had
actually started can be only a matter of speculation.   Even
an ardent 'pacifist' like M. Pierre Dominique is not certain
that Parliament would not have been swept off its feet by the
reaction of public opinion to an actual outbreak of war.   But
one thing is certain: and that is the desperate fear of the
majority of the French deputies of being suspected of *belli-
cisme*; a charge of 'warmongering' might prove fatal in the
next Election.   And it is significant that, although opinion
was greatly divided in every party on the merits of Munich,
the motion of adjournment (which, in effect, implied the
approval of Munich) was voted unanimously with the exception of the Communists, and of M. de Kerillis.   There were
one or two abstentions.   Unlike the Labour Party, the French
Socialists, though profoundly divided, all voted 'for Munich'.

The electoral aspect of the vote is well illustrated by the
interruption made by a Right-Wing deputy during M. de
Kerillis's speech: 'Remember Neuilly!'—Neuilly being M. de
Kerillis's constituency, which as a *belliciste* he was now considered to be certain to lose.

M. Daladier spoke that day with great self-assurance, though
not perhaps without a slight touch of uneasiness.   He began
by saying that when his Government was formed the Czech-
Sudeten conflict was already in progress.   The Anschluss had
made the conflict an acute one.

> We did what we could from the outset to avoid anything
> irreparable.   Several times I defined the position of my Govern-

ment: 'We are animated by two equally strong feelings: the desire not to be compelled to take military action and the will never to betray our word if, unfortunately, our hopes were to be deceived.'

After briefly recalling the London meeting in April and the crisis of May 21 'which was overcome thanks to the effective collaboration of the peaceful wills of all the Powers concerned', M. Daladier referred to the pressure brought to bear on the Czechs:

> In a spirit of friendship we advised the Czech Government to grant important, rapid and just concessions within the frame-work of the Czech State. The action of the British Government ran parallel to ours; Lord Runciman's Mission gave birth to a great hope . . . but, unfortunately, there was never any synchronism between the Czech proposals which became increasingly generous and the Sudeten demands which became increasingly important.

In September the situation became truly dangerous, and on the night from the 13th to the 14th M. Daladier told Mr. Chamberlain that he thought direct contacts between the responsible statesmen to be more useful than any diplomatic notes. 'Mr. Chamberlain, who had the same feeling, went to Berchtesgaden.'

There followed a tribute to Mr. Chamberlain which was cheered by the greater part of the House, most of the deputies rising to their feet.

In this account M. Daladier had already skated over a great deal of thin ice; and in the rest of his account there were to be no end of gaps. No mention was made of the critical French Cabinet meeting of September 13; and in what was to follow, the whole story of Godesberg and of the two London meetings in September was left very obscure. Nevertheless, M. Daladier made the remarkable claim:

> Perhaps for the first time in the history of the world was every-thing done and said in public. And I think I may say that if peace was saved, it was because we never had recourse to the methods of secret diplomacy. We acted in open daylight, under the control of the Nations; and I wish to assert that the nations, all the nations, desire peace.

After briefly mentioning Berchtesgaden M. Daladier described 'the great emotion' with which he and M. Bonnet heard of

Lord Runciman's conclusion that the Czechs and Sudetens could no longer live together. 'All our efforts had consisted in making Czechoslovakia evolve towards a federation which would have safeguarded the integrity of her territory.'

> But it was necessary to look the facts in the face. We were in the following dilemma: we could have said No, and so encouraged Czech intransigence and German aggression, or we could have looked for a compromise. . . . If we had taken the former course, who could assert that the integrity of Czechoslovakia could be maintained even after a terrible but victorious war?

The French ultimatum of September 21 was naturally discreetly omitted. Instead a tribute was paid to the 'heroic devotion of the Czechs to the cause of peace' with which they accepted the London Plan.

But at Godesberg Herr Hitler put forward new claims, in the form of 'modalities of application'.

> We had proposed to Germany the cession of territories inhabited by more than fifty per cent of Germans, in accordance with the findings of an international commission. We provided for an exchange of populations, and for an international guarantee of the new Czechoslovakia.
>
> Germany, on the other hand, asked at Godesberg for the immediate cession of territories, for the creation of vast plebiscite zones, without any real guarantees for either the population or the new Czechoslovakia.

There was thus a blatant difference between the two plans.

Then came an interesting definition of the attitude of the French Government:

> During those days of anguish there were two currents of opinion in France. Both could be found inside every political party, one might even say in the heart and conscience of every Frenchman: one was the hope in further negotiation, the other the faith in intransigent firmness. As the head of the Government I recognised from the outset that both these movements of opinion represented the infallible instinct of the French people; and I felt that the truth lay in the synthesis of these two currents of opinion and not in their juxtaposition. What the French people desired was that the irreparable should be avoided. The irreparable was German aggression. If this had happened we, for our part, would have asked you to fulfil France's obligations.

The phrase suggested that he was not sure whether Parliament would have agreed to a war declaration on Germany if Czechoslovakia had been attacked.

But the theory of the 'synthesis'—whether, on close analysis, it makes any sense or not—is in curious contrast with M. Daladier's later claim in December that 'the policy of firmness meant the policy of war'. For, in spite of his self-confident manner on October 4, M. Daladier had not yet been fully converted to the view that Munich was both good and completely inevitable.

After referring to the mobilisation of September 24 M. Daladier claimed that the General Staff had

> 'placed France's armed forces in a position to carry out their supreme duty towards the country. . . . France and Britain were agreed in their common will for peace, but also in their common will to oppose aggression.'

And then came the confirmation, which caused visible embarrassment on the Right, and loud cheers from the Left, that the *fausse nouvelle* about the official British statement of September 26 was perfectly authentic.

A reference was then made to President Roosevelt; and the ovation that the mention of his name produced on nearly all the benches, but particularly on the Left, was greater than that produced by the mention of Chamberlain. And, significantly enough, a later reference to Beneš was received with almost complete silence by the Right.

Then came M. Daladier's account of the 'historical night' of September 27-28. On that night

> 'we decided to make a last effort. We asked our Ambassador in Berlin to request a personal interview with Chancellor Hitler; and we instructed our Ambassador in London to ask Lord Halifax to give instructions to the British Ambassador in Rome to ask Signor Mussolini to support the idea of a conference.'

And giving Mr. Roosevelt's intentions a rather loose interpretation, M. Daladier added:

> 'We responded in this manner to the spirit of the second message of President Roosevelt who made such a generous contribution toward a peaceful solution of the conflict.'

M. Daladier continued:

> 'At 11.15 a.m, on September 28 M. François-Poncet was re-
> ceived by the German Chancellor and submitted to him in the
> name of the French Government certain proposals of a precise
> nature and capable of immediate and practical application.
> Herr Hitler did not reject these suggestions, and said he would
> reply in writing.'

Two points might be emphasised.

These proposals 'capable of an immediate and practical
application', which meant in reality the virtual acceptance of
an immediate German occupation of at least certain Sudeten
territories and of other demands contained in the Godesberg
memorandum, and which were submitted to Hitler 'in the
name of the French Government' had not been discussed by
the French Cabinet. They were agreed upon by M. Bonnet
and M. Daladier, or—if one takes the *Intransigeant* version
at its face value—they were decided upon by M. Bonnet personally, as he sat there, all alone in his study at the Quai
d'Orsay, 'wondering how to save millions of human lives'.
From M. Daladier's account it would appear that the brainwave to call Mussolini to the rescue was also a French brainwave; and that it was M. Bonnet (and M. Daladier?) who
suggested this solution to the British Government. As already
said, there is no reference to any French move on the night of
September 27-28 in Mr. Chamberlain's speech on the afternoon of September 28.

> 'I accepted the invitation to Munich,' M. Daladier went on.
> 'It was not a question of discussing procedure or of submitting
> counter-proposals. [What an admission!] It was a question of
> saving peace which many considered to be definitely lost. I said
> "yes," and I regret nothing.' (Loud and prolonged cheers on
> many benches).
> 'No doubt, I would have preferred that all the nations
> directly concerned be represented. But there was no time to
> lose. The least delay might have been fatal. Was not a frank
> conversation with Herr Hitler and Signor Mussolini better than
> any such proposals [what proposals—Roosevelt's?] or any
> written discussions. You know the results of the Munich
> meeting, which was a useful conversation rather than a formal
> conference. We avoided the use of force. We produced, with-
> out a shadow of doubt, a Peace Plebiscite in the four
> countries. . . . It was an effective victory of peace, and a

moral victory of peace.   Also a human victory, for thanks to the
reciprocal concessions and to the good will of all (!) Munich is
an unquestionable improvement on Godesberg.'

The 'improvement' was, however, described only briefly:

> 'It contains stipulations for organising the right of option for
> individuals, and it *eliminates all the provisions which might have
> figured in an armistice imposed by the victor on his defeated foe (!).
> England and France have given complete guarantees, and Italy and
> Germany have promised to give their guarantees as soon as the question of
> the Hungarian and Polish minorities is settled.*   I am convinced that
> thanks to direct conversations, a just and honourable settlement
> will soon be found.'

To think that in the weeks that were to follow England and
France remained completely aloof from the 'honourable settlement' of the Hungarian claims!   The Czechs did not even con-
descend to invoke the Franco-British guarantee when Germany
went on taking away territories for the transfer of which no
provision had been made at Munich.   They were the first to
consider the Anglo-French guarantee as a scrap of paper.

> 'No doubt,' M. Daladier said, 'Munich has reduced the terri-
> tory of Czechoslovakia. *But the Czechoslovak Republic can continue
> her life, as a free country, and we shall do our best to help her.*'

There followed compliments to the spirit of peace and heroism and self-sacrifice of the Czechs.

These compliments were, in turn, followed by a discourse
on the mutual esteem France and Germany felt for one another.
'One can no more think of intimidating Germany than one
can think of intimidating France.'   Daladier's ambition had
always been a *rapprochement* with Germany; and he dwelt on
this *rapprochement* at length even in the speech that followed
immediately upon France's 'diplomatic Sedan'.

M. Daladier added, of course, that in seeking friendship with
Germany France had no intention of 'substituting new friendships for old'.

Peace, he said, had unfortunately not been

> 'definitely saved; and we must go on defending it every day. . . .
> It is possible, as some have written, that at Munich the face of
> the world had been changed in a few hours.   However, that
> may be, one thing is certain: France must meet a new situation
> by developing a new sense of duty.   (Loud cheers on the Right.)

Peace will not be maintained unless our production enables us to
speak as equals to the people around us. We can maintain
peace only with healthy finances. . . . We must reach a
general settlement in Europe, and build it on new principles;
and having avoided war in Central Europe, we must make it
retreat in all parts of the world where it is still in progress. . . .
This country is in need of a moral transformation. This unity
was achieved during a few days around the mobilised forces.
My dear friends, let us not allow this unity to be scattered
through idle quarrels and unimportant polemics.'

M. Daladier then announced that he was going to ask Parliament for plenary powers; 'the interest and the very life of the
country are at stake'.

He was, naturally, going to secure these plenary powers on
the following day. They were to be valid until the 15th of
November; the Communists voted against them; the Socialists,
after being promised by the Government (so at least they
claimed) that Parliament was to be called by the middle of
November, abstained.

The dicussion that followed M. Daladier's speech—technically it was on the motion of adjournment—was a rather tame
affair.

M. Edmond Miellet, Vice-President of the Army Committee,
complimented the Government on the Munich agreement,
which, he said, was the best possible solution to the Czech
problem.

M. Michel Walter, an Alsatian with mildly autonomist tendencies, dwelt on the grave consequences of the crisis which
had completely upset the economic life of Alsace; and while
Alsace was loyal to France, it was necessary for France to pay
the greatest attention to Alsace's economic plight; the prosperity of Alsace would not be restored unless the threat of war
ceased to hang over her, as it had now done for years. Such a
threat must be eliminated for ever.

'Alsace-Lorraine appeals to France and to her Government
not to refuse *a priori* to take the new road of the new diplomacy.'

Meaning of course, Four-Power Pact diplomacy.

A flood of home truths on Munich and of charges of unpar-
donable weakness came from M. Péri, the Communist speaker,

and from M. de Kerillis, the upholder of the Nationalist tradition, who was frequently cheered—by the Communists only.
At one point M. Flandin interrupted him, and reminded M.
Herriot, the Speaker, that M. Kerillis was exceeding his time
limit. These were the only words uttered by M. Flandin during that post-Munich discussion. It was surprising, for M.
Flandin was in an admirable position for standing up and
congratulating the Government *on having carried out his
policy*. Probably he did not wish to embarrass the Government; and perhaps he also felt uneasy because the truth was
beginning to leak out about the telegram of congratulations
he had sent to Hitler (as well as to Mussolini and Mr. Chamberlain) on the day of the Munich settlement. And—worse
still—Hitler had answered his telegram and had told him
encouragingly that *he had watched M. Flandin's activity for
the past year with great interest and sympathy*.

Through the indiscretion of a post office official the copy
of the telegram was to be read out before the Foreign Affairs
Committee of the Chamber some time later.

It created a fearful uproar—here was Hitler treating Flandin
as though he were a kind of potential Seiss-Inquart. Several
members resigned from the Alliance Démocratique; and even
M. Maurras, in the *Action Française*, which had approved of
the famous Flandin poster of September 27, now declared that
Flandin 'had not understood the first thing about the real
meaning of Munich'; and added that he had, in fact, always
thought him to be rather an ass.

In the discussion on Munich, M. Marin, the old Lorrainer
who had supported Poincaré through thick and thin at the
time of the Ruhr, spoke with sorrow but with a feeling of
helplessness and futility. His main argument was that the
Government had left France completely in the dark about the
negotiations. M. Daladier's statement had not explained
anything. Without the British White Paper and the Commons
Debate and the Czech documents, France would be in absolute
ignorance of what had actually happened.

M. Blum's statement, which he made in the name of the
whole Socialist group, with all its conflicting tendencies, was
inevitably vague and colourless—except for its final passage,
which was of considerable significance.

He blamed the men who in the past had refused to treat with Weimar Germany, he spoke of the noble example of Jaurès, who never despaired of saving peace; he expressed joy because Peace had been saved and sorrow because Czechoslovakia had been sacrificed, and said that if France's will for peace was so deep and general it was largely thanks to the Socialists.   And in deploring the sad fate of Czechoslovakia, M. Blum said that if only his proposal for a National Government in March had been accepted, all might have been different.

'Perhaps one understands better than one did then why certain statesmen persistently refused to follow us.'   France, M. Blum said, 'must now be honest with herself and examine all the treaties to which she is a party and frankly denounce those which she does not intend to fulfil.'   And he then made a rather general appeal for the establishment of indivisible peace in Europe, for disarmament, economic co-operation and a higher morality in international relations.   Europe must be built up on the basis of 'equity, concord and solidarity and may France take the lead in bringing this about'.

But once again we ask whether such an initiative can be effectively taken without the support of the French masses; and for the third time we say: no.   You can neither organise peace nor prepare war without the support of the people.

'*We are ready in advance to struggle against any attempt to exploit the European Crisis for the benefits of political Reaction; and we proclaim that the lesson to be learned from the last crisis is that the unity of all the forces of liberty, progress and justice—which are the real national forces—is more essential than ever.*   It is with these feelings and with this hope that the Socialist group is prepared to vote the motion of adjournment.'

Blum's proposal meant that it was more important than ever to form a real National Government, complete with the Socialists.   And his fears that if this was not done France would, after Munich, go along the road of political reaction was, as we shall see, not unjustified.

But Blum's new proposal for a National Government was met with nothing but jeering from the Right.

The Right were determined that Munich should be followed by a long spell of political reaction.   Not only in home affairs, but also in the handling of foreign affairs.   For the next two months at least home policy was dominated by anti-Communism, and foreign policy by *rapprochement* with the dictator countries.

THE NEGLECT OF RUSSIA

Before starting on the story of the post-Munich period, it may be advisable to inquire more closely into two important points which have hitherto been mentioned only incidentally.

One is the cold-shouldering of Russia by France and England throughout the Czech crisis; the other is the state of the French Air Force in September—whose weakness was widely declared to be one of the principal reasons why the Munich surrender was inevitable.

Although Russia was tied to Czechoslovakia by a treaty of mutual assistance concluded in 1935, in terms of which the signatories were bound to help each other in the event of an unprovoked aggression by a third party, provided that the Franco-Czech treaty had entered into force, Russia was ignored throughout the Czech crisis by both England and France. So much so that even Dr. Beneš refrained from establishing too close a contact with the U.S.S.R. lest he confirmed the impression that Czechoslovakia was an 'outpost of Bolshevism in Europe'.

The two reasons for the cold-shouldering of Russia by France and England were (1) the deep antipathy felt for Russia in the greater part of the British Conservative Party and, for that matter, among the greater part of the French Right, and (2) the deplorable effect created in Western Europe by the 'purges' in the Red Army, and the belief that a 'decapitated' army could be of little use. But actually, this judgment on the Red Army was largely encouraged by natural antipathy for the U.S.S.R.; and no serious attempt was made by either England or France to find out what the Russian Army or Air Force was really worth. Staff talks were consistently refused; and, instead, questionable sources of information like Colonel Lindbergh were used in high quarters in London. I merely state a fact; I am not trying to assert that the Russian Army is better than what the French and British Governments believed it to be; all I say is that they did not make any serious attempt even to find out.

The cold-shouldering of Russia was consistent.

(1) In March, the Soviet Note proposing immediate consultations on the situation after the Anschluss, and handed to the

British, French, United States and Czechoslovak Governments, produced only the reply from Mr. Chamberlain that the proposal was 'not opportune'.

(2) In May, Litvinov's proposals to Bonnet of staff conversations was noted by Bonnet, and thereafter ignored.

(3) In July, there was no consultation with the U.S.S.R. about sending Lord Runciman to Prague.

(4) In August-September, the U.S.S.R. was not once consulted about the steadily increasing pressure which forced out of the Czechs the 2nd, 3rd, and 4th Beneš plans.

(5) In September, there was no response whatsoever to the definite proposals made by Litvinov to the French Chargé d'Affaires in Moscow for immediate Government consultations, staff talks and a démarche at the League. Nor was there any response to the notification of these proposals to Lord Halifax by the Soviet Ambassador in London on September 7.

(6) On the evening of September 23, in reply to a question by Lord de la Ware at Geneva, Litvinov again declared the Soviet Government's intention and readiness to help Czechoslovakia. Asked about the military aspect of this, Litvinov replied: 'We are laymen; let us get the military to discuss it at once.' Lord de la Ware said he agreed, and said he would report to Lord Halifax. Nothing happened.

(7) The 'authoritative statement' which was circulated on the night of September 26, and printed in next day's London newspapers, about Great Britain and Russia certainly standing by France if she were involved with Germany over Czechoslovakia, was issued without any consultation with the U.S.S.R. in any shape or form.

(8) In October, from French Foreign Office quarters, foreign journalists in Paris were given to understand that the U.S.S.R. had in some way authorised Daladier to act on its behalf at Munich, and that it was in the closest contact with the British and French on the subject. The Soviet Government was forced to issue two categorical denials (October 2 and 3)—which of course never called forth any counter-denials.

In British and French Government quarters it was frequently suggested that Russia had neither the intention nor the means of helping Czechoslovakia. There is no ground for this suggestion. Her air force would, in any case, have been an important factor—in fact, the only *direct* help that Czechoslovakia could have obtained immediately from abroad in case of war. To move a Russian army into Czechoslovakia, would, of course, have presented greater difficulties; but it is not true that (a) Rumania would have refused transit. On

September 11, though without wishing to commit himself at that stage, M. Comnene, the Rumanian Foreign Minister, nevertheless clearly indicated to M. Bonnet that there would be no difficulty once the war had started and (*b*) that the Russians had made no military moves at all during the September crisis.

The Riga Correspondent of the *Times* wrote on September 6 that the view held in Moscow was

> that the Red Army, especially the air fleet will intervene if Czechoslovakia asks for help. The reorganisation of the Kiev and White-Russian military districts is interpreted as preparation for this, especially as these commands have been strengthened to nearly a war basis, and all frontier garrisons have been reinforced.

Later in the month, on September 25—i.e., at the time of Russia's warning to Poland to denounce the Russo-Polish non-aggression pact if the Poles invaded Czechoslovakia—foreign observers estimated (the Riga Correspondent of the *New York Times* wrote) that

> in the Kiev and White-Russian military districts, there were 330,000 to 350,000 Soviet troops, with artillery, tanks, chemical sections, and 2,000 aeroplanes, mostly heavy bombers and fast fighters of the newest type. At other places there were five cavalry corps and two tank corps (2,000 tanks) ready to break through at the start of hostilities.

This, in itself, does not prove that Russia would have been of great military help to Czechoslovakia; but it rather suggests that there was no ground for the assertion that the Russians were 'doing nothing'. Considering that the French scarcely did anything before September 24, and that the Russians did not receive the slightest encouragement from the Western Powers, their military preparations appear to have been more substantial than could have been reasonably expected from them by France and England—who had simply ignored Russia throughout the crisis.

THE FRENCH AIR FORCE

The weakness of the French Air Force was one of the chief arguments used in favour of surrendering Czechoslovakia. That France's Air Force was inadequate in September is true enough; but her helplessness in the air was deliberately exaggerated for political ends. General Gamelin himself admitted that France was extremely weak in the air; but his conclusion, nevertheless, was that France was fit to fight a successful war, if, unhappily, this could not be avoided.

To understand the reasons why the French Air Force was so weak, one has to look some years back. Between 1929 and 1938 France had spent an equivalent of £200,000,000 on her air force, and of this about £150,000,000 since 1932 alone. Why, then, had she so little to show for it? It was alleged in some quarters that the French General Staff had for a long time urged the Government to spend as much as possible on the army and as little as possible on the air force, and that the air force suffered from a lack of funds. This allegation is not confirmed by the budget figures.

What, then, had been the trouble, even allowing for wastage, incompetent handling—and even graft, which in France is a popular explanation for so many things? One of the main sources of trouble was the simple fact that the aeroplane is the least standardised of all weapons and is in constant progress; and the difficulty of catching up with this progress has been felt in other countries, and not only in France. But in France, for a variety of reasons, this difficulty was particularly great. There was also some bad luck, as the following case will show. The most ambitious French air programme since the foundation of the Air Ministry in 1928 was decided upon by General Denain, who was Minister of Air from February 1934 to January 1936. At the beginning of 1934 France had 1,665 aeroplanes, nearly all of out-of-date makes. Denain's renovation' programme provided for 1,050 new planes, mostly fighters. But here was the tragedy: when in 1934 the plan was set in motion General Denain rather went on the assumption that 250 km. per hour was a speed not likely to be exceeded for many years. And it was precisely during 1935 and 1936 that enormous technical progress was made in aeroplane construction. This knocked the Denain programme on the head long before it was completed.

But it is obvious that once a plan is in motion it cannot be suddenly stopped—with nothing ready to replace the plant set up at great cost. (In England, as distinct from France, the

expansion of plane construction luckily began after the great
'step forward'.) Adjustments were attempted in France, and
various excellent prototypes like the Morane-Saulnier 405
fighter were built, but the mass production of an entirely
different category of planes from those provided in the Denain
programme was found to be impossible. As it is, the Denain
plan, which should have been completed in July 1936, was not
completed until a year later. It is true that in the meantime
the Pierre Cot programme was, as it were, superimposed on
the Denain plan; it provided for 1,500 planes—that is, an
addition of about 500 planes to the Denain programme. But
progress was slow. The aeroplane industry suffered directly
or indirectly from the great strike movement of 1936, and
while the nationalisation of most of the aeroplane factories
that year had no adverse effect on production the (admittedly
useful) decentralisation of many of the works concentrated
until then in the Paris area rather upset production for a time.
Shorter working hours also had a bad effect. In the whole of
1936 only 500 military planes were produced.

In 1937 little progress was made as regards quality, and
the total output for the year was only 470 machines or an
average of under forty a month. But most of these, at least,
were thoroughly modern machines.

M. Guy la Chambre, who succeeded M. Cot in January
1938 produced a new plan for 2,617 first-line planes; this again
was superimposed on, rather than added to, the Cot plan.
After the Anschluss, no less than 3,000,000,000 francs of
special credits were granted to the Air Ministry, which out
of this sum ordered new plant for 1,300,000,000 francs.
Shortly after taking office M. Guy la Chambre claimed that
French production would be increased to 250 planes a month
within a short time.

What was the strength of the French Air Force in September? There are no official figures, but according to reliable
sources the entire French Air Force consisted of about 3,500
planes of which 1,400 were first-line. Naturally only a small
proportion of these 1,400 planes were completely modern; a
large part still consisted of planes built under the Denain plan.
These old bombers, flying under 250 km. an hour, could not
of course, be dismissed as 'useless'; they were quite fit to do

night-raid service, only the danger of being destroyed on the return flight was much greater than with faster bombers. The modern French planes, like the immensely fast Morane 405 single-seater fighter, the Potez 63 are among the best in the world, and the Lioret bombers and Dewoitine fighters are also considered to be excellent. But there were not enough of them. As in other branches of industry, France had achieved remarkable quality but what she lacked was mass production. However, the suggestion that the French are 'incapable' of mass production is absurd: until 1931 France was the biggest maker of mass-produced cars in Europe.

At the time of the September crisis France was producing little more than 50 military planes a month. What happened between September and the spring of 1939 was briefly this:

Soon after the September crisis a large Press campaign was launched in Paris with the slogan '5,000 planes!' These were to be procured 'somehow and at any price'; it was declared to be a matter of life and death; if France could not produce them they were to be bought abroad.

What was the position in the spring? Experts at the time of the crisis had declared that with her present plant France would not be able to exceed 250 planes a month; and that if she wanted to build up a large air force rapidly foreign purchases were the only solution. This solution was partly adopted; and M. Reynaud, the Finance Minister, said in February that with the capital that had returned to France during the previous months France would be able to buy 6,000 aeroplanes abroad.

It was, of course, a theoretical figure in the sense that even the United States could not deliver 6,000 aeroplanes as though they were a pound of butter. But the phrase could nevertheless, be regarded as the statement of a policy; for France, left to her own resources, could never rival Germany in aeroplane production, and the fact was admitted. She lacked both the plant and the skilled labour; and it was clear that it would take at least two years before Germany's output of 500 a month could be equalled—and what would Germany's output be then?

Since the £10,000,000 investment in new plant and various measures of reorganisation adopted early in 1938 French aeroplane production had increased, but not on any impressive scale. Between January and July 1938, France was producing a monthly average of forty-one military planes a month. During the four months that followed the average went up to fifty-three a month; in December (partly as a result of an extension of working hours) the figure was seventy-three and in January ninety-four, and it was not expected to exceed a monthly 100 to 120 before the summer of 1939.

But that period was, according to M. de Torres, a well-qualified writer, still a *période de démarrage*—a 'starting period'—in which the mass production had not yet come into its own. He claimed that the plant purchased in 1938 would be in full working order by the summer and that France would then be able to turn out 250 to 300 military planes a month. But if this figure was to be maintained or exceeded, important new investments would be necessary.

One could only hope that this forecast of '300 in the summer' would prove correct. But the Government was, clearly, not relying exclusively on French aeroplane production any longer. According to the same writer, the following were the orders placed abroad by the end of February 1939 and partly fulfilled —200 fighters, 235 bombers, and 200 training planes in the United States and 505 fighting planes in Holland, as well as a considerable number of engines—mostly from England. For there was a dangerous shortage of French engines, particularly of the high-power engines required in the case of the ultra-rapid modern planes; the French production of engines in January 1939 was only 237 a month; and unless the whole system was reorganised France was going to continue to import a large proportion of her aeroplane engines from abroad. Already in January France was buying several hundred engines abroad, mostly Rolls-Royces.

CHAPTER XVI

THE CONFUSION AFTER MUNICH

L IKE every country in Europe France heaved a physical sigh of relief at the thought that war had been averted. But what were the *rational* reactions to Munich? On the whole, it may be said that while everybody in France *must* have felt a little humiliated, the humiliation was keenly felt by only an important section of the working class, by some traditional nationalists in the army and elsewhere, and by a number of intellectuals. In October Paris was described by some on-lookers as being in a state of mental confusion, by others as being in a state of *abrutissement*, inertia and resignation. To many sensitive Frenchmen there must have been something false and a little degrading in the manner in which the Government and the greater part of the Press were presenting Munich as a triumph. What could have been falser in tone than Daladier's speech at the Chamber on October 4? It minimised in every respect the fearful tragedy of Czecho-slovakia; it made no mention of France's obligations to that country—obligations which in the two previous years had been 'confirmed' so frequently and with such astonishing ease; it smugly suggested that the new Czechoslovakia could carry on very well inside her new frontiers; and, altogether, it repre-sented Munich as being the height of statesmanship and of French diplomatic skill. And the words 'I regret nothing' sounded callous. It was an ungenerous speech. In fact, no member of the Government had the honesty to say that Munich was a fearful defeat for France. Why could they not have admitted it freely, and said to their people: 'It *was* a defeat, but now, let us pull ourselves together and work for a better France, so that it doesn't happen again.' Such an admission would have been a basis for some kind of National Unity. But they went on praising and praising Munich—

*because some lacked moral courage; while for others it was
necessary to do so for internal political reasons. It was part
of the reactionary offensive.* Jouhaux said in October: 'They
lied and lied before Munich, and they have gone on lying.'

And yet, except among an important part of the working
class and in certain nationalist quarters, Munich was accepted
with astonishing ease. M. Duhamel was one of the few men
who was profoundly conscious of the moral wound Munich
had inflicted on France, and had realised how dim her
authority had grown in the world. France—source of all
generous ideas! He was one of the few who openly said that
what France had lost was not only her Maginot Line in Central
Europe, but also what he called her Descartes Line. French
schools were closing down in Czechoslovakia; Munich was not
only a diplomatic Sedan, but a cultural setback of immense
importance. Her century-long spiritual leadership of Europe
seemed at an end. And it is strange to think how little the loss
of the 'Descartes Line' affected the Government, and even
many intellectuals, especially of the Right. It looked as though
these intellectuals were ready and eager to conduct France
along the spiritual groove of Fascist ideology. Maurras might
well speak of Germany as being 'the mad dog of Europe'—but
the soul of the *Action Française* was like the soul of Goebbels.
The 'monstrous dupery of the International Commission'—as
the *Ordre* called it—which went on chopping more and more
slices off Czechoslovakia at Germany's behest was more or less
ignored by the general public, which simply preferred not to
hear any more about it.

It is curious that while England suffered from a guilty feeling which expressed itself in the enormous contributions—
totalling some £400,000—to the Lord Mayor's Fund for Czech
refugees, there was no such reaction at all in France. The
Temps collected a few thousand pounds—and that was about
all. While, after Munich, hundreds of thousands of 'Penguins'
on Czechoslovakia continued to be sold by bookstalls throughout Great Britain, France lost all interest in her former ally.
With a curious lack of sensitiveness the Government-inspired
Press continued to praise M. Daladier and M. Bonnet to the
skies. A remarkable demonstration of complacency and insen-
sibility was provided by M. Bonnet at a reception organised in

his honour by his constituents at Périgueux. The officially-inspired Press made much of this reception: the accounts of it were calculated to show that *la province* was a hundred per cent 'pro-Munich'. Here are a few specimens from the four-column account in the *Petit Parisien* of that 'unforgettable day':

> Already outside the station thousands were shouting, *'Vive Bonnet! Vive Bonnet!'* Périgueux will not soon forget this cry. Bunches of flowers were piled round him in his open car. Women—mothers and young girls—went on crying: *'Merci, Bonnet! Merci, Bonnet!'* Looking a little pale, the Foreign Minister answered these greetings with his hands and with his eyes,[1] while, behind him, enormous bouquets continued to be presented to Madame Bonnet whose charming modesty was also being loudly cheered.[2] And the triumph of the people began. . . . In the Place du Théâtre three little girls recited a compliment, which no one could hear, so loud were the shouts of enthusiasm. And the din was dominated by that cry of gratitude: *'Merci, Bonnet! Merci, Bonnet!'*

And later, speaking with the voice of injured innocence to a number of ex-servicemen and local worthies, about the unjust attacks that had been made on him, M. Bonnet said:

> 'There is one criticism which I refuse to accept: and that is that France was not loyal to her signature. France's signature is sacred. Czechoslovakia wasn't invaded, was she?'

To which the local worthies replied: 'Of course she was not! *Vive Bonnet! Merci, Bonnet!'*

> And then they all sang the 'Marseillaise' and later M. Bonnet gave a dinner to all the mayors and assistant mayors of his constituency, without distinction of political opinions—an intimate dinner at which the Foreign Minister was able to measure once again the extent of his popularity and the profound gratitude of the people of France.

Guy de Maupassant would have made a pretty story of this Périgueux apotheosis.

That was on the 8th of October. On the 9th Hitler made his Saarbrücken speech which rather tended to damp the post-Munich and Four-Power Pact enthusiasm. If before Munich

[1] Such is the journalistic style of officially-inspired enthusiasm.
[2] Ditto.

he threw bouquets at France, and gave her Strasbourg Cathedral as a present and tried to flatter her into inactivity, he now made no mention of France whatsoever—though he was speaking at only four miles from the French frontier. All he said was that the two gaps in the Siegfried Line—the gap at Aix-la-Chapelle and the Saar gap (the latter had figured prominently in the plans of the French General Staff)—would now be filled up. The French Munich enthusiasts felt cheated —though not entirely discouraged. From their point of view there were some good points in the Saarbrücken speech. For instance this curious post-Munich novelty: Hitler declared, in effect, that he could not allow England to be ruled by Mr. Churchill or Mr. Eden or Mr. Duff Cooper; if these came into office there would be trouble. This suited the more cynical among the Munich enthusiasts perfectly. As we shall see, the 'Hitler veto' was actually going to become an important factor in French home affairs, and was to be used by the supporters of certain Ministers as an argument for maintaining them in office. On the eve of the Radical Congress at the end of October, M. Lamoureux, one of M. Bonnet's close political associates, published in a local sheet of the Allier, a statement alleged to have been made by Hitler to François-Poncet, the retiring French Ambassador, when he went to take leave of the Führer at Berchtesgaden:

> So long as men like M. Daladier and M. Bonnet remain in office I am confident in friendly relations between our two countries.

Just like that. The Radical Congress could put it in its pipe and smoke it.

The wave of political reaction that was to reach its height in December, began during the days that immediately followed Munich. It was a phenomenon to be expected. Munich was the work of the Bonnets and Flandins and the greater part of the Right—and the support given to the 'Munich' policy by these people was not so much dictated (as in the case of many Socialists and trade unionists) by an innate pacifism, or even by provincialism, as, to a large extent, by rather precise political motives. The battle between pacifists and *bellicistes* was not only a battle over foreign policy; it was a much more complex affair. It is extremely characteristic that almost the very first reaction of the Press of the Right after Munich was to start an anti-Communist campaign:

'There are accounts to settle,' the *Matin* wrote on the very day after Munich. Doriot's *Emancipation Nationale* also wrote: 'There are accounts to settle.' The *Action Française*, on the very day of Munich, wrote a little nursery rhyme, inciting its readers to murder the *bellicistes*:

> S'ils s'obstinent, ces cannibales,
> A faire de nous des héros,
> Il faut que nos premières balles
> Soient pour Mandel, Blum et Reynaud,

and, like the others, it went on shouting: *'Comptes à régler!'* —even though M. Maurras suddenly became rather less pro-Munich, and declared that it was not such a great 'victory' after all. And Doriot's *Liberté* declared on October 4 that it was high time the *belliciste* Ministers in the Cabinet were turned out.

Some days later it was reported that two hundred-odd papers in France had published a sort of manifesto demanding the dissolution of the Communist Party. All this was pretty well orchestrated.

. . . .

The Chamber votes on Munich and on the plenary powers were of the greatest importance in encouraging the reactionary campaign. The Communists were the only party to have voted against Munich: it was 'positive proof' that the Communists had *wanted* war. That was one of the arguments of the reactionary campaign. Although the Socialists voted for Munich and merely abstained in the vote on the plenary powers, the papers of the Right thought it good enough. The Front Populaire, they said, was now completely and irretrievably lost; even in a purely nominal parliamentary sense. They urged Daladier to draw the only possible conclusion from the two Chamber votes—and that was that he must sever his connection with the Left completely and form an alliance with the Right and Centre. As usual, Daladier hesitated. He hesitated for nearly a month. On October 26 on the eve of the Radical Congress at Marseilles, Sennep, the cartoonist, published in

Candide one of his best drawings entitled 'Daladier speaks to
the 3,000 Daladiers at the Daladier Congress.' In this drawing the Premier was shown addressing a hall crowded with
Daladiers, most of them with different expressions and in different clothes—some of them clamouring for the dissolution
of the Chamber, others for a National Government with the
Right, others for a Front Populaire Government. The Daladier shouting 'Democracy' was knocked on the head by a
Daladier shouting 'Authority', while there were several other
Daladiers shouting 'Vive Blum!' and 'Heil Hitler!' and 'Long
live Munich!' and 'Rearmament, rearmament!' Two other
Daladiers were presented in the form of a fierce-looking bull
and a bleating sheep. Another Daladier—dressed up as a *Con-
ventionnel* shouted: *'Salut Public!'*

The cartoon reflected M. Daladier's hesitations during the
few weeks that followed Munich, and the complete uncertainty
of French opinion at that time as to the line of policy he was
intending to pursue.

These hesitations were not confined to M. Daladier alone.
The public was rather muddled. Daladier's first idea was to
fight an election on the Munich and *'anti-belliciste'* issue; but
this would have meant the dissolution of the Chamber; and
this met with much opposition from the deputies themselves
who did not much care to risk their seats and, in any case, to
go to a lot of expense. The Senate was lukewarm in its support of dissolution; and M. Maurice Sarraut, the influential
editor of the *Dépêche* of Toulouse, and a sort of Father Con-
fessor of the Radical Party, was altogether hostile. The dissolution proposal was advocated most strongly by part of the
Right Press, notably by the *Temps* which hoped to see the
Socialists and Communists both beaten and driven into Opposition. For at that time it was still uncertain whether Daladier
had finally severed his connection with the Left.

It is true that on October 13, the Bureau of the Radical
Party passed a violently anti-Communist resolution, in which
it said that the Communists had through their two Chamber
votes wilfully abandoned 'the formation to which they still
claim to belong'—which meant that the Radical Bureau considered the Front Populaire at an end. But information from
the constituencies suggested that the Bureau did not fully

reflect the feelings of the Radical rank-and-file. The resolution also attacked M. Flandin, and suggested the formation of a 'concentration' Government comprising everybody except M. Flandin's followers and the Communists. This made little sense, and was scarcely practicable. The Right would, clearly, not abandon Flandin's followers and at the same time agree to co-operate with the Socialists; and, though in a rather indiscreet form, Flandin represented, after all, much the same foreign policy as M. Bonnet, one of the great men of the Radical Party.

It was enough to confuse anybody—not least M. Daladier. In the days that followed, M. Daladier, however, consulted both M. Marin and M. Blum with a view to forming a wide national coalition; but while M. Blum was favourable, and M. Marin reserved at first, he informed the Premier, after the Senate election of October 23, that he would not enter a Government containing Socialists. For the Senate election had shown a notable swing to the Right.

During October M. Daladier was, in fact, being carefully pushed into an alliance with the Right and Centre. It is true that there were other ideas in the air. Many people felt that France needed something different from the existing parliamentary form of Government—though, heaven knows, Parliament, which had played no part whatsoever throughout the Czech crisis, had fallen pretty low, and M. Flandin could, not without an element of truth, declare in his open letter to Kerillis, that France was now a 'parliamentary democracy only in name'. On the Right (and also among some people on the Left) the real question was whether a 'new form of Government should be established on the basis of the existing institutions, or whether the pretence of 'parliamentary democracy' should be discarded.

The irrepressible Kerillis demanded a Government of National Safety, presided over by a General, and working in close contact with the working class. But Parliament, he said, should be sent on holiday for two years, and his plan provided for a censorship and for a number of other drastic measures of the same sort. Regarding Parliament, he remarked, not without justice, that 'it was not playing any part anyway'.

And M. Henri Pichon, the leader of the Union Fédérale

des Anciens Combattants, the principal 'Leftish' ex-servicemen's organisation with 2,000,000 members, and claiming to
speak in the name of 6,000,000 ex-servicemen, also advocated,
in a statement made on October 11, a Government of *salut
public*.

> There are four problems confronting France: France has no
> budget; her currency goes on depreciating, half the revenue is
> used for paying the arrears of the public debt.   Lastly, there
> is the question of labour.   People are squabbling over the 40-
> hour week, while forgetting that her production is below that
> of 1913.   I do not wish to criticise the present Government;
> but I cannot help recalling that it began by asking for plenary
> powers, which produced 400 decrees last April.   Nothing
> good can have come of them; for why was the Government
> obliged to ask for plenary powers again last week?   Is it
> going to solve all our problems in 45 days?   The most that
> can be hoped for is a respite.
>
> What the country needs is a Government of Public Safety.
> The time has come for men of action—men who are honest,
> intelligent and with character; who are Republicans, but
> without party labels.   The day of party combinations is over.
> Such a Government must be given time to work; it must be
> given plenary powers until the 1940 election.   If the Chamber
> refuses, it shall be dissolved; and we shall see to it that the elec-
> tion is fought clearly.   We are not proposing that Daladier
> should go, if he is determined to pursue a policy that will save
> France.   By saving peace he has gained the confidence of the
> masses.   Let him work!   But whatever may be his new decrees,
> I maintain that in forty-five days France on her sickbed can
> be given only a respite.   What we must gain is not three
> months; we must save France.

The statement caused something of a row.   Other ex-servicemen's organisations, particularly those of the Right, claimed
that M. Pichon had no right to speak in their name.

The statement was, however, typical of that post-Munich
atmosphere in which many felt that 'this could not go on any
longer', and that France must turn over a new leaf.

Among important sections of the Left, a *salut public*
Government—though not with Daladier at its head—was, if
anything, welcomed.   It seemed better than the sort of reactionary 'parliamentary' Government into which the Radicals
were being gradually driven.   It is curious that about the
middle of October rumours were current to the effect that

several leading Socialists were considering favourably the formation of a *salut public* Government with General Noguès, the Resident-General of Morocco, at its head.   They thought that a respected army man heading a *salut public* Government and working in co-operation with the trade union leaders— that is, working not 'against' but 'with' the working class, would, despite parliamentary appearances, be less 'reactionary' than the sort of 'Radical-Centre-Right' Government the Right were having in mind.   But these projects did not go very far.

.   .   .   .

A typical post-Munich phenomenon was the campaign for a large air force.   This campaign came from different directions.   M. Frossard, M. Daladier's former Minister of Public Works, who had resented Daladier's hostility to the working class, and had resigned from his Government in August, and who was, in October considered to be a coming man—one who could, with advantage replace M. Daladier at the head of a 'Leftish' National Government—launched in his paper, the *Homme Libre*[1] the slogan for '5,000 aeroplanes'.

> If I were Premier I should say: Do not ask me what my home policy or my economic policy or my foreign policy is.   My only policy is more aeroplanes.   I shall make aeroplanes everywhere; in Paris and in the country, in towns and villages.   I shall buy aeroplanes abroad or wherever I can get them.   I implore the workers not to argue about hours and the manufacturers not to worry about making profits and the investors to bring all the money they have to finance this gigantic work of national salvation. . . .   Our chief weakness is in the air; and that is why in the last crisis Hitler felt that he could take grave risks. . . .   France must be prepared to say no to his next ultimatum.

But the Government would not allow him a monopoly in his clamour for '5,000 aeroplanes'.   The Government-inspired Press ran a similar campaign; and by the 20th of October the campaign was in full swing.   Giant headlines: *'Des avions! Des avions!'* shrieking from every newspaper kiosk in Paris were a typical post-Munich sight.

The biggest campaign was run by *Intransigeant*: but *Paris-Soir* soon followed suit.   One night it published a gruesome

[1] He was, some weeks later, to be squeezed out of the *Homme Libre* which became the personal organ of M. Bonnet.

account of a gigantic air raid on Paris during a cloudy night.
Searchlights and anti-aircraft batteries were helpless against the
bombers flying at 24,000 feet, and the Morane 603—the fastest
of the French fighter planes—were doing their best, but there
were only a few of them. The moral of the story was clear.
So also was the political purpose of this Press campaign. In
the case of M. Frossard it was inspired partly perhaps by personal ambition, but chiefly by the sincere and gloomy belief
that without a large air force France would be helpless against
more German blackmail. In the case of the Government
Press the campaign was partly calculated to justify the surrender of Czechoslovakia, but, above all, to impress upon the
public that what France was needing, above all, was a very
strong Government, and one which, among other things, would
abolish the forty-hour week. The articles naturally suggested
that M. Daladier the Premier and War Minister and M. Guy
la Chambre, the Minister of Air, were the right men in
the right places. In those post-Munich days a 'strong Government' was a slogan that was bound to be universally accepted:
only *what kind of strong Government?*

By the end of the month it became clear that M. Daladier
had finally decided to break with the Left—and not only
with the Communists, but also with the Socialists. At the
Radical Congress at Marseilles on October 27—a Congress
which was to be marred by the disastrous fire in the Canebière,
in which eighty people lost their lives—M. Daladier attacked
the Communists with extraordinary violence. He accused
them not only of having hampered the international talks
that preceded Munich 'by grossly insulting Mr. Chamberlain',
but also of paralysing French production by their propaganda
among the workers. In short, the Communists were to M.
Daladier the agents of a foreign Power, and Public Enemy
No. 1. As for the Socialists, they were not mentioned at all.
The speech delighted the French Right and all the anti-
Comintern enthusiasts in France and abroad.

In Germany the Press almost suggested that France had as
good as joined the anti-Comintern Pact!

Throughout October M. Daladier had hesitated; but now
he had taken his decision; the Communists, who as part of the
Front Populaire, had brought Daladier back to power in 1936,

were now Public Enemy No. 1; and M. Daladier was henceforth going to work with the Right and Centre. He had made his choice. The anti-Communist drive of the Government was, as we shall see, going to reach its climax a month later, when the Government broke the General Strike.

.   .   .   .

November and especially December were the two months during which France seemed to be sinking more and more deeply into the quagmire of political reaction. The two outstanding events were the abortive General Strike of November 30, and the signing of the Bonnet-Ribbentrop declaration on December 6. The large-scale reprisals that followed the strike, the bullying of the Press, the rigorous control of wireless, the 'reorganisation' and 'purges' in the semi-official news agencies, the decrees drafted by M. Bonnet for restricting the freedom of the Press especially in its comments on Germany (decrees which, in the end, M. Marchandeau, the Minister of Justice refused to sign), the attempt to stop Mr. Duff Cooper's lecture on December 6; all this ran parallel with the cultivation of an extreme 'post Munich' foreign policy, which consisted, in effect, in driving Germany east. The *Temps* openly declared on the very day after Munich that the Franco-Soviet Pact and the Franco-Polish alliance had now 'lost much of their practical value'; and in November and December the 'free hand in the East' policy reached its height with the campaign in the *Matin* and other papers in favour of *La Grande Ukraine*. The *rapprochement* with Italy being slow in coming, France was playing the German card.

The anti-French demonstration in the Italian Chamber on November 30, when the deputies rose like one man and shouted: 'Tunisia! Corsica! Nice!' opened in reality a new chapter in French foreign policy—and had, as will be seen, a wholesome effect. For it created a certain *sursaut* of French public opinion, which at the time of the Ribbentrop declaration had sunk into a state of gloomy inertia. It will be objected that the Ribbentrop declaration came a week after the Italian 'Tunis-Corsica' demonstration: but such was the *gleichschaltung* of the French Press in those days that the news of the Italian demonstration was, if not suppressed, at any rate enormously minimised and it was not until about a fortnight later

that the general public became fully aware of the real significance of the Italian demonstration.

During the weeks that followed two distinct policies in relation to Italy seemed to exist: the Daladier policy of firmness,
and the Bonnet policy of 'appeasement'. While Bonnet did
his best to suppress in the Press all the unpleasant news from
Italy, Daladier went on his voyage to Corsica and North Africa,
and said in effect that the Italians could go to hell. The
Italian campaign against France was in reality a tremendous
setback for the Flandin policy which consisted in saying that
France could become an 'Empire Power' instead of pursuing
a Continental policy. It was largely on this assumption that
the Right in France welcomed Munich: and now it looked as
though the Axis Powers were preparing a new Munich not at
the expense of Poland or Rumania or Russia, but—at the
expense of the French Empire with Spain as the big trump
in their game.

.   .   .   .

During a few weeks which followed Munich the French
Government and the inspired Press heavily backed the
Italian horse. Compliments were showered on Mussolini for
having 'saved peace'; and the withdrawal from Spain of 10,000
Italians—mostly war-weary invalids—in the first week of
October was treated by the official Press as the beginning of
a happy settlement of the Spanish problem and as the beginning of a Franco-Italian *rapprochement,* and of a happy co-
operation between England, France and Italy. All objections
were met with the most optimistic hopes and assurances. Thus
M. Lucien Bourguès, who was in close touch with M. Bonnet,
wrote in the *Petit Parisien* on October 9:

> The Italian decision marks a decisive turning-point in the
> Spanish affair. . . . The departure of the ten thousand
> Italians corresponds to that 'substantial withdrawal' which
> England demanded on April 16. The Anglo-Italian Agree-
> ment should therefore before long become a reality, and the
> Abyssinian Empire will be recognised by England as well as
> by France, whose Ambassador to Rome is going to be appointed
> on Tuesday. He will be accredited to the 'King of Italy and
> Emperor of Ethiopia'.

The rest of M. Bourguès's article was even more outspokenly
optimistic:

> In deciding to recall 10,000 volunteers Mussolini has made the gesture of appeasement that was expected from him. This gesture is of the greatest value, for it marks the beginning of the total liquidation of the Spanish war as an international conflict.

And to meet the most important objection of all, that the withdrawal of 10,000 volunteers was not of the slightest use unless all the technicians and airmen also went, and that new men and new war material were not sent to Franco, M. Bourguès concluded:

> It is estimated in Rome [estimated by whom?] that this first step will shortly be followed by the complete repatriation of all the Italian troops, including technicians, airmen, and tank operators. . . . Spain will then be left to herself, and we can help to mediate a peace. . . . Mussolini is pursuing his noble work as a peacemaker, etc.

All this was not reassuring. And it was curious how in these flattering articles on Mussolini's 'pacifism' the awkward question of Germany's co-operation with Italy in Spain was completely ignored.

It is significant that all this outburst of flattery of Italy coincided with Hitler's Saarbrücken speech, which, as we have seen, was a disappointment to the Munich enthusiasts; for, with his talk about the western fortifications, Hitler clearly indicated that the dismemberment of Czechoslovakia did not by any means mark the end of the trouble as far as Germany was concerned. During those two months French diplomacy tried, without much success, in playing off Rome against Berlin or Berlin against Rome—though without, at the same time abandoning the Four-Power idea. Only this idea did not and could not work well: for the tactics of Rome and Berlin consisted at the same time in playing off London and Paris against one another. In October, just after the Hitler-Chamberlain declaration, Italy encouraged France to court her; but in November, while the *rapprochement* between France and Germany was in progress, relations improved between England and Italy, and became extremely strained between England and Germany! The Four-Power harmony was being constantly disturbed by Italy and Germany in this curious manner.

In October, as already said, Italy was the object of France's particular attentions. The sacrifice of Spain on the altar of Franco-Italian friendship was going on—for in reality nobody really attached any importance to the withdrawal of the 10,000 Italian veterans. In accordance with the promise given by M. Daladier to Mussolini during their meeting at Munich, the French Cabinet appointed M. François-Poncet, who had been Ambassador in Berlin since 1931, to Rome. M. Coulondre who had for a year been Ambassador to Moscow, and, before that Director of Economic Relations at the Quai d'Orsay, was appointed to Berlin. Together with these two appointments went the 'purge' at the Quai d'Orsay. M. Massigli, one of the most prominent 'pro-League' men at the Quai was sent to Ankara, and M. Comert, the head of the Press Department was *limogé*—and appointed to the relatively obscure post of assistant director of the American Department. M. Bonnet, clearly, wished to be surrounded in Paris by people more in sympathy with his new policy. M. Comert was succeeded at the Quai d'Orsay by M. Bressy, a councillor at the French Embassy at Warsaw; he was very much 'Bonnet's man', an 'appeasement' enthusiast, and he had (at least when he first started on his new post), little experience, and a profound distrust, of the Press.

Unfortunately, the Italian Government missed no opportunity of displaying their bad humour towards France; and took an abnormally long time to grant their *agrément* to the appointment of the new French Ambassador. The delay caused great worry at the Quai d'Orsay for some days; but at last the *agrément* came, and at the end of October M. François-Poncet was able to leave Berlin. After taking leave of Hitler at Berchtesgaden—and during his visit, the possibility of a Franco-German declaration was discussed—M. François-Poncet went for a few days to Paris, and arrived in Rome on November 7. According to Reuter, a crowd of Italians applauded him as he drove from the station. That same night it was announced in Rome that the Franco-Italian visa restrictions would be removed—which indicated an end of the tourist war, which had gone on since August. 'The decision is the first outcome of the arrival of the new Ambassador,' Reuter said. On the following day Reuter said that since M. François-Poncet was accredited to the 'King of Italy and Emperor of Ethiopia', it was probable that Franco-Italian negotiations would be shortly resumed; and that the Italians were very anxious to clear up a number of points relating to the Suez Canal, the port of Jibuti and the Jibuti-Addis-Ababa railway. The Reuter message said that the French Ambassador was expected to visit Count Ciano shortly, but added cautiously that 'for the present there is no authoritative indication that negotiations will be resumed'.

The real sequel was to come on November 30.

. . . .

If, during November, the French Government was playing about with 'appeasement' and Four-Power Pact ideas, the same was even truer of the British Government.

On November 1 Mr. Chamberlain still flushed with the Munich triumph and feeling very strong in the country—Mr. A. D. Lindsay had just been beaten in the Oxford By-election —spoke in a dictatorial manner which Opposition speakers found insufferable. It was the speech in which the Prime Minister attacked the Opposition for 'fouling the nest'. Regarding Eastern and South-Eastern Europe, Mr. Chamberlain said that it was quite natural for Germany to have a 'dominating position' there. And the Four-Power *motif* was played with great gusto.

> We should not wait until the crisis becomes acute before we attempt to settle it. We should try and consolidate the goodwill of the four Powers . . . by the removal of fears and suspicions. . . . We shall never get far in this way unless we can accustom ourselves to the idea that democracies and totalitarian States are not to be ranged against one another in two opposing blocks but that they can, if they choose, work together not merely for the settlement of differences after they have arisen but also for the operation of a constructive programme which will facilitate the international exchange of goods and provide for the regulation of international relations in various ways for the good of all.
>
> That is the policy which is sometimes called a policy of appeasement; that is the policy to which this Government intends whole-heartedly to devote itself.

Mr. Chamberlain said nothing about colonies; and that disturbed the Opposition; for it was well known that Germany was about to make a new bid for colonies. As Sir Archibald Sinclair said:

Is nothing going to be done about the colonies?   The Government's policy on that matter should be made known.   The solution of the colonial question must be based upon three principles—that of trusteeship for the interests of the natives, with guarantees for their welfare and against fortification, militarism and conscription: free access to the raw materials and food supplies for merchants and traders of the world; and that all Powers with colonial interests and claims should be consulted.

Whatever the solution, it must not be the offer of a colony in order to buy a few months' peace from Germany.   It must be part of a general settlement, and the acid test of the sincerity of that settlement must be the measure of general disarmament.

Although Mr. Chamberlain's speech was very much in M. Bonnet's 'line', it caused considerable uneasiness in France, not only on the Left, but among important sections of the French Right, particularly in the Marin Group, which on the following day passed a resolution saying that 'it had carefully examined Mr. Chamberlain's speech and had found several of its points particularly disquieting'.   These were, clearly, the *carte blanche* for Germany in Eastern Europe, no reference to France, and a mysterious silence on the question of colonies. This last point worried the Right most of all; and the Marin Group, in its resolutions, called upon the French Government to make a new declaration

refusing to negotiate on the transfer to Germany of any parts of the French Colonial Empire, including the mandated territories.

It even threatened to vote against the Government if it failed to give adequate assurances.

The absence of any reference to France in Mr. Chamberlain's speech was resented by many other people.   One French commentator remarked that day: 'With all our faults Mr. Chamberlain should still remember that we provide Great Britain with an army—it is no good putting us on the same level as Italy and Germany.'

On November 8, at Munich, Hitler raised the question of colonies; and so pushed the question to the foreground of European politics.

'We are very grateful,' he said, 'if there are statesmen in

France and Great Britain who wish to live in good understanding with the German people. It only remains for us to agree over colonies which have been taken away from us on pretexts contrary to justice. Beyond the colonial question Germany has no demands to make on France and Great Britain.'

.   .   .   .

What was the attitude of the French Government to colonies during that post-Munich honeymoon? It was not as simple as might be imagined. At that time M. Bonnet was desperately anxious to secure a Franco-German 'no war' declaration; and negotiations on the subject were in progress. It was important to do nothing that would hamper the Franco-German talks. At the Radical Congress at Marseilles M. Daladier had spoken of colonies; he had referred to 'a vast zone of security outside Europe which France will defend as she will defend her home territory'. What exactly did this 'vast zone of security' mean? A person working in close touch with M. Daladier put forward the view that this did not mean every French possession in the world, but rather all her possessions in Africa which formed a vast single *bloc*—with the exception of a few British enclaves (Nigeria and the Gold Coast being the most important) and three unimportant Spanish enclaves, besides Liberia. According to this view, this African *bloc* was considered by M. Daladier to be 'unalterable'. It was true that it included the former German colonies of Togoland and the Cameroons, but if these were returned to Germany France's strategic position in Africa would before long be rendered hopeless, and such a transfer of territory might lead to no end of new trouble.

But since Germany had more or less (or so at least M. Daladier's friend thought) admitted the principle of substituting territories of equivalent value for those that once belonged to her, it was possible that, if he found sufficient general reasons for doing so, M. Daladier would be willing to consider the transfer of certain other French territories to Germany—territories lying outside the 'security zone', and which would be equivalent in value to Togoland and the Cameroons.

But these ideas did not go far. The German demand for

colonies produced a surprisingly sharp reaction in France—
perhaps an unconscious and belated reaction against 'Munich',
and against German bullying. Scarcely a month had passed
since Munich, and here he was again asking for something
else! It annoyed people.

On November 9, the day after Hitler's speech, the Marin
group (or Fédération Républicaine) passed unanimously a
strongly worded resolution which expressed surprise at the
Government's failure, in spite of repeated requests from that
group, to state its position with regard to the colonial question.
This, the Fédération Républicaine said, was all the more
alarming in view of the British visit a fortnight later. The
group declared that it would vote against the Government if
it failed to make such a statement.

There was an enormous amount of excitement at the
Chamber that day. A Socialist deputy, and M. Monnerville,
a Negro deputy, wrote to the chairman of the Colonial Committee demanding that no decision be taken without the
approval of Parliament. M. Moutet, the former Minister of
Colonies in the Blum Government, demanded on behalf of
the Socialists that this committee be called immediately. A
Radical deputy, M. Gerent, announced his intention to question the Government on its colonial policy at the first opportunity.

President Lebrun himself indirectly joined in the campaign by making a speech in which he referred to 'the magnificent unity of our Empire' and to the loyalty and devotion to
France of the natives. He implied that it would be monstrous
to hand them over to the mercies of Nazi Germany.

It so happened that it was during that week that the
pogroms in Germany were at their height. On November 7,
a seventeen-year-old Polish Jew, Herschel Grynspan wounded
fatally a secretary of the German Embassy in Paris. To all
appearances the boy had been driven desperate by the sufferings inflicted on his parents in Germany; though some of the
circumstances of the murder were mysterious, and there were
many who believed that Grynspan was like another Van der
Lübbe. Vom Rath, his victim, died three days later; and the
result was a fearful Government-organised pogrom throughout Germany. All the Jewish shops in Berlin were smashed

in the middle of the night by bands of hooligans; all the syna-
gogues were burned, and thousands of Jews—men and women
of every age—were dragged out of their houses, and beaten
up and sent to concentration camps, and their houses de-
molished.

Although the greater part of the French Press was instructed
by the French Foreign Office not to 'play up' the pogroms, and
not to offend Germany in the midst of the Franco-German
negotiations, the pogroms were of considerable importance in
providing the opponents of any surrender of colonies to Germany with an unanswerable argument. M. Monnerville, the
Negro deputy, was extremely active in protesting against any
attempt to hand Negro people over to German rule. But it
was not until November 16 that the Government made its
position perfectly clear; it was after a meeting between M.
Daladier and M. Taittinger, the vice-president of the Colonial
Committee and a leading member of the Right, that the following *communiqué* was published:

> The Government has not waited for the present campaign
> over colonies to make its position clear on this question.
> Several weeks ago it already announced that France would
> oppose any attempt to lay hands on its colonial empire and
> that she was resolved to maintain the integrity of her posses-
> sions such as they were constituted at the end of the World
> War. No surrender of territory was ever, or could ever be,
> considered. No negotiations have therefore been entered
> into.
> The Government hereby renews the denial of the false news
> suggesting that the question of colonies will be discussed during
> the coming Anglo-French talks.

Although Togoland and the Cameroons were not strictly 'possessions', but mandated territories, the reference to the 'end of
the World War' suggested sufficiently clearly that these territories were also covered by the *communiqué*. This *communiqué* was emphatic enough; but it was strange, all the same,
that it should have taken the Government fully a week to produce it. It was suggested, after its publication, that M. Bonnet
was not by any means pleased; in pursuing his policy of *rapprochement* with Germany, he almost certainly wished to keep
colonies in reserve as a possible bargaining counter. But
M. Daladier knew that the campaign against the surrender of

colonies could no longer be ignored; and he took his decision under the influence of a number of factors:

1. The unexpectedly violent opposition in Parliament to the surrender of any colonial territories and the repeated demands addressed from various quarters to the Government asking it to promise not to enter without the preliminary approval of Parliament into any negotiations involving colonies.

2. The open warning made by the Fédération Républicaine (the Marin group) to vote against the Government in the absence of any such pledge—and that precisely at a time when, with the outcry against the Reynaud decrees, the Government had no chance of depending on a Left majority but was sorely in need of support from the Right.

3. The opposition of French business interests to the surrender of either Togoland and the Cameroons or of territories outside the 'security zone'. Thus a paper like the *République*, reflecting business interests, emphasised the enormous economic development the Cameroons and Togoland had undergone since coming under French rule. For instance, in 1913 the two colonies exported 1,170 tons of cocoa; in 1936 they exported 35,104 tons; exports of palm oil rose from a few hundred tons to 65,800 tons; copra from 130 tons to 5,650 tons. The export trade of the Cameroons alone had risen from 70,000 tons in 1913 to 230,000 tons in 1936.

4. The strategic aspect of Togoland and the Cameroons. If these were occupied by Germany, it was argued, it would mean no end of trouble to France's 'zone of security'. This was a point which carries great weight with M. Daladier and the French General Staff. The strategic importance of these two colonies was, in their eyes, far greater to France than many territories outside the 'security zone'. In reply to the 'academic' argument that Togoland and the Cameroons were mandates and not colonies, the French Right said that it is no use being too 'legalistic' with Hitler. It was much better to tell him outright that the two colonies were conquered by French arms.

5. The outcry from the natives against being handed over to Nazi Germany, where in Hitler's own words, Negroes were considered as 'half-apes'. This outcry was strongly voiced in Parliament by M. Monnerville, the Negro Radical deputy and a member of the Colonial Committee, and it had a particularly profound moral effect in view of the German pogroms which were going on in Germany just then. For, even if the native policy of France was not in practice above criticism, France had many liberal and

generous-minded colonial officials, and the basic principle of her policy was to educate the natives and to increase their prosperity. The aim was to 'raise' the natives as far as possible and not to lower them to the status of 'half-apes'.

M. Daladier probably also knew that in the Senegal and other Negro colonies French officials had been distributing pamphlets with translations into the Negro languages of certain passages of *Mein Kampf* concerning the 'apishness' of the Negroes. The effect was devastating.

And so the colonial question was shelved—at least for a time —as far as France was concerned. The only danger, many Frenchmen thought, might come from the visit to Paris, during the following week, of Mr. Chamberlain and Lord Halifax. But, actually, nothing happened. Anti-German feeling in England was running so high at the time that there could be no question of conceding colonies to Germany.

CHAPTER XVII

DALADIER BREAKS GENERAL STRIKE—RIBBEN-TROP IN PARIS

As we have seen, the Daladier Government obtained plenary powers from the Chamber on October 4. These were to expire on November 15. M. Daladier had stressed the extreme gravity of the financial situation; the mobilisation had cost several milliards: business had come to a standstill during the crisis; production was low, and France was faced with a deficit of forty or fifty milliard francs in 1939. Like other ministers before him, he declared that the time had come for drastic remedies.

But nearly a month passed, and nothing happened; and nobody knew what use the Daladier Government would make of its plenary powers. M. Daladier himself did not seem to know. At last, on the eve of the Marseilles Congress M. Gentin, the Minister of Commerce, dropped an interesting hint which caused much excitement: the time had come, he said, to adopt a policy of *économie orientée*. This was understood to mean that the Government had decided in favour of an economy which would be half-way between liberal economy and planned economy (*économie dirigée*). Without saying what he had decided, M. Daladier made a resounding speech at Marseilles, in which he declared that he had 'chosen his road'. '*J'ai choisi mon chemin; la France, en avant!*'

But three days later a violent campaign was suddenly set loose in the *Petit Parisien*, in the *Action Française*, in a number of other papers against—M. Marchandeau, the Finance Minister, of all people. Marchandeau, who had had the reputation of a gentle, cautious, over-orthodox financier was now accused of taking part in a revolutionary plot against France. The *Action Française* spoke about a Blum-Marchandeau conspiracy; and even the more sober *Petit Parisien*

364

charged him with being almost revolutionary, and with borrowing his policy from the defunct Blum Plan of the previous April. It said that he was planning to establish a camouflaged form of exchange control (despite the assurances given to the contrary to Parliament before the plenary powers were granted), two kinds of currencies—one 'loyal' to the Tripartite agreement, and the other a purely internal currency—of wishing to resort to large-scale credit inflation, to increase income tax to 'absurd' proportions, and to subject companies to some kind of capital levy. In short, M. Marchandeau was accused of being as unorthodox and as anti-capitalist in his quasi-totalitarian schemes as was M. Blum's plan which the Senate had angrily rejected six months earlier. Was that the road M. Daladier had chosen?

In any case the Cabinet met on November 1, and after a stormy meeting that lasted several hours it was announced that M. Marchandeau had resigned from the Finance Ministry, or rather, had swopped jobs with M. Reynaud, the Minister of Justice. 'Liberal' finance had triumphed, and was going to be given another chance.

M. Reynaud was hated by the Right on account of his foreign 'anti-Munich' policy; but as a financier he was welcome both to the Right parties and to High Finance generally.

Personally he had always enjoyed a considerable measure of goodwill from the Left, who well remembered his courteously devastating criticisms of Laval and who appreciated his hostility towards M. Flandin; but if he did not become Finance Minister in April, when the Daladier Cabinet was formed, it was, at least partly, because his financial remedies were too unpalatable to the Left parties, whom, nominally at any rate, Daladier still desired to keep inside his Government majority. Now that the Communists had dropped out the majority, and the Socialists, in abstaining, had half deserted it, there was no longer any parliamentary reason for not appointing M. Reynaud to the Finance Ministry. M. Reynaud locked himself up in the Ministry of Finance for a week, and on November 12 produced his decrees. These increased the income tax, put on a super-tax of two per cent on all earned incomes, increased the production tax (which in 1936 had taken the place of the old turnover tax) and heavily increased indirect taxation, postage, telephone dues, and bus and metro fares. They 'revalued' the gold in the Bank of France at the rate of 170 to the £, providing thereby for the paying-off of the Bank's advances; scrapped a large part of the public works programmes, and while maintaining the 'principle' of the forty-hour week, abolished the five-day week (the '5 x 8' principle) and provided for compulsory overtime. Further the axe was going to be applied to the 750,000 *fonctionnaires*, the 500,000 railwaymen and the 150,000 employees of the City of Paris. Forty thousand railwaymen were the first to go. Such were the principal measures of M. Reynaud's decrees.

In addition to a long and detailed report to the President of the Republic, on the state of France's finances and economy, which was published in the *Journal Officiel* together with the decrees, M. Reynaud gave a dramatic broadcast on the night of November 12.

> 'You wish to know the truth about your finances,' he said. 'I shall tell you. Your situation is very grave. The good news is that we are certain to get over the situation.
>
> 'The main evil is not in the finances of the State; it is in the country's economy. We are in the last rank of industrial production. France is using up her reserves; she is living on her capital. Your houses are getting old, and they are not being rebuilt. While building has been reduced by half in France in the last nine years, it has increased by 60 per cent in Germany.
>
> 'On sea France ranked third in 1900, fourth in 1914, and we are now eighth. Besides this, we are affected by a serious malady. I refer to armaments. I am asked for 25,000,000,000 francs (about £140,000,000). How can I refuse it? Factories which are profitable are decreasing in numbers, and those which are not [arms factories] are increasing.
>
> 'A needy State has a family of poor relations hanging on its skirts. They all dip their hands into the treasury, and in order to satisfy them the State borrows at ever-increasing rates of interest. And when the State cannot borrow any more it has recourse to the Bank of France. It has done that for thirty months, and what began well has ended badly in depreciation of our currency. We are going blindfold towards an abyss.'

M. Reynaud said that public expenditure must be reduced and revenue increased. Civil servants must be adequately remunerated, and if that were to be so their number must be reduced. The number of railway workers would be reduced in 1939 to 40,000.

Turning to the question of large public works, M. Reynaud said that in 1939 about £140,000,000 would be spent on armaments. 'We cannot simultaneously offer ourselves the luxury of big public works.'

M. Reynaud said that taking the population as a whole the increase in taxation proposed would represent only 25 centimes a day per head. Naturally the rich would bear the heavier burden.

The deficit on the ordinary Budget, said M. Reynaud, had been wiped out and the deficit on the railways had been largely reduced. Expenses on big works had been cut. 'We have wiped out to-day a deficit of some £114,000,000. Apart from a few milliards of francs, our only borrowings now will be for national defence.

> 'However hard all this may appear, it is but the beginning. After this first week's battle we shall have many others to fight. Our final salvation is not for next week or next month, or even for the coming year.
>
> 'In next Thursday's statement of the Bank of France you will no longer see that list of advances to the State totalling about fifty milliard francs. The gold reserve has now been valued at its true worth. The profit of this revaluation has gone to the liquidation of the State's debt to the bank. This means that the tombstone has now been put on the policy of "easy money".
>
> 'M. Reynaud announced that the Treasury would abstain from appealing to the money market for six months. 'You will no longer see the quotations of Treasury and corporate loans depressed by fresh issues bearing a higher rate of interest than the preceding issues.'

As regards production, M. Reynaud declared that it must increase by between thirty and forty per cent. If all the unemployed were taken on to-morrow they would increase production by only eight per cent. Therefore more hours must be worked.

> 'Do you think that with Europe as it is to-day France can at one and the same time maintain her standard of living and spend 25,000,000,000 francs on armaments *and take two days' holiday a week? People abroad are listening to me and I tell you that*

the 'week with two Sundays' has ceased to exist in France. The decrees which have just been signed are only the first step on our way. Our plan is a three-year plan.'

The decrees were well received by the Bourse, where *Rentes* and industrials boomed. But they, naturally, met with angry criticism from the Left, and particularly from the C.G.T. whose Congress met at Nantes that week. The Left Press considered that disproportionately heavy sacrifices had been asked from the poor man; nothing serious had been done to fight tax evasion in the case of the rich; the flat two per cent supertax on all earned incomes, no matter how small, was a thoroughly undemocratic measure; the compulsory overtime gave arbitrary power to the employers; and the general abolition of the five-day week was absurd, as in many factories there was scarcely enough work for four full days.

M. Blum thought that the whole plan was far too much based on the 'return of confidence' principle, and so was unsound. For one thing, he said, it was enough for one of the Dictators to frown to shake this 'confidence'.

.　　.　　.　　.　　.　　.　　.　　.　　.

M. Jouhaux spoke at the C.G.T. congress at Nantes on November 16; and, rather carried away by the hostility shown towards the decrees by a large part of the rank-and-file, threatened the Government with a General Strike, 'if this were to prove indispensable'.

'Trade union labour,' he said, 'is ready to take a large share in a programme of sacrifices but it does not accept sacrifices that are contrary to the general interest. A sound economy cannot be built on the basis of "Get rich, you capitalists. and may the working class sink lower than ever". . . .

'The Government is trying to achieve economic recovery by inspiring banking and industrial capital with confidence. At the same time coercion is being used against the working class—is that the basis on which labour and capital are expected to co-operate? Democracy, Mr. Roosevelt said, must give its confidence to those of whom it stands in need. In the view of French capitalists, confidence consists in scrapping the advantages gained by the working class in the last two years.

'The decrees in their present form are unacceptable. The system of overtime introduced by M. Reynaud aims much more at the restoration of the employer's authority than at any economic restoration.'

M. Jouhaux added:

> 'Poor France, what humiliations have you not suffered already? An attempt is now being made to prepare the worst humiliation of all—to divide you internally and so to prepare the conditions for your complete decline. France, once the light and the conscience of humanity, will sink into darkness and will become the servant of the dictatorships.'

He concluded that the C.G.T., the trade-union federation, should work out in minute detail the use of 'its supreme weapon', the general strike, in case its use became indispensable.

The mention of a general strike was made rather cautiously; but the idea was to take shape in the days that followed— largely under the influence of events, and of extremist—mostly Communist—agitation.

The truth is that, although the decrees were extremely unpopular, they did not warrant the use of the 'supreme weapon'; and the general strike was determined by a large number of considerations: to the Communists, in particular, the general strike, was above all, a mass protest against the Government's growing reactionary tendencies at home and the increasingly pro-German policy abroad. It should be remembered that what was ultimately called was only a twenty-four-hour strike —i.e. a demonstration or a warning, and it was not intended to be a full-fledged general strike; and essential services like electricity, water and gas were never to be suspended; a point conveniently overlooked by the Government, which tended to represent the strike as a revolutionary rising.

The general strike was a complete failure; and that for a number of reasons. For one thing, M. Jouhaux had threatened the Government a fortnight before it actually happened; and in the interval the Government had been able to take all the necessary precautions. Secondly, the issues were extremely confused. Officially it was a protest strike against the decrees; but everybody felt that these were not an adequate reason for resorting to the 'supreme weapon'; and if the Communists and a considerable part of the rank and file—who were, after all, the descendants of the Communards who in 1871 had rebelled against the capitulation of Francfort—were smarting under the humiliation of Munich, this feeling was not shared by

everybody. The increasingly domineering attitude of some of
the big employers—who felt that the day of reckoning had
come after all the humiliations they had suffered in 1936, and
who now made a point of eliminating trade union labour
from their works as far as possible—also increased the discontent among certain sections of the working class. But, all
this was not sufficient to make the strike a success. In the
last analysis it is probably also true to say that, disillusioned
in the Front Populaire, the working class were not feeling
sufficiently heroic about anything to risk losing their jobs—
especially after the Government had requisitioned all the
public services and was threatening prospective strikers with
severe reprisals.

The real trouble started on November 23, first in the north
of France, and on the afternoon of the 24th, in the Paris Region.
That day, while Mr. Chamberlain and Lord Halifax—who
had already been welcomed at the Gare du Nord on the
previous night with loud cries of *A bas Munich!* and *Vive
Eden!*—were being fêted at the Paris Town Hall, a vast
stay-in strike broke out at the Renault works with its 33,000
workers. Simultaneously, a number of other works were
occupied. The stay-in strike at Renault's was a challenge to
the Government; for no Government had ever even attempted
to evacuate by armed force a factory even half that size. A
year earlier M. Chautemps had sent the *garde mobile* to
Colombes to evacuate the much smaller Goodrich Tyre works;
but the strikers had threatened to resist; there was danger of
serious bloodshed, and the Government withdrew the troops.
The strike was ultimately settled after lengthy negotiations.
But now there were no longer any Socialists in the Government; and M. Daladier, without even attempting to negotiate
an evacuation, sent 10,000 *gardes mobiles* to the Renault works
and ordered them to 'chuck the strikers out'. He told them, if
necessary, to use tear gas. By midnight the works were cleared,
with comparatively little bloodshed—about a dozen people
were badly hurt on each side. Actually, the tear gas machinery
did not work properly; on one occasion the wind blew the gas
the wrong way—at the guards. In one part of the Renault
works all the windows were broken by iron bars, stones and
other missiles hurled at the advancing guards. Over 200 ar-

rests were made; and in the days that followed practically all the arrested men were automatically sentenced to a fortnight's or a month's imprisonment. The judge in one court favoured a fortnight, the judge in another, a month; hence the difference. But none of the men were tried on any individual charges, there were not even any *procès-verbal d'arrestation*—it was a mass trial if ever there was one. A great many of the men pleaded not guilty; one man said that he was arrested by the *gardes mobiles* as he was mounting his bicycle to ride home; with a few exceptions, all were sent to prison for rebellious conduct. The trial scandalised a great many leading French barristers—not least M. de Moro-Giafferi who declared the trial to be outrageous, and a model of totalitarian justice. Many innocent men had been sent to prison. This trial was a sign of the times. So also, though in a different way, was the Council of War set up by General Doumenc to deal with the strikers on the requisitioned railway belonging to the D'Anzin Mines near Valenciennes.

Actually, the word 'requisitioning' has a curious effect on the French mind. A requisitioning order is too much like a mobilisation order to be ignored. And M. Daladier was completely successful in requisitioning the railways and the public services; on the day of the general strike nearly everybody was at work on these services. For one thing, as already said, the issues of the strike were not sufficiently clear, and few people saw sufficient reason for risking their jobs. For two days before the strike of November 30—which was called on the 25th, the day after the Renault evacuation—the Socialists fulminated against the Government, saying that everything would have been settled by the arbitration of Parliament—but Daladier, they said, had deliberately failed to call it, for fear of being overthrown. They declared that he had broken his pledges to them—which was to call Parliament on November 15. They also accused him of deliberately provoking the working class.

But Daladier was determined to break the strike—if it occurred. On the 27th he made the following broadcast:

> When Mr. Chamberlain and Lord Halifax were examining with us the common problems of our national defence and the consolidation of peace in Europe strikes and illegal

occupations of factories were launched in Paris and the North of France.

When on Friday we announced the forthcoming Franco-German declaration which is to guarantee the integrity of our frontiers we were confronted with the threat of a general strike. Why these movements when all occupations of factories have been declared illegal? Why these threats when the humblest will be certain to suffer most? Why paralyse all public services? The pretext is that we are about to destroy existing social legislation.

The general strike has no material or moral justification. We have not threatened the liberty of the people. We intend no dictatorship, no Fascism. The sacrifices demanded are necessary to the life of the country. Yet one party opposes these sacrifices and prepares to offer violence and is attempting to blackmail the Government.

I am determined that the law shall be respected. Occupation of factories, partial strikes, and a general strike are attempted against the Government's policy of peace.

The Government is anxious that the blood of Frenchmen shall not be shed for interests which are not those of France. The general strike is a challenge by the dictatorship of a minority to democracy. Posters and calls to action betray the political origin of the movement. . . .

In conclusion the Premier said:

While the ever-lengthening shadow of dictatorship is spreading over the world France, true to her spirit, remains the land of freedom. Frenchmen—do not compromise that freedom. If in spite of my efforts threats lead to action I shall fulfil my duty. I have no other thought than to assure respect for law and to protect the interests of France.

The speech was sharply anti-Communist. It was clear that M. Daladier was banking on a split within the C.G.T. itself.

M. Reynaud also spoke, in rather milder and more appealing terms.

M. Daladier was right: the trade unions were sharply divided.

On November 27 M. Henaff, one of the trade union leaders, still spoke in the most categorical terms:

We are now engaged in a great battle, an unprecedented battle in the history of the French working class. We prefer a fight to capitulation, and that is why on Wednesday the strike will be complete. Not a single train will run in France and the postal service will be stopped.   If the Government wishes to requisition the workers it will create conditions suitable for stay-in strikes.

But a day later—after the requisition orders had been issued—it was fairly clear to everybody that the strike would not succeed.   For one thing, the strikers were not on solid legal ground: it was clearly for Parliament to reject or approve the decrees—though they could meet this with the moral argument that the Daladier Government was persisting in postponing the meeting of Parliament.

But Daladier was determined to win in what he called 'this trial of strength'.   A delegation of ex-servicemen and M. Frossard, fearing the evil effects of antagonising the working class, attempted on November 28 and 29 to mediate a settlement between the Government and the C.G.T.   But in vain; Daladier even refused to see them.   In the meantime Jouhaux and the other more clear-sighted trade union leaders were becoming desperate; and by the night of the 29th were praying for some face-saving device that would enable them to call off the strike which was obviously going to be a fiasco.   But a face-saving device was the one thing Daladier would not provide them with.   He wanted his victory.   And the Communist leaders in the C.G.T. would not agree to Jouhaux's proposal to call off the strike 'in any case'.   So he went on with it—partly in order not to split the C.G.T.   The Right—and no doubt M. Daladier himself—were desperately afraid lest Jouhaux were at the last moment to overrule the Communists and call off the strike unconditionally.

.   .   .   .

The strike was a failure.   On the railways and in the public transport services the number of strikers was less than two per cent.   Teachers, postmen, and the other *fonctionnaires* were nearly all at work.   In Paris, shops, restaurants, and banks were nearly all open, and although the strike was almost complete in the building trade and in the docks, in private industry it did not exceed an average of fifty per cent.   It is curious that, as distinct from the Communist railwaymen, few of whom struck, the Socialist miners were nearly all on strike.   They were less in sympathy with the strike order than the Communists, but followed it largely in virtue of an older trade union discipline. It is true that the railways were 'requisitioned', while the mines were not.

At noon I went to the headquarters of the C.G.T. and saw M. Jouhaux. He looked rather gloomy, and, trying to make the best of a bad job, he said:

> For two hours this morning there was a complete stoppage in the bus and Underground services, but owing to the requisition order and the military measures taken by the Government work was resumed at eight o'clock. We do not deny it.
>
> In many factories, as in some of the Government offices, the crossed-arms strike is in progress. It may be invisible from outside, but is effective for all that. Eighty per cent of the miners are striking. Among the dockers and in the chemical and metal industries the stoppage is almost complete. The movement will continue unless something exceptional happens.

His last sentence suggested that the possibility of calling off the strike at noon had been discussed. Actually in the case of the Post Office the strike was called off at noon. Not that many postal employees had struck in the morning, but it was possible that there were some belonging to the afternoon shift who might, and who would thus unnecessarily expose themselves to reprisals.

In Paris the most unusual sight were the newspapers. Only six, I believe—all Right-Wing—appeared that morning; and most of them had only four or six pages. They were the *Matin*, the *Jour*, the *Journal*, the *Action Française*, the *Epoque* and the *Petit Parisien*. At noon there was a special edition of *Paris-Midi* on two pages only, and at night two-page editions of most of the evening papers.

In spite of the relative success of the strike—as far as *they* were concerned—these papers were triumphant, and several of them demanded the dissolution of the Communist Party.

The failure of the strike was certainly a severe blow to the Communist Party—though the Government did not go so far as to dissolve it—and also to the C.G.T. The tension between the 'syndicalists' and the 'Communists' became very severe, the syndicalists like M. Belin openly admitting the strike to have been a failure and an error—an error which, they said, was made under Communist pressure, and against the better judgment of the 'true' syndicalist leaders. The C.G.T., whose membership had soared from 1,200,000 to 5,000,000 in 1936, and had gradually declined to some 3,500,000 during 1937 and 1938, was estimated to have lost at least another million in the weeks that followed the General Strike. Widespread dismissals and other reprisals followed the strike—particularly in private industry. The 'ringleaders' were the principal victims. The Government refused a complete amnesty, and it was not until February that a bill giving the Government certain discretionary powers in this matter was passed by the Chamber.

M. Daladier was intensely pleased with himself. One had the impression during those days that he had at last achieved his long-cherished ambition—which was to prove in practice that he was a 'strong man'.

.   .   .   .

When, on December 9, at the end of the debate on the Government's general policy, M. Daladier rose to speak, he looked almost a new man. He now betrayed no hesitation, no uncertainty on any subject. He spoke as the strong man of France, as the man of law and order. The firm but quiet, almost Baldwin-like, manner that was his in the days when he was War Minister in the first three Front Populaire Governments had given way to a pugnacious and truculent manner which only now and then was relieved by moments of emotion —for instance, when he recalled his War days or spoke of the dangers that were besetting France or when he described his frequent longing to retire to his native Provence and to live there a quiet life with his children in the shadow of the olive trees.

Throughout he was loudly cheered by the Right and Centre and part of the Radicals. The Left were silent except for some heckling from the Communists and an important intervention by M. le Trocquer, the Socialist deputy, on the summary sentences passed on the Renault strikers.

In the very first sentence M. Daladier declared that his 'brutal frankness' might hurt some feelings. He was sorry, but it was better than hypocrisy.

> The Chamber must decide to-day whether the Government is to continue in office. I am responsible for my own actions and am not the prisoner of any man or any party.

The general strike of November 30, M. Daladier said, turning to the Communists, was political in character, and the objection to the decrees was only a pretext.

The Premier then produced a large pink folder and proceeded to read some of the more explosive utterances of trade union leaders before the strike. With his face turned to the Communists he read out the quotations with a triumphant air. One of the quotations said that 'Munich and the decrees are inseparable'. He said scathingly:

> You wanted to paralyse the country, you wanted to stop all trains and buses, you thought that this stoppage would lead to the fall of the Government whose foreign policy you dislike. You call that a professional strike.
>
> The Nantes Congress of the C.G.T., he said, had accepted only the principle of the general strike, but the Communists were determined to force the hand of the trade union leaders. The trouble started with Mr. Chamberlain's visit. M. Daladier described the demonstration against Mr. Chamberlain on November 23 as 'ridiculous and indecent'. But Mr. Chamberlain, M. Daladier said, knew that the people of Paris were grateful to him for saving peace and for continuing to work in close co-operation with France. And then, even before Mr. Chamberlain had left, and while important diplomatic talks were in progress, stay-in strikes broke out in the North of France and in the Paris area.

M. Daladier now spoke with much grimness. He said:

> When factories are occupied they must be cleared. Democracy has one sovereign and that is the law. The police of every country in the world use tear gas, and I ordered tear gas to be used. You need not blame the Prefect of Police or the commander of the Mobile Guards; it was not they, it was *I* who ordered the use of tear gas.

And with a grim jocularity that slightly reminded one of Dr. Goebbels's witticisms, he added: 'I wish I could have given them laughing gas instead.'

> Altogether, M. Daladier continued, it was intolerable that while he was discussing important matters with Mr. Chamberlain France, with her stay-in strikes should be the laughing-stock of the world.

The cheering on the Right was frantic.

His next point was rather more difficult. It was when he

defended the legal action taken against the Renault workers
who had been arrested that night.   He admitted that 'a certain
confusion was inevitable' in the scuffle that accompanied the
evacuation of the Renault works, but he made no serious
attempt to justify the weighty charges made against the summary trials of the 300 strikers, nearly all of whom had automatically been sentenced to terms of imprisonment.

Several leading lawyers in France had, as already said, protested against the manner in which these trials were conducted.
One of them, M. le Trocquer, the Socialist deputy, rose to his
feet and interrupted M. Daladier.   He said that the judge had
sentenced the men on a general charge without any evidence
on the individual cases and without even a police report on
the circumstances in which each man had been arrested.   Some
had been arrested outside the factory and claimed not to have
had anything to do with either the stay-in strike or the disorders.

There were many at the Chamber who felt that M. Daladier
had here a good opportunity of proposing an amnesty for all
the imprisoned strikers—some of whom at least were certainly
innocent (and M. Daladier almost admitted as much)—but he
did not seize this opportunity.   Later in his speech, it is true,
he said something about 'throwing the veil of oblivion' on the
errors of misguided men and about the necessity of punishing
only the leaders, but this did not mean that the Government
had decided in favour of an amnesty.

Coming back to the failure of the strike—an achievement
of which M. Daladier was obviously exceedingly proud—he
said that it was due to the common sense of the French
people.

There was some heckling from the Communists, one of them
saying something about the 6th of February riots against Parliament, which had driven the Daladier Government of 1934 out
of office.   M. Daladier made a quick retort: 'Yes—when the
Communists were rioting against Parliament side by side with
the *Action Française.*'   (Loud cheers on the Right.)   One
wonders, however, what would have been M. Daladier's reply
if the 12th of February instead of the 6th of February had been
mentioned.   The 12th of February, 1934, was the date of the
general strike which laid the foundations for the Front

Populaire—that Front Populaire which played so decisive a part in M. Daladier's political fortunes.

Be that as it may, M. Daladier's 'strong man' speech on the strikes was impressive in its own way and was certainly an able piece of Parliamentary oratory—full of platform effects, which had not previously been in M. Daladier's manner.

The second part of his speech was much less substantial. He defended Munich with greater determination than on October 4, when there was still a note of apology in his voice. Now his tone was more self-assured, and he no longer seemed to have the slightest doubt about the virtues of the Munich policy. The policy of 'firmness', he now declared without hesitation, was in reality a 'policy of war'. Were millions of French peasants to be sacrificed again?

It was a strange remark. Large numbers of rural deputies rose to their feet and cheered, and in the midst of the cheering a war cripple rose from the Communist benches and angrily shouted something at M. Daladier. 'I am sorry if I used this phrase,' M. Daladier said. 'I spoke as an old infantry-man. For after 1915, ninety per cent of my company were peasants.'

The slip was almost certainly deliberate. The Daladier régime—for one can already speak of such a 'régime'—was becoming, more and more, based on the support of the peasantry. The Munich policy had more support from the peasantry than from the working class; the decrees demanded heavy sacrifices from the working class and from the middle class—but, apart from the rises in indirect taxation, next to nothing from the peasantry. The direct taxes paid by the peasants in France were negligible, and negligible they remained. The income tax schedule, called *bénéfices agricoles*, remained a joke. And now the Premier was awarding the peasantry the first prize in patriotism. One could not help remembering Napoleon III and his plebiscites.

After referring to Anglo-French friendship and deploring the sarcasm that the Communists were exercising at the expense of that 'great old man' Mr. Chamberlain, and referring to 'peace with Germany which I and every ex-serviceman wants', Daladier ended on a note of emotion:

The man who speaks to you has been the same for twenty

years—(ironical cheers on the Left)—I am a son of France, of the people of France; a little rough, perhaps, but a free man who has never betrayed his party. I am the son of a workman, and I am a patriot.

I want to ask you two questions: Does one cease to be a Republican by desiring law and order to be respected? Does one cease to be a patriot by refusing to lead one's country down the war path?

He then recalled the storms France had weathered in the last year; and sometimes, he said, he longed to be back under the olive trees, in his native Provence, with his boys, far away from Paris.

And this strange and mostly aggressive speech ended with an appeal for a feeling of greater brotherhood among all the people of France.

The speech was made shortly after two important international events: the anti-French demonstration in the Italian Chamber of November 30, and the signing of the Bonnet-Ribbentrop declaration on December 6. The former was not mentioned by Daladier at all, the latter only briefly.

.   .   .   .

M. Bonnet had worked very hard, almost since Munich, for a Franco-German 'no war' declaration. M. François-Poncet had sounded Hitler on the subject when he went to see him at Berchtesgaden at the end of October; and Bonnet was hoping to produce something in time for the Radical Congress at Marseilles. But the Germans were slow in reacting to his advances. Why did he want such a declaration? Surely, nobody could seriously believe in the value of a German non-aggression pledge. And yet, he wanted it. For one thing, he thought that even if of little practical value in the long run, such a declaration would be of a certain psychological value, and might even be of practical value, at least for a time. If Germany was up to more mischief, it was better that her mischief be directed towards the East, rather than towards the West. Besides, Mr. Chamberlain had at Munich signed his 'no-war' declaration with Hitler; and if Bonnet managed a parallel Franco-German declaration, it would look good, and increase his personal prestige, and—improve his chances for the Premiership.

The *gleichschaltung* of the French Press which was never so apparent as during November and December—that is, for some time before and for some time after the Bonnet-Ribbentrop declaration—had a great deal to do with this declaration. First it was necessary not to do anything that would disturb the Franco-German negotiations; and later, it was important not to spoil the 'moral effect' of the agreement. In December, moreover, Bonnet's desire to prevent Franco-Italian relations from becoming unduly strained became another reason for 'keeping the Press in order'.

How can the Press be 'kept in order'? I am here on delicate ground. But the Press in France was, in a large measure, muzzled by a technique which must be familiar to all French Foreign Ministers, but which was never practised, at least since the War, more extensively and more effectively than by M. Bonnet. The Government has all kinds of means at its disposal for 'influencing' the Press. First of all, the secret funds, which are, in many cases, heavily supplemented by funds placed at this or that Minister's disposal by various financial and business interests. Parallel with funds received from or *via* the Government, certain papers are alleged to have been receiving important 'subsidies' from foreign Governments; and Germany is alleged to have been quite unusually lavish with her money in Paris not only at the time of the Czech crisis, but also during the few months that followed. M. de Kerillis, invoking a high American authority, claimed that £2,000,000 had been spent by German propaganda in France during the greater part of 1938. But there are other ways of influencing papers. The Government can resort to intimidation, or flattery, or certain other methods. The Havas Agency has a quasi-monopoly of agency news in France; and it is officially subsidised by the Government. The Foreign Office, therefore, has a considerable hold on Havas. It is able—especially in cases when the news is not likely to leak out elsewhere in France (for if it leaks out abroad it does not necessarily matter)—to get Havas to suppress some unpleasant piece of news;—the suppression of such news in France was done on a very extensive scale especially at the early stages of the anti-French campaign in Italy; an attempt was even made not to 'release' the story of the anti-French demonstration at the

Italian Chamber on November 30. But the story was too big to be suppressed altogether; and it was merely toned down. The Foreign Office has also great possibilities for toning down news. Apart from papers directly subsidised, and to which the Government can give 'friendly advice', certain Ministers have also a personal way of influencing the Press. Personal relations exist between Ministers and newspaper editors; and these are asked by *Monsieur le Ministre* not to play up this or that piece of news. The editor—or his 'diplomatic correspondent', for that matter—cannot easily refuse, if he values the Minister's friendship, and even if he is financially independent of him. It was in these various ways that during the great Franco-German *rapprochement* the bulk of the Press was *gleichgeschaltet*; extraordinarily little was said, for instance, about the pogroms in Germany. On another occasion, a paper with a very large circulation was specially 'requested' not to publish a big *reportage* it had prepared on German refugees in France. King Carol's visit to Paris on November 19-20, while the Franco-German negotiations for a 'declaration' were in progress, was virtually ignored by the semi-official Press; in the past, the *Temps*, which now gave the visit only a few lines, would certainly have written ponderous editorials on '*L'Amitié Franco-Roumaine*'. When the bulk of the Press can be *gleichgeschaltet* by these methods, the Opposition Press becomes, in itself, less dangerous: for its aggregate circulation becomes negligible compared with that of the 'semi-official' Press. The one sells in millions, the other only in hundreds of thousands.

But there are ways of dealing with the Opposition Press, too. Thus, a small paper belonging to a former Cabinet Minister which more or less depended on Government subsidies, became rather rebellious after Munich. The subsidies were stopped, and the paper passed into other hands, which wrote exactly what *Monsieur le Ministre* wanted to be written. Then there is the case of a political weekly of high standing, but run at a substantial deficit. The deficit is 'covered' by one or two wealthy patrons who are not out of sympathy with the paper's 'anti-Munich' policy. But it so happens that the patrons are invited to lunch; and there they meet *Monsieur le Ministre*; and *Monsieur le Ministre* is perfectly charming; and during coffee he remarks casually that such-and-such a journal is doing the country a great deal of harm, and that its patrons are really very ill-advised to spend their good money on such a mischievous publication. Sometimes it does not work; but sometimes it does. Similar methods—though not by *Monsieur le Ministre* personally—are applied to big advertisers. M. de Kerillis, in the *Epoque*, has referred to the advertising revenue his paper has lost through such pressure on the bigger advertisers.

I hasten to add that such Government pressure on the Press was not by any means limited to France before and after Munich; 'friendly admonition' and 'friendly requests' and lunch invitations to Editors and similar tricks have been applied on an extensive scale in England, too. Advertisers, whether directly inspired from above or not, have also tended to boycott papers which were 'too gloomy', and not sufficiently in agreement with Mr. Chamberlain. But the *gleichschaltung* has never been quite so blatant in England as it was in France especially during November and December 1938. For one thing, English papers are financially independent of the Government.

To reinforce this *gleichschaltung* of the Press M. Bonnet conceived two decrees which he desired the Government to approve; but M. Marchandeau, the Minister of Justice, refused to sign them. These two decrees were calculated to protect the Dictators against attacks. Under the existing Press Law heads of foreign States and (this was added by a Laval decree to oblige Mussolini) heads of foreign Governments may ask the French Government to take action against a paper which has published anything which they consider offensive. In terms of the decree drafted by M. Bonnet this action could be taken without any complaint from abroad, but on the initiative of the French Foreign Minister. This proposed decree had vast implications. The other decree proposed that any trials likely to have 'international repercussions' be heard *in camera*: the purpose of this was to keep a trial like that of Grynspan, the Jewish murderer of the Secretary of the German Embassy, out of the Press. The counsel for the defence was obviously going to say some unpleasant things about the Nazi régime; and, for the sake of Franco-German friendship, it was better that all that sort of thing should not be given any publicity.

.   .   .   .

It was on November 22, on the eve of Mr. Chamberlain's and Lord Halifax's arrival in Paris that M. Bonnet received the Press and announced that the terms of the Franco-German declaration had been agreed upon. 'There are some,' he said not without a touch of bad humour, 'who do not want friendship with Germany; but I am not one of them.'

Mr. Chamberlain, on the following day, naturally declared himself to be in full agreement with the French Government, and said that he greatly welcomed the Franco-German declaration.

It may be said that if, after creating some difficulties in October, the Germans were now much easier to deal with, it was for a number of reasons, one of which was a very curious one: the pogroms had created a tremendous wave of anti-Nazi feeling in England and the United States; and by getting Ribbentrop fêted by Democratic France, Germany was made to look more or less 'respectable' again in the eyes of the world. If the French Government was friendly, and treated the pogroms as an 'internal German affair', why should England and the United States be so squeamish? From the German point of view, the declaration also had other advantages: it helped her propagandists to convince her Eastern neighbours that France had lost all interest in Eastern Europe; or, as Kerillis was to put it, it was calculated to disgust Eastern Europe with France, and to neutralise it if, by any chance, Germany desired to tackle the West. That German propaganda was supplied with an effective weapon in Eastern Europe was true enough: not only did the German Press interpret the Franco-German declaration as a declaration of France's indifference towards Central and Eastern Europe, but this view could be confirmed by plenty of extracts from the French Press à propos of Ribbentrop's mission to Paris. Ribbentrop's visit was to have taken place on November 28; but was postponed owing to the general strike; and he arrived in Paris on December 6.

Already on the day before his arrival a part of the Press 'interpreted' the real meaning of the Franco-German

declaration in a manner that was eminently suitable to the
Germans.   Thus, M. Sauerwein wrote in *Paris-Soir* that no one
should imagine that France would ever attack Russia—oh no!
if Germany attacked Russia France would not betray her
Russian friend, she would remain neutral.   Such, at any rate,
seemed to be the meaning of his words which read as follows:

> It should not be difficult to show that by seeking appease-
> ment with Germany we are not going to enter into any coali-
> tion against Russia.

Just like that.   With such comments in the French Press
Ribbentrop could well gain the impression that Germany
could help herself to the Ukraine, at least in so far as the
Russians would let her.

And two days later, after the declaration was signed, the
Matin explained that the third clause of the declaration—with
its reference to 'special relations with third Powers'—did not
really mean what it seemed to mean.

> In the course of their conversations, M. Bonnet and Herr
> von Ribbentrop tried to find out whether within the frame-
> work of their commitments towards third parties it would not
> be possible for them to allow one another a certain liberty of
> action in order to extend and develop the premises of the Franco-
> German agreement.

The phrase was somewhat involved, but there seemed to be
little doubt as to its meaning.

.   .   .   .

There was a strange unreality about that German visit to
Paris;—and yet what a big occasion it would have been in
different circumstances!

There is nothing since the War that the average Frenchman
had in his heart desired more than a loyal understanding
between France and Germany.   Briand was popular because
for three or four years—at least until Stresemann's death—he
held out the hope of such an understanding.   Melancholy
thoughts of missed and wasted opportunities in the past must
have run through many a Frenchman's mind when he read in
the evening papers the official, polite, but rather embarrassed
descriptions of Herr von Ribbentrop's arrival in Paris that
morning, and when he observed the total indifference with

which the people of Paris treated what in other circumstances would have been a great day in the history of France, Germany and Europe.

This indifference was understandable, for Ribbentrop was not paying a visit to the people of Paris, and the French Government, indeed, made it clear that it did not wish the people of Paris to have anything to do with the visit. Lest they should give Ribbentrop the wrong kind of welcome, it was better that they should not give him any welcome at all.

The German Foreign Minister, who was accompanied by Frau von Ribbentrop, was met at the Gare des Invalides by several hundred policemen and by M. Georges Bonnet, Mme Bonnet, and a number of Foreign Office officials. Members of the German Embassy and of the German colony were also there. Ribbentrop greeted the Germans one by one with the Nazi salute.

The station was decorated with evergreens, and a striped dais was erected outside the entrance. There were a few German flags—but only very few, and outside the station there were no German flags anywhere except on the Foreign Office building and at the German Embassy.

The German Foreign Minister and his wife, accompanied by two French Foreign Office officials, were then taken in two cars to the Hôtel Crillon, in the Place de la Concorde, just across the river, where the whole first floor with a separate entrance had been reserved for them. Traffic was held up in the Champs-Elysées until the two cars had passed.

Large bodies of police were concentrated in the small area between the station and the hotel. There were no public reactions of any kind—simply because there was no public. The couple of hundred people who from a respectful distance were allowed to see Herr von Ribbentrop arrive at the hotel just looked on curiously, expressing neither approval nor disapproval.

Surrounded by similar police precautions Ribbentrop called at 12.30 on the President of the Republic, with whom he had a short private conversation, and then lunched at the Hôtel Matignon, the Premier's residence, as the guest of M. Daladier.

At the receptions given by M. Daladier in the afternoon

and by M. Bonnet at night the two 'non-Aryan' members
of the French Government—M. Mandel (the Minister of
Colonies) and M. Zay (the Minister of Education)—were not
invited. This left many people with a bad taste in the mouth.
The *Populaire* indignantly asked whether Hitler's racial laws
had been accepted by the French Government and whether
Ribbentrop was to be left with the impression that France
already discriminated between 'Aryan' and 'non-Aryan'
Cabinet Ministers.

A number of persons invited refused the invitations, including the wife of a Cabinet Minister, who declared that she was
dining instead at the Czechoslovak Legation.

In the afternoon Bonnet and Ribbentrop had a long conversation in which they 'reviewed all international problems,
particularly those directly concerning their two countries'.
Count von Welczeck, the German Ambassador, and M. Léger,
the Secretary-General of the French Foreign Office, were
present.

The Franco-German declaration was then signed, with great
solemnity, in the famous Clock Room of the Quai d'Orsay—
the room where the Kellogg Pact was signed in 1928. Members
of the French Foreign Office and of the German Embassy were
present, as well as representatives of the German and French
diplomatic Press. The two copies of the documents, one in
French and the other in German, written on single sheets of
cream-coloured vellum, lay in the middle of a Louis XVI desk.
They were signed by M. Bonnet and Herr von Ribbentrop
with a golden pen.

The declaration read:

1. The German and French Governments have come to
   the unanimous conviction that friendly and good-neigh-
   bourly relations between Germany and France are one of
   the most essential elements of a consolidation of the good
   relations in Europe and of the maintenance of a general
   peace. Both Governments therefore will do all in their
   power to safeguard such a formation of relations between
   their countries.
2. Both Governments state that there are no more questions
   of a territorial kind between their countries, and they
   solemnly recognise as definite the frontier between their
   two countries as it now runs.

3. The countries are resolved, without prejudice to their special relations to third Powers, to remain in touch with one another as regards all problems concerning their two countries, and to enter into negotiations if the future development of these problems should lead to international difficulties.

In testimony of this the representatives of the two countries have signed this declaration, which comes into force immediately.

GEORGES BONNET,
JOACHIM VON RIBBENTROP.

Signed in German and French in Paris on December 6, 1938.

The statements Bonnet and Ribbentrop later made were taken down on gramophone records and broadcast. The two statements differed considerably in tone. Whereas M. Bonnet expressed the pious hope that the Franco-German declaration would do good to the cause of peace in general, Ribbentrop said nothing whatsoever of European peace but dwelt merely on Franco-German relations.

Ribbentrop said:

With to-day's declaration France and Germany, taking into account the solid basis constituted by the friendship which binds them to other States, have agreed to put an end to their secular frontier conflicts, and, by recognising reciprocally their territory, to facilitate the road to mutual recognition and the consideration of their vital national interests.

As partners equal in rights, two great nations declare themselves ready, after serious differences in the past, to establish relations of good neighbourliness for the future. With this declaration of their goodwill they express the conviction that there exists in fact between them no opposition of a vital nature to justify a serious conflict.

The economic interests of both countries are complementary. German art and the spiritual life of Germany owe to France valuable inspiration, in the same way as Germany has often enriched French art.

The consideration which the courage of the French and German peoples won for them during the world war can in peace find its natural complement and further increase, thanks to the courage and efforts which both peoples are showing in their work.

I am convinced that the Franco-German declaration of to-day will serve to put aside historical prejudices and that the *détente* in our neighbourly relations which are expressed in this declaration will not only find unanimous approval among the leaders, but also among the peoples of our States.

The sentiment that the German people has as regards the new orientation of relations between the two States showed itself in the warm welcome given to the French Premier, M. Daladier, at Munich. The numerous manifestations of sympathy of which I have been the object in my few hours in Paris in the same way show how those sentiments are shared by the French population.

I hope to-day's declaration will open a new era in the relations between our two peoples.

M. Bonnet said:

The efforts of the French Government, like those of its predecessor, are always sincerely inspired with the aim of maintaining and organising peace. The arrangement of relations of good neighbourliness between France and Germany and the expression of their common desire to develop peaceful relations constitute essential elements in this undertaking.

That is why I am very glad about the signing of this Franco-German declaration, which, by solemnly recognising existing frontiers, ends a long and historic debate and opens the way to collaboration, which must be facilitated by the conviction that there exists between the two countries no difference of a nature to call in question the peaceful basis of their relations.

This conviction finds itself reinforced by the mutual appreciation of the value of intellectual exchanges which have always existed between the two nations, and by the mutual esteem which two peoples owe each other when, after opposing their heroism during the World War, they propose to work to-day in an atmosphere of comprehension and peace.

Furthermore, I do not doubt that this common declaration will bring to general appeasement a contribution of which the future will confirm the full value. It marks a particularly important stage in that work of co-operation and reconciliation to which France ardently hopes to see all peoples associate themselves.

On the following day, after driving in the company of M. Bonnet up the Champs-Elysées, heavily guarded by forces of police, Ribbentrop, wearing full uniform, laid a large laurel wreath on the tomb of the Unknown Soldier at the Etoile. The Swastika ribbon was inscribed, 'From the Foreign Minister of the German Reich'.

The Place de l'Etoile was cleared of traffic during the ceremony and at the foot of the arch military honours were rendered to the German Foreign Minister.

After changing into civilian clothes Herr von Ribbentrop visited the Goethe House—a 'cultural' institution, in the Avenue d'Iéna—and the 'Brown House' in the rue Roquepine, decorated with a large Nazi flag, where Ribbentrop received members of the German colony of Paris. This 'Brown House' is the main centre of 'cultural' Nazi activity in Paris, and, according to evil tongues, the headquarters of German espionage. Ribbentrop then visited the Louvre and attended a luncheon given in his honour at the Hôtel Crillon by the Comité France Allemagne, most of whose members, like M. de Brinon, are Nazi sympathisers and strong supporters of a 'Four-Power Pact' policy; M. Bonnet, who was attending at the Elysée a luncheon given in honour of Prince Paul of Yugo-Slavia, was not present.

In the evening, however, the French Foreign Minister had another meeting with Ribbentrop and at night they both attended a banquet and reception at the German Embassy. One of the items on the menu was *jambon de Prague*. Photographs taken at the German Embassy included one of Ribbentrop and Herriot glowering at one another, and of Ribbentrop and Flandin grinning like two Cheshire cats.

On this second day, in spite of the innumerable photographs in the Press, the visit continued to be treated by the public with great indifference and scepticism. Those most favourably impressed by the visit said in effect: 'After all, why not?' But it did not go much farther than that.

For the lack of spontaneity in the Franco-German protestations of friendship, the numerous mental reservations that certainly existed at least on the German side, the police wall that separated the representative of Germany from the people of France, certainly made any enthusiasm over the Franco-German declaration very difficult.

Herr von Ribbentrop was conscious of this strained and rather artificial atmosphere when in his statement he expressed the hope that 'not only' the Government but also the people of France would approve the declaration of friendship.

And what was the net result of the Franco-German meeting? The French papers, including those most favourable to a Munich policy, betrayed an unmistakable feeling of uneasiness. The uneasiness was chiefly due to the anti-French agitation in Italy.

Not without much humming and hawing the semi-official Press tried to suggest that Ribbentrop had expressed disapproval of this Italian agitation, and had even suggested that it had no support from Germany. But coupled with the violent outburst of the German Press on that same day against the anti-Italian demonstrations in Corsica and Tunisia, Ribbentrop's 'disapproval' of Italy failed to convince. Even the ultra-reactionary *Action Française* declared that it 'didn't believe a word of it'.

As regards Spain, there was the same humming and hawing in the semi-official Press. Herr von Ribbentrop was supposed to have said that he fully sympathised with the French view that the Spanish problem ought to be 'cleared up', but in reply to the remark that it would be desirable to establish some kind of 'neutral' régime in Spain he was reported to have said that 'while he appreciated this point of view and while Germany no longer took very much interest in Spain she would still like to see General Franco win'. Obviously no great step towards a 'settlement'.

Nor did Ribbentrop commit himself in any way to hastening the withdrawal of the 'volunteers' on Franco's side. Instead he made the usual remarks about the menace of Bolshevism.

Colonies were not discussed, except that, according to one report, the Germans expressed the desire to be given a share in the management of Tangiers. Apart from that, however, the Germans were anxious to give France the impression that France and Germany were 'facing different ways as regards territorial interests', France being primarily a Colonial Power and Germany primarily a Continental Power.

On the face of it the declaration contained nothing which would allow Germany a free hand in the East and cancel the Franco-Polish alliance or the Franco-Soviet Pact. Nevertheless, both the German Press and a part of the French Press clearly suggested that France was no longer interested in Central or Eastern Europe.

Bonnet tried to make the most of the Franco-German declaration. According to one report of the meeting of the

Foreign Affairs Committee of the Chamber on December 14, he claimed that Ribbentrop had said to him:

> If in signing the Franco-German declaration we Germans have abandoned Alsace-Lorraine, do you imagine that we are going to attack France not for the sake of Alsace-Lorraine but simply in order to help out Italy?

During some weeks Bonnet seemed to treat the Franco-German declaration as the corner stone of his whole policy; and, far from regarding it as useless in the light of the Italian claims, he considered it all the more valuable. His point of view at that time may be reasonably summed up as follows:

He held that peace on the Rhine must be secured whatever else happened. This was all the more important since British aid on land could only be negligible at first and slow for several months afterwards. He felt that France could not pursue a Continental policy unless there was conscription in Great Britain and a large expeditionary force, and that without these it was not even certain that France could conduct a successful defensive war for more than a few months—especially if Italy also intervened on Germany's side.

In fact, he felt that while France could hardly help Eastern Europe, Eastern Europe could hardly be expected to give important help to France.

According to M. de Kerillis, who is himself a member of the Foreign Affairs Committee, M. Bonnet gave on December 14 the following remarkable answer to his question whether France would intervene in the event of a conflict in Eastern Europe: 'If Poland, Russia, and Rumania defend themselves, why, then we shall go to their aid.'

This remarkable statement implied that—

1. M. Bonnet was not convinced that Poland, Rumania and Russia were fit to defend themselves against Germany.
2. That he anticipated a number of 'peaceful' German conquests in Eastern Europe.
3. If Poland and Russia and Rumania were to put up a good fight against German aggression and so prove their value as military Powers, why, then the questions of France's military 'commitments' in Eastern Europe could be reconsidered.

Perhaps after what had happened over Czechoslovakia the French Government did no longer feel in a position to encourage Poland and Russia and Rumania to prepare their resistance —and that if it did, it might endanger the Franco-German declaration of December 7.

Altogether, in the heyday of the Franco-German *rapprochement* M. Bonnet appeared to believe that while Germany was busy in Eastern Europe France need fear nothing on the Rhine and could even afford to take a high hand with Italy.

And it was about that time that the *Matin* printed a most impressive series of articles on *La Grande Ukraine*, in which Biskubsky, Skoropadsky and other adventurers and Nazi puppet hetmans were treated in all seriousness as Ukrainian nationalists and patriots. In the early part of December, France's sense of responsibility had fallen to its lowest point. The 'let's-be-last-on-the-menu' policy was never advocated with such blatant cynicism; and this virtual acceptance by a certain part of the Press of the 'vassalage' principle ran parallel, in a curious way, with the creation of a December 1851 atmosphere in France itself. Some months later I lunched with three prominent French journalists—and they all agreed that December was 'something of a nightmare'; the atmosphere in France had never got nearer a 'Fascist' atmosphere than during those days. The *Canard Enchaîné* referred to M. Daladier, the baker's boy, as '*Daladier, fils du Général Boulanger*'.

Not content with the *gleichschaltung* of the greater part of the French Press, the French Foreign Office began to treat distinguished foreign correspondents, who had always been good friends of France, as though they were her enemies, simply because they commented candidly on the policies of the French Government. M. Bonnet came to hate the bulk of the American Correspondents (with the exception of P. J. Philip), but the worst thorn in his flesh was the British Press. Not only was a whispering campaign started which consisted in saying that such-and-such British journalists were on the 'blacklist', and would 'soon' be expelled from France; but, certainly not without official inspiration, *Gringoire* started a violent personal campaign against Thomas Cadett, the admirably informed Paris Correspondent of the *Times*, who, because he had lunched a few times with M. Blum when the latter was Premier, was accused of being 'Blum's spokesman' and a frequenter of 'Bolshevik drawing-rooms'. *Gringoire* demanded his expulsion—a thought that was perhaps son to M. Bonnet's wish, if one may say so.   But since such an expulsion would have created a fearful scandal in London, where questions would certainly have been asked in the House of Commons, a few rather perfidious attempts were made instead to pull wires from the London end to get Cadett 'recalled'.   It was a typical instance of the December atmosphere.   Some reasonable advice ultimately put an end to the campaign; though it was to flare up again for a short moment in February, when, one day, in a message to the *Times*, Cadett commented, not without a touch of impish irony, on the striking difference between M. Daladier's public utterances on Italy's claims on France and M. Bonnet's semi-private utterances on the same subject.   But that was perhaps only a flash in the pan.   For after the second half of December this oppressive atmosphere in France began to improve somewhat—largely, it is only fair to say, thanks to M. Daladier and, indirectly, thanks to Count Ciano.

CHAPTER XVIII

'TUNIS! CORSICA! NICE!'—THE END OF THE MUNICH LIE

T HE Italian campaign against France which was, at first, not
taken nearly sufficiently seriously—for one thing, the
French Press was doing everything to tone it down—was at last
beginning to annoy the French; and French opinion was at last
beginning to shake off that drowsy torpor into which it had
sunk as a result of Munich and the Franco-German declaration.
'Little France' feelings may have been strong in France; and
it was even possible to persuade French opinion into believing
that 'a free hand for Germany in the East' was a sound policy.
But had not M. Flandin said that France would be 'an Empire
Power rather than a European Power'? And if, two months
after Munich, the very existence of this Empire was, for the
first time, being openly challenged—then, surely, somebody
must have been wrong; and the whole problem of peace was
not as simple as all that. That France should be selected as
the *next* victim—immediately after Czechoslovakia—that was
really too much! I can well believe that Hitler, who is a much
cleverer man than Ciano, was annoyed; for the 'awakening' of
France at that stage did not suit his purpose at all. He had
successfully sent France to sleep; and here was Ciano giving her
a savage kick. And France did jump up. Not that French
opinion fully realised that peace was 'indivisible'; it did not
go quite so far in its analysis of the Montecitorio demonstration; but it did realise that something was wrong with the post-
Munich world; and this was demonstrated to it in the most
tangible way. One day I remarked to a Left-Wing and rather
anti-Munich Radical: 'If you didn't risk a war for the "Czech
bastion", are you going to risk a war for Jibuti?' His reply
was instantaneous: '*Jibuti, c'est à nous. It isn't the same thing
at all. In the case of Czechoslovakia most people didn't know

what it was all about. It may seem absurd to you, *mais c'est comme ça. Jibuti, c'est à nous!*' he repeated. It reminded one a little of the joke about Chamberlain who after giving away Czechoslovakia, refused to leave Hitler his umbrella as a souvenir.

'Oh, no, you can't have that: it's British.'

'*Jibuti, c'est à nous.*'

.   .   .   .

Mr. Chamberlain and Lord Halifax came to Paris as the official guests of the French Government on November 23, and stayed till the morning of the 25th. At the Gare du Nord their arrival was marked by an anti-Munich demonstration apparently organised by the Communists. On the following day the two Ministers attended various functions, and the political talks lasted only a few hours. But the visit was of great importance to the Daladier Government. It had been badly shaken by the outcry against the financial decrees, and its position in Parliament was considered to be very unsteady. Parliament had not yet been called; but on the eve of the Chamberlain visit the Finance Committee of the Chamber met and it was touch and go. To save the Government from a moral defeat, M. Daladier took an extraordinary course; if, he said, the Finance Committee did not approve the decrees, he would telephone London and call off Mr. Chamberlain's visit! If defeated by the Finance Committee, the Government, he said, would lack sufficient authority on the following day to enter into important conversations with the British Ministers. It was under this threat that the Committee approved the financial decrees—(or rather rejected the Socialist motion for their revision by the Chamber), by only twenty votes to eighteen. What was ultimately going to save the Daladier Government was its victory over the General Strike; but until then its position remained very shaky.

At the end of the debate that followed the strike M. Daladier secured a majority of seventy-four—the entire Right, including even M. Chiappe and the eight members of the P.S.F. (the ex-Croix de Feu) voting for him. There were three hostile Radical votes, and thirty hostile Radical abstentions (including M. Delbos, M. Cot, and M. de Tessan). This time the New Majority had come officially into existence. Later in

December, during the budget debate, M. Daladier had some difficult moments; but, by the end of the year the position of the Government was stronger than ever.

The talks during the Chamberlain-Halifax visit were of no great importance. The official *communiqué* said that the discussions 'once more made plain the complete identity of conception on the general orientation of policy of the two countries, which are inspired by the same care for the maintenance and consolidation of peace'. Perhaps the most important talks related to Anglo-French defence problems. The French urged upon the British the necessity of constituting an expeditionary force; while the British pointed out to the French that the French Air Force was still in a mess. The conclusion on both sides seems to have been 'we'll see what we can do'. The other talks were rather general. Regarding Eastern Europe, they agreed on a policy of 'wait and see'; 'wait and see—and hope for a Franco victory' seems to have been the 'decision' taken on Spain; and the Left were kept quiet by the assurance that the two Governments were going to stick, as before, to the London Plan, and that 'there could be no question, before the withdrawal of volunteers, of granting belligerent rights to Franco.' The Ministers already felt that the matter was no longer of any decisive importance in one way or the other, and that they could well afford to sound firm and fair on this point. After all, had not Lord Halifax made it perfectly plain in the House of Lords on November 3 that the British Government not only 'accepted' a Franco victory, but also 'accepted' Mussolini's refusal to withdraw his troops from Spain; and that, in spite of it, the British Government was still ready to bring the Anglo-Italian agreement of April into operation at once, since Spain was no longer 'a danger' to European peace. Glibly Lord Halifax declared:

> Signor Mussolini has always made it plain from the time of the first conversations between His Majesty's Government and the Italian Government that for reasons known to us all, whether we approve of them or not, he is not prepared to see Franco defeated.

As the *Manchester Guardian* wrote in its editorial on November 7:

> Lord Halifax's extraordinary admission is the most complete

vindication of Mr. Eden's protest and resignation. For this new principle, against which Mr. Eden struggled in the Cabinet, marks a revolution, and a sinister and dangerous revolution, in the foreign policy of Great Britain. Can anybody imagine Lord Salisbury or Sir Edward Grey telling Parliament that the British Government, so far from protesting against such a flagrant outrage on public law, was entering on a cordial agreement with Italy—an agreement which implies mutual trust and some common purpose.

But that did not worry the French and British Ministers, and when they met on November 24, they were obviously already looking forward to a Franco victory.

One had, however, the impression during that meeting that there was a certain reserve—particularly on the British side; and that Mr. Chamberlain was not exactly 'falling over' his French hosts. And it is curious that there was one very important piece of news which, to all appearances, he withheld from them—and that was his decision to go to Rome in January. He probably knew that the French had good reason to advise him against such a move. But, as he was to say at the famous London Press dinner on December 13:

> Next month Lord Halifax and I have planned a visit to Rome for the purpose of discussing with the head of the Italian Government and his Ministers all matters of common interest and concern. *It may be that some will once again be speculating upon who is the winner and who the loser in these talks. That is not the spirit in which we propose to undertake our journey.* Rather has it been our hope that we might find an atmosphere in which it could be possible, by personal interchange of thought, better to understand each other's point of view, and by establishing a greater mutual confidence to co-operate in one way or another in further steps towards the general sense of stability and security.

And he added the somewhat undemocratic remark, which sounded almost like a—wholly undeserved—apology for the Nazi outrages:

> I find it difficult to rouse much excitement over different systems of government, apart from particular actions which may not necessarily be inherent in the system.

'Who will be the winner and who will be the loser' in the Rome talks seemed unessential to Mr. Chamberlain. The French did not look at it quite in that way—for Mussolini obviously wished them to be the losers. Mr. Chamberlain's famous speech was not made until a fortnight later; but the French Ministers must have had a pretty good idea of Mr. Chamberlain's theory about 'winners and losers'; for the announcement on November 28 of the Rome visit came to the French—or at least to many of them—as a rather unpleasant surprise; all the more so as, three days earlier, Mr. Chamberlain had not told them about it. Even M. Bonnet apparently received the news with slightly mixed feelings.

The effect in Italy of the announcement of Mr. Chamberlain's visit was immediate. Two days later, Count Ciano made a speech before the Italian Chamber. First he praised the British Government:

> 'We do not allow ourselves to be moved by panic or alarmism. On the other hand, we note with satisfaction every effective and fruitful contribution to peace. Among such we must mention in the first place the recent putting into operation of the Anglo-Italian agreement, which places the political relations of Great Britain and Italy on a basis of firm and friendly co-operation.
> 'The agreement takes into account the new realities of the European, Mediterranean, and African situation, settling, on the basis of the most absolute moral, political, and military equality, relations between the two empires. The entry into force of the Anglo-Italian Pact represents an effective contribution to the consolidation of peace.
> 'This,' Ciano added, 'is to be the prime object of our policy, which we will pursue with tenacity and realism not untinged with that circumspection which is indispensable when it is our intention *to safeguard with unshakable firmness the interests and natural aspirations of the Italian people.*'

At this point, rising to their feet almost like one man, the black-shirted deputies burst into loud cries of 'Tunisia! Corsica! Nice!'

M. François-Poncet, the French Ambassador was in the diplomatic box. Instead of standing up and leaving, he stayed. The French Government cannot have liked it, and there was some grumbling in official quarters against Mr. Chamberlain who was held at least partly responsible for what had happened. The announcement of the Rome visit, without any consultation on the subject with France, gave the Italians the idea that the French could now be squeezed in the name of 'appeasement', and that Mr. Chamberlain would consent to 'mediate'. Italians in Tunis were already saying— though half-jokingly on the face of it: 'We want Runciman! We want Runciman!'

The anti-French demonstration aroused comparatively little attention in France at first. Partly because the semi-official Press had been given the strictest injunctions by the Quai d'Orsay to say about it as little as possible. '*Il ne faut rien dire pour envenimer la situation,*' M. Bonnet would say to the diplomatic Press night after night. 'And please don't start answering back any Italian Press attacks. *Pas de polémiques, je vous en prie.*' A member of the Havas Agency told me that the Quai d'Orsay's first move was to try to suppress the news of the anti-French demonstration in the Italian Chamber altogether; but it was found that one or two papers had already received the news from their own correspondents in Rome, and that complete suppression was impossible. But the Quai tried, nevertheless, to reduce the damage to a minimum, first by getting the news toned down in the Press as far as possible; and then by declaring, on December 5—after assurances had been received by M. François-Poncet that the Chamber demonstration was spontaneous and did not represent the official policy of the Italian Government—that 'the incident was closed'.

Instinctively, the French people refused to be so easily convinced. Not that they took the Italian campaign very seriously at first. Except in Corsica and Tunisia, where some angry anti-Italian demonstrations took place in the first week of December, the demonstrations elsewhere were little more than student rags. In the Latin Quarter the students carried posters and shouted: 'We want Vesuvius!' 'We want Venice!' and in the Place de la Sorbonne a youthful orator defended the 'natural aspirations of the Youth of France'—their most natural aspiration being to take their girl-friends for a holiday to Venice or Naples without having to bother about visas and passports. '*A nous Venise! A nous le Vésuve!*' It was all a joke—but a rather significant one to come from the very students of Paris who, three years earlier, had forced Professor Jèze to abandon his lectures at the Faculty of Law because he was legal adviser to the Emperor of Abyssinia. If the anger was not greater, it was very largely because there is a time-honoured tradition in France not to take the Italians seriously —least of all as soldiers.

But in Corsica and in Tunisia it was all taken considerably more seriously. On December 5 M. Daladier published a statement saying that he had 'since last Thursday' (i.e., since the very day after the Rome demonstration) received a great number of telegrams from Corsican municipalities and associations, from groups in the island itself, and from all parts of the French Empire.

> The Prime Minister regrets that he is unable to reply to each, there being several thousand, many rightly recalling that 40,000 Corsicans fell during the Great War for the liberty of France and her allies.
> M. Daladier has also received a large number of telegrams from French people and Tunisians, who reaffirm in moving terms their attachment to France and loyalty to our flag.
> The Prime Minister, who, thanking public bodies and private individuals for their thousands of telegrams voicing attachment to France, will be visiting Corsica and Tunis during the January holidays, sees in these spontaneous testimonies the best possible response to the [Italian] demonstrations which have already led on his part to the necessary protests, and, moreover, to which the Italian Government has declared itself to be entirely foreign. Is there need to add that these demonstrations would come up against the determined will of Frenchmen to ensure respect by every means for the absolute integrity of all territories flying the national flag?
> The Prime Minister appeals to the calm and sang-froid of the inhabitants of Corsica and Tunis to abstain from any demonstration, which could only be harmful to the dignity and nobility of their patriotism.

But although the Italian Government had declared itself to be 'entirely foreign' to the anti-French demonstrations, the Press campaign in Italy grew daily in intensity. The French occupation of Tunis in 1881 was described by the *Tribuna* as 'an insult'; the *Piccolo* used headlines curiously reminiscent of Hitler's speeches on Czechoslovakia:

FRENCH RÉGIME OF TERROR AGAINST THE ITALIANS IN TUNIS

CONCENTRATION CAMPS NEAR THE FORTIFICATIONS

ANOTHER MAGINOT LINE NEAR THE LIBYAN FRONTIER

AN INTOLERABLE SITUATION

Gayda, in the *Giornale d'Italia* on December 12—sounding rather more moderate than usual—demanded a free zone in the port of Jibuti and the cession to Italy of the shares in the Jibuti-Addis-Ababa Railway. But, at the same time, the Italian papers declared M. Daladier's coming voyage to 'Italian Corsica' to be an 'intolerable provocation'. And Gayda declared, already early in December, that the Franco-Italian agreement of 1935 had become 'worthless'.

The clamour for Corsica and Nice was, of course, not taken seriously. But with 95,000 Italians in Tunisia, Italy was obviously trying to turn Tunisia into a 'problem'. That there were over 100,000 Frenchmen in Tunisia and over 2,000,000 natives who (whatever their grievances against France), were unanimously anti-Italian, made no difference. The Jibuti port and railway were a different matter; nobody denied that, since the conquest of Abyssinia, Italy had a reasonable claim in respect to these. But why discuss Jibuti in *such* a tone? Regarding Tunisia, a number of writers were prepared to accept Italy's challenge.

Thus, M. Viénot, who was Under-Secretary for Foreign Affairs in the first Blum Government, wrote in the *Œuvre* on December 13:

> 'Italy intends to obtain for her 95,000 nationals living in Tunisia the right to organise a "national community"—after the manner of Henlein's original demands. In this way Italy hopes to lay the foundations for her eventual conquest of Tunisia.'
> M. Viénot went on to say that the Italians in Tunisia were enjoying favoured treatment in virtue of treaties concluded between Italy and the Bey of Tunis before the establishment of the French protectorate. France agreed to prolong this favoured treatment from year to year, but these privileges were not, in M. Viénot's opinion, a legal right but a 'gratuitous favour'.
> It had been argued, he continued, that M. Laval consolidated until 1955 the immunity of the Italian schools and until 1965 the exemption of the Italian settlers from progressive denationalisation. But the 'mode of application' explicitly provided for in the Franco-Italian agreement of 1935 had not yet been negotiated.

But even apart from that France had a perfect right to deprive Mussolini of every legal pretext to meddle in Tunisian affairs:

Let us reduce the Italians in Tunisia to the status of aliens by putting an end to their present privileges. The Franco-Italian Convention of 1896 is in force only by virtue of its tacit and automatic renewal, and we may denounce it at three months' notice. Let us, before waiting for new claims, denounce it. Let us at the same time take the necessary measures of self-protection; let us expel Italian agitators, dissolve the Fascist organisations and prohibit their paper the *Unione*.

We are faced with an unprecedented piece of blackmail on the part of a man who understands only the language of force and trusts in our weakness. The risks can only increase if we fail to act at once.

M. Brossolette, taking a similar view in the *Populaire*, said that since Italy was threatening to repudiate the 1935 agreement, France should only welcome it; it would give her a completely free hand in dealing with the Italians in Tunis. Like M. Viénot, M. Brossolette said that the Italians in Tunis could then be reduced to the status of aliens.

The 1935 agreement was actually denounced by Italy a few days later—on December 17; but, naturally, the French Government did not take advantage of this to apply to Tunisia the drastic remedies advocated by M. Viénot and M. Brossolette.

This repudiation was, in fact, a brutal reply to the conciliatory speech M. Bonnet made before the Foreign Affairs Committee of the Chamber on December 14, when he said that, in spite of the attacks on the 1935 agreement in the Italian Press, France still considered it valid; and that there was no question of 'retorting' by depriving the Italian settlers of their existing privileges. M. Bonnet repeated several times that the anti-French outcry in the Italian Chamber 'did not represent the official policy of the Italian Government'. He added, however, that France would not surrender an inch of territory to Italy.

That is to say that not a single one of Italy's *territorial* claims would be considered; but there were also *non-territorial* claims; and these M. Bonnet did not mention.

We are going to hear a lot more about this distinction.

On December 19 M. Bonnet spoke to the Chamber itself. He was even firmer than before about Italy's territorial claims.

Not a single inch of French territory, he said, would be given up.

> Any attempt to achieve such ambitions can only lead to an armed conflict. And when I speak of French territory I include in it Tunisia, the French possessions on the Somali coast in their entirety, Corsica, Nice, and Savoy. This statement should be sufficient to calm and to reassure completely the people living in these territories.

By speaking of 'the French possessions on the Somali coast in their entirety' M. Bonnet must have had in mind certain suggestions tentatively put forward in London—such as a 'free zone' for Italy in the port of Jibuti.

Apart from that, however, his speech rather suggested that there were signs of a *détente* between France and Italy. Incidentally, it was in the course of this speech that M. Bonnet re-affirmed the statement of his predecessor, M. Delbos, that in the event of an unprovoked aggression against Britain French land, sea, and air forces would be immediately used for her defence.

> How would it be otherwise in the case of France and Britain whose relations as Mr. Chamberlian says, are so close as to surpass mere legal obligations because they are founded on identity of interest?

This speech was made on the 19th; and it was actually on the 17th that Italy had repudiated the 1935 agreement. At the meeting of the Chamber on December 29 M. Bonnet was going to be publicly accused of having deliberately concealed from the Chamber, in his speech on the 19th, this new development of extreme gravity. The news finally leaked out in the *Ordre* on December 22; and it was only then that the fact was officially admitted by the French Foreign Office.

M. Bonnet was accused of excessive timidity, which, his critics thought, would only encourage Italy in her demands. The French Government, they said, should frankly state that if the agreement of 1935 was null and void, then the status of the Italians in Tunisia was now again subject to revision by France at three months' notice.

It was also said that the French Government should also demand the return by Italy of the 2,500 shares in the Jibuti-Addis-Ababa Railway which were handed over to her in 1935.

Further, it was proposed that all the territories which had, actually or nominally, passed under Italian sovereignty under the 1935 agreement, should be promptly returned to France.

But the French Government preferred to 'go easy', and not to 'dramatise' matters. Although in view of the dangerous-looking troop movements in Abyssinia and French Somaliland, a gunboat and two batallions of Senegalese troops were sent on December 28 to Jibuti, at the request of M. Mandel, the Minister of Colonies, the French Foreign Office claimed that these dispatches were 'a matter of routine' and had nothing to do with reports of alleged Italian troop movements. In reply to allegations that Italian outposts had already been occupying, for some time past, various points thirty or forty miles inside the frontiers of French Somaliland, the Foreign Office declared that it had decided to send there a commission of geographers who would find out exactly where the frontier was. Pertinax replied to this that the geographers had returned from there several months before and knew 'exactly where the frontier was'. It was an open secret that M. Mandel had played this little trick on M. Bonnet by giving the information to Pertinax.

On December 29 M. Bonnet was asked at the Chamber why he had concealed from it, in his speech ten days earlier, the repudiation of the 1935 agreement. M. Bonnet looked rather embarrassed.

At first he said that he had not been informed of the denunciation in time; then he said that, even if he had been informed, he could not have disclosed the facts since the matter had not been discussed by the Cabinet, and in the end, pressed by further questions, he said that he would 'neither confirm nor deny'.

The incident started in the middle of the Budget debate, when M. Sibué (Socialist) alleged that in his speech on December 19 M. Bonnet 'had concealed from the Chamber an extremely grave event. Perhaps he was not then aware of the Italian Note, but in that case what was one to think of the Government's services?'

> M. Péri (Communist) asked how in the circumstances M. Bonnet could have invited the Chamber on December 19 to declare itself satisfied with his statement. Did he not know that Italy was making fresh claims? Such a policy of con-

cealment was not a good one. For did it not suggest to the
Italian Government that France was ready to enter into further
bargaining?

It was clear that the Italians were hoping, on the eve of the
ominous British visit to Rome, to employ tactics with which
Germany had already succeeded in the past. The Italian
papers were boasting that the offensive in Catalonia was being
conducted by Italian troops. What was the French Government going to do about the withdrawal of these troops?
Would Parliament be left in ignorance of all the Government's
moves and in the end be asked to ratify its capitulations in a
quarter of an hour, as happened after Munich?

Significantly enough, this onslaught on the Government by
the Left received the strongest support from the Right. M.
Marin declared that it was not enough to say that France
would not yield an inch of territory. One had to teach people
to respect other people's property acquired at the cost of blood
and tears and milliards of money.

M. Vallat, another leading member of the Right, supported
M. Marin, while M. Gouin, a member of the 'Socialist Union'
asked that the sitting should be suspended so as to indicate to
M. Bonnet that a reply was desired.

Although M. Campinchi, the Minister of Marine, asked that
the discussion of the Budget should be resumed, the suspension
was voted by 309 votes to 279.

This was a blow to the Government—even though it had
not made the vote a question of confidence. M. Bonnet then
spoke. He began by saying emphatically that he had learned
of the Italian repudiation of the 1935 pact after his speech in
the Chamber. Then, however, he added that 'even if he had
heard of it before he could not have mentioned it, as it had
not been discussed by the Cabinet'.

M. Sibué said that he was not satisfied with M. Bonnet's
explanation. He understood that the Italian Note repudiating
the 1935 pact had been handed in on December 17. M. Bonnet
had not denied it.

M. Bonnet: 'I neither deny nor confirm it.'

M. Sibué then said that he could not believe that M. Bonnet
had not heard of a Note which had been handed in two days
before. It was a serious matter that no mention should have
been made of the Note in M. Bonnet's speech on December 19.
Parliament could not accept such methods. The excuse given
by M. Bonnet that the Government had not discussed the Note

previously cut no ice. The matter was so important that the Cabinet should have been informed.

M. Péri said that M. Bonnet's 'I can neither confirm nor deny' was a terrible answer to give to Parliament. Had M. Bonnet nothing more to say? He had talked about 'not an inch of territory', but territorial concessions were not everything. Was Parliament going to wait until after the Chamberlain visit to Rome before being informed?

'I am sorry to say,' M. Péri concluded, 'that M. Bonnet's denials are no longer of any use to anybody.'

For once, the Left were having the time of their lives. *'Il mentait comme un arracheur de dents,'* a French journalist later irreverently remarked in the Lobbies. And Reuter telegraphed at midnight:

> The attack in the Chamber on M. Bonnet is regarded by the politicians as somewhat serious, particularly as regards its affect on his prestige. M. Daladier and M. Bonnet conferred for an hour after the debate.

For some days, and especially during M. Daladier's triumphant visit to Corsica and North Africa M. Bonnet's stock had fallen very low. The Premier, now genuinely infuriated by the Italians, was also dissatisfied with his Foreign Minister's 'over-cautious' handling of the conflict with Italy. Speaking at Algiers, he said, in effect, that he had no use for subtle juridical distinctions—meaning M. Bonnet's distinction between territorial and non-territorial claims—and that the Italians could go to hell. The full report of his speech was naturally toned down when it got to Paris! And M. Bonnet, as we shall see, was going to come into his own again, once the enthusiasm of Ajaccio and Bastia and Tunis and Algiers had subsided. Largely, by converting M. Daladier to his own outlook—at least for a time—particularly on the question of Spain.

.   .   .   .

On board the *Foch*, which was escorted by the cruiser *Colbert* and three destroyers M. Daladier sailed for Ajaccio on New Year's Day. If there was anyone in Italy who doubted Corsica's loyalty to France he must have been completely disillusioned, after the truly Mediterranean enthusiasm with which M. Daladier and his suite were greeted at Ajaccio and Bastia.

Corsica is politically one of the most clannish of French

provinces. Every Corsican is a politician, and there are long-standing party feuds in every town and almost in every café, but all Corsicans, whether they belonged to the 'Piétri clan' or to the 'Landry clan', or to the 'Campinchi clan', welcomed M. Daladier with the same joyful unanimity. For on that occasion he represented one thing only, and that was France.

At Ajaccio, in replying to the words of welcome by the Mayor of the town, M. Daladier said:

> France has no need to be aggressive or threatening, she has no need to shout. You have asked us to reflect with solicitude on the destinies of your island. You can count on us. You can be assured that the Government of France thinks of you with particular tenderness, for French history, rich as it is, is further enriched by your history.
>
> Whatever province we belong to, whatever may be the diversity of our opinions, we are above all attached to France. In carrying the greetings of France to her Empire I had to stop at your island, which is on the sea routes—the Mediterranean routes, which are growing every day more important for French development. It is a natural link between the Mother Country and North Africa.
>
> We are glad you have kept your traditions and customs, since local characteristics strengthen the unity of France. Whatever our origins, we have become French because we wanted to. France was not created by a series of historical accidents, but is a free and voluntary union of all her provinces which form the country's greatness in an atmosphere of civilisation and brotherhood.
>
> You gave Bonaparte to France and France gave you back Napoleon, but you also gave France 40,000 lives in the Great War, whose blood proves your unbreakable attachment to your Motherland.

And he added, in characteristic Daladier stlye, that he himself had blood bonds with Corsica: half the blood in the veins of his two sons was Corsican.

At Bastia the enthusiasm was as great. To quote Reuter's Correspondent:

> M. Daladier went ashore with a salute of 19 guns. While he reviewed a detachment of troops 30,000 Corsicans gave him a delirious welcome and sang the 'Marseillaise'.
>
> Hardly had the military march-past ended than the crowds broke through the barriers and police cordons, and with shouts of 'Long live France' and 'Long live Daladier' swept the official party along to the war memorial, where the Prime

Minister laid a wreath. In the silence that accompanied this ceremony the Prime Minister turned to the crowd and said:

'We swear by our weapons, our women, and our cradles; we swear to live and to die French.'

The crowd shouted back 'Yes, we swear it.'

M. Daladier was then borne in triumph to the municipal theatre. So thick was the crowd that it was with difficulty that the Prime Minister managed to enter the theatre.

Here M. Montera, the Mayor of Bastia, said that Corsica was indissolubly attached to France in all the fibres of its being. Recalling that 40,000 Corsicans gave their lives in the Great War, the Mayor declared that Corsica was ready to make even greater sacrifices, even to the last man, if France, in spite of her ardent desire for peace, was threatened in the least particle of her territory or colonial Empire.

M. Daladier made a short speech thanking the citizens of Bastia for his warm welcome. There was vigorous applause when the French Premier declared:

'We will remain free, for it is the destiny of France to prefer death to servitude.'

The huge crowd afterwards accompanied the official party to the landing-stage to see M. Daladier leave. On the voyage to Bizerta the *Foch* was escorted by the cruiser *Colbert* and three destroyers.

In Tunisia the reception given to the Premier was equally impressive—M. Daladier drove through the streets of Bizerta, densely packed with people shouting *Vive la France! Vive Daladier!* Women in top-storey windows threw flower petals into his car. Later the sentiments of the people were to be translated into words by their veteran ruling prince, Sidi Ahmed Bey, who told M. Daladier:

> You can be certain that all Tunisians will if necessary rally to France. I give you this assurance here. France has the right to the infinite thanks of the people of Tunis for the work it has done here, and Tunis will show her gratitude.

That day the Bey of Tunis received the Premier in solemn audience; and later there was a military parade. To quote Reuter again:

> Hundreds of tricolour flags were flying as M. Daladier slowly made his way to the parade ground to take the salute from the North African battalions. The sky was filled with bombers as the different units—infantry, artillery, armoured cars, and tanks—filed by to the cheers of over 100,000 Arab spectators.

Many of the onlookers clambered on to the tops of date trees to get a better view.

M. Daladier appeared deeply moved by the many evidences of the people's loyalty to France. Everywhere people wore tricolour favours, and parties of Arabs carried placards bearing inscriptions of goodwill to the Mother Country. At Bizerta a little girl handed the Prime Minister a silver casket inlaid with gold containing an address in which M. Daladier was described as 'the saviour of peace'.

The one jarring note was a demonstration outside the Bey's palace as M. Daladier was leaving. A party of natives carrying a banner inscribed '*Vive le Destour*' (Destour is the Tunisian Nationalist Party) was roughly handled by the Bey's guards and several arrests were made. The crowd expressed strong disapproval of the demonstration.

The Italian language paper *Unione*, published in Tunis, did not mention the visit, but published an article discussing the community of feeling between Arabs and Italians. All other papers welcomed M. Daladier, the Arab Press in particular declaring that Rome received a shock from the reaction of Tunis and Corsica to the 'mad Italian claims'.

On the following day M. Daladier inspected part of the 'desert Maginot Line' which guards the frontier between Tunis and the Italian colony of Libya. This system of defences, known as the Mareth Line, was designed by General Morin, one of the chief engineers of the Maginot Line, and M. Daladier, as War Minister, was specially anxious to see it.

From Gabet, in Southern Tunisia, M. Daladier gave a broadcast:

> 'Since dawn,' he said, 'I have been going from village to village, or rather from blockhouse to blockhouse, on the fortified line built to defend our Tunisian frontiers. I remember above all the review, remarkable for the enthusiasm of the soldiers and people, and perhaps more so for the presence there of the chiefs of the Southern tribes, who came voluntarily with their men. They told me, "If one day France has need of us again we will come with all our force, all our soul, and all our love for her!"'
>
> M. Daladier expressed his delight at finding when visiting new towns only about nineteen miles from the Tripoli frontier that the populations were as enthusiastic as those he met in North Tunis. Everywhere, he said, the French Army gave

an impression of strength and energy which he believed was
unsurpassed by any army in the world.

M. Daladier also gave Tunisia assurances that France could
keep an eye on her economic problem. This was important,
for Tunisia has certainly been handicapped by the tariff
system under which Tunisia is, as it were, an open market
to French exports, but France is not an open market to Tunisian
agricultural exports.

But there could be no doubt about it. Whatever their
economic grievances against France, the Arabs infinitely preferred her to Italy. They knew, for one thing, that they were
incomparably luckier than their fellow Arabs in Libya; and
French official quarters made at that time a point of 'rubbing
it in' that while in fifty years of French rule in Tunisia the
native population had doubled, in Libya it had declined by
sixty per cent in twenty-five years of Italian rule. Moreover,
the Italians in Tunisia (95,000 in all as against 105,000 French
and over 2,000,000 Tunisians) provided much of the cheap
labour in the docks and mines, and they were in sharp competition with the native workers.

A French friend of mine who was travelling in Tunisia
shortly before the Munich crisis, told me the following significant story. He was staying in Southern Tunisia as the guest
of a local chief. The outlook in Europe was very serious. The
Frenchman asked his host whether he thought Tunisia would
supply any troops to France in case of war. After much
humming and hawing the Arab chief said that it would be
'very difficult to get his men to go and fight in France'. 'But
supposing,' the Frenchman said, 'they have to fight not Germany but Italy?' The Arab's embarrassment vanished in-
stantly. 'Oh, that's quite different,' he said. 'You have only
got to supply the rifles. *Tu n'a qu'à nous donner des fusils.*'

One of the effects of the Italian agitation against France
was to reduce to a large extent the importance of the Neo-
Destour, the organisation of the Tunisian Nationalist extremists. Another effect, in the few weeks that followed the Montecitorio demonstration was to produce in Tunisia 25,000 Italian
applications for French citizenship.

Daladier's tour ended at Algiers, where, shortly after arriving, the Premier attended an important conference with
General Georges, a member of the Higher War Council, Vice-

Admiral Darlan, Chief of the French Naval Staff, and General Vuillemin, Chief of the Air Staff. The co-ordination of the defences of North Africa was discussed.

After the conference it was decided to call a meeting of the Higher War Council as soon as M. Daladier returned to Paris.

The native population of Algiers greeted M. Daladier with the same enthusiasm as the native population of Tunis. The visits had been arranged at short notice, and, without the totalitarian police mechanism at their disposal, the French authorities could obviously not have 'cooked' such native demonstrations in which hundreds of thousands of people took part.

M. Daladier himself was carried away by it all, and at Algiers he made a speech of which only expurgated versions were published in the Quai d'Orsay-controlled Press. They regarded it as contrary to 'appeasement' and its final phrase as a fairly obvious criticism of M. Bonnet's more cautious policy:

> 'We shall resist any attack, whether direct or indirect, whether by force or by cunning, with a determination and a will which nothing in the world shall bend.
> 'France wants peace with all countries. . . . But if anyone interprets her attitude as a sign of weakness or abdication then I cry "Halt".
> 'When I said "I maintain the integrity of the French Empire",' he went on, 'I not only said I would not yield an acre of its territory, but I meant I would not be led into juridical procedures which some people would like to set on foot.'

The phrase was also a warning to Mr. Chamberlain not to try and drag France into any Four-Power Pact scheme or into a Mediterranean Munich after his talks with Mussolini.

. . . .

Paris was delighted with the journey. It was like a fresh wind blowing through the stale 'pre-Fascist' hothouse atmosphere that had developed in the last three months of 1938. In spite of the humiliation of Munich, France, it was felt, could still speak in a clear loud voice. Even the Press of the Left spoke with great approval of the North African tour. The journey cured France to some extent of her growing inferiority-complex. During the days that followed the Tunisian voyage Daladier's popularity and personal prestige were greater than they had ever been.   He had become something of a national figure—even though the Left Press liked to point out that what the people of Corsica and Tunisia and Algeria had cheered with such impressive unanimity was not M. Edouard Daladier, but the Representative of France.   On the other hand, M. Bonnet's stock sank very low.

It was believed for a time that, taking advantage of his enhanced position and his genuine popularity in the country, Daladier would attempt to form a 'real' National Government; but soon after his return to Paris the Right-Wing influences again began to make themselves felt.   Besides, internal problems soon became confused as a result of the *débâcle* of Catalonia.   It came as an unpleasant reminder that the 'defence of the Empire and the Empire routes' was not perhaps as simple a matter as some of the North African speeches had suggested.

The North African tour was a severe blow to Italy.   In Rome it was called a provocation; in a frenzy of rage the *Tevere* published its famous article: *We spit on France*; but on the voyage itself, the Italian Press said as little as possible.   The accounts of the voyage were about as 'cooked' as were the accounts of the British Coronation in 1937.   The Italian papers dwelt principally on the public burning of an Italian flag in the streets of Tunis, on a minor street incident caused by Tunisian Nationalists, and on M. Daladier's 'provocative' gesture in brandishing a knife which was presented to him, among other gifts, in Corsica.

For fear of any indiscretions none of the Italian papers had been allowed to send their own correspondents to accompany M. Daladier to Tunisia.   The papers had to content themselves with the accounts given them by their official news agencies.

The Italian authorities were certainly angry with the French as a result of M. Daladier's successful tour, and stopped even distinguishing between the pro-Fascist and anti-Fascist among the French.   So much so that M. Tharaud, the well-known writer, was arrested at Genoa on January 5 and sent back to France just as he was going to board an aeroplane on his way to Jibuti.   M. Tharaud is one of the most pro-Fascist of French writers.

Nevertheless, the success of the voyage was not without some effect in Italy. Although the *Tevere* 'spat' on France, the *Telegrafo Fascista* of Leghorn, belonging to the Ciano family, though fulminating as much as ever against France, said on January 4 that

> although circumstances may arise in which the claims to Corsica, Tunis and Jibuti may have to be 'soft-pedalled' for a time, this will not, however, mean that these claims have disappeared from the tenacious memory of the Italians.

But while this sounded like an Italian climb-down, the abuse in the Italian Press went on as strong as ever.

But it was significant that even so semi-official a paper as the *Petit Parisien* should have given the greatest prominence on its front page to the famous *Tevere* article 'We spit on France'. France was no longer frightened. And M. Bailby boldly addressed his condolences to Mussolini on having such a stupid son-in-law, without whose clumsy indiscretion M. Daladier would not have gone on his triumphant tour—a tour which had made France 'Empire-conscious'.

That sounded very good: and the Munichois did not fail to interpret it as the crowning achievement of their policy: had not M. Flandin proclaimed long before that France should be 'an Empire Power rather than a European Power'? Only—in the last resort, the security of the Empire still depended on three things: (1) no German hegemony in Europe, and (2) no German support of Italy's claims, and (3) no extension of the Berlin-Rome Axis to Spain.

. . . .

Barely a couple of days after M. Daladier's return to Paris this last point was going to become a question of the most immediate importance. M. Daladier returned on January 6, and on January 8 Mr. Chamberlain and Lord Halifax left for Rome, and, on their way they stopped in Paris for a cup of tea. The tea party took place in M. Bonnet's study at the Quai d'Orsay. It will be remembered that the Montecitorio demonstration took place exactly two days after Mr. Chamberlain's visit to Rome had been announced; which showed that the Italians were preparing the ground for a 'Chamberlain mediation' to their own advantage and at France's expense. But

already at the end of December the French Government officially requested Mr. Chamberlain not to attempt any 'mediating' between France and Italy during his visit to Rome.
Apparently rather reluctantly, Mr. Chamberlain agreed; and
he confirmed this promise to the French Ministers during his
tea party at the Quai d'Orsay on January 10.

The Rome visit was a remarkable failure; since Mr. Chamberlain could not commit himself to 'mediating' a settlement
with the French, the visit was of little interest to the Italians.
Mussolini assured him that he would withdraw his troops
from Spain 'after the final Franco victory'—but that was about
all. Chamberlain could 'believe it or not'. From Rome Mr.
Chamberlain went straight back to London. In passing
through Paris he saw only Sir Eric Phipps, the British Ambassador, with whom he had an hour's talk—but a talk which was
of some importance in the light of the Ambassador's visit to
M. Daladier that same day.

Lord Halifax had, in the meantime, gone to Geneva, and
there he saw M. Bonnet. According to reliable accounts Lord
Halifax was greatly dissatisfied with the Rome visit, and gave
M. Bonnet a gloomy view on the future prospects of 'co-operation' with Italy. But being as devoted as ever to 'appeasement', M. Bonnet, in receiving the French Press at Geneva
that night, gave them a rather rosy version of what Lord
Halifax had told him.

.   .   .   .

The Spanish tragedy was, in the meantime, moving to its
close. The great Franco offensive against Catalonia had
begun on December 23, and, in spite of a diversion attempted
by the Madrid troops in the Peñarroya region, the Franco
troops, with their vastly superior equipment, were rapidly
moving up the coast. On January 11, Franco's troops were
within fifteen miles of Tarragona. A few days later Tarragona fell. By January 22 Barcelona was in sight. Within
thirty-six hours the hungry city was bombed nineteen times.

How was the French Government reacting to Franco's
advance?

It started with a rather nasty bit of hypocrisy. On January 10—it was the day of the Chamberlain tea party—it was
solemnly announced at the Quai d'Orsay that on the initiative

of M. Bonnet (the point was strongly emphasised) the French Government had, at its meeting that morning decided to send 45,000 tons of French flour to the Spanish Government—'a purely commercial transaction,' it was explained, 'fully compatible with the non-intervention agreement and answering the elementary demands of humanity.'

That was on January 10; and one may say at once that on January 24—two days before the fall of Barcelona—700 tons out of the 45,000 had left for Spain. Señor Pascua, the Spanish Ambassador in Paris, remarked bitterly that these bags of flour were 'tied up with red tape'.

Certainly M. Bonnet had no desire to see the Spanish Government win, or even prolong their resistance.

The position of M. Daladier was rather less clear. On Saturday, January 14, he received two visits: one from M. Blum, the other from the British Ambassador. M. Blum pleaded for the Spanish Government, and said that France would be in grave danger if Franco was allowed to win with Italian and German help: could not an eleventh-hour attempt be made to save the Spanish Government? M. Daladier who had, a week earlier, returned from Algeria, and who was full of ideas on the Empire and on Empire Routes, was much perturbed; and Blum left with the impression that Daladier had made up his mind to do something to help the Spanish Government. And, for a day or two afterwards, it was whispered in the Chamber lobbies—perhaps simply in order to keep the Left quiet—that 'two munition trains had left Toulouse for Catalonia last night'.

But on that same Saturday M. Daladier also received a visit from Sir Eric Phipps, who had seen Mr. Chamberlain that morning on his home journey from Rome. That night Havas published the following highly significant statement:

> After seeing Mr. Chamberlain the British Ambassador gave M. Daladier an account of the Prime Minister's impressions of his Rome visit. He emphasised particularly the repeated assurances that Signor Mussolini gave Mr. Chamberlain of his intention to withdraw the Italian forces now in Spain, in the Balearics, and in other Spanish territories after the final victory of General Franco.

The emphasis placed on these assurances left little doubt

that Mr. Chamberlain was desiring a rapid Franco victory
and was hoping that nothing would be done by the French to
delay it.

But M. Daladier was wobbling. On the following day,
January 15, the *petit congrès* of the Radical Party met; and
the majority of the delegates were greatly alarmed and excited
about Spain. The mention of M. Bonnet—who was at Geneva
at the time—was booed; and the thousand delegates cheered
unanimously when Senator Berthod said:

> We know that in spite of the undertakings entered into on
> the Non-Intervention Committee Italy has not ceased to send
> soldiers and armaments to Spain. What is becoming of non-
> intervention in such circumstances? We want the Govern-
> ment to tell us what it intends to do, together with the British
> Government, in the days to come. Spaniards alone should
> have been allowed to settle the Spanish problem.
>
> But there is also a French problem. Last April Italy under-
> took not to keep any hold on Spain or on any Spanish posses-
> sions. Judging from the manner in which she has·observed
> her other obligations we can only feel very anxious about the
> whole thing. For if Italy remains in possession of the Balearics
> on the main French sea route to North Africa, it will clearly
> mean the end of the French Colonial Empire.

M. Daladier himself did not touch on the Spanish problem
in his speech before the Congress, but it was widely assumed
that he had, in advance, given his approval to Senator Berthod's speech.

The success of this speech was a remarkable *sursaut* of the
Radical conscience: for the Radicals are easy-going people,
and until then they had always hated to discuss Spain and
were only too glad to let Spain take care of itself, or let non-
intervention take care of it.

It is curious that even the *Petit Parisien* which had been
consistently pro-Franco, should on January 16 have published
a message from Rome admitting that

> in certain Fascist quarters the view is taken that after a Franco
> victory Italy's diplomatic position will be very much stronger
> for trying to achieve what is called in Rome 'the natural
> aspirations of the Italian people'.

London was apparently becoming alarmed by these signs
of an 'evolution' of French opinion on the Spanish question.

The *Agence Economique et Financière* reported from London on the same day that the Radical Congress had caused great excitement in 'responsible British quarters'.

And M. Bonnet and M. Flandin and the Right generally thought that it was high time to 'stop this nonsense'—all the more so as even on the Right there were men like M. Raymond Laurent, the Catholic deputy, who had recently come back from Barcelona, together with M. de Tessan and a number of other deputies, and had been giving highly favourable accounts of the tolerance and humanity of the Spanish Government. It may be added that among the French Catholics there were large sections who during 1937 and 1938 had developed an intense dislike of General Franco, and resented his pretensions to being the 'Soldier of Christ', while allowing the German and Italian auxiliaries to bomb open towns and to machine-gun women and children. The two outstanding attacks on Franco from the Catholic side were made by M. Mauriac, in a memorable article in the *Figaro* in June 1938, and by M. Georges Bernanos in his magnificent piece of polemical writing— *Les Grandes Cimetières sous la Lune*. But that by the way.

M. Bonnet hurried back from Geneva on Monday January 16, and the 'reaction' against the mood shown by the Radical Congress started in full earnest. In fact, it was so successful that one has the suspicion that all the demonstrations of righteousness at the Radical Congress were little more than a flash in the pan.

In any case, by the Tuesday all the bags of tricks had been set in motion. In the semi-official Press the 'solemn promise' given by Mussolini to Mr. Chamberlain that the Italians would clear out of Spain and the Balearics once the war was over was given the greatest prominence. The report according to which Count Ciano said something that was very nearly the opposite was dismissed as a fabrication. The fear of 'entanglements' in Spain and the fear of 'provoking' Italy and Germany and of offending Mr. Chamberlain were being cultivated to the utmost. At the same time happy visions were conjured up of the future co-operation between France and the new Spain. There was a sudden clamour for the sending of a diplomatic representative to Burgos.

At the same time appeals were made to instincts of decency and humanity—'it would be inhuman to prolong the war'—and the same old story was told over and over again that Spain would be Spanish and that the Spanish would never be run by foreigners. In the Chamber lobbies it was whispered all over the place, 'Chamberlain is a wise bird. He has got his agreement with Franco in his pocket—so no wonder he does not want us to interfere.'

And in M. Bonnet's *entourage*, night after night they were producing stories of how the Spaniards loathed the Italians; how at Tarragona there were fearful rows between the two, and how Spanish women would empty their chamberpots on the Italian troops as they marched past. The effect of all this propaganda soon became very noticeable at the Chamber. Already on January 17—the second day of the foreign debate—the Chamber was in a completely unheroic mood; and seemed to be only too glad to take the line of least resistance. Thus, M. Flandin's speech on Spain received much wider support than could have been expected a few days earlier. He was cheered by half the House—that half which formed part of M. Daladier's majority. It almost looked as though these people were lapping up gratefully the arguments with which he was supplying them for leaving the Spanish Government to its fate.

M. Blum, who attacked M. Flandin with unusual vigour and charged him with hypocrisy, was loudly cheered by the Socialists and Communists and by about half the Radicals. But the other half of the Radicals seemed unimpressed. It was an altogether different reaction from that of the Radical rank and file at the Radical Conference two days earlier.

M. Flandin's great argument was that 'non-intervention' as he understood it, was something quite different from what some people imagined·it to be. 'If we have agreed to non-intervention,' he said in effect, 'it means that we will not intervene even if the others break their promise.'

M. Flandin then used what was expected to sound like a highly moral and conclusive argument—that the purpose of non-intervention was 'not to have Spanish blood on one's hands', which would mean that after the war England and France would be entitled (whether they got it or not) to the friendship of Franco-Spain, while Germany and Italy would not be.

M. Blum, intervening in the debate said that he could not accept M. Flandin's way of reasoning. The purpose of the Non-Intervention Agreement was to prevent all Powers from taking part in the Spanish war, and this agreement demanded reciprocity. Germany and Italy, in joining the agreement, had given a definite pledge to England and France. How could France look on complacently now that the pledges made to her and to England were being grossly violated? He added:

> If I could believe that the non-intervention policy could yet be carried out honestly I should still be in favour of it. But how can one accept an arrangement under which our hands are tied while the others boast of a complete freedom of action. The British and French Governments must either denounce the Non-Intervention Agreement or else model their action on that of the other signatories. And the Chamber must take a decision on this point (Loud cheers on the Left).

M. Flandin, speaking almost like an Italian newspaper, said that M. Blum had not himself observed non-intervention as pedantically as all that, and he remarked that in March 1938, in particular (during the great Aragon offensive) M. Blum had 'relaxed' the frontier control and 30,000 tons of war material had reached Government Spain.

M. Flandin then returned to his 'moral' argument.

> 'If we send any munitions to Spain now,' he said, 'the Spaniards will be able to say, "Our fathers and brothers and sons have been killed by French shells.' '

This 'moral' argument was reinforced by the 'intimidation' argument:

> 'If you thought that Italian intervention in Spain could damage France's vital interests, why did you tolerate it for two years? Why are you choosing this moment for putting an end to non-intervention—the very moment when we have been solemnly warned that French intervention would lead to a general war?'

Once France started sending armaments to Spain, he continued, there would be no end to it. Sooner or later she would have to send troops as well (an argument suggesting that Italy's resources were inexhaustible). In conclusion M. Flandin rather let the cat out of the bag when he said:

> 'I condemn Italy's attitude, but I think that after the end of the war this attitude will have done her more harm than good. It is a crime to take part in any civil war. (Cries from the Left: 'It is no longer a civil war.') It is France's duty to remain strictly neutral, to recognise that both sides are belligerents —-(loud cries of protest from the Left)—to enter into contact with Franco, and to prepare the development of economic relations between our two countries.'

M. Flandin ended with an appeal for 'creative co-operation' between France and Germany.

These arguments, providing *an easy 'moral' case for doing nothing,* carried the day—all the more so as, in London, Mr. Chamberlain was taking exactly the same line. In his reply to Mr. Attlee asking that Parliament be summoned at once to discuss Spain, the Prime Minister wrote:

> I have given careful consideration to your request, which is apparently based on your view that the time has come when the policy of non-intervention should be reversed and all embargo on the supply of arms and ammunition to the Spanish Government removed.
>
> In the opinion of his Majesty's Government such a course would inevitably lead to the extension of the conflict, with consequences which cannot be accurately foreseen but which would undoubtedly be very grave. His Majesty's Government are not as at present advised prepared to adopt such a course, and in these circumstances they see no advantage in anticipating the date on which Parliament is due to meet in less than a fortnight.

On that same day, January 18, the French Cabinet met and decided to stick to 'non-intervention'. As *Paris-Soir* put it, the policy of the Government would consist in 'neutrality in the affairs of Spain but vigilant defence of the Empire and of the Empire communications'. There were some people who felt that this might be a little easier if only instead of taking Mussolini at his word, Mr. Chamberlain had asked for certain guarantees—for instance, an international occupation of the Balearic Islands, for without such a precaution anything might happen to France's 'Empire communications'.

In the meantime the anti-French raving in the Italian

Press was growing wilder every day. The *Lavoro Fascista* wrote:

> France's blindness and incomprehension of the new realities will bring about the end of France. The French public spirit is in a state of dangerous lunacy. . . . Spring is near, and this spring may be tragic for France.

But M. Flandin and M. Bonnet liked to think that the Italians were merely being playful, and simply did not want France to interfere in Spain, which they thought to be quite a legitimate desire.

And although the Chamber was shaken up for a brief moment by the speech of M. Izard, the young Socialist deputy, on January 19, the effect did not last long.

> 'The Italian troops in Spain' he said, 'are a diplomatic instrument of the first order. The Italian Government is determined that these troops shall be in Spain at the moment of Franco's victory. It is not only a question of prestige. Europe must be shown the bonds uniting Franco Spain with Fascist Italy. The troops are not there to "stamp out Bolshevism". Mussolini is not fighting Bolshevism but democracy.'
>
> The traditional Spanish nationalists (M. Izard continued) were being eliminated from all the key positions in Franco Spain. The men in charge were supporters of the totalitarian system. Gil Robles and other real Spanish nationalists who were against Italian domination had been eliminated. It was possible that with the support of the people Spanish nationalism would revive. But how soon? Perhaps in five years. But what would happen in the meantime? Would Mussolini wait for five years to make his demands?
>
> 'I am surprised at M. Flandin's faith in Mussolini's promises,' M. Izard said.
>
> *A member of the Right:* Has not Mr. Chamberlain the same faith in Mussolini's promises?
>
> *M. Izard:* I am not concerned with Mr. Chamberlain; but even if the troops are withdrawn, will it not be enough if Spain is the ally of Italy at the time when Mussolini makes his demands? This alliance would be fatal to France. German military journals have emphasised it time and again, and they have also promised Franco Gibraltar and Oran. The Franco Press is already supporting Italy's claims on Tunis, and Franco himself has expressed his enthusiasm for a new Spanish imperialism. Having lost the Czech fortress, are we now going to see the Balearics taken over by the totalitarian States?
>
> It is all very well talking about sending a diplomatic representative to Burgos, but since May 1936, Franco has been

in the hands of Italy. In July, 1936 he received his first
Italian aeroplanes—long before there were any Russian aeroplanes in Spain. It is not too late to help. General Niessel
estimates that even in the present conditions the Spanish war
can last six months longer. Six months are a long time for
Italy, with her crumbling economy. Mr. Chamberlain has
provided Mussolini with a tremendous weapon of pressure
against us. We must not allow this. We must open the frontier. If we do not, M. Daladier's journey to North Africa
will have been the last demonstration of France's greatness,
a greatness which he himself will have destroyed.

M. Daladier, on the Government bench, shook his head in
faint protest.

It was a curious debate. It began on January 13, and went
on for six whole sittings until January 26. In fact, apart from
Spain, the whole dispute between the *Munichois* and the
anti-Munichois was exhausted on the very first day. The
Munichois speaker was M. Montigny, M. Caillaux's hench-
man; and his ideas—as M. de Kerillis later said were, in effect,
the ideas of M. Bonnet.

M. Montigny's main argument was that while as a result
of Munich, and especially as a result of Italy's hostility, France
was no longer able to conduct a big European policy, she was,
together with England, invincible in a defensive war.

It is an argument which may be questioned. As. M. Paul
Reynaud said in the famous foreign debate in February 1938:
'No line of fortifications can hold out indefinitely against an
indefinite accumulation of guns and tanks'—not to mention
the various ways of turning the Maginot Line.

But the invincibility of France in defensive war was the
corner-stone of M. Montigny's argument. Nevertheless, he
betrayed some uneasiness, for instance, when he said that 'the
pro-Munich people would never accept a form of German
hegemony which would mean the vassalisation of France'.

He also denounced German propaganda in Alsace, which
he said must be stamped out—another remark pointing to
some doubts about the real value of the Franco-German 'no
war' declaration.

M. Montigny said that the Italian people did not want war
with France, and he expressed the hope that for this reason
Italy's claims would in due course, once normal relations had

been re-established between France and Italy, be examined firmly and calmly.

As regards France's Eastern alliances, M. Montigny thought that these no longer counted for much, since the League Covenant, with which they were linked, had become a dead letter.

> In reply, M. de Kerillis, the great *anti-Munichois* recalled all the disturbing things that had already happened since Munich —Hitler's speech at Saarbrucken in which he vetoed Mr. Churchill and Mr. Eden, so intervening in British home affairs; the Italian campaign against France; the pogroms in Germany; the manœuvres in favour of an independent Ukraine, and so on. If this sort of thing continued, he said, France would be left alone in Europe 'with no ally except a soldierless England'. That, he said, was the policy of the present Government.
>
> An alternative policy was to agree right away to become a vassal of Germany—such a solution had at least the advantage of avoiding war.
>
> Finally there was the policy of bringing all the nations threatened with German aggression together, for only such a coalition could prevent Germany from destroying the nations of Europe one by one. He went on:
>
> Without Eastern alliances there can be no balance of power in Europe. The Russian alliance remains a necessity. It was hoped after Munich that M. Bonnet would go, like M. Barthou in 1934, on a European tour. He did not. King Carol and the Regent Paul came to Paris instead and went back in a state of discouragement.
>
> M. Bonnet, interrupting, said that, on the contrary, they went back in full agreement with the French Government.
>
> M. de Kerillis then said that Colonel Beck, the Polish Foreign Minister, had been cold-shouldered. He was recently in the South of France but he was not invited to Paris; he was instead invited to Berchtesgaden.
>
> Hitler's ambitions were unlimited. The only question was whether he would first go east or west. It was no longer certain that he would go east, for he was doing his best to neutralise the east through Colonel Beck.
>
> 'Germany will never fight a European coalition again,' M. de Kerillis said. 'Hitler has said so. Therefore the only way of preventing war is to create such a coalition.'

All the rest of the debate consisted, more or less, of variations on the same two themes.

And yet, the Government showed remarkable patience in

letting the debate drag on indefinitely: M. Bonnet was going to speak—but it was always 'at the next sitting'. His speech was announced four times; it was not until January 26 that he spoke. It was the day on which Barcelona had fallen. It was the *fait accompli* for which he had been waiting for a fortnight: It was no longer any use discussing the pros and cons of sending help to the Spanish Government.

On the previous night I saw Del Vayo off at the Gare d'Orsay. He was going back to Barcelona. 'Come and see me soon in Barcelona,' he said with a false note of bravado in his voice. He got no farther than Figueras. The game was up. Most of the other passengers on the train were going to the winter sports with their skis.

    .   .   .   .

On the day Barcelona fell, most of the people at the Chamber looked rather miserable and bewildered. Even the Right looked puzzled: for while Franco's Spanish and Italian troops were marching into Barcelona, Mussolini was addressing a crowd of 40,000 outside the Palazzo Venezia, on 'the splendid victory of Barcelona'; and the crowds shouted: 'Tunis!' 'Corsica!' and 'To Paris!' That afternoon Bonnet made a completely empty speech.

> He praised Munich, he praised Anglo-French friendship, which he said was the corner-stone of France's foreign policy; he praised the Franco-German declaration, which, he said, 'should open up prospects of confident collaboration in the future'.
>
> M. Bonnet said that France had done everything to make friends with Italy. He praised Mr. Chamberlain and Lord Halifax and repeated Mussolini's pledge to the British Premier. France, he said, would maintain intact her sovereignty and her territory everywhere. He even added that the undertakings connecting France with Poland and Russia remained fully in force. France was doing all she could for the refugees; no country had done more for refugees. France would not allow any of her interests to be harmed in the Far East, and she ardently desired to see peace restored in Spain.
>
> France would continue to observe non-intervention. France had sent flour to the Spanish Government; she was looking after 11,000 Spanish children; she had proposed the creation of a neutral zone in the north of Catalonia for refugees. France had no lessons to receive from anybody about her energy, her liberalism, and her generosity. She had her own interests

in Spain and could not allow the integrity of Spain to be threatened. England's interests in Spain coincided with France's interests.

M. Bonnet then criticised those French journalists who had attacked him and said that the Communists wanted France to 'intervene everywhere—in China, in Spain, in Central Europe'. This remark created an uproar which lasted nearly half an hour, the Communists shouting all kinds of insulting remarks at M. Bonnet and demanding that he should 'produce a text'.

In the end M. Bonnet was able to complete his speech. The radiance of France's prestige, he said, was now as great as ever, and if anybody counted on France's decadence he was preparing for a rude disappointment.

Daladier's speech was of a different order. He spoke with great emotion, suggesting that in the coming year France would have some very dangerous corners to turn. While accepting the idea, put forward by M. Blum for an international conference—that is, something different from Munich —he declared that nothing would be given away under the threat of force: 'Not an acre of our territory, and not a single one of our rights.'

A notable passage in his speech was that in which he paid a warm tribute to the Italian people, and protested against flippant remarks in various papers to the effect that the Italians were not soldiers. His speech ended on a tragic note —so tragic that many listeners wondered whether M. Daladier was not taking the blackest possible view of the developments in the days to come.

France, he said, which had defended her ideals in a world ruled by law, would know how to defend them even in a world ruled by force.

It was noticed that while M. Bonnet said that not an inch of territory would be given away, M. Daladier added 'and not a single one of our rights'. One rejected merely Italy's territorial claims, the other both her territorial and her 'non-territorial' claims.

·   ·   ·   ·   ·   ·   ·

Why was Daladier's speech so strikingly tragic in tone? Why did he speak of 'the hard and heavy task that lies ahead'?

Why did he say: 'A free nation cannot argue over the sacrifice to be made if this sacrifice is indispensable to the maintenance of its dignity and independence'?

Was he overdramatising the situation? On the following day, the *Homme Libre*, the mouthpiece of M. Bonnet began its leading article with a veiled criticism of Daladier:

> M. Bonnet defined French foreign policy yesterday. There are moments in the life of a great nation when it is best to avoid fireworks and empty phrases and grandiloquent perorations and when it is best to be like a meticulous accountant carefully adding up all the facts of a given situation.

But did not M. Daladier know of something which he did not wish to disclose openly, but which had deeply disturbed him?

The Diplomatic Correspondent of the *Manchester Guardian* wrote on January 27 reporting German troop movements and the danger of a German attack on either Holland or Switzerland. And during the days that followed the atmosphere in Paris was an 'alarmist' one; and it was not until January 30, when Hitler 'merely' demanded colonies, that Paris heaved a sigh of relief. As a Frenchman remarked to me that day: 'We are all so scared by Hitler that if he does not conclude his speech with the words: "And now, fellow-Germans, my bombers are on their way to London and Paris," we consider it a "moderate" speech.' But the causes for immediate anxiety were still there. During those first days of February the general public was not aware of any serious danger; but President Roosevelt knew that the Germans were preparing a *coup*—possibly against Holland; and his famous statement before the Military Commission of the Senate was calculated to be a warning to Germany. 'Our first line of defence is France.' It was believed both in London and Paris that the 'leakage' was deliberate. Mr. Chamberlain, a few days later— on February 6—added his own warning; it was calculated to discourage Italy's belief that England would not support France were Italy to attack her in the Mediterranean and North Africa. This warning was repeated by Lord Halifax on the 23rd of February.

In the meantime General Franco had practically won the war, and France hastened to apply 'appeasement' to Spain.

Franco's victory was hailed with loud cries of joy from all the Right papers. How they revelled in the *'débâcle des rouges'*. How they poured buckets of mud over the vanquished Republican army—vanquished by hunger and 'non-intervention'.

And when the French Government decided that it could not, after all, drive back the retreating army with machine-gun fire, and allowed the 170,000 women and children and the 270,000 soldiers and civilians to enter France, with what howls of rage they were greeted by *Gringoire* and the rest. *Gringoire* published a loathsome drawing of a burglar and murderer, with a large bag of stolen art and church treasures on his back, entering France, and saying: 'I'll find plenty of work here.' *Le Jour* wrote—'Will France open her door wide to the murderers?' The *Petit Bleu* wrote:

> After the Italian anti-Fascists, and the German refugees, and the undesirables of the whole world; after the procession of beggars and international crooks and professional unemployed and murderers, here are our next visitors, the Spanish 'republicans', among them the most dangerous revolutionary agitators, dripping with blood, and running away from the punishment they deserve for their 'political' crimes.

And the foulest phrase of all was produced by the *Matin* which said that France must not allow herself to be 'blackmailed with pity' (*le chantage à la pitié*). But I shall say no more. Nor shall I attempt to describe the sufferings of these hundreds of thousands of refugees. The first few weeks at Argelès and St. Cyprien were hell. But the French have perhaps been blamed unduly for this. It was a stupendous problem to receive nearly half a million people within a few days. Many died for want of care. Thousands lived for weeks in conditions of incredible filth. At first there were no shelters —they dug holes in the wet, filthy sand, and slept there. But there were many French doctors and nurses and many many other people; yes—mainly *le peuple*—who did for the refugees a thousand little acts of kindness. Also many of the *gardes mobiles*—not all, but many. The refugees were not all good soldiers; among 300,000 people one gets every kind of people —'heroes and jailbirds, and poor bewildered peasants, and hungry women and children and many wounded with fearful wounds and gangrenous limbs', as M. Sarraut was to say at the

Chamber on March 14. 'People of every kind—good, bad and indifferent.' An ocean of suffering.

The French Government felt that they ought to be got rid of as quickly as possible. Repatriation was the word. One had to make sure that Franco took them back without delay. Except those who might be shot. Only what was the criterion? France and England hoped that Franco would grant a generous amnesty. It would have solved an immense problem for the French. But nothing could be extracted from Franco. 'How many can *not* go back?' M. Sarraut asked on March 14. And he added: 'I haven't the slightest idea at present.'

The Right, fully supported by M. Bonnet, clamoured for the immediate recognition of Franco. Well, obviously, since France and England had done so much to secure his victory, it was little use not recognising him now. Only it was foolish to imagine that they could now lay down conditions. They still had the idea that Franco would 'need money', and so would eat out of their hands. But when M. Bérard went to Burgos he at once found that there was no great *empressement*. M. Bérard was an aged senator, a former wit and boulevardier, a great admirer of General Franco, and an intimate friend of M. Laval's. He had a very long nose, and one paper published a cartoon showing Bérard and Bonnet touching noses—an *arc de triomphe* through which Franco walked. Bérard went twice to Burgos; but Franco was not available. Each time he was received by General Jordana, Franco's Foreign Minister. It wsa a great disappointment to the Right Press, who thought that a Franco-Bérard meeting could be produced as proof that their policy was right. Bérard—rather half-heartedly—tried to lay down conditions: (1) an amnesty and (2) a 'moral' undertaking of neutrality. The Press of the Right hummed and hawed and said that both conditions had been 'practically' fulfilled, and that the refugees should be sent back by the thousand. It was added, however, that Franco could 'obviously' not commit himself openly while the Italians were still in Spain. According to Havas from Burgos Bérard's last meeting with General Jordana 'was not merely cordial, it was affectionate. General Franco's Foreign Minister shook him by both hands, and said how glad he was to have negotiated with him a settlement of such vital importance.'

It may be said that this settlement provided neither for an amnesty nor for any 'moral' undertaking of neutrality; nor even for the withdrawal of the Italians. The French, as far as one could see, got nothing. But the Spaniards, according to the Burgos version of the agreement, were promised not only the return to Spain of all the war material brought to France by the Republicans; but also the £7,500,000 of gold which had been denied the Republican Government some months before, besides all the other Spanish property in France. When M. Bérard returned from his first visit to Burgos, it was suggested in responsible French quarters that the armaments (including 50 up-to-date aeroplanes) and the gold would be used for paying for the refugees. But the Burgos version of the agreement said nothing about this; and at the French Cabinet meeting on February 27 M. Daladier refused to give any information on the contents of the Bérard-Jordana agreements.

The truth is that the French Government decided to recognise Franco unconditionally. No arrangement was reached even about the return of the refugees. M. Sarraut and his paper, the *Dépêche de Toulouse*, had protested against such unconditional recognition; for at Toulouse they were worried at the thought of living next to the 'third hostile frontier'. But Bonnet's advice prevailed. *On n'insista pas.*

Daladier got over the difficulty very nicely. On February 24, at the Chamber, Daladier announced that he was determined to recognise Franco precisely *because* he did not wish this 'third frontier' to be hostile. And when the Cabinet met three days later to approve the recognition of Franco, M. Sarraut said no more. In any case what more could he say? Amid a storm of applause from the Right and Centre and part of the Radicals the Chamber had ratified the recognition in advance by 323 votes to 261. In the *Populaire* Blum burst into lamentations: 'To think that the Front Populaire Chamber of 1936 could have done *this!*' But it was a groan rather than an argument. One need hardly add that the Government partly justified its decision by saying that the British Government had no intention of delaying the recognition; while Mr. Chamberlain said, in effect, a few days later: 'We didn't start it; it was the French.' The truth is that

Daladier read into the British communication of February 22
—to which Daladier referred in his speech—precisely what
he wanted to read into it—and what Mr. Chamberlain had
wanted him to read into it.

A quibble which was a fitting conclusion to the Anglo-
French policy of 'non-intervention'—that Giant Quibble.

. . . .

A few days after the recognition of Franco Bonnet was
reported to have told to the Foreign Affairs Committee of the
Chamber a cheerful story to the effect that at the Barcelona
parade Franco said to the Italian commander as the Italian
troops were marching past: 'I'd like you to regard this magnificent parade as a farewell revue in your honour.' The story
naturally got into the Press, and made first-rate pro-Franco
stuff—and most cheering news. But at 1 a.m. the Quai d'Orsay
issued a statement saying that 'only the official *communiqué*
of the Foreign Affairs Committee must be regarded as accu-
rate'. Which had the advantage of allowing the Barcelona
story to get about, yet without engaging anybody's responsibility.

The French Government had in the meantime taken a bold
step. 'A stroke of genius,' some said when they heard that
Daladier had appointed Marshal Pétain Ambassador to Burgos. The hero of Verdun, a national figure if ever there was
one. It was a little as if Chamberlain had sent to Burgos a
member of the Royal Family. Many felt it was much too great
an honour to render to Franco. But in official quarters they
said: 'It's got nothing to do with Franco. It's in order to
foil the Germans.' It wasn't quite clear *why* this was going
to foil the Germans; but it sounded very Machiavellian.

But the Spanish response to this unprecedented honour was
not brilliant. The person Franco sent to Paris was a Señor
Lequerica—nothing more than the Mayor of Bilbao; and
worse still, alleged to have been associated for a long time with
the *ABC*, a Madrid paper noted for its violently pro-German
and anti-French sentiments. It is true, that Lequerica had
treated Bérard to lunch during his first journey to Burgos; an
important fact which the *Jour* produced as though it were
positive proof that Lequerica was *un ami de la France*.

A few days after the 15th of March, the extraordinary piece

of news reached Paris, namely, that Marshal Pétain had been for a week at San Sebastian but had been unable to travel to Burgos 'owing to a snowstorm' (in Spain and in March!). According to a less official version the Hero of Gernika was refusing to see the Hero of Verdun so long as the Republican fleet, which, after the Casado *coup* on March 5 had sailed from Cartagena and was interned at Bizerta, was not returned immediately to General Franco. It was a national affront if ever there was one. Franco refusing to see Pétain!. Was the French Government going to recall Pétain? No. It decided to hand over the fleet!

. . . .

During that first fortnight in March optimism was running high in both Paris and London. Franco was not perhaps as appreciative as he might have been, after England had conquered Minorca for him and France had sent him Pétain; but it was thought that he 'would be all right in time;—he had to keep up appearances with regard to his allies, and not sound ungrateful so soon;—but he would soon want some money. Bla—bla—bla——'

And Poland and Rumania seemed quite energetic. The Poles were showing a renewed interest in the French alliance and the Polish Army was said to be splendid. And King Carol was full of energy; Codreanu was dead; and Calinescu was the worst enemy of the Nazis. The Italian claims on France could be ignored. Chamberlain was behind France; and Daladier had told Italy to go to hell. The Italians would, it was thought, be only too pleased if they got the shares of the Jibuti Railway—something to show for their efforts—but if they wanted them, they must ask for them politely, the French said. And Cardinal Pacelli had been elected Pope—what a biff in the eye for Hitler and Mussolini! the optimists said. And beyond the sea, Mr. Roosevelt had uttered his grave warning.

Optimism was running high. There was no spot in Europe, it seemed, at which Hitler or Mussolini could strike with impunity. Even the Hungarians had gone anti-Nazi. Even the anti-Munich *Aube* thought that France and England were 'turning out to be luckier than they deserved to be'.

It seemed to have occurred to nobody that Hitler might strike at—Czechoslovakia. Poor Czechoslovakia! She had been forgotten. It was, somehow, assumed that she was now a vassal of Germany, and of no importance any longer. The Czechs were being *so* tactful, not trying to do anything to offend Germany. Moreover, had not Hitler said at the Sportspalast on September 28: 'I don't want any Czechs'?

Had everybody forgotten the Bohemian Bastion? Had everybody forgotten that it was not an end but a means—that bastion which, in September, it was such 'bad style' to mention. M. Bonnet knew on March 11 what was coming. And yet, on March 14, in the *Homme Libre*, the organ of the French Foreign Minister, the unspeakable M. Thouvenin in an article entitled *Fausse Alerte!* thundered against the 'lies' in the British Press about the strange things that were happening in Slovakia.

> Some day it will become necessary to discover who the people are who are deliberately spreading these mischievous stories— and why they are doing it. . . .

Fausse alerte! Fausses nouvelles—intolérable! And then came March 15. The Great Lie of Munich was in ruins. The policy of Appeasement, of Peace in our Time was shown up. That policy which was a blend of well-meaning British gullibility and French *facilité*—and some worse things.

And during the days that followed the seizure of Prague by the German troops I often remembered *la mère* Thiébaud, and what she said on the night Munich was announced. And when I thought of the 'common' people of France—that admirable *peuple*—who were now perhaps going to bear the brunt of it all, I wondered whether there was not another lie, I mean the story that 'Every people has the Government it deserves'.

. . . .

March 15 was a rude awakening for France. In the days that followed it was clear that Mitteleuropa—and more than Mitteleuropa—was coming into being. Wherever the victorious German armies went without firing a shot, they brought with them the gospel of the Concentration Camp.

And yet the reaction in England was sharper than in France. When Lord Halifax proposed the peace front, French official quarters were polite about it at first; but the old pro-Munich Press soon began to poo-pooh it—'That's all very well, *but not with the Soviets!*'

France was in a state of depression and bewilderment. And the strangest thing of all was that the Government observed at first a non-committal attitude in relation to foreign affairs.

The first reaction to the Prague *coup* among certain people around M. Bonnet was to say rather cynically '*Ça vous étonne?* It is, after all, only a consequence of the blunders made in 1919.'

As for M. Daladier's first reaction, it was to ask Parliament for plenary powers 'for the defence of the country'. *Pleins pouvoirs*—and completely unlimited. The Left, including a number of Radicals, tried to argue: 'Will these powers apply to the freedom of the Press? Will they enable the Government to put parliament in cold storage, not merely for eight months but for years?' M. Daladier refused all explanations. He dismissed all objections as 'byzantinism'. 'You will go on with your hairsplitting discussions even with the enemy at the gates.' And M. Daladier added contemptuously: 'This is not a time for words; it is a time for action. Democracy must cease to be a régime of contradictions'—a strange phrase singularly reminiscent of certain totalitarian formulae. And he said that he could not attach as much importance to parliamentary speeches as to the words that reached him 'from the very bowels of the country'—which was, in effect, a reference to his fan mail—a fan mail which, for some time, Daladier had come to consider as the best barometer of what the country felt and thought.

Parliament gave way; it was no use risking a Cabinet crisis at a time like that. The Chamber passed the unlimited plenary powers, valid until November 30, by a small majority; while the Senate passed it by a large majority. M. Daladier had refused to commit himself to any interpretation of his plenary powers; and all the Senate could do was to explain unilaterally, through M. Caillaux and M. Gardey, the spirit in which it was granting M. Daladier these powers. In the course of these discussions hardly any reference was made to Czechoslovakia. Only on the second days did M. Daladier express his sympathy for the Czech people. As for M. Bonnet, he remained silent; he sat on the Government bench, with his thin lips tightly shut, and with a cold, lizard-like look on his face. Like a lizard expecting to be attacked.

Prague—German trade agreement with Rumania—Memel

—all within a few days; and what more was in store? London was active. Mr. Chamberlain proclaimed the British guarantee to Poland: late, terribly late, the man who had given the League its *coup de grâce* in dismissing Eden was becoming converted to collective security. Hitler had said he would not allow Germany to fight on two fronts again. Poland was to become the Second Front. But Russia? How much was Poland worth without Russia? Mr. Lloyd George stressed the point and questioned the value of the Anglo-Polish Pact, with Russia's position remaining uncertain for a number of reasons. For obviously, Russia alone could give Poland direct and immediate help.

.   .   .   .

Postscript—1968: The last couple of pages of the 1939 edition can be summarized and completed here in a few lines. The French government took the British guarantee to Poland with very mixed feelings, though it felt, as usual, bound to associate itself with Mr. Chamberlain. But it sensed, too, that there was something quixotic and unrealistic in the guarantee to Poland, unless something was also done about Russia. The 'pacifists' started on a new gambit: was not Britain proposing to fight the next war right down to the last French soldier? And they firmly demanded that the British immediately introduce conscription. For how could France hold out without strong land reinforcements from England? All of which suggested that there had now suddenly been aroused a certain distrust even in the sacrosanct Maginot Line. This demand for British conscription was, indeed, fair enough, and met with almost universal support in France, so much so that the British Government hastened to give way. But other French pacifists went a great deal further. Marcel Déat, the future French Nazi leader, wrote a celebrated article in the *Oeuvre* entitled: 'Die for Danzig?' In short, there were some who were now simply advocating a 'Polish Munich.'

Certainly France was now beginning to feel, as never before, in a very dangerous position. Could a German invasion be avoided, after all, Maginot Line or no Maginot Line? Hitler had made it amply clear that he was going to attack Poland. One thing could still save Poland, and that was an alliance with Russia. Daladier suddenly became a Russian-Alliance enthusiast—more so than Chamberlain. Bonnet was, at heart, prepared to consider a 'Polish Munich,' though, for a time, he also went through a few pro-Russian motions. As we know, he was well aware of the fearful danger France was facing when Stalin made his pact with Hitler, and tried, if only for a few hours, even *after* England had declared war on Germany, to delay France's declaration of war. Could not Mussolini arrange a 'Second Munich?' But it was no good. Hitler was determined to smash Poland. Some years afterwards, in his Memoirs, Bonnet still tried to show that Munich was a good thing, even though it had, in reality, led to the total isolation of France on the Continent and to the disaster of 1940. Today M. Bonnet, aged seventy-nine (he was born in the same year as Hitler), continues to be an important local worthy at Périguex—the scene of his Munich 'apotheosis'—and a defender of 'French democracy' against de Gaulle. Daladier, living in retirement, is now eighty-four the last survivor of the Big Four of Munich. He seems less proud and less certain than Bonnet of always having done the right thing. Flandin, after a discreditable Vichy record, died a few years ago. He never quite lived down his telegram to Hitler, and was debarred from French public life after the war. Nearly all the *dramatis personae* of this story—French, British, Czech and German—are now dead.

INDEX

INDEX

439